AL-MATHNAWI AL-NURI

THE RISALE-I NUR COLLECTION

AL-MATHNAWI AL-NURI

Seedbed of The Light

BEDİÜZZAMAN SAİD NURSİ

Translated by Huseyin Akarsu

The Light

New Jersey

10 09 08 07   1 2 3 4

Published by The Light, Inc.
26 Worlds Fair Dr. Unite C
Somerset, New Jersey, 08873, USA

www.thelightpublishing.com

Library of Congress Cataloging-in-Publication Data

Nursî, Said, 1877-1960.
[Mesnevî-i nuriye. English]
Al-mathnawi al-nuri : seedbed of the light / Bediuzzaman Said Nursi ; translated by Huseyin Akarsu.
p. cm.
Translated from Turkish.
Includes bibliographical references and index.
ISBN-13: 978-1-932099-18-8
1. Nurculuk--Doctrines. 2. Islam--Essence, genius, nature. I. Akarsu, Huseyin. II. Title.
BP253.N85613 2007
297.8'3--dc22
2007001099

ISBN-13: 978-1-932099-18-8

Cover design
Engin Çiftçi

Illumination of Cover
Hatice Aksu

Printed by
Çağlayan A.Ş. Izmir - Turkey
March 2007

Table of Contents

THE SECOND TREATISE

THE THIRD TREATISE

The Fourth Treatise

THE FIFTH TREATISE

THE SIXTH TREATISE

THE SEVENTH TREATISE

THE EIGHTH TREATISE

THE NINTH TREATISE

THE TENTH TREATISE

The Eleventh Treatise

The Twelfth Treatise

Introduction

Said Nursi and his work

SAID NURSI (1877-1960) WAS BORN IN NURS, EASTERN ANATOLIA,[1] and educated by the district's best scholars. He soon surpassed them in debates and earned the name Bediüzzaman (Wonder of the Age). Believing that modern science and logic was the way of the future, he advocated teaching religious sciences in secular schools and modern sciences in religious schools.

During the unrest of March 31, 1909, he was arrested and court-martialed for inciting the uproar. However, as he managed to restore some calm, he was acquitted. Returning to eastern Anatolia, he taught that Islam allowed freedom in government and rejected dictatorship. He later collected these speeches in *The Discussions*.[2]

In 1911, while preaching in Damascus' Umayyad mosque, he stated that the Muslims were being defeated due to the growth of despair, the loss of truthfulness in social and political life, love of belligerency, ignoring bonds among believers, pervasive despotism, and egocentricity. He then offered his cure: hope, truthfulness, trustworthiness, mutual love, consultation, solidarity, and freedom in accordance with Islam. Building on these, he asserted that the true civilization contained in Islam would dominate the modern world.[3]

---

1 At this time, this area belonged to the Ottoman State. Turkey only emerged as an independent nation in 1923. (Ed.)

2 Said Nursi, *Münazarat* (The Discussions), new ed. (Istanbul: 1977).

3 Said Nursi, *Hutbe-i Samiye* (The Damascus Sermon), new ed. (Istanbul: n.d.). One hundred famous scholars were among the audience.

Returning to Istanbul to seek the new sultan's support for a university in Van, eastern Anatolia, he finally secured sufficient funds—19,000 gold liras. Unfortunately, World War I broke out before it could be completed.

Said Nursi during the Ottoman period

During World War I, Said Nursi commanded a volunteers' regiment on the Caucasian front and in eastern Anatolia. His heroism was admired by Ottoman generals, including Enver Pasha, Minister of Defense and Deputy Commander-in-Chief. Together with his volunteers, known as "The Felt Caps," he fought heroically against Russian and Armenian forces. He also dictated (to his students) his famous Qur'anic commentary, *Isharat al-I'jaz* (Signs of Miraculousness), during the war.

Eventually captured, he spent over 2 years in a prisoners' camp in Kostroma, northwestern Russia. When General Nicolaevich, Commander-in-Chief of the Caucasian front and the Czar's uncle, passed by, Said Nursi remained seated. When charged with insulting the general, he said: "I am a Muslim scholar with belief in my heart. One who has belief in his heart is superior to one who does not. I cannot act against my belief." He was sentenced to death by firing squad. Watching him pray before his execution, the general understood that his attitude was due to his belief, and lifted the sentence.

Amid the Russian revolution, Said Nursi escaped and returned to Istanbul. After receiving a medal and rejecting all government appointments, he joined the Dar al-Hikmat al-Islamiya (the religious academy) on the army's recommendation. When imperial Europe invaded the collapsed Ottoman State to grab what it could, Said Nursi protested the British presence in Istanbul and wrote and spoke against them fiercely. He was never silenced or caught.

In 1922, after receiving 18 official invitations, Said Nursi went to Ankara and was received at the Grand National Assembly. Gradually seeing that most representatives ignored their religious obligations, he addressed them on January 19, 1923.[4] After this, 50 or 60 of them began to pray. Eight months later he moved to Van and devoted himself to meditation and prayer. When the "Eastern rebellion" broke out, he rejected the rebels'

---

[4] His address to the Turkish Parliament is presented on pp. 155-58. (Ed.)

call to support them, saying that Muslims should not fight each other and that many innocent people would die for the benefit of a few criminals.[5]

The government nevertheless exiled him to Burdur, western Anatolia, where he was kept under strict surveillance. When Ankara learned that he was still spreading his view of Islam, he was exiled to Barla, an out-of-the-way place in central Anatolia surrounded by mountains. Instead, he produced the main part of his greatest work: *The Risale-i Nur*, a 6,000-page Qur'anic commentary.

The Republic of Turkey

After the collapse of the multiethnic, religion-based Ottoman State and the Turkish National War, Turkey became a compact, secular, and largely Turkish nation-state. The principles of republicanism, nationalism, populism, statism, secularism, and revolution (meaning continuing change in the state and society) were "officially" accepted as the essential principles to guide the new Turkey.

The founders of the republic asserted that Islam and Sufism had made the Ottoman State stagnant and backward. They imposed their own style of Europeanization by abolishing the Sultanate and Caliphate, closing religious schools and religious courts, and outlawing traditional male headgear and Sufi brotherhoods. They replaced the Islamic legal code with a mixture of Swiss civil, Italian penal, and German commercial codes; increased women's emancipation; outlawed polygamy; made marriage and divorce civil affairs; and replaced the Arabic-based Ottoman alphabet with a Latin-based one. They also stipulated that the Turks should take family surnames, thereby abandoning the traditional system, and allowed women to vote for parliamentary members and hold parliamentary seats.

To further weaken Islam's hold, the new republic also abolished the office of the Shaykh al-Islam, converted many mosques to secular uses, forbade calling the people to prayer in Arabic, and discouraged all public manifestations of the Religion of Islam.

---

5 This Kurdish rebellion broke out on August 7, 1924, over whether Turkey or Iraq would receive Mosul and its oil fields. Another one broke out in February 1925. Said Nursi, a Kurd, was falsely charged with being its leader. (Ed.)

The Risale-i Nur

Before the republic, Said Nursi had already changed from "Old Said" to "New Said." Withdrawing from public life, he had devoted himself to defending and explaining Islam's main principles of thought, belief, worship, morality, and way of life through writing. His words reached millions of people through the 600,000 copies handwritten by him and his students. And this at a time when any religious undertaking was extremely difficult.

In his *Risale-i Nur*, considered a classic of Turkish religious literature, he identified the cause of the Muslim world's decline: the weakening of belief's foundations. When joined with the unceasing attacks of materialism, atheism, science, and progress, he saw a great cloud of denial and doubt hovering over the Muslim world. To neutralize it, he undertook a "jihad of the word with the diamond principles of Islam" designed to strengthen—even save—belief by reconstructing Islam from its foundations of belief.

The *Risale-i Nur* explains Islam and belief to modern people in their own terms and according to their own worldview. Analyzing both belief and unbelief, he used clearly reasoned arguments to prove that the Qur'anic conception of God and His Unity, Prophethood and bodily resurrection, and all others are the only rational explanations for existence, humanity, and the universe.

Using easily understood stories, comparisons, and explanations, Said Nursi produced categorical proofs showing that modern scientific discoveries actually support and reinforce the truths of the Religion. He used the Qur'anic methodology of addressing each person's intellect, and all inner and outer facilities, to encourage people to study the universe and its functioning in order to understand creation's true nature and purposes. This, in turn, leads to learning the One Creator's Attributes and their own duties as God's servants.

Said Nursi explained the universe's true nature as being a comprehensive sign of its Creator, and showed via clear arguments that all fundamentals of belief can be proven rationally when the universe is read in this way. As belief is then grounded in modern science, it remains firm and immune to materialism, naturalism, and atheism.

Such believers view all scientific and technological advances as merely uncovering the cosmos' workings. Viewing the cosmos as a vast and infinitely complex and meaningful unified book describing its Single Author, all discoveries and advances reinforce, deepen, and expand belief. Thus their most fundamental needs—to worship God by recognizing His Most Beautiful Names and Attributes, and to obey His laws—are met.

Said Nursi's concept of science

Said Nursi used religious and scientific terminology together, as indicated by his usage of *ulum-u musbete* (positive sciences). Given this, and his emphasis on contemporary scientific achievements, we can say that he accepted the existence of *positive* and *metaphysical* sciences. He states that the "*Risale-i Nur* uses demonstrative proof," which for him is the scientific method, and thus addresses the human mind convincingly. He argues that all phenomena in the universe give as much certainty for the truths of belief as science gives for any established fact. He accepted and then tried to modify the prevalent concept of science by joining religious and modern scientific knowledge, and then justifying this theoretically:

> The light of the conscience is religious sciences (*ulum-u diniye*). The light of the mind is modern sciences (*funun-u medeniye*). Combining both manifests the truth. The student's skills develop further with these two (sciences). When they are separated, the former breeds superstition and the latter breeds corruption and skepticism.[6]

Classical Muslim scholars joined scientific and religious knowledge during the Islamic world's Golden Age (ninth to mid-thirteenth centuries). Although Said Nursi stated that Islamic metaphysics must remain Islamic, he approved of such attempts in *being related to certain religious issues, with the result that the scientific theory is believed to be part of the the Religion*. He stressed that the knowledge of these two fields must not be mixed, and that great care must be taken when using scientific theories to interpret religious issues.

The role of knowledge

Said Nursi emphasized that knowledge yields happiness of this world and the one to come, and that humanity came to this world to be perfected through knowledge and supplication. Thus "knowledge without the heart's insight

---

6 "Munazarat," in Ibid., 2:1956.

is ignorance,"[7] for our minds need to absorb religious truth with Revelation's help, to which our heart—not our mind or reason—is a mirror. Moreover, "revealed truth is reasonable, but reason on its own cannot attain it."[8]

The heart's insight comes from the Qur'an; the mind's insight comes from the other sciences. He writes:

> The reality of the universe and all beings is based on the Divine Names. The reality of every being is based on one or many Names. All sciences and arts are based on and rely upon a Name. The true science of philosophy is based on the Name All-Wise (al-Hakim), true medicine on the Name Healer (al-Shafi), geometry on the Name Determiner (al-Muqaddir), and so on. Just as each science is based on and ultimately ends in a Name, the realities of all arts, sciences, and human perfections are based on the Divine Names.[9]

Said Nursi concludes that knowledge gained by studying the universe in God's name is true knowledge, while knowledge gained in other ways is ignorance. Science interprets the universe, which is a symbolic creation of God pointing to a Truth beyond itself.

Expressing scientific truth

Said Nursi's conclusion leads us to how science should express its discoveries and theoretical formulations. He suggests the language of the Qur'an as a model, on the grounds that since the Divine language guides all aspects of our social life, it should guide us in this matter as well.

According to him, in most cases the Qur'an speaks of certain scientific phenomena in an allegorical style, for it addresses all levels at all times and seeks only to make our Creator known to us through His creation and establish the pillars of belief and good conduct in minds and hearts.[10] Thus it speaks in terms of our relationship to the Creator, whereas Western philosophy and science use language to encourage people to look at things only in relation to the things themselves. In addition, Western language is directed toward specialists, whereas the Qur'anic language addresses everyone and so must be general to ensure understanding.

---

7 Said Nursi, *The Letters*, The Light, Inc., New Jersey: 2007.

8 Nursi, *The Words*, The Light, Inc., New Jersey: 2005.

9 Ibid. See The Thirty-second Word's third station.

10 Ibid.

For example, the Qur'an presents the universe as a huge kingdom, Earth as a palace, the sun as a lamp, the moon as a nightlight, and the stars as decorations. People are to reflect upon all of these to grasp what they can of their Creator. Western science and philosophy present the sun and other beings as things on their own and without an owner. It inspires awesome dread and fearful wonder, and gives the spirit no perfection of knowledge or moral lesson. Said Nursi considers such philosophy to be divorced from the Religion.

Said Nursi and the Republic of Turkey

Said Nursi's life, both while writing the *Risale-i Nur* (1925-48) and until his death in 1960, consisted of arrest and imprisonment, surveillance, and harassment. But he persevered. In the words of a person familiar with such anti-Said Nursi activities: "Despite all we have done in the past 25 years, we have not been able to prevent Said Nursi from his activities."

Following is a brief chronology of this phase of his life:

- 1925-35: Kept under strict control at Barla, a very small, mountanous district, and forced to live alone.
- 1935: Arrested and imprisoned for 11 months with 125 students during their trial at Eskisehir Criminal Court.
- 1936-43: Following his release, began a 7-year exile in Kastamonu, where he spent the first 3 months at a police station. After that, he was transferred to a house opposite to the police station.
- 1943: Arrested and tried with 126 students at the Denizli Criminal Court for having a treatise on God's existence printed secretly in Istanbul. He taught the other prisoners and produced his *Fruits from the Tree of Light* and other works on small pieces of paper torn from paper bags, which were then smuggled out. He was acquitted and exiled to Emirdag.
- 1948: Arrested in Emirdag with 53 students, and jailed for 20 months in Afyon prison. Now 72, Said Nursi endured solitary confinement in a cell with broken windows that were not fixed during the two harsh winters he stayed there. Sick and eventually poisoned, he had to serve his full term even though the Supreme Court had annulled his sentence. In 1956, they were declared innocent.

- In 1950, the multiparty system was introduced and restrictions on the Religion were relaxed. Said Nursi was arrested only once after this, and was acquitted by a unanimous decision. Dying on March 23, 1960, he left this world with complete honor, dignity and victory, and bequeathed to the Muslim world his works, which remain highly influential and a lighthouse guiding us on our way back to God.

Al-Mathnawi al-Nuri

SAID NURSI WROTE *AL-MATHNAWI AL-NURI* BEFORE THE MAIN PART of the *Risale-i Nur* collection. In this book, each thought reveals itself as a shoot, a drop, a bud that would become like a bubbling stream, a perfumed rose garden, a forest murmuring with majesty. They stimulated and excited Muslims' feelings based on belief and meditation, and led many unbelievers to re-evaluate their opinions.

He says that the greatest truths are belief and God's absolute Unity. To him, all existence is like a shuttle weaving Unity's truth, a needle and silk thread crocheting lace, embroidered everywhere with meanings belonging to Him. But everyone cannot grasp, understand, and feel Unity to the same degree:

> Belief in God's Unity has two degrees. The first is the superficial belief that God has no partners and that the universe belongs to Him alone. Such believers may be susceptible to deviation and confusion. The second is the firm conviction that God is One, that everything belongs to Him exclusively, and that only He creates. Such believers see His seal and observe His stamp on all things. Free from all doubt, they feel themselves always and everywhere in His Presence. Their conviction cannot be diluted by deviation or doubt.

Writing that belief is like a prism revealing the true dimensions of the nature of existence and humanity, he says in the Eleventh Ray's ninth point that belief makes the universe a readable book and an enjoyable show, and humanity an index and proclamation. Although all facets of belief's truth might appear as separate if they are sensed, perceived, and felt differently, in reality they are tightly connected and different faces of the whole:

> Belief in God, the Prophet, Resurrection, and affirming the universe's existence require mutual belief. That is, there is a perfect relation between these pillars of belief: believing one requires believing the others. Divinity requires Messengership; this world testifies to the other world.

Said Nursi observes in the *Risale-i Nur*'s Thirtieth Word and Gleams that people who have no depth in their spiritual and emotional lives, who take too much interest in mental and philosophical matters, have a "disease" in their hearts (the center of belief and emotions) that makes them ill.

> I have observed that the more people are preoccupied with philosophy, the more their hearts suffer from spiritual disease. I also have observed that the greater this spiritual disease of the heart becomes, the more people are preoccupied with rational sciences. Spiritual diseases lead to preoccupation with rational sciences, and preoccupation with rational sciences gives rise to spiritual diseases.

Another original observation is that while causes must be respected, attributing real influence to them is an aberration and deviation. The true way is to respect them and attribute the result to God, as stated in The Twenty-fourth Word's first branch.

> KNOW, O FRIEND, that attachment to material causes engenders humiliation and rejection. Consider this: Why are dogs, which should be considered blessed due to their many good qualities (notably their proverbial loyalty), considered ritually unclean? Why are other domestic animals, such as hens, cows, and cats, which feel no gratitude and loyalty in return for the we do to them, considered blessed? This is because—provided it is not to backbite dogs and break their hearts—dogs are greedy and so attached to apparent causes that they cannot see the true Bestower of bounties. Thus, they suppose the means to be truly effective [in procuring their food], and so suffer the stigma of ritual impurity as punishment for their blindness and indifference to the true Owner and Bestower of bounties.
>
> Blessed animals do not recognize means and causes or give them any value or importance. Cats ask for food and, when they get what they want, behave as if they do not know you or you do not know them. They feel no gratitude toward you. Instead, they thank the true Bestower of bounties by saying: "O Compassionate One, O Compassionate One."

Said Nursi also stresses living in the Sunna's orbit, reminding Muslims, as do all Ahl al-Sunna wa al-Jama'a scholars,[11] that the Prophet is a perfect guide and that only his Sunna leads to happiness in both worlds. He also calls us to unite in the Sunna. A life not based on the Sunna is more like revolving around a whirlpool's edge. Even if it appears to be like swimming and making progress, in reality it is nothing more than sliding toward death:

> KNOW, O FRIEND, that I have observed during my journeying in the "layers of darkness" that the Prophet's sayings and practices, as well as the principles of Islamic law, are like stars that guide us among innumerable dark and misleading ways. Deviating from his way or Tradition [the Sunna] makes one a plaything of devils, an object of illusion and suspicion, a target of fear, and a mountain of unbearable burdens. Deliverance from such things comes only from following the Sunna.
>
> I have also observed that the Sunna's principles are like ropes hanging down from heaven. Whoever holds fast to even a part of them can be elevated. Whoever opposes them and relies on their own or even public reason is like one who desires to obtain the means of traveling through the heavens' spheres in earthly vehicles and is ridiculed like Pharaoh, who said: *O Haman. Build for me a tower to obtain the means [of traveling] in the heavens* (40:36).

This subject is frequently mentioned in the *Risale-i Nur* collection. In particular, the Eleventh Gleam's Third Point discusses it and emphasizes that following the Sunna is the path of God.

Said Nursi puts forth an original idea concerning our relations with and view of the world: The world is not something to be disliked, but rather to be loved. He reminds us of the three elements comprising the basic principles of this love:

> The world has three facets. The first relates to God's Names. With respect to its second facet, the world is the arable field of the Hereafter. These two facets are beautiful. The third facet relates directly and exclusively to the world itself, and is where people gratify their bodily desires and seek to meet the needs of this transient worldly life.

In a related approach, these words greet us later on:

---

11 Those who follow the Prophetic example and the community of the Companions.

> What falls to one's part from life's fruits and purposes is proportionate to the degree of one's part in the ownership and disposal of one's life. Other purposes and fruits pertain to the Bestower of life, exalted is His Majesty. Humanity is but the object of His Names' manifestations. God will display His Mercy's colors and radiations, which will consist of the fruits growing from the seeds of this worldly life, in Paradise.
>
> The relation of human beings with their individual lives is like that between a navigator and the royal ship he steers. The navigator places his fingers on the instruments that move and steer the ship. What he receives from the ship's uses and income is proportionate to his relation with the ship and the service he renders. In other words, it is quite small. This is exactly how it is with any living being and the ship of its existence and life. What a living being receives from its life's uses and purposes is quite small; moreover, what is received has not been earned [but bestowed by the Bestower of life].

Said Nursi further observed that seeing and accepting human beings as greater than they really are is an act of oppression and a step toward idolatry. One who takes this first step may not be able to turn back in some circumstances:

> KNOW, O FRIEND, that people unjustly attribute the fruits of a group's labor to a single person and assume that that individual has produced those fruits. From this injustice arises a kind of secret association of partners with God, for assuming that the result of a community's labor and the product of their free will has originated from a single person means accepting that that person has an extraordinary power which has reached the degree of creativity. The deities of ancient Greece and other pagan peoples were devised from such devilish assumptions.

Later on, he states that belief is a secret source of strength. Those who possess this source can possess worlds, and through dependence on God realized with belief, individuals can make everything serve them:

> Those who submit to God's Will and pursue His pleasure are served by everything; those who disobey God find that everything turns against them. Those who affirm that whatever exists belongs to Him exclusively and is His property, find that everything serves them.

The Qur'anic verse: *Say: "If it weren't for your prayers, of what significance are you?"* proves this truth. Just as a child who cannot reach something asks for help, a servant should take refuge in the Lord with helplessness and need and ask Him for everything. This subject is described in great detail in The Twenty-third Word's fourth and fifth points.

Prophet Muhammad is of the nature of the universe's basis, essence, and root. Every point in the universe contains the truth of his light. Just as the spirit and meaning in a seed are found in the body of a tree and shoot, he is a mirror to the First and the Last with respect to his light, which comprises the essence of existence. The Thirty-first Word's third principle and the Tenth Word's second part of the addendum spread before the eye of our hearts a special depth and richness on this wonderful subject:

> If you see the universe as a great book, you will see the light of Muhammad as the pen's ink with which that book was written. If you see the universe as a tree, you will see his light as originally its seed and consequently its fruit. If you see the universe as an animate being, you will see his light as its soul. If you see the universe as a macro-human, you will see his light as its intellect. If you see the universe as a flower garden, you will see his light as its nightingale. If you see the universe as a lofty, richly decorated castle with many rooms and apartments showing the splendor of the Eternal Sovereign's sovereignty and His Glory's marvels, as well as the beauties of His Grace's manifestations and the wonderful designs of His art, you will see Prophet Muhammad's light as a spectator.

According to Said Nursi, nature's and humanity's essential character is twofold: a deceiving idol and a secret prism showing the eternal Artist and eternal truth. For the spiritually prepared and aware, both nature as a richly embroidered art work and humanity as a crystal prism are unerring books, eloquent speakers, sources of light illuminating the realm behind the visible world. The Thirtieth Word's first aim approaches this subject with a unique breadth and richness, while the Twenty-third Gleam, "The Treatise on Nature," makes it impossible to idolize nature. He puts this observation in the form of a victory song:

> For 30 years I have fought two "rebels": the ego and nature in the outer world. I have seen the former as a shadowy mirror reflecting someone other than itself. But people view it as having an independent existence, showing itself and so becoming an unbending tyrant in rebellion against its Creator.
>
> I have seen nature as a work of Divine art, a painting of the All-Merciful. However, as a result of viewing it heedlessly (i.e., ignoring

> the Creator), it has come to be seen by materialists as a deity, self-originated and existing by itself, and made into an excuse for an ingratitude resulting in unbelief.
>
> Thanks be to God and praise be to Him, for through the help of the One, Eternally-Besought-of-All, and the enlightenment of the glorious Qur'an, my struggle has ended in the death of these two rebels, the smashing of these two idols.

In the Second Gleam's first point, Said Nursi portrays sins as the reconnoitering hands of unbelief, nets on the road of unbelief. In places where they are seen frequently, thought "sets sail" for immorality and belief is confronted with danger:

> The seed of unbelief is present in the essence of sins, especially those that are committed frequently, for such sins lead to indifference. This attitude leads to addiction, which can be remedied only by abandoning the sin. Those who indulge in sin seek to avoid punishment and so, unconsciously, try to find an excuse to believe in the non-existence of eternal torment. This continues until they deny eternal torment and the abode of punishment. Also, the shame arising from indulging in this sin with no feelings of remorse or seeking God's forgiveness leads them to deny that the sin is really a sin. This leads to the denial of the existence of those beings—like guardian angels—who oversee people and are aware of their sins. Due to the resulting shame's intensity, the sinners wish for there to be no reckoning in the other world. When they encounter even a false argument for its non-existence, they take it as a strong proof and deny the final reckoning. Thus their hearts gradually become darker and darker. May God save us from such a consequence. Amen.

Said Nursi sought a deeper understanding of the Qur'an. In a line extending from *Isharat al-I'jaz* (Signs of the Qur'an's Miraculousness) to the *Mathnawi* and to *The Words* (particularly The Twenty-fifth Word), he breathed the Qur'an. With new and original interpretations, he frequently displayed its depth and excited thirsty hearts by making Divine truths easily understandable.

In The Twenty-fifth Word, the analysis attains a wonderful state. Its elaboration of what is summarized here in the *Mathnawi* is like an ocean to a drop, a forest to a seedling. Soon after this brief reminder, a new topic pertaining to the Qur'an whispers to us as if through a door slightly opened and then passes on.

> While listening to the Qur'an, each of its melodies assumes a new attitude and mood according to its audience's degrees of guidance. Try to assume the mood of intermediaries ranging from Gabriel, who brought it to the Prophet, to the one from whom you hear it directly. While listening to the reciter, try to hear it as if listening to the Prophet reciting it at the summit of Prophethood to humanity and other beings throughout the world. Then, assume the manner of Gabriel while he recites it to the Prophet on the "highest horizon." Finally, if possible, try to hear it as if listening to it from behind 70,000 veils from the Eternally Speaking One, Who speaks to the Prophet at "the distance of two bows' length."

Al-Mathnawi al-Nuri resembles an index of many topics, each requiring a separate book, and each of which would be elaborated upon in the *Risale-i Nur*. Under "Flower," in notes that would later be discussed in the *Risale-i Nur*, many important truths are summarized. The "Spark" is like a tiny seedbed of piety and good works that questions our worldly emotions, directs our thoughts to Divine Unity, and shows belief's vastness. The "Whiff" touches our hearts and points out the depth and richness of the Qur'anic verses. It discusses why human organs were created, and thereby removes habits that can be considered "crust on our eye of discernment."

The third part of the "Whiff" analyzes Divine Destiny and Decree and the Law of Sparing, and reveals why Qur'anic verses end as they do. Immediately after that we are offered a path to the Truth, one that differs from earlier paths. The offer is made, and our attention is turned to our essential weakness and poverty. A little further on, our unique creation is pointed to, and we are reminded that humanity is an index of existence. After that, our attention is turned to prayer, which is analyzed in great detail in several parts of the *Risale-i Nur*. The meaning of God's answering prayers is explained, and our desire to supplicate is excited. Also explained is the difference between self-pride and our proclaiming God's blessings upon ourselves as a sign of gratitude to Him.

The "Fourteenth Droplet" discusses the Qur'an's basic issues and essential purposes, which the *Risale-i Nur* considers pivotal subjects. Under "Radiance," we are led through the vastness of the Divine Existence, whose "proper" name is Allah, and given a unique knowledge of Him. Elsewhere, the reader is introduced to grace and intercession, which can be considered active prayer. After showing the significance of soil as an element through which God manifests His Names, the concept of humility, or being like the soil upon which one prostrates before God, is raised. Here it is stressed that "a servant is closest to his Lord when prostrating."

Under "Point," in the name of the Divine Essence which Said Nursi frequently discusses, a fourth important universal proof is added to the existing three.[12] This proof deals with the human conscience, which is regarded as the meeting point of the Unseen and the visible, material world. The impossibility of evolution, mutation, and leaping from one species to another is stressed. Basing his arguments on sound thought, Said Nursi rejects evolution.

It is our earnest desire that these works be examined in depth by members of an institute entrusted with the task of studying the *Risale-i Nur*.

— M. Fethullah Gülen

12 The universe, the Qur'an, and Prophet Muhammad.

The First Treatise

The First Treatise

Rays from God's Unity as bright as the sun

In the Name of God, the All-Merciful, the All-Compassionate.

> God is the Creator of all things, and He is guardian and watcher over everything. To Him belong the keys of the heavens and Earth. (39:62-63)

> Glory be to Him in Whose Hand is the kingdom and inner dimensions of all things. (36:83)

> There is nothing but with Us are the stores thereof. (15:21)

> There is not a moving creature but He has grasp of it by the forelock. (11:56)

KNOW, O HEEDLESS ONE WHO ATTRIBUTES ALL THINGS AND EVENTS IN this world to the law of causality. The causes to which you ascribe creativity are only veils covering the Divine Power's operation, for God's Dignity and Grandeur require such veils. But the Eternal Divine Power, absolutely independent of everything, is ever-active and creates, for Divine Unity and Glory require that it be so.

The Eternal Monarc has officers, but they have no authority to execute His orders independently. They are not partners in His Sovereignty; rather, their only functions are to serve as media through which His Lordship's acts and executions are watched and known. They also function as observers and witnesses. By doing so, they obey His laws and commands of creation and thereby perform their duty of worship, which is required by their nature and disposition. They exist because they must manifest the dignity of Divine Power and majesty of Divine Lordship and Sovereignty. Human monarchs, on the other hand, need officers and other means to help them to enforce their rule. There is no resemblance or relation between these two kinds of officers.

Since most people cannot discern the beauty and wisdom behind every event, they complain and object. To divert such complaints from God, causes are placed as an intervening veil between people and God's acts. However, those who see the real beauty and wisdom in events know the truth of what is going on. A parable clarifies this point: The Angel of Death complained to God that His servants would complain of his role as the taker of souls. God answered him: "I will put illness and misfortune between you and them so that they will complain of them, not of you."

In sum, God's Dignity and Grandeur require apparent causes to prevent complaints and to hide, from those who reason superficially, the hand of Power's involvement in certain seemingly insignificant or vile things and affairs. At the same time, God's Unity and Glory require that these apparent causes have no part in either the creation or disposition of things.

A note

Belief in God's Unity has two degrees: believing superficially that God has no partners, and that the universe belongs only to Him—such believers may be susceptible to deviation and confusion; and firm conviction that God is One, that everything belongs to Him exclusively, and that only He creates. Such believers see His seal and observe His stamp on all things. Free from doubt, they feel themselves always and everywhere in His Presence. Their conviction cannot be diluted by deviation or doubt. For you to acquire such conviction in God's Unity, I will point out some of its rays that I have obtained from the Qur'an.

First ray

God Almighty sets a special seal on each thing He makes, showing that He is the Creator of all things. He sets a special stamp on each creature, demonstrating that He is the Maker of all things. Each "letter" that Power "writes" bears an inimitable signature specific to the Eternal Sovereign.

For example, look at the seal He has put on life, through which one thing is made into many and many things are made into one. He transforms the water we drink into a means for forming innumerable animal organs and systems. Through His command, a single entity becomes "many." Conversely, He changes varieties of foods into a particular body or skin, a whole system or subsystem. Thus "many" things become, by God's command, a single entity. Whoever has an intellect, consciousness, and a heart must conclude that making a single, simple entity from many things and using a single entity to make many things is a seal special to the Creator of all things.

Second ray

Among His innumerable stamps, look at the one He has put on living things. Being complex and inclusive in character, a living thing is a miniature universe, a shining fruit of the Tree of Creation, a nucleus of creation made by the Creator as a sample or pattern for most species. It is as if that living thing were a drop filtered through wisdom from creation with absolutely exact measures, an all-inclusive point extracted from existence via knowledge with absolutely precise calculations. As one without the supreme disposition of creation cannot create anything, the one who made the honeybee an index of most things, and who inserted most parts of the Book of Creation in human nature, must be the Creator. He has encoded a fig tree's future life in its tiny seed, and made the human heart a small-scale copy of thousands of worlds as well as a window opening onto them. He has recorded our past life and everything related to it in our memories. The One Who has done these and many similar things can only be the Creator of all things, and His doing so is a stamp specific to the Lord of the worlds.

Third ray

Look at the signature put on the acts of bringing to life and reviving. Out of innumerable possible examples, we mention only one: In each transparent (mirror) or apparently transparent (glass) thing, from planets to drops and glass, there is a stamp—an image or reflection—specific to the sun. The Unique, Eternal Sun also sets on each living thing a seal, a stamp, of reviving and bringing to life, which reveals itself by showing all of His

Names on that thing.[13] If all material causes—supposing they had power and will—*came together to produce the like of that stamp, they could not do so, even if they helped each other* (17:88).

Assume that the sun's images reflected in a drop, glass, or any transparent thing are not attributed to the sun. Given this, one would have to accept that there is a real, tiny sun in each drop facing the sun, in each piece of glass reflecting the sun's light, and that every transparent thing has become a sun.

Assume that every living thing and life, every act of bringing to life, is not attributed to the Divine Names' manifestations. Assume that the belief that life is the focus of the Divine Names' manifestations, which could be regarded as the Eternal Sun's rays, is not acceptable. If this were so, each living thing would have to possess an infinite power of creation, all-encompass-

---

[13] God Almighty should be considered from five perspectives. One is His Essence as Divine Being (*Zat* in Islamic terminology). Only He can know His Essence. A Prophetic Tradition says: "Do not reflect on God's Essence; instead, reflect on His works and acts." God has no partners, likes and resemblance, as pointed to by the verse: *There is nothing like or compared unto Him*. The second perspective is His Essential, "Innate" Qualities as being God, which are the Attributes' source. The third perspective is His Attributes, which are of three kinds: Essential Attributes (e.g., Existence, Having No Beginning, Eternal Permanence, Oneness, Being Unlike the Created, Self-Subsistence); Positive Attributes (e.g., Life, Knowledge, Power, Speech, Will, Hearing, Seeing, Creating); and innumerable "Negative" Attributes, summed up as "God is absolutely free from any defect and shortcoming."

The Attributes are the sources of the Names: Life gives rise to the All-Living, Knowledge to the All-Knowing, and Power to the All-Powerful. About 1,000 of God's many Names are known to us. The Names are the sources of the Acts: giving life has its source in the All-Living, and knowing everything down to the smallest originates in the All-Knowing. God is "known" by His acts, Names, and Attributes. Whatever exists in the universe, in the material and immaterial worlds, is the result of the Names' and Attributes' manifestations: Universal and individual provision points to His Name the All-Providing, and the All-Healing is the source of remedies and patient recovery. Philosophy has its source in Wisdom, and so on. The acts, Names, and Attributes are the "links" between God and the created, or the "reflectors" with which to have knowledge of God.

Although we try to know or recognize God by His acts, Names, and Attributes, we must not think of Him in the terms associating likeness or comparison unto Him, for there is nothing resembling Him. He is absolutely One, Single, and totally different from all that exists or has the potential to exist. In this sense, His Oneness is not in terms of number. He also has Unity and relations with the created. To have some knowledge of Him through His acts, Names, and Attributes, some comparisons are permissible. This is pointed to in the verse: *For God is the highest comparison*. The writer's using *the sun* as a unit of comparison to understand God's acts, Names, and Attributes should be considered from this perspective. (Tr.)

ing knowledge, absolute will, and attributes found only in the Necessarily Existent Being. Also, each atom would have to have divinity, for the existence of everything would have to be ascribed to itself. Likewise, if the existence of everything were ascribed to causes, absolute divinity would have to be attributed to each cause. Thus there would be countless partners in Divinity, which necessarily requires absolute independence and rejection of any partnership.

Consider an atom or a seed. See how astonishing are its well-arranged composition and relationships. It has relationships with all parts of the living thing of which it is a part, as well as relationships with all members of its species and all other creatures. Its relationships and duties resemble those of a private with respect to military officers. If the atom's or seed's connection to the Absolute Power were severed, we would have to admit that it has eyes to see all things and an all-comprehensive consciousness.

In summary: If the sun's reflection in a drop is attributed to the actual sun, many suns would have to exist in the smallest things. It is the same with the Absolutely Powerful One, in relation to Whose Power whatever exists, without exception, is the same. Accepting the above assertion means accepting countless divinities.

Fourth ray

Writing a book requires only a writer and a pen. However, if it is printed on a printing press, there would have to be as many iron letters as the actual letters in the book, and many people would be needed to make and arrange them. Sura *Ya Sin* is written in very small letters inside the two Arabic letters *Ya* and *Sin*. If a book is written in small, fine letters within one word, as many iron letters as actual letters in the book would be needed to print that one word.

If you say that the universe is a book written with the Pen of a Single One, then you are following the easiest and most reasonable path. If you attribute the universe's existence to nature or material causes, you are following the most unreasonable and difficult way. In such a case, "printing" one living thing would require as many instruments as necessary for printing most of the universe. So this is a supposition having nothing with the truth.

Suppose a flower's or a fruit's existence is attributed to nature or material causes. Given this, each soil, water, and air particle would have to have as many "programs" and hidden factories [to produce it] as all flowers and fruits in all of their colors, tastes, and shapes. Or, each particle should have as much power as to make all plants, and as much knowledge as to know in exact detail all flowering and fruit-bearing plants and trees. Then, each air, water and soil particle or atom could be a means for the formation of all (or most) plants.

Suppose different seeds have been buried in a soil-filled pot. Empty the pot and fill it with soil taken from Earth's surface. In both cases, the result will be almost the same, as can be seen world-wide. Despite the variety in shape, color, taste, and appearance, any soil can be used to produce all flowers and fruit-bearing trees. Thus, if you attribute their existence to nature or material causes, each seed, despite its physical simplicity and similarity, would have to have special machines or workshops to form the entire plant or tree.

Fifth ray

LOOK, O FRIEND! While each letter in a book points to itself as a letter and in one respect only, it points to its writer in many respects. Similarly, every "created" letter of the Book of the Universe points to itself only as a letter, while pointing to its Maker in many respects. It does so individually and in the words and sentences in which it is included, and manifests its Maker's Titles, describing them as if it were a fine poem.

Sixth ray

LOOK, O FRIEND, how the Glorious Maker puts His special stamp on each particular thing, and His specific seal on each part of a whole. Likewise, He puts His special stamp on each species and each whole. He puts the stamp of His Unity on the universe, as well as on any part of it, thereby demonstrating His Unity. By concentrating the manifestations of all or some of His Names on a single entity, He displays His Oneness.[14]

Look at the stamp pointed out in: *Look at the prints of God's Mercy, how He revives Earth after its death. He is the Reviver of the dead in the same way, and He is powerful over all things* (30:50). Earth's revival is an astonishing

---

[14] *Unity* and *Oneness* denote two different meanings. *Unity* means God's manifesting all His Names throughout the universe or on any part of it. *Oneness* means God's concentrating all or some of His Names on a single entity, which causes differentiation among species and individuals.

"resurrection" or coming to life again. Countless animal and plant species are raised to life. There are far more members of many non-human species than there are of humanity. Nevertheless, to fulfill certain subtle purposes, most plants are not raised in their exact former identities, but in forms bearing a substantial and close resemblance. However they are revived, their revival indicates the ease of the Resurrection [that will occur at the end of time after the universe's destruction].

Despite their being infinitely mixed with each other, reviving these innumerable species without confusion and with exact differentiation is a special stamp of the One of infinite Power and all-encompassing Knowledge. Species are infinitely mixed and intermingled, and there is great similarity among them. On the "page" of Earth, countless "books" are written without confusion or mistake, with infinite order, and with absolute accuracy in distinguishing among them. This is also a special seal of the One in Whose Hand are the dominion and keys of all things. He can do one thing while simultaneously doing something else.

Those who deny the Resurrection should observe its countless examples in Earth's quickening. Your denial of it is like this: A man saw another man rewriting innumerable lost books from memory, or composing new ones like the lost ones, all at once. He is told that the miracle-working author can rewrite his book, composed in an instant, after he had dissolved it in water. The man replies: "Impossible! How can a destroyed book be rewritten in a moment?" for he compares his own ignorant and impotent self to that miracle-working author who never forgets anything and can do all things.[15] If someone says to a man, who shows his strength by lifting a mountain, that he cannot remove a rock blocking the guests' way to the garden in which he will offer them the most delicious foods and beverages, would you not call him a fool?

---

[15] The Qur'an declares: *I shall not allow to go to waste the deed of any doer among you, whether be a male or female: you are one from the other* (3:195). It is clear that Islam does not discriminate between men and women in religious responsibility. Each gender shares most of the responsibilities, but each one has certain responsibilities that are particular to it. The Qur'an usually uses the masculine form of address, for this is one of Arabic's characteristics. In almost every language, the masculine form is used for a group comprising both men and women, like the English word mankind, which includes both men and women. So, brotherhood also includes sisterhood, and, since the believers comprise both male and female believers, the believers are brothers and sisters. However, in order to maintain the original text and avoid repetition, usually we do not mention the feminine forms in translation. (Tr.)

During spring there is an exalted, subtly embroidered seal belonging to the Lord, one showing itself in absolute accuracy and orderliness, abundance and extensiveness, and with absolute speed and ease. You see that completely mixed things are perfectly distinguished and separated. This seal is particular to the One Who can do many things at once, from Whom nothing is hidden, and for Whom nothing is difficult.

In this same season, we see extraordinary art and activity on Earth based on purposefulness, insight, wisdom, and munificence. This occurs everywhere, in exactly the same way, orderliness, and abundance. This art and activity are seals of the One Who, despite being nowhere, is present everywhere through His Power and Knowledge, Whom nothing wearies, and Who never needs help.

Seventh ray

LOOK, O FRIEND! Just as the stamp of the Oneness of Him Who is the Eternally Besought-of-All is observed on the "page" of Earth and throughout the heavens and Earth, so is the stamp of His Unity observed on the universe as a whole. The universe is like a magnificent palace, a well-ordered factory, a well-planned city, all of whose elements or parts work together for great purposes. Elements hasten to help each other, even over long distances, when they are needed and do not get lost. Those who discern this truth see how some parts help other parts to meet their needs. It is as if they respond to each other's requests for help and, in close cooperation and obedience to a single manager, work in orderliness and serve living beings for specific purposes.

Look at this principle of mutual helping and cooperation. The sun and the moon, day and night, and summer and winter work with plants to help animals and to convey their food to them, which they take from the treasury of Mercy. Animals hasten to help human beings. For example, honeybees and silkworms take honey and silk from the treasury of the All-Merciful and carry them to humanity. Soil, air, and water particles help fruits and vegetables, each of which differ in taste and quality of nourishment. In turn, they help the body's cells in perfect orderliness and for great purposes.

This perfect, purposeful, and well-arranged mutual helping is manifested by all of these things, especially inanimate objects. It is an evident proof and clear argument that they are servants of an All-Wise Sustainer, workers of a Munificent Manager who work by His command and leave, and by His Power and Wisdom.

Eighth ray

LOOK, O FRIEND! The food needed by living things is distributed on time and according to their need. This well-arranged universal providence, contained in an all-encompassing mercy, implies love for and knowledge of those beings supplied. Such all-encompassing mercy combined with perfect graciousness implies favoring and gratifying. Such graciousness combined with universal wisdom implies a certain purpose and consciousness. Such universal wisdom combined with a perfect arrangement makes all things interdependent. Such interdependence requires mutual helping and solidarity among all parts of existence.

All of this is a special stamp of the One Who is the Lord, Sustainer, Provider, and Director of all things; a seal unique to the One to Whose Command the sun, the moon, and the stars are subjugated. He is the One Who *has made all things good which He has created* (32:7) and *When He wills a thing, He only says: "Be," and it is* (36:82).

Ninth ray

The stamp of Oneness is seen on all individual things and species, on Earth and the universe, and is distributed throughout the world on such universal elements as air, water, and soil.

Planting seeds in an arable land indicates that the land is controlled by the owner of the seeds, and that the seeds belong to the one who controls the land. All universal elements [like water, air, and soil, which imply an all-encompassing knowledge and wisdom] are at the disposal of a single Maker. Their simplicity, uniformity, and comprehensiveness, and all the things "planted" in them (i.e., fruits of Mercy, miracles of Power, and words of Wisdom), as well as their world-wide distribution for certain purposes, are evidence that the comprehensive and comprehended, as well as the "land" and the "seeds" planted in it, are controlled by God. Each species and element testifies that it belongs to the One Who owns everything. Each flower or fruit, animal or micro-organism, is a seal proclaiming, a stamp pronouncing, a signature declaring in the tongue of perfect harmony, orderliness, and purpose: "The One Who owns me owns this space. Whoever created me created it. Whoever uses me as a letter wrote it. Whoever made me a stitch wove it."

The One Who controls the smallest creatures and manages the life of the weakest beings has supreme power over all elements. The One Who employs all elements manages the lives of all animals and plants, and holds them in His Hand of Lordship. This stamp of Unity is clear to those whose eyes are not blind and hearts are not sealed.

Can you claim absolute ownership of and control over anything? Ask an individual being, and it will reply: "Only the absolute owner of my species can claim to own me." Ask the species, and they will reply: "Only the absolute owner of Earth, both its exterior and interior, can claim to own me." Ask Earth, and it will reply: "Only the absolute owner of the whole universe can claim to own me."

Tenth ray

We have pointed out some stamps of Unity put on parts, individual beings, and wholes; on the universe; and on life, living beings, and bringing to life. Let's look at another of these innumerable seals of Oneness on species and wholes.

The difficulty or ease of creating a tree and a fruit is the same, as both depend on the same law of growth and issue from the same center. Depending on the same law of raising and upkeep lessens difficulty and expenditure to such an extent that there is no difference between one person growing a tree with abundant fruit and many people raising one fruit tree. A single fruit grown by many people requires as many tools as does growing a tree with abundant fruit. Similarly, the instruments, machines, and factories needed to equip an army would be the same if only a single soldier were to be equipped. The difference is only qualitative. Also, printing thousands of copies of a book is not much more expensive than printing one copy. If each copy were printed on a different printing press, the amount paid would be thousands of times greater than that paid for thousands of copies from the same press.

In sum: If innumerably multiple things are not attributed to one source, then, in addition to having to attribute one thing to innumerably multiple things, there would be as many difficulties as those things. So, the extraordinary ease of creating so many species distributed world-wide comes from the Oneness of their Creator.

Eleventh ray

The essential similarities among members of a species and species of a class show the stamp's oneness and the "pen"'s singleness, and testify that such similarities are a Single One's work. Also, the absolute ease [of their creation in such abundance] and the small expenditure spent on them show that they are a Single Being's work. If this were not so, their creation would be impossibly difficult. This observed ease and economy of means also shows that God has no partners in His Essence and acts, for such a condition would destroy the order, which, in turn, would ruin the universe.

Twelfth ray

LOOK, O FRIEND! Life proves Divine Oneness and the necessity of His Existence, and death proves His Permanence and Eternity.

The sun's images reflected in bubbles floating on a river and the sea, as well as in transparent things on Earth, bear witness to the sun. These images disappear when the sun sets or the river enters a tunnel, and new ones appear when the sun rises or the river comes out of the tunnel. This testifies to the permanence of the sun's light and demonstrates that these images are the work of a single sun. Their existence shows the sun's existence; their disappearance shows that there is only one "permanent" sun.

Similarly, the existence of creatures shows the necessary existence of the Necessarily Existent Being. Their disappearance along with the causes of their existence, and their replacement with new creatures bear witness to His Permanence, Eternity, and Oneness. This is because along with the alternation of day and night, seasons and years, beautiful beings are renewed, and fine creatures are replaced as they "set" while their likes "rise." All of this testifies to the existence of an Eternally Beautiful One Who continuously manifests Himself, and to His Permanence and Oneness.

The disappearance of causes and their effects along with the succession of years and centuries, and their being followed by their likes testify that causes and their effects are created for subtle purposes. All of those fine beings coming in successively are creatures of the All-Majestic, All-Gracious, and Beautiful One, all of Whose Names are beautiful and holy. Such activity testifies that they are His changing works, moving mirrors, and successive stamps and seals.

Thirteenth ray

LOOK, O FRIEND! Without exception, everything points in the tongue of its essential helplessness to its Creator's necessary Existence. In the general order of creation, each element has a tongue to express its functions and tasks. These tongues, despite each element's helplessness, indicate their Creator's Oneness. Everything testifies in two ways to the Creator's necessary Existence and Unity. In every living being, there are two signs of His Oneness and absolute independence of creation. Through the Qur'an's enlightenment, I have seen that each part of creation testifies to the Necessarily Existent Being, the One and Eternally-Besought-of-All, in around 55 tongues, which I described briefly in *Qatra* (The Drop).[16]

Fourteenth ray

KNOW, O FRIEND, that just as creatures testify to the All-Glorious One's necessary Existence and Oneness, so do they testify to His Attributes of Majesty, Beauty, and Perfection; the perfection of His Essence; and the fact that His Being, Essential "Qualities," Attributes, Names, and acts have no defect or deficiency.

A work's perfection points to the act's perfection. The act's perfection points to the title's perfection. The title's perfection points to the attribute's perfection. The attribute's perfection points to the being's essential capacity or indispensable quality. The perfection of the essential or indispensable quality points to the perfection of the being who has them. A palace's perfect structure and decoration manifest the perfection of the engineer's work. The work's perfection shows the perfection of his title as an engineer. That is, you know him as a skillful, expert, and capable engineer. The title's perfection displays the perfection of the engineer's qualities, meaning that you know him by his knowledge, intelligence, capability, and efficiency. The perfection of the qualities displays these essential capacities, and that the engineer has fully realized his or her superior capacities and distinguished potential. The capacities' perfection reveals one's perfection as an engineer.

Similarly, the perfection of the works we observe in the universe bears witness to the perfection of the activity behind them, which, in turn, bears

16 *Qatra* is included here as the fourth treatise of this book.

witness to the perfection of the titles of the one doing the work. The titles' perfection testifies to the qualities' or attributes' perfection, for names or titles issue from attributes. The attributes' perfection reveals the perfection of the essential capacities, which are the attributes' sources. The essential capacities' perfection testifies to the All-Glorious Being's perfection. Actually, compared to His glorious Perfection and majestic Beauty, all perfection or beauty in the universe is only a dim or vague shadow.

In conclusion:

- Causes or causality only veil the operation of Divine Power.
- Belief in God's Unity has two degrees: superficial belief and firm conviction.
- Life is an argument for God's Unity.
- If the One God created everything, everything becomes easy. If nature or material causes created everything, everything becomes extremely difficult.
- Everything points to itself only as a "letter," while pointing to its Maker in many respects and manifesting its Maker's titles.
- Spring displays countless examples of the Resurrection.
- The universal interconnectedness of everything for great purposes points to the One Creator and Director.
- The Provider's love for and knowledge of everything is shown by how He takes care of them.
- Every species and element testify that it belongs to the One Who owns everything.
- Attributing innumerably multiple things to many sources results an equal number of difficulties.
- Creatures' testify to the Necessarily Existent Being's necessary Existence via their existence. They bear witness to His Permanence, Eternity, and Oneness via their disappearance, along with the causes of their existence, and via their being followed by new ones.
- Everything points, in the tongue of its essential helplessness, to its Creator's necessary Existence.
- The perfection of what we see in the universe testifies to the All-Glorious Being's perfection.

The Second Treatise

The Second Treatise

Droplets from the ocean of knowledge of the Prophet

A NOTE: Many things make our Lord known to us. The three greatest and most universal are:

- The universe, some signs of which [concerning our Lord's Existence and Unity] have been discussed already.
- The Seal of the Prophets, upon him be peace and blessings, our Lord's greatest sign and key to His hidden treasures.
- The Qur'an, which interprets the Book of the Universe and is God's argument against creatures.

WE SHOULD RECOGNIZE THE SECOND SIGN, PROPHET MUHAMMAD, as an articulate, indisputable "argument" [for our Lord], and then listen to what he says.[17] From the ocean of knowledge of this sign, we shall mention a few droplets.

First droplet

KNOW, O FRIEND, that Prophet Muhammad, this indisputable, articulate argument for our Lord, has a universal personality. He can be described in the following terms:

---

17 In any publication dealing with Prophet Muhammad, his name or title is followed by the phrase "upon him be peace and blessings," to show our respect for him and because it is a religious requirement to do so. A similar phrase is used for his Companions and other illustrious Muslims: "May God be pleased with him (or her)." However, as this practice might be distracting to non-Muslim readers, these phrases sometimes disappear in this book, on the understanding that they are assumed and that no disrespect is intended. (Ed.)

As his person is universal in nature, Earth is his mosque, Makka his place of worship, and Madina his pulpit. He leads all believers, who stand behind him in rows and follow his words on the principles of happiness [in both worlds]. The chief of all Prophets, he removes the lies and slurs leveled against them by their own people and affirms them and the essentials of their religions within Islam. The master of all saints, he guides and educates them via the light of his Messengership. He is the "pivot" around which turns a circle formed of the Prophets, the good, the truthful, and the righteous, who recite God's Names and agree on his Message.

Muhammad, upon him be peace and blessings, is a luminous tree growing on the firm, healthy, and lively roots of the previous Prophets and the heavenly principles they preached. This tree shoots out green, fresh branches yielding the fine "fruit" of saints distinguished with knowledge of God. Whatever he claimed is confirmed by all Prophets based on their miracles, and by all saints based on their good or marvelous works. All his affirmations bear the seals of all perfected people. If one hears him declaring *there is no deity but God*, thereby affirming Divine Unity, one will hear the same declaration from the past and the future, from the illustrious shining "suns" and stars of humanity reciting God's Names in His circle. Despite their different approaches and temperaments, they agree with all of his affirmations, as if saying in unison: "You declare and speak the truth."

How can one object to what has been affirmed by innumerable witnesses, whose miracles and marvelous good works display their pure characters and truthfulness?

Second droplet

KNOW, O FRIEND, that this illustrious person, who affirms Divine Unity and guides humanity to it, is confirmed by Prophethood and sainthood. Billions of people have agreed upon this for 14 centuries. Earlier revealed Scriptures (the Torah, the Gospels, the Psalms, etc.) predicted his coming and confirm his Prophethood. He is confirmed by marvels that, prior to his Prophethood, either he worked or that took place in connection with him. It is also reported through reliable channels that his coming was predicted.

He is affirmed by the hundreds of miracles he worked: splitting the moon; abundant water flowing from his fingers; trees moving in answer to his call; the coming of rain upon his prayer; satisfying many hungry people with very little food through his blessing; understanding the languages of rocks, trees, lizards, gazelles, camels, and wolves, and so on. All of these were narrated by truthful Traditionists and historians. He is also confirmed by the Islamic law, which enables people to find happiness in both worlds. You already have seen the rays from its "sun" diffusing happiness. If your eyes and heart are open, this will be enough for you.

Third droplet

KNOW, O FRIEND, that his very person or character proves his Prophethood. Like the sun [showing itself through its light, heat, and other manifestations], all of the praiseworthy virtues concentrated in his person, as well as the merits and excellences he displayed while fulfilling his mission, confirm his Prophethood. Further proofs are his firm belief demonstrated by his austere life, great awe of God, righteousness, and matchless servanthood to his Lord. The Prophet's complete submission to God, to which his life testifies; the perfection of his earnestness, firmness, and courage; and his utmost certainty in his movements shown by his full confidence in his cause all confirm him. Just as green leaves, bright blossoms, and fresh fruits bear witness to a tree's vigor, the Prophet's full adherence to his cause and following it in total certainty and strictness confirm him in his claim.

Fourth droplet

KNOW, O FRIEND, that time and space greatly influence human reasoning and thought. So, let's free ourselves of these constraints and travel back in time to the Arabian peninsula during the Age of Happiness. Putting on the clothes of that time, we will visit the "Axis of the Sphere of Divine Messengership" at work.

Open your eyes and look carefully. What catches our eyes first is an extraordinary man excelling all others in good looks and good conduct. He has a revealed book, and speaks in an extraordinarily concise and wise way while addressing creation, humanity, jinn, and all other creatures.

What strange things he speaks about: a very important affair, a very awesome tiding. He removes the veil of mystery from the universe's creation, explains why it was created, and answers the questions that occupy the mind of every conscious being: Who am I? Where do I come from? What is my purpose or final destination?

Fifth droplet

Look at this most illustrious being. See how he disseminates the truth with such light that our night is changed into daytime, our winter into spring. It is as if the universe changed form so that its vexed, distressful face became cheerful and smiling.

If we do not look at the universe according to the light [of the truth] that he brought, it seems full of sorrow, its living creatures like strangers and mutual enemies, and its inanimate objects like frightening corpses. We see animals and human beings as orphans weeping at the pain of death and separation. The world's movements, changes, alterations, decorations, and adornments seem like meaningless playthings of chance. Our helplessness is a continuous source of trouble, and our poverty renders us powerless. Human reason or intellect continually upset us with sorrows of the past and anxieties of the future, causing us to be the lowest and most wretched of animals.

Now look at the universe with his light and observe it through the telescope of Islam. See how its appearance has changed. It is no longer a house of mourning, but a mosque in which all beings praise and thank the Creator and reflect [on His works]. Creatures that formerly seemed like strangers and mutual enemies have become friends, brothers, and sisters. Inanimate objects, seen as terrifying corpses, have become like amiable living beings fulfilling certain important functions. In the tongue of those functions or tasks, they articulate their Creator's signs.

Living beings who were like orphans weeping with pain and complaints now appear as reciting the Creator's Names throughout their lives and thanking him for discharging them from their duties (death). The universe's movements, changes, and alterations are no longer subject to chance, but messages from the Creator's rulership or mastership, "pages" on which He writes His signs of creation and rules of the universe, and mirrors in which His Names are reflected. In sum, the universe is a book of Divine Wisdom.

Now look at the past, that great tomb of darkness. See how it has been illuminated with the suns of Prophets and stars of saints. Look at the future, the darkest of nights. See how it has been illuminated with the Qur'an's light and appears as gardens of Paradise.

Now look at people and see how they progressed from being helpless, destitute, and degraded animals to the rank of Divine caliphate on Earth.

They have progressed through the force of their weakness, the power of their helplessness, the motive of their poverty, the incentive of their destitution, the strength of their servanthood, the light of their heart, and the splendor of their intellect. Then look how the reasons for their descent (helplessness, poverty and weakness) have become the reasons for their ascension due to their being enlightened by the light brought by that luminous person: Prophet Muhammad, upon him be peace and blessings.

Without his presence, the universe and everything in it (including humanity) would have been rendered worthless and meaningless. Had it not been for that wonderful, superior person who makes known the universe and its Creator, this beautiful universe would not have existed, for we could not have understood its meaning. How truthful is He Whose words are true, and for Whom is the sovereignty of creation, in His declaration: *But for you, I would not have created the worlds*.

Sixth droplet

Look at and listen to him. He speaks of eternal happiness and brings good tidings of it. He unveils infinite mercy and calls everyone to it. He proclaims the beauties of Divine rule and upbringing, and reveals the secrets of the Divine Names' treasuries.

Look at him from the viewpoint of his mission: He is the proof and lamp of the truth, the Sun of guidance, and the means of happiness. Look at him from the viewpoint of his person: He is the epitome of the All-Merciful's love [of His creatures], the embodiment of the Lord's mercy upon them, the honor of humanity, and the most radiant and illustrious fruit of the Tree of Creation. Now look at him and see how the light of Islam has reached the east and the west with the speed of lightning, how one-fourth of humanity has accepted the gift of his guidance wholeheartedly.

Given this, can the carnal soul and Satan argue, with reason and without sophistry, against the affirmations of one like that man, especially against the foundation of his affirmations: *There is no deity but God?*

Seventh droplet

What stimulates him? Sacred power. Consider his accomplishments in that desert full of savage people who adhered fanatically to their customs, tribalism, and hostility. They were so hard-hearted that they buried their daughters alive without remorse or grief. How did he remove such things from them so quickly and equip them with high, laudable virtues? How did he make them teachers of humanity and masters of civilized peoples? Not by power and terror, as do most rulers, but by conquering hearts and minds; subjugating spirits and egos; and becoming the beloved of hearts, the teacher of reason, the educator of selfhood, and the ruler of spirits.

Eighth droplet

It is very difficult even for a powerful, determined ruler or government to remove an established bad habit from a small community. The Prophet removed many established bad habits from vast communities of people who adhered fanatically to their customs and traditions, with a small force, little effort, and very quickly. Moreover, he replaced them with praiseworthy virtues and exalted merits. Look at 'Umar ibn al-Khattab [a leading person of pre-Islamic Makka, and the second Caliph after the Prophet] before and after his conversion to Islam—after his conversion, the seed of virtue in his character became a "tall, excellent tree" [of most laudable merits].

Almost all of the Prophet's accomplishments are extraordinary. Whoever denies this should go to the Arabian peninsula today and see what they can accomplish there. Let them take a hundred philosophers [psychologists, sociologists, scientists, and pedagogues], and see if they can accomplish in 100 years even one-hundredth of what the Prophet accomplished in a year.

Ninth droplet

A basic understanding of human nature shows that people cannot lie easily about something that will embarrass them if they are caught. Even if it concerns an insignificant matter and is told to a small group, it is still hard. If they can lie comfortably without blushing or shame, they are compulsive liars, a trait that will be publicized by their enemies. Given this, how can someone, especially one famed for his trustworthiness and truthfulness and who carries the greatest responsibility, lie about the most important and greatest mission before humanity until the Last Day? How could he lie before people who hate him and are just waiting to expose him?

When the Prophet, upon him be peace and blessings, speaks, he has no fear of his opponents and neither hesitates nor is anxious. Rather, he speaks with absolute sincerity and enthusiasm, and in a way that confounds his enemies' reason, arguments, and attitudes. How could he have lied and deceived people concerning his mission? No! *[Whatever he says] is but a Revelation revealed* (53:4).

Truth is free and independent of deception, and the eye that sees the truth is not deceived. Therefore the Prophet's path is true and, therefore, he is wholly free of deception, just as his truth-perceiving eyes could not be deceived by illusions.

Tenth droplet

Listen to his words that inform and warn people of awesome events. He speaks about matters that captivate hearts and inspire minds to reflect, and brings humanity good tidings [of a happy future in this world and the Hereafter].

Many people would give almost anything to know the reality of things and events. If someone told you that a person had come from the moon or Jupiter and was saying very interesting things and foretelling the future, would you not give almost anything to find out what he was saying? It is very strange, then, that while you probably would do so in this case, you do not care what the Prophet says, despite the fact that the people of truth and expert knowledge (namely, Prophets, truthful and truth-seeking scholars, and saints) confirm him and agree on what he has said and predicted. He speaks about the acts of a Sovereign in Whose kingdom the moon is no more than a fly circling a moth that, in turn, circles a lamp He has lit in one of the thousands of mansions He has prepared for His guests. He speaks of a world full of wonders and marvels, about a revolution so unusual and extraordinary that if Earth exploded and its mountains flew like clouds, this would not be equal in strangeness to one-thousandth of that revolution.

> When the sun is folded up, and when the stars fall, losing their luster, and when the mountains are moved, and when camels ten-months pregnant are abandoned, and when the wild beasts are herded together, and when the seas are set boiling, and when souls are reunited, and when the girl-child that was buried alive is asked for what sin she was slain, and the records of all people's deeds are laid open, and when heaven is torn away, and when Hell is set blazing, and when Paradise is brought near—then every soul will know what it has prepared. (81:1-14)

> When the sky is cleft asunder, and when the planets are dispersed, and when the oceans are poured forth, and when the graves are over-

> turned, each soul will know what it has sent forward and what it has kept back. (82:1-5)

> When Earth is shaken with its earthquake and Earth yields up its burdens, and humanity asks: "What is the matter with it?" That day it will proclaim its tidings because your Lord inspired it. That day all people will come forth in scattered groups to be shown their deeds. Whoever does good an atom's weight will see it then. And whoever does ill an atom's weight will see it then. (99:1-8)

> The sudden, mighty strike! What is the sudden, mighty strike? What enables you to perceive what the sudden, mighty strike is! A day when humanity will become like scattered moths, and mountains will become like carded wool. Then, the one whose whose scales are heavy [with good deeds], he will be in a pleasing life. Whereas the one whose scales are light, the bottomless pit will be his home. What will convey to you what that is like! It is raging Fire. (101:1-11)

He gives tidings of a future, compared to which this world's future is like a drop from a mirage of water as compared to a limitless ocean. He brings good tidings of contentment, compared to which worldly contentment is but a flash of lightning as compared to an ever-shining sun.

Beneath the veil of this universe of wonders are extraordinary events totally beyond what we are used to. We can learn of such events only if an extraordinary person sees them and tells us about them. We see what he does and how he lives, and conclude that he witnesses them and thus either warns us or brings us good tidings [of the happy future awaiting us beyond them]. He tells us what pleases the Lord of the worlds, what He wants us to do, about some awesome affairs we cannot escape, and about some strange realities we will face and without which happiness is impossible.

Can they really be blind and deaf to such truth and realities? How can people not care about such an extraordinary person?

Eleventh droplet

KNOW, O FRIEND, that this man, known to us by his most sublime character and recognized by the world for his matchless accomplishments, who is an articulate and truthful argument for God's Oneness and a most true evidence of His Unity, is a decisive argument and definite proof of eternal happiness. Through his call and guidance, he shows us how to gain eternal happiness, the creation of which he caused through his prayer and servanthood.

Look at him leading the most comprehensive prayer in front of the peninsula's inhabitants, in front of the world's inhabitants. Look again. All virtuous descendants of Adam, from the beginning until the end of time, stand in rows behind him and follow him. All down the centuries they follow him in worship and say "Amen" to his supplications. Be attentive to what he does and says, for he prays out of a deep, comprehensive, and mighty need. The world, the heavens, and all creatures accompany him and say in the tongues of their behavior and dispositions: "Yes, O Lord, accept his prayer. We ask what he asks of You, together with everything we have—our eyes, ears, tongues, hands, legs, hearts, minds, and so on, as the manifestations of Your Names; we ask of You whatever He asks."

Look at his manners and see how he supplicates in utmost consciousness of his poverty before his Lord, in a most ardent desire and deep sorrow. He stirs the universe to tears, and it participates in his prayer. What does he ask for? The realization of a purpose that, if not realized, will reduce us and all creatures to a state without value or meaning. If this purpose is realized, however, all creatures will attain their rank of perfection according to their capacity.

See how he supplicates with such a deep yearning for help and such a moving request for mercy that the Divine Throne of Universal Rule and the heavens are moved to pity and love and say: "Amen, O God, Amen." To whom does he address his request for the realization of his purpose? To the All-Powerful, All-Hearing, All-Munificent, All-Knowing, All-Seeing, and All-Compassionate One, Who hears everything's most secret supplication and then satisfies it. He sees whatever any of His creatures desire, and enables them to realize their desire in a way they had not considered. He gives freely and shows compassion in such a wise, orderly, and regular way that one cannot doubt that such training, raising, and sustenance is the work of One All-Hearing, All-Knowing, All-Seeing, and All-Wise.

Twelfth droplet

How extraordinary! What does he ask for, this man who stands with all the Prophets behind him and, raising his hand toward God's Supreme Throne, offers a supplication to which humanity and jinn say "Amen"? We know by his acts that he is the honor of humanity, the pride of all beings, and the unique one of creation. He intercedes with God [for all beings] for the sake of all Divine Names manifested in the "mirrors" of beings. He asks for eternal existence, meeting with God, Paradise, and God's good pleasure. Eternal happiness is necessitated among other reasons by Divine Mercy, Favor, Wisdom, and Justice, as well as God's Beautiful Names, almost all of which demand the existence of the other world. But even if it were not so, one prayer of the Prophet would suffice for his Lord's creating Paradise for him and his followers, just as with each spring He builds for us Paradise-like gardens decorated with the miracles of His Art. Just as his mission of Messengership caused the creation of this world for trial and worship, so the prayer he makes as a requirement and dimension of his servanthood would cause the construction of the other world for reward and punishment.

The universe's matchless beauty is so perfect that it prompted the famous theologian Imam al-Ghazzali[18] to say: "It is not possible for a creation more beautiful than the present one to come into existence." Can such extraordinary order and harmony, all-inclusive mercy and faultless artistry, and matchless beauty be combined and marred with ugliness, injustice, and confusion?

The most insignificant petition is heard and answered most attentively. Would it not be an act of supreme ugliness (injustice) to be deaf to the loudest voice making a supplication for the greatest need, and not to accept the best request made with the most beautiful desire and longing? God is absolutely free of such ugliness, and the universe's faultless beauty does not allow it.

Thirteenth droplet

O FELLOW TRAVELER, do you need to see more? Do you want to acquire complete knowledge of the Prophet? Even if we stayed in the Arabian peninsula for 100 years, we still could not comprehend fully even one dimension of his mission and accomplishments. Let us return and, traveling through forward in time, see how each century "flourished" [with his Message] and to what extent it benefited from that Age of Happiness.

While doing so, we see that innumerable "flowers" opened in the "Sun" of that Age of Happiness, and that through the light of guidance he diffused,

---

18 Imam Abu Hamid Muhammad al-Ghazzali (d. 1111): A major theologian, jurist, and sage who was considered a reviver (of Islam's purity and vitality) during his time. Known in Europe as Algazel, he was the architect of Islam's later development. He wrote many books, the most famous being *Ihya' al-'Ulum al-Din*. (Ed.)

each century yielded thousands of illustrious fruits, such as Abu Hanifa,[19] al-Shaifi'i,[20] Abu Yazid al-Bistami,[21] Junayd al-Baghdadi,[22] Shaykh 'Abd al-Qadir al-Jilani,[23] Imam al-Ghazzali, Muhiy al-Din ibn al-'Arabi,[24] Abu al-Hasan al-Shadhili,[25] Shah Naqshband,[26] and Imam Rabbani.[27]

Let's postpone our observations to call God's peace and blessings upon that illustrious, miracle-working being, namely our master Muhammad:

> O God, bestow peace and blessings on that illustrious being, on whom the wise Qur'an was sent down from the Supreme Throne of God by the All-Merciful, All-Compassionate. He is our master Muhammad, upon him be peace and uncountable blessings to the number of the good deeds of his Ummah.
>
> Peace be upon him whose Messengership was predicted in the Torah, the Gospels, the Psalms, and other Divine Scriptures. His Prophethood was prophesied by miraculous events before his Prophethood, by seers among the jinn, humanity, and saints. By his gesture the moon split in half. He is our master and lord Muhammad, upon

---

19 Nu'man ibn Thabit Abu Hanifa (d. 768): Founder of the Hanafi School of Law and one of the greatest Muslim scholars of jurisprudence and deducers of new laws from the Qur'an and Sunna. He also was well-versed in theology. (Ed.)

20 Muhammad Idris al-Shafi'i (d. 820): Founder of the Shafi'i School of Law. He was well-versed in Islamic jurisprudence, Hadith (the Prophet's sayings and actions), language, and poetry. He wrote *Al-Umm* and *Ahkam al-Qur'an*. (Ed.)

21 Abu Yazid al-Bistami (d. 873): One of the most famous Sufi (Muslim spiritual masters) saints. (Ed.)

22 Junayd al-Baghdadi (d. 910): One of the most famous early Sufis. He enjoyed great respect and was known as "the prince of the knowers of God." (Ed.)

23 'Abd al-Qadir al-Jilani (d. 1166): One of the most celebrated Sufi masters. A student of jurisprudence and Hadith, he became knows as the "spiritual axis" of his age and the "the greatest succor." He wrote *Kitab al-Ghunyah*, *Futuh al-Ghayb*, and *Al-Fath al-Rabbani*. (Ed.)

24 Muhiy al-Din ibn al-'Arabi (1165-1240): The "greatest Sufi master." His doctrine of the Transcendental Unity of Existence, which most have mistaken for monism and pantheism, made him the target of unending polemics. He wrote many books, the most famous of which are *Fusus al-Hikam* and *Al-Futuhat al-Makiyya*. (Ed.)

25 Hasan al-Shadhili (d. 1258): Founded the Shadhiliyah, one of the most important Sufi brotherhoods. (Ed.)

26 Muhammad Baha' al-Din Shah al-Naqshband (d. 1389): One of the most prominent Islamic spiritual masters and founder of the Sufi Naqshbandiyyah order. Among his books are *Risalat al-Warida*, *Al-Awrad al-Baha'iyya*, *Hayatnama*, and *Tanbih al-Ghafilin*. (Ed.)

27 Imam Rabbani, Ahmad Faruq al-Sarhandi (d. 1624): The "reviver of the second millennium." Born in Sarhand (India) and well-versed in Islamic sciences, he removed many corrupt elements from Sufism. He taught Shah Alamgir or Awrangzeb (d. 1707), who had a committee of scholars prepare the most comprehensive compendium of Hanafi Law. (Ed.)

him be peace and uncountable blessings to the number of the breaths of his Ummah.

Peace and blessings be upon him whose call trees answered, at whose prayer rain came speedily, and whom the cloud shaded from heat. Hundreds of people were satisfied with a gallon of his food, and water flowed abundantly from his fingers. God made the lizard, the gazelle, the wolf, the camel, the mountain, the rock, and the tree speak to him [and he understood them]. He ascended as far as the seventh heaven and the Supreme Throne of God, and his eyes did not swerve. He is our master and intercessor Muhammad, upon him be peace and uncountable blessings to the number of the letters of the Qur'an's words that have had forms by the All-Merciful's leave in the "mirrors" of air molecules while being recited by reciters from the first day of its revelation until the end of time.

O God, for the sake of every blessing and peace called upon him, forgive us and have mercy on us. Amen, amen, amen.

The arguments for his Prophethood are uncountable. We related several in The Nineteenth Word and The Nineteenth Letter. The miracles manifested through him number around one thousand. Moreover the Qur'an, whose about forty miraculous aspects we explained in The Twenty-fifth Word, also testifies to his Prophethood, as do the universe and all its signs.[28] Among the creatures distributed throughout the universe, there are innumerable signs of the Divine Being's Unity and countless proofs of his Messengership.

For example, consider the fine artistry in creation. Such perfection is a decisive evidence of Muhammad's Messengership, for the beauty of these ornamented creatures manifests a fine artistry in their creation. Their richly ornamented form and constitution show that the Maker has a boundless will to make all creation beautiful and ornamented. Such a will clearly indicates the Maker's elevated love for His creation, His sacred desire to manifest the perfection of His Art. This sacred love and desire show that humanity—the most perfect and finest creature, the most comprehensive being—is the comprehensive and excellent object and focus of this love and desire. Thus we are the conscious fruit of the Tree of Creation, and are finer and more comprehensive than all other parts of creation.

All of these characteristics signify our all-encompassing view and universal consciousness, a full view of the Tree of Creation, and a full awareness

---

28 For all Words and Letters mentioned in this book, refer to Said Nursi, *The Words*, The Light, Inc., NJ: 2005, and *The Letters*, The Light, Inc., NJ: 2007.

of the Maker's purposes. We are the direct, special addressee of the Maker, because we possess this all-encompassing view and universal consciousness. But one individual focuses his all-encompassing view and universal consciousness exclusively on servanthood to the Maker, on love of Him, and on appreciating this exhibition of His Art. He uses all his consciousness, attention, and strength to thank that Maker, Who demands thanksgiving in return for His bounties, and in calling humanity to serve and thank to Him. Surely this individual will be the Maker's first and foremost addressee, the nearest to Him, and the most beloved by Him.

How can it be said that this unique individual is not Prophet Muhammad, upon him be peace and blessings? Is there another person more worthy of this position? Look at this world, and you will see two spheres and scenes facing each other. The first sphere is the infinitely magnificent and well-ordered Divine Lordship, manifested as the scene of the Maker's infinitely perfect and splendid Art. The second sphere is that of servanthood, radiant with utmost submission, integrity, and righteousness. This is the scene of utmost contemplation and appreciation, and the firmest belief and fullest thanksgiving.

After discerning these two spheres and scenes, look at the relationship between them. Notice how the second sphere moves thoroughly in the name of the first one, and works with all its strength for its sake. Then, notice how the scene of contemplation, thanksgiving, appreciation, and belief, with all its content and meanings, is turned wholly to the scene of art and favoring.

When you witness this reality, how can you deny the greatest relationship between the chief of the sphere of servanthood and the Owner of the sphere of Lordship? By fully appreciating and exhibiting [the works of] His art, that chief serves the Maker's purposes most sincerely. How can you remain unconvinced that he has the greatest relationship and connection with the Maker, that he speaks to the Maker directly, and that the Maker honors him with His Messengership? Indeed, he is accepted and beloved by the Lord of the whole domain [of the heavens and Earth]; he is the most beloved by Him and the nearest to Him.

Given this, could the Maker of these infinitely beautiful creatures, the Bestower of all these bounties, Who considers the delicacies of taste in all creatures' mouths, ignore that most perfect and beautiful creature? Muhammad turns to Him with perfect yearning, servanthood, and love. He enraptures the heavens and Earth with his loud songs of applause and appreciation of the Maker's art. He throws the land and sea into ecstasy with his chants of gratitude for the Creator's favors, and with the splendor of his glorification and magnification of the Grandeur of the Creator and Bestower of bounties.

Could such an All-Benevolent and All-Powerful Maker ignore such an appreciative and grateful person? Would He not turn to him with affection and speak to him, love him and draw him near, desire that his good conduct and refined manners be approved and imitated by all people, make him an example to be followed by everyone, and send him as a Messenger to humanity? Could the Maker of these completely well-formed creatures, the delicacies of whose artistic design point to an infinite knowledge and boundless wisdom, be so unaware and unconscious of His creation's most perfect and most beautiful member that He does not know, see, and speak to him?

Could the One Who makes Himself known and loved through the ornaments of His creatures not know and love the one who loves Him as much as He deserves and makes Him known as He must be known, who makes himself loved by Him through his faithfulness, and worships Him most truly?

Fourteenth droplet

This contains "driblets" from the ocean of the greatest miracle [the Qur'an].

First driblet

KNOW, O FRIEND, that the arguments for the Prophethood of Muhammad, upon him be peace and blessings, are uncountable. Scholars have devoted many volumes to this topic. Once I humbly offered some "rays" from this "Sun" in my treatise *The Rays*. I briefly explained some aspects of the Qur'an's miraculous nature in another treatise, *The Flashes*, and expounded upon its eloquence, which is only one aspect, in *Signs of (of tne Qur'an's) Miraculousness*, an introduction to the interpretation of the Qur'an.

Second driblet

The Qur'an came from the Creator of everything. It is clear from the foregoing explanations that the Qur'an, which makes the Lord of the worlds known to us, deals with many issues in different degrees of priority. We have described what the Qur'an is in The Twenty-fifth Word.

It is the eternal translation of the universe, the everlasting translator of the "languages" expressing the Divine Being's "natural" signs, the interpreter of the Book of the Universe. It discloses the secrets of the Divine Names' treasuries hidden on the "pages" of the heavens and Earth, and the key to the truths behind events.

It is the tongue of the world of the Unseen and the world of the seen, the treasury of the eternal Divine Speech, and the eternal favors of the All-Merciful One. The Qur'an is the foundation and plan, the sun of Islam's spiritual and intellectual world, and the map of the Hereafter. It is the expounder, lucid interpreter, articulate proof, and clear translator of the Divine Essence, Attributes, Names, and acts; our educator and trainer, and the water and light of Islam, which is the true and greatest humanity. It is the true wisdom of humanity, the true guide leading us to the purpose of our creation.

The Qur'an is a book of law and wisdom, worship and servanthood to God, commands and invitation, invocation and contemplation, one book containing many books to answer our needs. It is like a sacred library of books and treatises from which saints, eminently truthful ones, purified and discerning scholars, and those distinguished with their knowledge of God derive their specific ways. It illuminates each way and answers their followers' needs.

Third driblet

This section explains the gleam of miraculousness in the repetitions or reiterations to be found Qur'an.

FIRST POINT: Know, O friend, that as the Qur'an is a book of invocation, prayer, and invitation, its repetition is a necessity, for repetition enhances and strengthens these characteristics. Repeated invocations bring spiritual enlightenment, repeated prayers bring satisfaction and peace, and invitations are strengthened through repetition.

SECOND POINT: Know, O friend, that the Qur'an is a [Divine] address to and cure for [the "diseases" of] all people, regardless of their intelligence or condition. Not everyone can recite the Qur'an, a cure for everybody at all times, from beginning to end. To make it easy, the All-Wise and All-Compassionate One included most of the Qur'an's purposes in most of its chapters. It encourages people, declaring: *In truth We have made the Qur'an easy for remembrance and warning. Is there any that will remember and take warning?* (54:17).

THIRD POINT: Bodily needs vary. Air is always needed; water only when one is thirsty or hot. Food is needed daily; others items only monthly or yearly; and some, like medicine, only sometimes. In the same way, one's spiritual needs vary. While some Qur'anic words and verses, like *He* and *God* are always needed; others, such as *In the Name of God* are needed regularly; and still others, such as *There is no deity but God*, are needed very frequently.

Thus the repetition of certain verses and words is based on our need for them. Such repetition reminds us of this need and urges us to feel the need for a certain "spiritual sustenance," namely, the certain verses and words repeated in the Qur'an.

FOURTH POINT: Know, O friend, that the Qur'an has established Islam firmly, and has laid down its foundations and those of the Muslim world. It has transformed human communities by uniting their inhabitants in a shared culture and civilization. Establishing something so firmly and extensively requires reinforcement, and thus repetition. The Qur'an also answers questions asked by all people, regardless of their condition or intelligence.

FIFTH POINT: Know, O friend, that the Qur'an mentions important matters and calls hearts to believe in them. It speaks of subtle truths and invites reason or intellect to gain knowledge of them. Obviously, securing belief and understanding requires repetition in different styles and contexts.

SIXTH POINT: The Qur'an's verses have inner and outer meanings and dimensions, which serve an ultimate purpose for our inner and outer improvement. For example, it was intended that many legal injunctions and norms of conduct would be derived from various verses, and that their relative significance and applicability in different contexts would require the Qur'anic verses to be repeated in different ways and contexts. Similarly, the inner dimensions of meaning challenge the intellect's effort to understand, and the recurrence of verses in different contexts enables an infinite variety and depth of nuanced meaning.

Fourth driblet

This section explains why the Qur'an does not mention certain issues of relevance to science, and why it refers to others implicitly and succinctly.

FIRST POINT: The Qur'an discusses the universe in terms and ways that differ from those of modern philosophy and science, for these disciplines approach the universe in reference to themselves and for their own sakes. But the Qur'an, which was revealed in truth and guides to truth, discusses the universe in reference to its Creator and for the sake of knowing and understanding Him.

Contrary to modern philosophy and science, which provide apparent information on heavenly objects and Earth, as well as on their shape and movements, the Qur'an deals with the universe in succinct and allusive ways. Why is this?

FIRST: The Qur'an mentions the universe only parenthetically, for its purpose is to make the Creator known by humanity with His Attributes and Names. An argument should be explicit and understandable so that everyone can follow it through to its underlying purpose, which, for the Qur'an, is to provide us with sufficient knowledge of God, His Attributes and Names. If it had proclaimed, as scientists desire: "Look at the sun in its motionlessness and Earth in its movements, and see how their Creator is powerful," the resulting argument and purpose would have remained beyond most people, regardless of the time in which they were living. The absolute majority of people should be given precedence in guidance by considering their level of knowledge and understanding. However, the Qur'an's consideration of their level never excludes any society's small minority of scientists, philosophers, and intellectuals. Giving precedence to the minority would deprive the majority [of benefiting from the Qur'an's guidance].

SECOND: The rules of good speech in texts of guidance require that the intended audiences understand the words used. Thus their views, feelings, and levels of understanding should be considered, and they should be addressed in plain, general terms so that they feel comfortable with the subject and understand it easily. [As the Qur'an is designed to guide us for all time, its form of expression must be universally accessible to everyone.]

THIRD: The Qur'an mentions the universe and what happens in it in relation to its Creator, for the most important factor is that everything that exists and happens in the universe should point to its Creator. Science and modern philosophy deal with the universe for its own sake, for they believe that the most important factor is that everything that exists and happens in the universe should point to itself. These two attitudes have nothing in common.

In addition, the Qur'an is God's Word made comprehensible to even the most common people. It considers the majority of people, so that they can acquire direct access to accurate knowledge of and belief in God. Science, however, speaks on behalf of scientists so as to force the masses to imitate and accept their views. And so it goes into detail—although its resulting "truth" is highly questionable—where the Qur'an speaks succinctly or allusively, or says nothing, according to if and how that knowledge will benefit humanity.

FOURTH: As the Qur'an is a guide for all classes of humanity, its speech must not persuade them to accept something through sophistry and vying for superiority. It is also pointless, except when absolutely necessary, to change their views of such facts [when those very facts are called into question]. Rather, it is better to keep silent or be succinct on matters that are not related directly to their essential duties to God or to each other.

For example, the Qur'an mentions the sun only on account of the One Who has made it a light-giving lamp. It says that the sun functions as the "pivot" of the universal system, the center of creation's order, and the shuttle of the loom by which the Eternal Designer's works are woven on Earth's face and the heavens with the threads of day and night and alternating seasons. The Qur'an shows us the magnificent system and arrangement in weaving, the extraordinary order and design of woven things, to show us the perfection of their All-Wise Creator, their All-Knowing Maker. It is not important to its purposes whether the sun moves or not. The Divine weaving of things is obviously splendid; therefore if the sun does not move, as modern science asserts, this does not harm the Qur'an's purposes or its expression of them. [In any case, as scientists tell us, the sun's motionlessness is relative only to the motion of Earth and other planets; it is not absolute.][29]

SECOND POINT: The Qur'an says: *[He] has made the sun a lamp*, (71:16) and: *The sun runs on unto a resting-place for it* (36:38). Why does the Qur'an say this, when scientists say that the sun is the center of a huge system of

---

[29] In recent decades, solar astronomers have discovered that the sun quivers, shakes, and continually rings like a well-hit gong. These vibrations provide vital data about its deep interior and hidden layers, data that affects calculations of the universe's age. [See M. Bartusiac, "Sounds of the Sun," *American Scientist* (Jan.– Feb. 1994): 61-68]. Exact knowledge of the sun's internal spinning is important for testing Einstein's Theory of Relativity. Like many significant findings in astronomy, this discovery also was unexpected. Some astronomers say that the sun is like a symphony orchestra with all instruments being played simultaneously. At various times, all vibrations combine to produce a net oscillation on the solar surface that is thousands of times stronger than any individual vibration. (Tr.)

which Earth is only a part? These two views seem to contradict each other. However, consider these arguments.

By calling the sun a lamp, the Qur'an means that the universe resembles a palace containing furniture and other necessary items, such as food, which the All-Munificent and Compassionate One has prepared for His guests and servants. The sun is the palace's lamp, and obeys the palace's Owner. Describing it as a lamp suggests the Creator's mercy in the grandeur of His Lordship, indicates His favor in His comprehensive Mercy, and His generosity in the majesty of His Sovereignty. By demonstrating that the sun, which often has been deified and worshipped, is only a lamp subjugated to God's command, it declares Divine Unity.

The word *runs* implies God's supreme, purposeful disposition and acts in the continuous alternation of day and night and the succession of summer and winter. It thereby reminds people of the Maker's infinite Power and that He is the Unique Lord of the universe. When the sun and moon are mentioned together, minds automatically go to day and night, summer and winter, and therefrom to events that occur during them. Thus *runs* implies all these meanings, not whether the sun really moves or not.

Look at the Qur'an's words and expressions. See how they function, despite their apparent simplicity, as doors or keys to treasuries of subtle meanings. Then look at those used by science and see how, despite their apparent glitter, they are of little use spiritually, intellectually, or with respect to one's main purposes in life. They cause human beings to fall from the heaven of illumining unity to the dark valleys of multiplicity. Listen to part of what modern philosophy and science say concerning the sun:

> It is a huge mass of intense fire 1,300,000 times as big as Earth, and spins on its axis. The planets, including ours, were detached from it and, at different distances, fly around it attracted toward it through general gravity. If, after some unpredictable event in the heavens (e.g., collision with a passing comet), one planet leaves its orbit, it will result in the solar system's collapse and our world's destruction.

The probability of such an event fills people at times with terror. Is such information useful in our normal, ordinary life?

May God be glorified! See how misguidance assumes the form of truth. The sun and planets were created by the All-Wise Maker, entrusted with certain tasks, and obey the Command and Power of the Creator. Despite its huge size, the sun is nothing more than a single shining drop on the face of the "ocean" of the heavens, on which a ray of the Divine Name "the Light" is manifested.

If scientists and philosophers had said: "God uses these huge inanimate objects in important tasks for the order of the universe, and they obey Him," their knowledge would have had some meaning. But since they attribute [these celestial objects' creation, movements, and the tasks they perform] to the objects themselves or to nature and material causes, they are included in the meaning of the Qur'anic verse: *One who serves other deities besides God is like the person who falls from the sky and the birds had snatched him, or the wind had blown him to a far-off place* (22:31).

THIRD POINT: Know, O friend, that the Qur'an has four main purposes: Divine Unity, Messengership, Resurrection, and justice together with worship. The other issues it discusses are means for realizing these purposes. Good speech requires that detailed explanations of the means and unnecessary additions or arguments not defeat the main aim. Thus the Qur'an tends to omit, or adopt an allusive or succinct attitude toward, certain points of explicitly scientific import.

Most people cannot understand profound Divine truths without metaphors, comparisons, and parables. Since most scientific and philosophical issues require a long time to be understood, and since many scientific truths have been unveiled centuries after the Qur'an's revelation, the Qur'an refers to most such issues through metaphors, similes, and parables, while remaining succinct on points to be understood with the passage of time (i.e., with progress in scientific inquiry).

FOURTH POINT: Know, O friend, that just as a clock ticks continuously due to its parts' ceaseless functioning, so does the world, which can be considered a huge, continuously active clock. When time is included, centuries resemble the hour hand, years the minute hand, and day and night the second hand. When space is included, the movements of Earth and the formation of mountains resemble the hour hand; Earth, through the changes observed in its plants and animals and with respect to life and death, resembles the minute hand; and the atmosphere, through the speed of its changes, resembles the second hand. The heavens, through the changes occurring in them, the movements of their objects, the birth of new stars, and the death of old ones, resemble the "day" hand.

The world is based on certain basic elements (e.g., changing, alteration, day, night, year, century, soil, atmosphere, and heavens) that manifest the acts of the Divine Names and the inscriptions of the Pen of Divine Power and Destiny. Although this world is moving, perishing and transient, journeying and flowing like water, it is transformed into a veil covering the Hereafter through heedlessness and naturalism. By encouraging the excessive study of nature and philosophy, human-centered philosophy and civilization increases this world's density and opacity.

The Qur'an's verses, however, makes the world appear as carded wool, and its expressions make the world appear as transparent.[30] The Qur'an melts the world through its rays, smashes its illusory eternity with reminders of death and eternal punishment, and removes the heedlessness caused by naturalism with its admonitions. With its essential character, the world convulsed in change recites: *When the Qur'an is recited, give ear to it and pay heed, that you may obtain mercy* (7:204).

This is why the Qur'an is brief where modern philosophy and science is detailed. In contrast, where philosophy and science are brief or negligent in [describing] the functions of things as obedient [servants of God] to His commands of creation and life, and as pointing to their Creator's Names and acts, the Qur'an is detailed.

In short, the Qur'an explains the meanings of the Book of the Universe and what it refers to, while science describes the material structure of its "letters" and their positions and reciprocal relationships. Science does not tell us that all things or creatures are meaningful words. To see the difference between the attitude of philosophy and science and the wisdom of the Qur'an, refer to The Twelfth Word, where this difference is explained from the perspective of the Qur'anic verse: *Whoever is given wisdom, has truly been given abundant good* (2:269).

FIFTH POINT: This point is explained in the last chapter of this book ("A Light from the lights of the Verses of the Qur'an").

SIXTH POINT: Know, O friend, that the Qur'an stresses the aspects of things pointing to the All-Mighty's acts and how they manifest His Names. It expounds how Divine acts originate from Divine Names, and how these

---

30 Said Nursi uses "carded wool" to indicate that the Qur'an removes and tears up the veil of materialism and the scientific worldview covering the Divine truths and the Hereafter. (Ed.)

Names, being rays of Divine Attributes, encompass things. In short, the Qur'an deals with how everything's aspects point to their Creator, while science studies how these same aspects point to themselves and their causes, and what scientific or technological benefit they provide. Such a science and philosophy, long wedded to materialism, cannot judge sacred Qur'anic expressions.

Fifth driblet

KNOW, O FRIEND, that one virtue of the Qur'an, affirmed by semantics and rhetoric, is its combination of an excellent fluency of style, and a firm mutual support and coherence, harmony and assistance among its sentences and elements. There is an extraordinary correspondence among its verses and their meanings. Although revealed over 20 years on various occasions and sometimes in reply to specific questions, it is so harmonious and consistent that it could have been revealed all at once or in reply to one question. It came to establish certain rules, explain certain commandments for different cases, and penetrate the understanding of different peoples. But its wonderful arrangement and smooth style make it appear as if it had come for one case, and to satisfy one taste and level of understanding. Its clear expression, beautiful diction, and pure style make everyone think that it directly addresses him or her, although in reality it considers every level of understanding and knowledge.

Although it came to guide all people, each to his or her level of attainment, it preserves the balance so perfectly that it seems to have been directed at only one point of attainment in its guidance. Its viewpoint takes in the entire universe, and its inner and outer dimensions, as if it were viewing a single page. It unveils all of its meanings and teaches them to whoever seeks to understand them.

Sixth driblet

The Qur'an cannot be compared to any other book or speech.

KNOW, O FRIEND, that speech derives its power, beauty, and sublimity from the time, place, and occasion determining the manner of speaking and subject matter, and also from the speaker, audience, and purpose. All of these must be considered. Furthermore, if the speech contains a command or prohibition, the speaker should have a certain authority and power. The greater this authority and power, the more forceful and exalted is his or her speech.

Consider the authority of the Divine commands in: O *Earth, swallow up your waters;* O *sky, withhold (your rain)* (11:44); and: *He said to it [the sky] and to Earth: "Come both of you, willingly or unwillingly." They answered: "We do come willingly* (41:11)." See how different they are from any human command, which has no authority over the sky and Earth. The difference resembles that between an order from a commander who is obeyed absolutely by a powerful, obedient army, and the order of someone to whom nobody pays attention. See the difference between: *when He wills a thing, His command is but to say to it "Be!" and it is* (36:82), and human words. Listen to:

> Have they not observed the sky above them, how We built it, and decked it out fair, and it has no cracks? And Earth—We spread it out, and set therein firm mountains, and We brought forth in it all kinds of delightful plants. An enlightenment and reminder for every penitent servant. And We have sent down from the sky blessed water with which We have brought forth gardens and the harvest grain. And lofty date palms with ranged clusters: Provision for the servants; thereby giving new life to a dead land. Even so shall be the Resurrection. (50:6-11)

Listen to these Divine words. See the difference between the descriptions of the True Owner, Whose commands are absolutely influential and Who describes His acts by enumerating His favors, and the shallow, human descriptions unrelated with the Divine acts and favor.

How vast is the difference between the "angels" of the words of the Creator of the sun and the moon, which diffuse the light of guidance, and those of human beings "blowing on the knots" of their vain ambitions. How different are the words of the Qur'an, "mother-of-pearls" of guidance and sources of the truths of belief and the essentials of Islam having issued from the Supreme Throne of the All-Merciful. They comprise the eternal address embedded in Divine Knowledge, Power, and Will. How different are they from the hollow human words of fancy and desire.

The Qur'an is like a tree that has sent forth its branches, come to leaf, blossomed, and yielded the fruit of the Islamic world: its spiritual values, principles, perfections, and purified scholars and saints. Many seeds produced by this illustrious tree as principles of conduct have grown into fruit-bearing trees. About this, the Qur'an declares: *Say: "If all humanity and jinn gathered together to produce the like of this Qur'an, they could not produce one like it, though they were helpers of each other"* (17:88).

The Qur'an is unique. The beauty of its order and composition; the originality and uniqueness of its styles; the superiority, excellence, and clarity of its explanations; the power and truth of its meanings; and the purity and fluency of its language are beyond compare. Its meaning is so comprehensive that all principles of exacting jurists, tastes of those famous for their knowledge of God, and paths of all purified, perfected scholars to God have all originated in it. It has remained original and fresh throughout the ages, becoming ever-fresher over time. It has satisfied all levels of knowledge and understanding in every age, and silenced those most distinguished in rhetoric and eloquence. Humanity has been unable to produce even one verse like it. So, the difference between it and human words is as great as that between the highest heaven and Earth; indeed, no human words can be compared with it.

> O God, for the sake of the Qur'an and of him to whom it was revealed, illumine our hearts with its light. Make the Qur'an a cure for our illnesses, and a companion for us during this life and after death. Make it a confidant in the world, a friend in the grave, an intercessor on the Day of Judgment. Make it a light on the Bridge, a veil and cover from the Fire (of Hell), a companion to Paradise, and a guide and leader to all good. (Do this) through Your Grace, Mercy, Generosity, and Favor, O Most Munificent of the Munificent, Most Merciful of the Merciful. Bestow blessings and peace on the one to whom You sent it and who You sent as a mercy for all the worlds, and on his Family and Companions,[31] as will please You and himself, and as will be approved, O Lord of the worlds. O Revealer of the Qur'an. For the Qur'an's sake, make this book say this prayer on my behalf when death has silenced me. Amen! A thousand times Amen!

In conclusion:

- The three greatest and most universal things that make our Lord known to us are the universe, the Seal of the Prophets, and the Qur'an.
- Prophet Muhammad has a universal personality.
- His Prophethood and sainthood are confirmed by predictions in the earlier revealed Scriptures, the marvels he himself or were connected with him

[31] The Prophet's Family: The Prophet, 'Ali, Fatima, Hasan, and Husayn. These people are known as the *Ahl al-Bayt*, the Family (or People) of the House. The Prophet's wives are not included in this designation. The Companions: Those who gathered around the Prophet to receive instruction and follow his example as closely as possible. They are considered the Muslim nation's elite and vanguard and are given the highest respect and admiration. (Tr.)

prior to his Prophethood, the approximately 1,000 miracles performed during his Prophethood, and his very person or character.

- Such questions as: Why was the universe created? Who are we? Where do we come from? What is our purpose or final destination? are answered in the Qur'an.
- If the Prophet had not lived, existence would have no value and meaning, and we would not know why the universe exists.
- The Prophet is the epitome of the All-Merciful's love [of His creatures] and the embodiment of the Lord's mercy for them.
- The Prophet transformed his hard-hearted people into teachers of humanity and masters of civilized peoples by conquering hearts and minds. He subjugated spirits and egos, and became the beloved of hearts, the teacher of reason, educator of selfhood, and ruler of spirits.
- The Prophet did not fear his opponents, for they could find no gap in his absolute sincerity, enthusiasm, and character.
- He speaks of, and warns people of, awesome events, of matters that captivate hearts and inspire minds to reflect. He brings good tidings [of a happy future both in this world and the Hereafter].
- He is a decisive argument and definite evidence of eternal happiness. Following his guidance leads to eternal happiness.
- He seeks eternal existence, meeting with God, Paradise, and God's good pleasure.
- Since that Age of Happiness, the Prophet's guidance has yielded hundreds of thousands of illustrious scholars in the religious and "natural" sciences as well as in the Religion's inner dimension (Sufism).
- The arguments for his Prophethood are uncountable.
- The Qur'an, which makes the Lord of the worlds known to us, deals with many issues in different degrees of priority.
- Answers to such questions as: What is the Qur'an? Why are its verses repeated? Does it mention scientific facts and, if it does, how are they mentioned? How do the Qur'an and science approach the universe? What are the Qur'an's main purposes? and Why is the Qur'an so eloquent?
- The Qur'an is unique, beyond compare, eternally original and fresh.

The Third Treatise

The Third Treatise

Arguments for the Resurrection

In the Name of God, the All-Merciful, the All-Compassionate.

ALL PRAISE BE TO GOD, TO WHOSE NECESSARY EXISTENCE AND UNITY all atoms and compounds of the universe testify with the tongue of their helplessness and poverty [before God]. Peace and blessings be upon His Prophet, the discoverer of creation's secrets and the key to its signs [of God's Existence and Unity], his fellow Prophets and Messengers, the angels nearest to God, and the righteous servants of God who live in the heavens and on Earth.

There is a fundamental, close relationship between the six pillars of belief, so much so that one cannot be considered without the others. Believing in one requires believing in the others. Given this, without proceeding to explain the arguments for the Resurrection, it is proper to expound briefly some arguments for God's Existence and Unity and the Prophet's Messengership.[32]

32 Since there is a mutual relationship among the six pillars of belief (belief in God's Existence and Unity, Prophethood, Divine Scriptures, angels, the Resurrection, and Destiny) in a way one requiring the other, and since the *al-Mathnawi al-Nuri* consists of booklets written at different times, and since the writer's aim is to guide people to belief, repetition is inevitable. There are similar repetitions in the Qur'an. You will see the reasons for this in the coming pages, as you have seen some in the previous treatise. (Tr.)

Some arguments for God's Existence and Unity

KNOW, O FRIEND, that those who follow naturalism and adhere dogmatically to causality find the door of thanksgiving [to the Creator] closed and the door of associating partners with Him opened. Associating partners with, unbelief in, and ingratitude to God are based on a foundation of impossibilities, for:

- *The One Who creates a fruit with all of its art and meaning can create and govern Earth*

If people awaken from their ignorance and analyze their unbelief according to true scientific knowledge, they must acknowledge that they have attributed functions and missions to one minute particle that it cannot fulfill. For example, they will have to admit that each atom contains millions of machines and can produce all subtleties of art found in all creatures. Each air particle can enter all plants and flowers, trees and fruits, and work therein. If it is said that these particles do not work in the name of One in Whose Hand is the kingdom of all things, then each particle must have full knowledge of whatever it enters.

Consider a fruit. It is a miniature of the whole tree, and its seed is like the page upon which the tree's life-history is inscribed. Also, it is connected with all members of its species as well as the whole Earth. Therefore, by virtue of the greatness of its art and meaning, the art of one fruit is as great as that of Earth. Thus the One Who creates a fruit with all of its art and meaning can create and govern Earth.

- *Destiny draws outlines or plans according to the purposes assigned to it by Wisdom, and Power builds it accordingly*

KNOW, O FRIEND, that everything has two aspects: its visible form, which resembles a garment made specifically for the functions and purposes assigned to it, and its immaterial aspect, which comprises all forms it will assume during its life. This is like a circle formed by something with light attached to one end spinning around itself at high speed. An item's immaterial aspect is, in one respect, its life-history determined by Destiny, which we call "fate" or the "destiny of things." Both aspects contain wise purposes for the item's existence and life. The material aspect requires Power, while Destiny determines its shape and growth. In other words, Destiny draws outlines or plans according to the purposes assigned to it by Wisdom, and Power builds it accordingly.

- *Denying God's Existence and Unity means attributing to every atom and natural cause as much knowledge and power as to create the whole universe*

Those who refer to true scientific knowledge and truth must admit, through their ingratitude and unbelief, that every minute particle and "natural" cause has enough knowledge to produce garments for everything that exists, as well as for the forms they will assume during their growth. It also must have as much power as necessary to renew continually all garments torn up by the "thorns" of events over time. Even human beings, the fruit of the Tree of Creation and supposedly the most powerful cause, the most knowledgeable, and having the most comprehensive willpower, let alone minute particles, cannot fashion a suitable garment for a thorny tree. However, the All-Wise Maker clothes it in ever-new garments while it grows, and makes its green, richly decorated and perfectly fitting garments swiftly and easily. *All glory be to Him, Who brings what He wills into existence by saying to it "Be!" and it is. Glory be to Him in Whose Hand is the dominion of all things, and unto Him you are returning* (36:82-83).

KNOW, O FRIEND, that everything bears a stamp and seal particular to the One, Besought-of-All, and has signs testifying that He is its Maker and Owner. Out of the innumerable stamps of His Oneness and seals of His being the Eternally-Besought-of-All, look at the "stamp" seen during spring.

- *Perfect artistry despite abundance; perfect order despite absolute ease; perfect measure, proportion, and firmness despite incredible speed; perfect individualization despite world-wide distribution; the highest price and value despite the greatest economy; and perfect distinguishment despite absolute mixedness and similarity point to the One, Single Creator*

On Earth's surface, we observe acts of ever-original and purposeful creation. These occur in infinite abundance together with beautiful and perfect artistry; with absolute ease and in perfect order and arrangement; at incredible speed with no loss of proportion, firmness, or substantiality; and in an infinite distribution of species together with each individual's infinite beauty. These acts occur with the greatest economy or lowest cost imaginable, yet every individual is priceless, and unique while having the highest correspondence and similarity between and among species despite the vast distances of time and space. They are in balance with an absolute variety, a perfect individualization of characters and features though generated from similar or even the same materials, structural principles, and organization.

Each thing is enough to manifest the stamp discussed, for the infinite abundance together with beautiful, ordered artistry is particular to Him Who has infinite power and Who is not distracted or prevented from doing many things at once. The absolute ease in perfect order and arrangement is particular to Him for Whom nothing is difficult and Who has infinite knowledge. The extraordinary speed that does not affect firmness and proportion is particular to Him to Whose Power and Command everything is submitted.

The vast distribution of species in which each individual's infinite beauty is maintained is particular to Him Who is unconfined by space, but near everything through His Power and Knowledge. Each individual's wonderful economy and abundance, which is of immeasurable value, is particular to Him Who is infinitely rich and disposes of inexhaustible treasures.

- *The firm coherence, perfect correspondence despite vast distances, and perfect individualization of characters despite being formed of the same material, show the Creator having absolute Will, Power, and Knowledge*

The coherence of the members of various species, despite the uniqueness of each individual and without the least confusion and fault, is particular to Him Who sees all things and is a witness over them. He can do many things at once, and hears the petition of all things simultaneously without becoming confused.

The perfect correspondence and similarity in structure and form among species despite vast distances in time and space, and in balance with an absolute variety as if each member expects the order to be given to it by a single director, is particular to Him. Via His Knowledge, Power, and Wisdom, He disposes of Earth as He wills.

Each creature, though generated from similar or even the same materials, has unique characters and features, and their structural principles and organization are particular to Him Who has absolute Will and freedom of choice. Each creature's perfect structure and beauty, despite the vast abundance of species, is particular to One Whose Power is so absolute and inclusive that atoms and galaxies are the same for Him.

While each of these points is enough to manifest the stamp of Divine Oneness, they present a forceful display of the stamp of Divine Oneness when considered together as a single act formed one within the other. Based on this, we can understand the meaning of: *Assuredly, if you should ask them who created the heavens and Earth, they will surely say*, "God" (39:38). That is, when intellectually and logically awakened to this reality, unbelievers cannot help but admit God's Existence and Creative Power.

Belief in God requires believing in Messengership

KNOW, O FRIEND, that belief in God, the Prophet, Resurrection, and affirming the universe's existence require mutual belief. There is a perfect relation between these pillars of belief, for believing in one requires believing in the others. The universe explains the absolute necessity of God's Existence, and God's Existence requires Messengership and the other world.

It is impossible for such a book, especially one in which each word is as meaningful as a separate book and each letter of which is like a eulogy, to have no writer. The existence of this Book of the Universe cannot be explained if there is no Eternal Designer. Just as a building containing marvels of art, exquisite designs, and wonderful decorations cannot exist without an architect and a builder, this world cannot exist without its Maker.

Images of the sun reflected in transparent things, as well as in bubbles on rivers and seas, and in drops of water and snowflakes, can be explained only by attributing them to the sun. Otherwise, we would have to accept the existence of as many suns as there are drops of water, bubbles, and snowflakes. The existence of this ever-changing and ever-renewed universe can be explained only by the necessary existence of its Creator and Builder. He planted this awesome tree according to the principles of His Will and Wisdom, elaborated it according to the prescripts of His Destiny and Decree, ordered it according to the demands of His manner of acting, decorated it in accordance with the gifts of His Favor and Mercy, and illuminated it by manifesting His Names and Attributes.

Each living part of creation is like a miniature of the whole, and therefore the Creator of that part can create the whole. Denying the existence of One Creator means that there are as many divinities as there are atoms and compounds in the universe.

- *God manifests Himself through Messengers*

Just as the sun diffuses light, God manifests Himself through Messengers. Infinitely perfect Beauty cannot fail to make Itself known through a teaching Messenger; infinitely beautiful Art cannot fail to draw attention to Itself through a herald who describes It; and the sovereignty of an all-encompassing Lordship must proclaim, through one raised with the principles of happiness in both worlds, Its Oneness and Its being the Eternally-Besought-of-All.

Infinite Beauty or Grace demands universal servanthood—those graciously created and subsisted to observe Its subtleties and love It; eyes to gaze upon It with appreciation; and the existence of a beloved servant (a Messenger) who will love It, make It loved by others, and through whom It will make Itself known. Thus the Messenger, through his servanthood, functions as a mirror reflecting the Beautiful One and, through his Messengership, calls others to observe Him. A treasure replete with miracles and most precious jewels will be exhibited by a goldsmith, who will describe it with all of its hidden subtleties.

Apart from our master Muhammad, upon him be peace and blessings, who else has possessed all these qualities [to make the Lord of the worlds known by all conscious beings]? Our master Muhammad is the most perfect, noble, and virtuous person. He is the king of Messengers, of those who make the Divine Being known, manifest His Beauties, and convey His commands. It is they who observe His miracles and bring others to observe them, worship Him and guide others to His worship, and love Him and draw others to love Him. May the most meritorious of blessings and peace, as long as Earth and heavens subsist, be upon him, them, and their families.

Arguments for the Resurrection

Consider the irrefutable arguments for the Resurrection and the afterlife. A just ruler must reward obedient subjects and punish rebellious ones. This is even more true when the ruler:

- Is infinitely munificent, controls infinite treasures, and whose awesome might is the source of infinite honor and dignity.
- Has boundless Mercy requiring boundless graciousness, and Majesty demanding the chastisement of those who slight it.

- Has exalted Wisdom requiring the preservation of His Sovereignty by treating kindly those who take refuge in it, and absolute Justice demanding the maintenance of His Glory by protecting His subjects' rights.
- Has infinitely vast treasures and absolute Generosity requiring a permanent abode of feasting and the permanent existence of those in need of His treasures.
- Has secret Perfections demanding to be manifested to those who fully appreciate them.
- Has peerless Beauty and incomparable subtlety of Benevolence that require being watched by others in "mirrors," which, in turn, requires the permanent existence of those who will gaze on them with yearning, wonder, and appreciation—permanent beauty and grace are not content with impermanent lovers.
- Has so much Compassion that He helps all in need, answers all who petition Him, and fulfills His subjects' needs, no matter how insignificant. Given this, He will gratify His favorite's need, especially if it is the need of all and is easy to meet.
- Has a small hospice, an ever-changing testing-ground, filled and emptied daily with His subjects, despite His Sovereignty's infinite splendor. They stay only for a short time in that place, which displays the marvels of the Ruler's art and Favor and is continually transformed. The implication is that behind this hospice, testing-ground, and place of exhibition are permanent palaces, everlasting abodes, and open treasuries filled with the original items.
- Is infinitely meticulous in His sovereign duties. He records and wants to have recorded everything that occurs in His kingdom. This means that one day he will call His subjects, especially the leading ones, to account. He will manifest fully His Mercy, Compassion, Forgiveness, Power, Justice, and Dignity.
- Makes repeated promises that He can carry out easily and that have profound significance for His subjects. He cannot break even one, for that would contradict His rule's glory and dignity.
- Has Messengers who agree unanimously that the center of His mighty Sovereignty is far from us, and that this world's transient mansions will be exchanged for everlasting palaces in the next world. Such a magnifi-

cent, permanent Sovereignty cannot be based on what is perishable, changeable, and transitory.

- Provides in this transitory world samples of many permanent worlds. Thus these gatherings and separations are not ends in themselves, but are rehearsals to be copied and preserved with their results. Proceedings in that vast place of gathering will be according to the consequences engendered by these rehearsals.
- Manifests in these decaying mansions, perishable grounds, and transitory places of exhibition the works and traces of His Wisdom, Favor, Justice, and Mercy. Anyone with discernment must conclude that one cannot find a more perfect wisdom, a more liberal favor, a more encompassing mercy, and a more glorious justice than His.

  For His Wisdom, Favor, Mercy, and Justice to be manifested, each with Its essential or original truth, the center of His Sovereignty must contain permanent lofty abodes, everlasting elevated mansions, and inhabitants to reside in them eternally. Otherwise, one would have to deny this Wisdom, Favor, Mercy, and Justice. Moreover, the doer of these acts, the owner of these instances of wisdom and munificence, would have to be considered a playful, capricious, and unjust tyrant. This, in turn, would require transforming truths into their opposites, which is inconceivable to those with sound judgment and reasoning but not to those who, like the sophists, deny the existence of everything, including themselves.
- Can transfer His subjects from these transitory mansions to the seat of His permanent Sovereignty, and displays uncountable signs that this temporary ground will be exchanged for a perpetual one.
- Has created this world and will create the next one (the Hereafter), where perfectly just reward and punishment required by the sovereignty of His Lordship will take place.
- Has a vast Munificence that demands a commensurate giving of favor and reward, and an immense Might and Dignity that require infinite sensitivity and zeal [to preserve that Dignity]. This world cannot fulfill even a minute portion of what such a degree of Munificence and Dignity requires.
- Has a Mercy that encompasses all things. Each mother's compassion, as well as the easy provision of sufficient food to all plants and weak

and young animals, are but a single radiation of this Mercy. Such Mercy requires a commensurate bestowing of favor and benevolence. Consider the ephemerality of those It favors and provides for in this world, which is but a drop from the infinite ocean of that Mercy. If that Mercy did not manifest Itself fully in another world, then favor and beneficence, blocked in this world and without hope of becoming unblocked, would change into a cause of distress and suffering.

Compassion [for things bound to eternal extinction]S is, in fact, a suffering, and love for them a desperate concern. The intellect, [which brings to mind past pains and future anxieties,] is, in this short life, a torment and passing pleasure, for with no hope of eternity it turns into pain. Denying eternal life means denying this Mercy, and is the same as denying the sun that fills the world with its light every day.

- Has a Majesty and Glory that require punishing those who disrespect them and destroying those who disparage them. His destruction of earlier rebellious peoples shows that He gives respite but does not neglect them. His actions show that He gives the greatest importance to His commands and prohibitions.
- Makes Himself known and loved through perfect, well-proportioned, and beautiful things, such as lovely flowers. He shows His Mercy through the attractive fruits therein. For those who deny Him their belief, worship, and respect, He has prepared an abode of punishment at the seat of His eternal Lordship.

From the purposes and benefits He has attached to everything, as well as the order and beauty of art He displays in all creatures, we may conclude that the wisdom behind His acts requires the rewarding of those who obey and seek refuge in Him. He places everything in its proper place, gives everything its due, and answers each supplication made by a member of His creation. And so we may deduce that He dispenses an absolute, true Justice that requires preserving the glory of His Kingdom and Lordship, and protecting the rights of His subjects in a supreme tribunal. Since this transient abode, a realm of trial for conscious beings where they can act freely, is too small for His Justice to manifest itself thoroughly, the All-Just, All-Wise One with absolute Beauty, Grace, and Glory must have at His disposal an eternal Paradise and permanent Hell.

- Has infinite Munificence and Generosity, and treasuries of blessings and favor. Among these are suns replete with light and trees full of fruit. This infinite Generosity and Wealth demand an eternal realm of feasting and the permanent existence of those who are in need. An infinite generosity requires an infinite bestowal of favor that, in turn, demands the perpetual existence of those who will be favored and return it by giving thanks. Otherwise, returning that perpetual favor would be restricted to each individual's limited life-span.
- Has secret Perfections. His miraculous works of Perfections must be manifested for appreciative observers. Perpetual perfection requires perpetual manifestation and the existence of appreciative observers. Perfection loses its value in the view of observers condemned to eternal extinction.
- Has a peerless, transcendent Beauty. Each Name is perfectly beautiful due to this Beauty's radiations. How can we grasp such Beauty? Earth, one of His "solid" mirrors of ever-changing scenes displayed annually and seasonally, as well as at every moment, is but a shadow of a few radiations of that Beauty, and spring is only one of its flowers.

  A perfectly Beautiful One must desire that His Beauty be seen by Himself and others. He desires the existence of "mirrors" to reflect His Beauty, and of lovers to show part of His admired Grace. Eternal Grace and Beauty require eternal lovers and admirers. Since one feels enmity toward that which cannot be attained or comprehend, the love of an ephemeral lover for an eternal Beauty turns into enmity. Therefore, just as this world requires the existence of a Maker, the Maker demands the existence of an eternal realm.

Further reflections

This world's Owner has such mercy and affection that He helps those who ask and answers those who pray to and take refuge in Him. He fulfills the smallest need on time, hears the softest voice of His most secret creatures, and complies with its request.

When one considers how infants and the weak are cared and provided for, one will see the Divine Mercy and Affection clearly. Thus this Mercy united with Generosity requires that the greatest need of His greatest and most beloved servant be met, especially if it is the need expressed, either in words or action, by all conscious beings. This is especially true if meeting that need will enable them to reach their highest potential, and refusing to meet it may cause them to fall so low that they cannot rise again; if that need is presented through all Divine Names manifested in the universe, such that the One Who can and will meet that need in an instant is the One Who has these Names; and if it is His most beloved servant who pleads its meeting in a most humble and acceptable manner and in a way that makes him loved. Those who accept his leadership, among whom are the Prophets, saints, and pure, exacting scholars, say "Amen" to his prayer and ask their Munificent Lord for Paradise, eternity, eternal happiness, and approval.

In such a case, the all-encompassing Divine Mercy fulfills the request, for not to do so would be unjust. This beloved person, the center or pivot of witnessing and having others witness the Existence, Unity, and acts of the Eternal Witness, is a Messenger who reveals to humanity the mystery of creation, Divine Unity amidst multiplicity, and how to attain eternal happiness in Paradise. Through his servanthood, He unveils the treasuries of Mercy, reflects the beauty of the Divine Lordship, and serves as the means of eternal happiness and the existence of Paradise.

If there were no other reason for Paradise to exist, this beloved one's request would suffice for the All-Generous One's Generosity, Who every spring creates richly ornamented gardens resembling gardens of Paradise, to create it. For Him, creating Paradise is as easy as creating paradisiacal gardens on Earth. The one about whom was declared: "But for you, I would not have created the worlds," deserves to be addressed with: "Had there been nothing but your prayer, I would have created Paradise for your sake."

> O God! Bestow blessings and peace on that beloved one, the lord of the two worlds, the pride of creation, the life of the two realms, the means of happiness in both worlds, who has the principles of a happy life in both worlds, the Messenger to both humanity and jinn, and on his Family, Companions, and fellow Messengers and Prophets. Amen.

- *There must be permanent castles, everlasting mansions, and open treasuries filled with the originals of the samples seen here, where the eternal Sovereignty's full Magnificence is shown*

Think of how this world's Owner, as may be concluded from His control of it as well as His subjugation of suns and moons, trees and rivers, and so on, enjoys a magnificent sovereignty in His awesome Lordship. However, as this abode is continually transformed and headed for destruction, it resembles a guest-house filled and emptied daily, an incessantly changing arena of trial, a place to exhibit models of its Owner's marvels and samples of His bounties. Its temporary inhabitants are on a continuous journey, and thus can stay only as long as they receive answers to their questions. As they may be told to depart at any time, there must be permanent castles, everlasting mansions, and open treasuries filled with the originals, where the eternal Sovereignty's full magnificence is displayed.

Suppose you come across a splendid guest-house that a benevolent ruler has built and richly decorated for travelers to stay in for only one night. You see that most of the decorations are samples, that visitors can taste only the food offered, that everything happening inside is recorded, and that the decorations are changed daily. You will conclude that its owner has limitless wealth and infinite generosity, and that it was built for a fixed period to arouse a yearning for the boundless and inexhaustible banquets prepared for all travelers in his permanent mansions.

A true human being understands that this world was not created for its own sake and is not an end in itself, but rather a realm filled through birth and emptied through death. The Munificent Lord invites its inhabitants to the realm of happiness. Its decorations provide only temporary pleasure, and are replaced by pain upon their disappearance, to sharpen one's appetite [for the originals]. They cannot satisfy this appetite, because both they and those enjoying them exist only for a short time. They are offered so that the travelers will reflect, give thanks, and yearn for the eternal originals.

These decorations are only samples of the bounties stored by the All-Merciful for believers in gardens of Paradise. These transient things were not created for eternal extinction, but have been assembled here to be copied with their forms, meanings, and consequences of their existence. Everlasting scenes will be woven from them for the people of eternity, or the One Who subjects them to incessant transformations will make from them whatever He wills in the eternal world.

- *Memories of conscious beings and the seeds of plants point to the Resurrection and the afterlife*

Here is another proof that they are for eternal existence and not for eternal extinction, that their apparent decay or extinction means the end of their tasks here or their discharge from their worldly duties. Consider a flower, a "word" of Divine Power that looks at us for a very short time and then goes away. Think of it as a spoken word that, by God's permission, goes to thousands of ears and whose meanings are understood by numerous intellects. When the flower dies, it entrusts itself to the memories of those who have seen it, and its forms and meanings to its seeds. Thus the memory of those who saw it and each seed becomes like a record preserving the decorations of its forms and a place for its permanence. You can compare with that flower other living beings that have a higher degree of life up to beings with eternal spirit.

- *The Owner of this world is the All-Preserving*

People have not been left to do whatever they want. Rather, their words and acts are recorded, and their consequences are preserved for a final reckoning. The Maker's autumnal destruction of spring's beautiful things means their discharge from their duties and makes room for new things to fulfill their duties. It is also a warning for the heedless that the Maker of this world is the All-Knowing and Eternal, Who drives and urges His servants to Him, and Who has prepared for them things beyond their imagination.

Reflect on the reality that the Owner of this world is the All-Preserving. He misses nothing, and records and preserves everything in a manifest book. The balance, order, harmony, and measure seen in the world are but a few lines of this book. Those who complete their life and therefore their duties and depart from the visible, material world carry their entire life on preserved tablets and their deeds preserved in their results. The Creator keeps them in various "mirrors" in the visible and unseen worlds. It is as if many things have been charged with recording whatever we do, how we behave toward the living and non-living entities with which we have some relation.

Look at our memories, the fruits of trees, and the seeds of fruits and flowers, so that you may understand the comprehensiveness of the law of recording and preserving. The Owner of these creatures is infinitely careful about His acts of Sovereignty, and records whatever happens in His Kingdom. Everything is so perfectly ordered and measured in His Lordship that He records (or has recorded) the most insignificant event and [His servants'] least service. Such recording and preserving require an eventual reckoning. This is especially true for the comprehensive acts done by humanity, the noblest and most honorable of creatures, who witnesses all acts of Divine Lordship, heralds Divine Unity in the realm of multiplicity, and observes the glorification of creatures. Due to this and innumerable other virtues, we have been honored with the Divine Trust—the human self distinguished with free will, knowledge, speech, and the Divine Religion—and God's vicegerency on Earth.

- *The honor and distinction conferred on human beings require their deeds to be recorded and preserved*

This honor and distinction does not exempt us from being called to account. *Does humanity think that it will be left to roam at will, that it will be left uncontrolled?* (75:36). Each person will be called to account for even the smallest act in the Place of Supreme Gathering and the eternal world. Destroying the world, raising the dead, and assembling them for judgment in the Place of Gathering are as easy for the Divine Power as creating spring and autumn. All past happenings, which are miracles of His Power, testify that He can do whatever He wills and promises to do in the future.

This world's Owner and Ruler has promised repeatedly to create something of infinite importance for His creatures and servants. Breaking a promise would contradict His Power's dignity and glory and His Lordship's mercy, for such an act comes from ignorance, inability, or impotence, all of which cannot exist in One with absolute Knowledge and Power. Building the other world through many revolutions and with all of its Gardens is as easy for Him as creating spring with all of its gardens and transformations. His promise has been agreed upon and affirmed by all Prophets and the consensus of all purified, exacting scholars. Hear the strength of His promise: *God—there is no god but He. He will gather you to the Resurrection Day, about which there is no doubt. Who is truer in tidings than God?* (4:87). But those who do not confirm the word of Him Whose truthfulness is confirmed by all creatures, and is affirmed by the universe through its articulate signs, must be relying on illusions, lying, and Satan's deceiving words and falsehoods. We seek refuge in God from being left without a true helper, and from the evils of the carnal soul and Satan.

- *The Lordship and Sovereignty observed in this fleeting world point to the everlasting world*

Here, we observe the manifestations of a magnificent, eternal Lordship and the works of a permanent and splendid Sovereignty. Consider the grandeur of this Lordship's Owner. He causes the ever-changing Earth, which submits to Him, to die and then brings it back to life, manages, and directs it. He manages the sun and its satellites, all of which are subjugated to His Power, and moves the whole sun-centered system.

This magnificent eternal Lordship and comprehensive perpetual Sovereignty, which amazes intellects through its awesome acts, cannot be confined to the ever-changing momentary affairs related to this changeable, transient world. Among the pavilions of this Lordship, this world is but an arena of trial, a place of exhibition. It will be destroyed at an appointed time, and then reformed into the foundation of the everlasting palaces to which its inhabitants will be transferred.

The Lord of this changeable, transient world has prepared another, perpetual world. Those with enlightened intellects, illumined hearts, and illuminating spirits, who have discovered the inner reality of creation and things and thus acquired nearness to the All-Glorified God, have informed us that God Almighty has prepared an abode of reward for the obedient and an abode of punishment for the rebellious. He has promised and warned of these abodes, and does not break His promise or cancel His warning. In addition to the Prophets, saints, and purified, exacting scholars who have related this information to us, experts in these matters agree that this information, which is corroborated by the universe's signs, is true. Can there be any other information truer than this?

Samples of the Resurrection displayed in the world

This world's Owner continually displays many samples of the Place of Supreme Gathering in this narrow, transient Earth. Reflect upon Earth's quickening in every "resurrection" of spring, during which countless instances of resurrection occur with perfect order within a short period, say about 6 days. See how innumerable plants and animals, while lying dead or almost dead, and either on or under the soil and mixed with each other, are revived with perfect distinction. How can anything tire the One who does this? Why should He be unable to create the heavens and Earth in "6 days?" Why should the resurrection of the dead not take place in the twinkling of an eye?

- *Whatever happens in the world is not an end in itself*

The One Who writes countless books on a single page—the face of Earth—without any confusion or mistake, obviously can rewrite a book that He wrote before and destroyed. To understand the intended meaning, reflect on: *Look at the imprints of God's Mercy, how He revives Earth after its death. Surely He is the Reviver of the dead (in the same way), and He is powerful over everything* (30:50).

All such acts required by His being the All-Merciful and All-Powerful Lord of creation show that these happenings (gatherings and separations) are not ends in themselves. There is no acceptable, reasonable relation between these important "festivals" and ceremonies and their particular, impermanent consequences within such a short, limited time. Therefore they are only copies to be preserved with their consequences, so that they can serve as the basis for what is to occur in the Place of Supreme Gathering, and so that these fleeting things should yield perpetual forms, everlasting fruits, and eternal meanings. So this world is no more than an arable field to plant for harvesting on the Day of Resurrection, a store that will be emptied into Paradise and Hell.

- *Wisdom, Favor, Mercy, and Justice require the afterlife*

Consider how the Eternal Lord and Everlasting Sovereign displays the works and traces of His Wisdom, Favor, Justice, and Mercy in this transient world. He does so to the degree that anyone with open eyes and an unsealed heart must conclude that there can be no wisdom more perfect than His, no favor more gracious than His, no mercy more comprehensive than His, and no justice more glorified than His. All these works and traces may be the means for manifesting the truths of this Wisdom, Favor, Mercy, and Justice.

If His Kingdom contained no permanent lofty mansions with everlasting inhabitants, His Wisdom, Favor, Mercy, and Justice would have to be denied. This also would require us to accept that the One Who does all these things originating in His Wisdom, Mercy, Favor, and Justice is—God forbid such a thought!—a capricious trickster and a heartless tyrant. We would have to turn truths into their opposites, an act that those with sound reasoning (excluding those, like the sophists, who deny the existence of everything, including themselves) say is impossible.

* * *

Arguments for the Resurrection are not limited to those given above. The Qur'an points to innumerable indications of it; states that our Creator will transfer us from this ephemeral place of exhibition to the seat of His everlasting Lordship; and gives countless signs that He will change this fleeting, transitory realm for the perpetual one. Also, the Divine Names requiring the Resurrection and the next life are not restricted to the All-Wise, All-Munificent, All-Compassionate, All-Just, and All-Preserving, for all Names manifested in the universe's administration demand it.

In sum: The fact of the Resurrection is openly and decisively declared by the All-Glorified One, and agreed on by His Grace, Beauty, Majesty, and all other Names; it is also agreed on by the Qur'an, which contains all books of the Prophets; by Prophet Muhammad, upon him be peace and blessings, the most perfect member of creation and the one who bears the meaning of the consensus of the Messengers, Prophets, discoverers of hidden realities behind things and events; by the saints and purified, exacting scholars, and truthful ones, who all have purified, exalted, and illuminating spirits; and by the universe with all of its signs.

All things in the universe, without exception, have two aspects. The first one is related to their Creator and has numerous "tongues," all of which testify to Divine Oneness. The second one is connected with each item's final purpose and the Hereafter, and has many God-given "tongues" that bear witness to the other world and the Last Day. For example, just as your existence as the best pattern of creation points to the necessary Existence and Oneness of your Maker, your rapid decline despite a very comprehensive capacity, great talents, and ungratified desires for a happy eternal life points to the Hereafter.

Divine Wisdom, Divine Favor's all-inclusive decoration and provision, His Mercy's all-encompassing benevolence, and His overall Justice and comprehensive and meticulous Preservation establish the universal order. These point to the All-Wise, All-Munificent, All-Compassionate, All-Just, and All-Preserving Maker, and demonstrate the truth of the afterlife, the Hour's near and imminent coming, and the realization of eternal happiness.

> O God, include us among the people of eternal happiness. Resurrect and gather us among the group of the eternally happy, prosperous ones. Through the intercession of Your chosen Prophet, admit us to Paradise in the company of the purified, virtuous ones. Bestow blessings and peace on Your chosen Prophet and his Family as befits Your

Compassion and deserved by his being a holy, respectable one, and keep us and our Religion in peace and security. Amen. All praise be to God, Lord of the worlds.

To conclude:

- Naturalism and dogmatic adherence to causality close the door of thanksgiving [to the Creator] and lead to associating partners with Him.
- Everything has two aspects: its sensed, physical form or body determined by its assigned functions and purposes, and its immaterial aspect, composed of all forms it will assume during its life-span.
- Only God can clothe everything in their proper garments.
- The relationship of a member of a species with its particular species, that species' relationship with all other species, and all species' relation with all other species, despite time and distance, manifest the Existence and Oneness of an All-Knowing, All-Willing, All-Powerful, and All-Wise Creator.
- Just as the sun has to diffuse light, so God manifests Himself by sending Messengers.
- The Almighty's infinite Justice, Munificence, Mercy, Grace, Generosity, Dignity, Majesty, Recording, and Preserving require the founding of a new, eternal world where everyone will see the consequences of what they did in this world.
- In sum: The truth of the Resurrection is agreed upon by God and His Names, the Qur'an, all the Prophets including the last and greatest of them, the saints and the purified and exacting scholars, and by the universe with whatever happens in it.

The
Fourth Treatise

The Fourth Treatise

A Drop from the ocean of [the proofs] of Divine Unity

In the Name of God, the All-Merciful, the All-Compassionate.

All praise be to God and blessings be upon His Prophet.

Introduction

KNOW, O FRIEND, THAT DURING THE 40 YEARS OF MY LIFE AND MY 30 years of study, I have learned four words or phrases and four sentences [each of which is a general ruling]. The phrases are: being, like a letter, a sign of the whole or pointing to others rather than to itself; like a word, pointing to or representing itself; intention; and viewpoint.[33]

In other words, everything except God should be considered on account of God Almighty, not on its own account. Considering the universe in terms of itself or material causes is wrong. Everything has two aspects: one points to the Creator, the other points to creation. Any creat-

33 In a word or a sentence, a letter points to the meanings of other things, not itself. A word points to itself in meaning. Considering something from the viewpoint of what a letter signifies, or on account of the Creator, means considering it a "mirror" that reflects God's Names and Attributes manifested on it. Considering something from the viewpoint of what a word signifies means considering it because of or on account of itself. (Tr.)

ed being should be considered with respect to its first aspect, that of being a sign of the Almighty Creator. For example, any bounty or blessing should be associated with the Divine gift or Divine act of bestowing bounties. The related means and causes should be seen as "mirrors" reflecting the management or administration of Divine Power.

Similarly, intention and viewpoint change the nature of things and, as an elixir turns soil into gold, good intention and correct viewpoint change evil acts into good ones. Intention transforms our everyday, ordinary acts into acts of worship, and viewpoint allows science to become a means of acquiring knowledge of God. If scientific findings are considered in terms of material causes and means, they become a means of ignorance; if they are considered in terms of or on account of God, they produce knowledge of God.

The four sentences are as follows:

FIRST SENTENCE: *I am neither the owner nor master of myself.* The one who owns me is the Owner of creation, the One of Majesty and Munificence. I imagine that I own myself in order to understand the Attributes of my Owner by comparison. I perceive the Infinite One through my limitations [in power, attributes, capacities, etc.]. "When the sun rises and morning comes, stars set."

SECOND SENTENCE: *Death is inevitable.* This life and body cannot be the world's foundation. As the body is made of flesh, blood, and bones, which eventually will decompose, one's life and body cannot be eternal. How can a "palace" as large as the world be built with desires and fancies upon such a loose foundation and rotting support?

THIRD SENTENCE: *My Lord is One.* Happiness is realized only by submitting to the One Lord. If this were not so, everyone would need as many conflicting lords as there are entities in the universe. As human nature is comprehensive, human beings need almost everything and have connections with whatever there is in the universe. Whether consciously or not, they are affected by all of them and suffer because of them. This is a hellish state. On the other hand, knowledge and recognition of the One Lord before Whose Hand of Power all those fancied or supposed lords are but a thin veil is a paradisiacal state.

FOURTH SENTENCE: *The ego is a black dot, a point of comparison [to know and recognize God] intertwined with the "threads" of a conscious artistry.* It shows that its Owner is nearer to it than itself.

These sentences are explained in the first chapter's conclusion.

First chapter

This is about [the profession of belief]: There is no deity but God.

In the Name of God, the All-Merciful, the All-Compassionate.

All praise be to the Lord of the worlds, and peace and blessings be upon the master of the Messengers, his Family, and his Companions.

I bear witness that there is no deity but God, Whose necessary Existence and perfect Attributes, and Whose Oneness, Unity, Singularity, and being the Eternally-Besought-of-All are decisively established by the following arguments:

The Prophet as the first proof for God's Existence and Unity

The first, foremost, and unanimously confirmed truthful witness, and the articulate, verified proof is the lord of the Prophets and Messengers, the leader of all saints and God-conscious scholars. He holds the meaning of the confirmation of God's Existence and Unity, and the consensus thereon of all Prophets, Messengers, saints, and scholars. He has clear signs [testifying to his Prophethood] and many miracles unanimously confirmed and transmitted by the Companions, later generations, and reliable authorities.

He has lofty, laudable virtues and perfect, admirable morals. He is the center upon which the Divine Revelation is focused, the traveler in the unseen worlds who saw spirits and conversed with angels, and the guide of humanity and jinn. Through his person, he demonstrates that he is the favorite of the Creator of the universe, the embodiment of all perfections shared by creation. The law he brought contains all principles of happiness, which proves that it is the order established by the Orderer of the universe. He is our master who guides us to belief. He is Muhammad ibn 'Abdullah ibn 'Abd al-Muttalib, upon him be the best blessing and most perfect peace.

At the head of all witnesses, he informs us in this visible, material world of what he witnesses in the World of the Unseen. As a bringer of good tidings and a warner, he announces to everyone with his fullest voice and all his strength, perfect earnestness and utmost reliability, and infinite conviction and perfect belief, and regardless of time or place, that *there is no deity but God.*

The Qur'an as the second proof for God's Existence and Unity

The Qur'an is another witness of God's necessary Existence and Oneness, an expounder of His Majesty, Beauty, Grace, and Perfection. It holds the meaning of the consensus of all heavenly Scriptures sent to all Prophets, as well as the meaning of the unanimous agreement of the books of all saints and authenticating monotheist scholars.[34] Those with sound reason and conscience, and truly enlightened intellects, have affirmed the commandments of the Qur'an, which is enlightening in all aspects.

The Qur'an is the Word of God. Those honored by the Divine Revelation, inspiration, and the ability to unveil hidden truths affirm that it is pure Revelation, pure guidance, and the source of belief containing all truths. It leads to happiness and continuously yields perfect fruit. Angels, uncountable people, and jinn have accepted and adopted it. Those with reason, wisdom, sound judgment, and conscience have agreed that the Qur'an is confirmed with rational proofs and the testimony of good character and disposition. It is an eternal miracle, the tongue of the Unseen, and bears witness in the visible, material world to the fact that *there is no deity but God*.

This great Book (of the Universe), with all its chapters, sections, pages, lines, sentences, and letters testifies to God's necessary Existence and Oneness, and His Attributes of Majesty, Beauty, Grace, and Perfection. This is also true of this macro-human being (the cosmos), with all its systems, organs, cells, atoms, attributes, and states.

Through its worlds and spheres it says that *there is no deity but God*, and through those worlds' main constituents it says that *there is no creator but He*. Through those constituents' parts it says that *there is no maker but He*, and through those parts' components it says that *there is no director but He*. Through those components' elements it says that *there is no giver of certain form and disposition but He*, and through those elements' cells it says that *there is none but He with the necessary power of ordering and disposing them*. Through those cells' atoms or minutest particles it says that *there is no Creator but He*,

---

34 The meaning of the consensus: The effect, support, affirmation that all Divine truths contained in previous Scriptures are found in the Qur'an and corroborate its truth. The meaning of the unanimous agreement: All truths contained in the books of saints and scholars are derived from the Qur'an, and therefore prove its Divine authorship or origin. (Tr.)

and through the ocean of ether in which all atoms or particles are "sown" it says *there is no deity but He*.

In sum: The universe, with all of its species, worlds, spheres, constituents, parts, components, atoms, and ether, testifies in 55 languages to the Eternal Designer's necessary Existence and Unity.

The universe as the third proof for God's Existence and Unity

Those 55 languages are explained below. However, first we will mention them briefly:

Through the languages of its individual parts and well-ordered compounds, and the poverty and neediness of its living creatures, the universe bears witness to the necessary Existence and Oneness of its All-Powerful and Beginningless Creator. Through the well-ordered conditions or states it undergoes, its amazing and perfect forms, and its specific and ornamented designs, the universe points to His Attributes of Perfection. Through the lofty purposes it serves, the great benefits it produces, the extraordinary variation it displays, and the well-arranged similarities it exhibits, the universe mentions and recites His All-Beautiful Names. Through the languages of the order and excellent measure observed in its wholes and parts, the good arrangement and regularity it manifests, and the firm and faultless artistry discerned in everything, the universe praises Him.

Through mutual assistance among different inanimate objects, solidarity among dissimilar and varying things, the languages of universal wisdom and perfect favoring, of comprehensive mercy, all-encompassing provision, and all-permeating life, the universe interprets the Qur'an's verses. Through the languages of beauty and making beautiful, the grace manifested everywhere, true love, attraction and being attracted, and nature's quality as Divine Truth's shadow, the universe contributes to the brightness of Islam's light.

Through the languages of acting for certain purposes, changes in an entity during its lifespan for certain benefits, and transformations for certain instances of wisdom, alterations for certain aims, and ordering and arrangements towards perfection, the universe interprets the Qur'an's verses. Through the languages of its being contingent and having a beginning; its needs, poverty, and destitution; its helplessness, death, ignorance, and ephemerality; and its being subject to ever-changing and final destruction to be built again, the universe declares God's Power.

Through the languages of the acts and forms of its worship, glorification, prayer, and seeking refuge [with Him], and with all its individual parts and compounds, the universe strengthens submission to the Summit of Prophethood, and belief in the Necessarily Existent Being, One and Single. In all such languages and under the command of the eternal Divine Word—the Qur'an—and presidency of the master of all creatures—Prophet Muhammad—and all other Messengers, the universe announces: *God, there is no deity but He, the All-Living, the Self-Subsistent and Sustainer.*

The universe manifests the truth of *there is no deity but* God in the following 55 languages:

1. As a whole and with all its parts, the universe displays an evident order and extraordinary concord among its individual parts. This points to the necessary existence of Him Whose Hand of Power holds the universe, and bears witness in the tongue of this universal order that *there is no deity but God.*

2. Everything is so exactly measured and proportioned that it announces that *there is no deity but God,* Who set this measure and made all things in proportions and exactly commensurate with one another.

3. The harmony, arrangement, and regularity displayed show that different hands cannot interfere in it, and announces in the language of this harmony, arrangement, and regularity that *there is no deity but God.*

4. The art and design exhibited in this "house" of the universe point to the fact that the One Who designed and decorated it is also its Owner, and testifies in the language of this art and design that *there is no deity but God.*

5. The perfection of the art displayed by the Pen of Destiny in everything, according to the capacity of each, shows that the Pen is one and announces that *there is no deity but God.*

6. The mutual relationship between all things and faultless artistry displayed in each demonstrate that the One Who inscribed the page of the sky with stars and suns is He Who inscribes the pages of the honeybee and ant with their cells. In the language of all its creatures, the universe bears witness that *there is no deity but God.*

7. We see that even inanimate objects, no matter how far from each other, aid each other for wise purposes. For example, [vaporizing waters fall upon Earth to "revive" it, and] corn and fruits become sustenance for human

cells. In the language of this mutual assistance, the universe bears witness that *there is no deity but God.*

8. As between the sun and the planets, which are its "fruits," there is solidarity among different, distant objects. This solidarity shows that whatever exists is under the command and control of only one being. In the language of this solidarity, the universe testifies that *there is no deity but God.*

9. The resemblance among certain things, such as among the stars, is another language in which the universe proclaims that *there is no deity but God.*

10. The proportion among certain things, such as flowers, demonstrates that whatever exists belongs to the same Owner and is controlled by the same Power. In the language of this proportion, the universe testifies that *there is no deity but God.*

11. Every living thing receives the manifestations of numerous Names.[35] Like the seven colors in sunlight, each Name has Its own beauty and imprints. And yet they work to the same effect in each individual thing, even cells. This shows that the One Who has these Names is one and same being: The All-Living Creator of something is also its Shaper, Provider, and Sustainer; the One Who provides something is the Creator of the sources of provision; and its Creator is He Who has dominion over everything. This reality opens a window on the necessary Existence and Unity of the One called by the Names mentioned, and in the language of every living thing the universe testifies that *there is no deity but God.*

12. The connection among and between all things, such as the eyes of a honeybee and an ant, the sun and the solar system, show that both are designed by a single Designer. In the language of this connection, the universe bears witness that *there is no deity but God.*

13. The indispensable relation among the parts of each thing and the things themselves demonstrates that everything is the work of a single Maker. In the language of this relation, the universe testifies that *there is no deity but God.*

14. The "brotherhood" between the gravity affecting an individual thing's minutest particles and atoms and the general gravity between stars and suns indicates that both are "inscriptions" of one pen, the texture of one weaver, the

---

[35] For example, the Names Creator, Shaper, All-Seeing, All-Hearing, Arranger, Provider, Sustainer, All-Healing, and many others manifest themselves on the same being.

rays from one "sun." This shows the necessity of Divine Existence and Unity. In this language, the universe bears witness that *there is no deity but* God.

15. A compound's minutest particles or atoms, as well as compounds within each other, are placed according to such delicate calculations that, for example, any atom or particle in an eye is interrelated with the eye's other atoms and with all bodily systems and cells. This demonstrates that the Creator of the eye with all its atoms, the body, and the eye of the world (the sun) and their positioner is the Creator of all compounds. In the language of all these minutest particles and their positions and tasks, the universe bears witness that *there is no deity but God.*

16. A species' comprehensive disposition and certain species' wide distribution, such as angels and fish, indicate that the Creator of one living being is the Creator of the species. The pen, which draws the lines of an individual's face and thus identifies or individualizes that person, has to see all faces at the same time to make each one unique. Otherwise, individualization would be impossible. This requires that the Creator of an individual be the Creator of the family and species. The universe testifies in this language that *there is no deity but God.*

17. Some may say that one being could not have created everything, and so deny the Creator's Existence and Oneness. Attributing things to nature, themselves, material causes, or to such notions as chance and necessity makes the existence of things impossible.

It is much easier for one creator to create everything than for many creators to create one thing. The interference of many blind hands in creating something only increases blindness. For example, if creating a honeybee were not attributed to the power of a necessarily existent being, everything that exists should have participated in its existence. If creating a minute particle or a hair were attributed to material causes, it would be as difficult as creating a mountain. A commander can organize and direct a military company much easier than its soldiers or multiple commanders can. Everyone judges water sprinkled [on flowers] to be shooting from a sprinkler. All lines ending on a circle's circumference originate from one center. Such results are obtained easily with a few acts by a single being.

Suppose that water from a sprinkler was attributed to drops of water, or a flower's existence to soil particles, water molecules, rays of sunlight, the flower's constituent particles, or to chance and the like. This would require that each particle involved have the attributes of the Necessarily Existent

Being, as well as perfect artistry, comprehensive consciousness, all-encompassing knowledge, and absolute will and power. Attributing creativity to these causes means accepting innumerable partners with the Necessarily Existent Being, Who does not admit partnership. Such order and perfect arrangement require that each particle simultaneously be dominant over others and be dominated by them. In sum, attributing the existence of things to nature, chance, material causes, or to themselves requires the suspension of human reason.

On the other hand, suppose that everything is attributed to its true Owner, Whose Existence is absolutely necessary and Who is One and Single. Then like drops of water, each of which contains and reflects the sun and shines with its image, each minute particle receives and reflects the rays of the infinite and eternal Power's manifestation, which includes the infinite and eternal Knowledge and Will. A minute particle that receives such a ray is more effective than the "sun" of material causes. Connection to that Power, even through a minute particle, produces a very great effect, for a transparent particle that receives and reflects that Power's manifestation possesses Its attributes and thus acquires universality or functions like a universal thing.

Furthermore, Power is an essential Attribute of Divine Being and thus is infinite and without opposite, division, or dilution. Due to essential qualities in existence, namely transparency and reciprocity, balance and measurement, orderliness, abstraction and obedience, that Power creates the sun with the same ease as It creates the minutest or largest thing, for they are the same in relation to a single ray from It.[36] Power's operation also can be likened to light penetrating through a small hole and illuminating a large area.

Life, being, and light are transparent and permeable, and operate in the inner, immaterial dimension of existence. Thus one can discern Power's operation under solid, material causes. To have an image of the sun in glass, its light only has to shine through a small hole. A cluster of grapes grows at the end of a thin, slender stem. A lit candle or lamp illuminates a room. As in these examples, Power operates behind such simple and delicate causes. If Power is not discerned in such effects, then they must be attributed to the glass itself, the slender stem, or to lighting a match.

Those who deny a single Creator or associate partners with Him in creation can find peace only by attributing everything to the One

36 These qualities are explained in the Second Aim of The Twenty-ninth Word. (Tr.)

Necessarily Existent Being, through Whose Power all difficulties can be solved, Whose Will is the key to all problems and mysteries, and through Whose remembrance hearts find peace and tranquillity. There is no shelter or salvation except by taking refuge in and relying on Him. The Almighty declares: *Flee to God* (50:3) and: *Assuredly in the remembrance of God do hearts find peace and rest* (13:28). This truth opens a window on the light of Islam, obedience to Prophethood, and belief in the Necessarily Existent Being of Oneness and Unity. In the language of all its parts, the universe testifies that *there is no deity but God.*

18. Apparent material causes, like bread and milk to satisfy hunger, are simple; limited in time, place, and quantity; and subject to disappearance, death, and change. They have no consciousness and will, and most are subject to nominal (not material) "laws" that are perceived only after the effects have been brought about. Compared to their causes, effects are extraordinary and display splendid artistry. For example, a cell's formation and relations with all others and the body are so complex that it requires much more knowledge, skill, comprehensive will, and power than that found in all members of creation. Therefore, they cannot be explained by the food taken or the working of an unconscious and ignorant body.

Look at human memory. How can it be explained? It is like a copy of your life that the Hand of Power reproduces and gives to your hand so that on the Day of Reckoning it may tell what you did during your life, and to convince you of the afterlife. The All-Knowing One arranges things and events in life perfectly, despite their utmost intricacy. Human reflection, reasoning, thinking, and speech cannot be attributed to or explained by some systems and organs and their movements.[37] Therefore, these faculties or powers, systems and organs, must be the work of One with infinite Power, Knowledge, and Will. Only a Creator with boundless Power can be the real agent. Material causes and means are only excuses [to allow some space for human agency] and veils [hiding Power's operation so that some should not crticize and complain of Him because of some seemingly unpleasant things and events]. Senses, faculties, and qualities are titles given to the "pieces of glass" receiving and reflecting, according to their capacities, Power's manifestations, including eternal and infinite Knowledge and Will. "Laws" are

37 All human beings are unique, although they are created from and nourished with the same elements and formed of the same constituents. (Tr.)

manifestations of Knowledge, Command, and Will on species, something issuing from the "realm" of Divine Commands and Will. This truth opens another window on the Divine Being's necessary Existence. In the language of all effects, the universe testifies that *there is no deity but God.*

19. The wonderful works of a universal, perfect art and the utmost care shown in them require a limitless power. Each part of these works also demands this power.

This points to an All-Powerful Creator with unlimited Power. Since It is infinite, It is independent of and does not need partners, for that would limit It. Divinity does not accept limitation, for that would cause It to be contained in time and space, and defective in the capacities and qualities required by a Divine being. Absolute independence and freedom are essential to divinity. Thus It has no partners, for the universe, through its parts, events, and as a whole, displays the stamp of Unity and shows that its ruling agent is One.

Humanity is the most capable part of creation, the most eminent of causes equipped with consciousness and free will. However, our role in our actions is very small. This being the case, what part can inanimate objects have in creating and operating the universe? How can the envelope in which the king's gift is placed be his partner or helper? This truth opens another window on the Divine Being's necessary Existence and Unity. In the language of this truth, the universe bears witness that *there is no deity but God.*

20. Although some Divine Names (like All-Knowing) encompass all things, the Divine Names manifested in the universe cooperate in the creation, life, and working of all its parts down to the minutest particles. Like sunlight's seven colors, they work to the same effect.[38] This demonstrates that the Being called by those Names is one. In the language of the coordination and solidarity among the Names manifested in it, the universe testifies that *there is no deity but God.*

21. Universal wisdom is apparent in the universe, both as a whole and in its parts. This wisdom, which includes a purpose, consciousness, will, and

---

38 For example, such Names as the All-Seeing, All-Hearing, All-Shaping, and All-Providing, and such Attributes as Knowledge, Will, and Power are manifested in an individual. Although each has Its own manifestation and produces Its own effects, they ultimately produce an integral entity.

preference, points to an All-Wise One's necessary Existence, for an act must have a doer and an act or a part of it cannot be the doer.

22. The purposeful and gracious, all-encompassing favor apparent throughout the universe testifies to an All-Munificent Creator's necessary Existence, as a favor cannot bestow itself without a favorer.

23. The extensive mercy encompassing the universe, which contains wisdom, favor, benevolence, munificence, kindness, gratifying, love, and recognition, indicates an All-Merciful, All-Compassionate One's necessary Existence. A quality cannot be the one qualified by it, and Earth and heavens could have been "clothed" only by that All-Merciful One.

24. Satisfying living creatures' infinitely diverse needs from the universal provision, which contains wisdom, favor, mercy, protection, engagement [to provide them], intention, love, and recognition, points to a Compassionate Provider's necessary Existence.

25. The life and vigor seen throughout the universe contain wisdom, favor, mercy, provision, delicate artistry, elegant design, firmness, and care. They are brought about by the manifestations of a purpose, consciousness, knowledge, and will. This indicates the necessary Existence of an All-Powerful, Self-Subsistent, All-Sustaining One, Who gives and takes life. Life is a simple and unified or uniform phenomenon. Contrary to the principle that only a single entity issues from something one and unified [suggesting that everything needs a different origin], something one and unified (like life) issues only from something one and unified or uniform. So, the creator of life is one and indivisible.

These five truths (articles 21-25) indicate that this universe's Lord is All-Powerful, All-Knowing, All-Wise, All-Munificent, All-Compassionate, All-Merciful, All-Providing, All-Living, Self-Subsistent, and All-Sustaining, One qualified by the attributes of perfection. These five truths open a window onto the light of Islam, together with submission to Prophethood and the light of belief that He is God, One, and Necessarily Existent. In the language of the light composed of these truths, the universe bears witness that *there is no deity but God.*

26. The grace observed throughout the universe, making everything graceful, indicates the necessary existence of the One to Whom grace is essential.

27. The innocent beauty of the universe signifies the necessary existence of the One with absolute beauty.

28. The true love felt by the universe deeply in the heart is a sign of the Truly-Beloved One.

29. The attraction and ecstasy felt by the universe demonstrate most profoundly the center of attraction toward which everything is attracted.

30. What we hear from all perfected people who describe their observations is that creation is a shadow of the Single Being of Unity's light.

These five truths (articles 26-30) indicate that the universe has a Lord, Necessarily Existent and qualified by the attributes of Majesty, Beauty, and Perfection. In the language of these five truths, the universe testifies that *there is no deity but God.*

31. Each member of a species, as well as the entire species, is disposed toward specific benefits and purposes. This points to the necessary existence of an All-Wise Disposer or Agent, as an act must have a doer, and an act or a part of it cannot be the doer of itself.

32. Continuous change is observed in plants and animals for certain benefits, which indicates the necessary existence of a Master Who directs them.

33. Continuous, purposeful transformations are observed in plants and animals, both individually and as a species. This points to the necessary existence of a Wise Master.

34. The alternation of day and night for many purposes and benefits is a sign of the necessary Existence of an Agent Who does whatever He wills.

35. Ordering must have an orderer, for the thing ordered and the order itself cannot be the doer of this act, which requires consciousness. The universe's order and arrangement serves to make each thing attain its particular level of perfection, and to make creation attain its final point of perfection. This testifies to the necessary Existence of an All-Powerful One, Self-Subsistent and Sustaining. Can a nightingale clothe itself in its elegant, ornamented body? Can Earth weave its richly decorated dress?

These five acts (articles 31-35) of disposing, changing, transforming, alternating, and ordering show that this universe has a Master. They show that He Who controls it is wise, efficient, powerful, self-subsistent and sustaining, One Who does whatever He wills and has attributes of perfection. In the language of these acts, the universe announces that *there is no deity but God.*

36. The universe has a beginning. Whether as a whole or in parts, it came into existence within time. While there were infinite probabilities as to how and what properties it might have, it assumed its present form of per-

fect order, harmony, and balance. This demonstrates the necessary Existence of One with free choice, One Who is All-Knowing, All-Wise, and All-Powerful.

37. Everything is in endless need of sustenance and survival. If it is a conscious living being, it also has spiritual and intellectual needs. Despite everything's inability to satisfy the most insignificant needs, the needs of everything are met on time and from an unexpected source. This points to the Exist-ence of a Sustaining, Providing, Munificent, Merciful, and Compassionate Lord.

38. Everything is in infinite destitution and unable to procure what it needs to survive. However, everything is provided in exact measure with whatever it needs. This indicates the existence of One Compassionate, Munificent, giving freely, All-Loving, and All-Aware [of even the smallest creature's smallest need].

39. Despite their essential and extreme poverty, things like trees and soil, while appearing utterly dead and dried up in winter, display signs of vigor and power in spring. This indicates the existence of One absolutely Powerful, in relation to Whose Power everything, without exception, is equal.

40. Despite its essential poverty, as displayed by the dried soil which is the source of provision for living creatures, the universe shows signs of absolute richness. This points to the Existence of One absolutely Rich. The sun and trees are "cells" of His treasures of Mercy; water and light are two "streams" originating in His ocean of Compassion.

41. Everything is essentially dead. The "lights" of life disseminated by all living creatures demonstrate the existence of One All-Living and Self-Subsistent, One Who gives and takes life.

42. Nothing has consciousness of its own.[39] Together with sight and hearing, the encompassing consciousness displayed by conscious living beings shows the existence of One All-Knowing and All-Aware.

43. The continuous, orderly change and decay of everything, especially of living things, point to the Existence of One making changes but Who is Himself Permanent and unchanging.

44. We observe that those living, conscious beings who do their duties of worship get the precisely weighed reward of worship and, attaining higher spiritual ranks, can have some kind of contact with the inhabitants of

[39] Consider a human embryo. Beginning as a lump of flesh and bones, it somehow acquires life and consciousness. It is illogical to claim that the embryo itself, nature, or certain biological laws with nominal existence only (all of which are ignorant, unconscious, and powerless) equip it with life and consciousness. (Tr.)

invisible realms. The imprints of their worship are discerned in their lives, manners, and even on their faces. This indicates the Existence of One Who alone deserves worship.

45. The glorification of the universe, whether in words or acts, points to the existence of One Whom *whatever is in the heavens and on Earth glorifies* (59:24). The testimony of "natural disposition" or actions is irrefutable. Therefore, how can you refute the testimony of all beings, through their dispositions, functions, lives, and physical compositions, to the necessary Existence of Him Who is glorified by everything in the heavens and on Earth?

46. The prayers and supplications of living creatures [verbal, physical, or in the language of need and helplessness] are answered and usually yield the desired results.[40] This indicates the Existence of One Who answers supplications.

47. The afflicted consciously or unconsciously seek refuge in their "unknown" Protector or Creator. This testifies to the Existence of the Refuge of the afflicted and fearful, the Helper of those who seek help.

48. Those who penetrate the inner reality of existence and base themselves on their intuitions, spiritual experience, and observation, agree that whatever exists in time and space is a shadow of the "Eternal Sun's" lights, and testifies to Its necessary Existence.

49. [Despite their lifelessness, ignorance, and unconsciousness,] inanimate objects, especially atoms and subatomic particles, serve comprehensive, conscious, and universal purposes. Their comprehensive movements or acts, due to the Names' manifestations on them, originate from Necessary Existence and Unity, not contingency. This bears witness to the necessary Existence of a Holy One Who uses all things and is called by the Names manifested on them.

50. [Those who deny the Existence of a Divine Being as the sole Creator differ in explaining the origin of existence and life.] The Qur'an says: *Flee to God* (51:50), *Assuredly in the remembrance of God do hearts find peace and rest* (13:28), and: *Unto God all things are brought back* (35:4). Those who acknowledge the truth of such Divine proclamations find relief from the difficulties, confusion, and problems of attributing existence to itself, nature, or material causes. Attributing existence to the Creator's Power easily resolves

[40] God does not always give what is asked, for it might not benefit the one who asks. Sometimes He gives what is better and sometimes He gives in the Hereafter. (Ed.)

all difficulties and problems, and allows minds and hearts to find peace. Truly, there is no creative agent other than God.

51. Everything is measured in exact proportions. [Also, as almost everyone has had a glimpse or clue of the future in dreams,] a universal Destiny that predetermined everything prevails in the universe. [This negates chance. Again, all seeds and fully grown plants or trees point to universal Destiny.] Due to this all-inclusive Destiny, everything is perfectly ordered and serves predetermined, evident purposes according to its form, characteristics, and capacities. Consider the human body, with all its lines and fingers. Each one has been built and shaped in accord with its purpose, and so signifies the Destiny that has determined those purposes and structure. According to Destiny's plan, Power puts into "writing" the meanings established and kept by Knowledge. The Destiny "Theoretical" that has preplanned all things, and the Destiny "Practical" that records the life-histories of all things, indicate the necessary Existence of Him, the pen of Whose Destiny and Decree has drawn the outlines of all things.

52. Our comprehensive capacities suggest that we are the fruit of the Tree of Creation, and thus creation's most perfect part. One aspect of our nature inclines us to non-existence, the world's dark face. However, our comprehensive capacity for worship implies that we were created for existence, not eternal non-existence. So we must turn toward light, permanence, and the Creator, not toward darkness, ephemerality, and the created. Worship connects the beginning to the end in creation. Our natural disposition thus bears witness to the necessary Existence of Him Who created the universe and its contents to make Himself known, Who created humanity and jinn so that they should [know and] worship Him.

53. In creation, there are the stations of contingency, multiplication, and of being affected. [Whatever is created is contingent, for its existence is not necessary and absolute; it is not unique or peerless, for it is something to be acted upon.] This requires the position of necessity, oneness, and agency. In other words, there must be One Whose Existence is absolutely necessary; Who is One, Unique, and Peerless; and Who is Ever-active.

54. We see that each thing continually moves toward its particular point of perfection. When it reaches perfection, it acquires stability and steadiness. Perfection requires stability and constancy. The existence of whatever exists is by perfection, and the perfection of whatever is perfect is by constancy. So, the One Who is necessarily existent is absolutely perfect, and all

perfections shared by contingent beings are only shadows of the manifestations of His Perfection's lights. This testifies that God is the Absolutely Perfect One, both in His Divine Essence and His Attributes and acts.

55. A thing's interior is much subtler and displays much greater artistry than its exterior. Therefore, its Maker is not distant from it. Also, maintaining the exact balance and proportions between it and other things indicates that its Maker is not contained within it. When we view a thing in respect of itself, its very being, we conclude that its Maker is All-Knowing and All-Wise. When we view it with respect to its relations with other things, we judge that its Maker is All-Hearing and All-Seeing, One Who sees all things from above, fashions them, and regulates their relationships for certain purposes. This truth indicates the necessary existence of the Maker Who is neither contained in the universe nor distant or excluded from it.[41] He is the Most Inward of the inward, the Most High of the high. He sees one thing and all things simultaneously.

These truths (articles 36-55) form one composite truth showing that this universe has one Owner, Ruler, and Sustainer Whose Existence is absolutely necessary. He is All-Knowing, All-Wise, All-Powerful, All-Merciful, All-Compassionate, All-Providing, All-Munificent, All-Wealthy, All-Living, Self-Subsistent, All-Aware, Everlasting, Permanent, and Deserving of Worship. He does whatever He wills, is glorified by whatever is in the heavens and Earth, and answers those who supplicate. He is the refuge of those in fear, and helps those who ask Him for help. This universe is a shadow of His lights, the manifestation of His Names, and the imprint or work of His acts. Hearts find peace and rest in His remembrance, and unto Him are affairs brought back. He created humanity and jinn to [know and] worship Him, and ordered the universe through the laws of His Destiny and Decree. He is Necessarily Existent and One, Unique, and absolutely perfect in His Essence, Attributes, and acts. He is All-Subtle, All-Aware, All-Hearing, and All-Seeing.

Through their lights, these truths show Islam and the necessity of submitting to Prophethood. This leads to believing that He is God, the One Whose Existence is absolutely necessary, Who is One and Single. These truths form a language in which the universe announces that *there is no deity but God.*

---

41 By His Essence or Divine Being, He is not contained within time or space. However, through His Names' and Attributes' manifestations, He is everywhere and nearer to everything than itself, just as the sun places itself in your eyes' pupils and penetrates your body through its light and heat.

KNOW, O FRIEND, that the pillar of belief establishes that there is no power and strength except with God.

KNOW, O FRIEND, that these proofs and belief in God require belief that Muhammad is His Messenger. Belief in his Messengership necessarily includes the other five pillars of belief and, like a mirror, reflects God's Attributes. Thus in the balance of belief, the belief that Muhammad is the Messenger of God is equal to the belief that *there is no deity but God*, for Prophethood has a universal, all-encompassing position by virtue of its being the mirror for reflecting His Attributes of the Ruler and Sustainer of the universe. The relation of sainthood to Prophethood is like that of God being the Lord of the worlds to His being the Lord of one person, like that of His Supreme Throne to a believer's heart, or like the Prophet's Ascension to the realms beyond all heavens to a believer's "ascension" while in the Prayer.

A Note

KNOW, O FRIEND, that the point we have so far discussed is like a center around which we have drawn a circle through our arguments. Each point on the circumference looks toward the center. Between the points there is a solidarity that removes the weakness of some among them. The entire argument produces a conviction that adds to the light of Islam, contributes to submission to Prophethood, and then to belief. The various arguments are sources from which this conviction originates.

The proofs for God's Existence and Unity, Prophethood, and other pillars of belief are not restricted to those mentioned. There are innumareble other arguments supporting the truth of Islam, which is based on God's Existence and Unity, and corroborating Prophethood and the Prophethood of Muhammad, upon him be peace and blessings. If an argument seems to us as weak, we should refer to the arguments as a whole and consider them from the viewpoint of the result to be filtered from them.

KNOW, O FRIEND, that as some individual arguments are like water, air, or light, we should consider them comprehensively and carefully so they do not slip through our fingers.

Two types of viewpoints

KNOW, O FRIEND, that to acquire knowledge of an elaborate, fruit-bearing tree's life, benefit, and strength, people look at it in two ways: from its roots upward, and from its fruits downward. The first way is better and leads to correct conclusions, while the second is defective and leads to misconceptions [especially as a tree may not yield good fruits every year]. In the same way, the tree of Islam is rooted in the heavens, while its branches spread throughout the world of multiplicity. To acquire knowledge of it, we can approach it from two viewpoints. In addition, there are two ways into its sphere.

The first viewpoint is from its roots. If we do this successfully, we will see that it originates in a massive pool whose source is perfectly pure: Divine Revelation. This pool continuously increases (in "water") through the "signs" joining it from the outer world and each person's inner world. Its fruits derive their "nourishment" from this "pool." To prove the life of a single fruit, it is enough to establish the tree's fruitfulness and vigor, as there is a basic connection between the roots and each fruit. However, [while the roots, trunk, branches are sound and there are numerous sound fruits,] one single fruit disappearing or being rotten does not mean that the tree is unproductive. In addition, the source from which the tree derives its vigor is a guarantee of its continued life. If those holding this correct viewpoint see one dead fruit in the tree, they will attribute it to external factors. This is the sound and correct viewpoint. May God provide us with it and hold us firmly to it.

The second viewpoint is the origin of misguidance and difficulty. People with this view look at the tree from its fruits and with the intention of criticizing it. Since the same connection among the fruits as that between the tree's roots and each of its fruits does not exist, they have to examine and taste the fruits one by one to judge the tree. Also, they cannot see how the roots carry life to the fruits. If they see a dead fruit, they might conclude that the whole tree is dead. May God save us from holding such a viewpoint.

Conclusion: About four diseases

First disease: Despair

KNOW, O FRIEND, that those who fear the punishment of Hell and cannot fulfill their duty of servanthood to God desire the non-existence of punishment and an argument against it. When they see signs that seem to confirm such an argument, they begin to be recruited by devils into their legions. [If you are in such a state,] give a sincere and attentive ear to the following Qur'anic verse:

> Report [to them what I say]: "O My servants who have transgressed against their own selves! Do not despair of God's Mercy. Surely God forgives all sins; for He is the All-Forgiving, the Most Compassionate." (39:53)

Second disease: Self-admiration (due to good deeds)

When despair causes us to look for support against Hell's punishment, we look at our good deeds and deviate into self-admiration. In reality, we have no right to own our good deeds. Also, you have no right to claim ownership of your body, for you neither created it nor found it on the way, and it is neither the result of blind chance nor the product of lifeless causes. Rather, through its amazing design and the marvels of the art it exhibits, your body testifies that it is the handiwork of an All-Wise Maker Who continually looks after it.

Our part in our body's operations is minute. Although humanity is the noblest cause and has the most comprehensive willpower among creation, the amount of free will we exercise is quite small. The area for freedom of action is, despite its apparent comprehensiveness, very narrow. If reason cannot control such a faculty as imagination, how can other faculties be considered within the realm of human free will? How can anyone take personal pride in them?

Furthermore, many things work for or against us. Although we might be unaware of many of them, they evidently serve many deliberate purposes. This means that the One Who causes them to occur is an All-Hearing, All-Seeing One with infinite consciousness, and not the individual or other deaf and blind causes. Thus there is no reason to claim personal ownership of good deeds, for one's share in them is quite limited.

We are rather susceptible to the faults and defects engendered by misusing our free will. Such misuse changes the quality of the virtues pouring into the world due to the incessant manifestations of Divine Perfections. Your body, your dwelling place, is a free loan in which you are a guest. Good deeds are gifts [that the Almighty enables us to do]; sin and evil are the result of misused willpower. So say: *He owns (all things in the universe), to Him is all praise, and there is no power and strength except with Him.*

Third disease: Vanity

Vanity or conceit engenders a "distant view" of past virtuous and illustrious individuals and causes people to belittle them. Such people are deprived of the blessing and benefits coming from their good deeds and virtues, for they are blinded by illusion and have a negative opinion of them. So, [to be saved from this disease] view them closely and see how in 40 days they accomplished what we cannot accomplish in 40 years.

Fourth disease: Suspicion

Suspicion of others causes people to think that others suffer the same defects and vices that they do. This view causes them to condemn everyone and blind themselves to the virtues of present and past illustrious people, from whom they could derive some benefit. Thus they turn daylight into night for themselves.

> May God save us from despair, self-admiration, vanity, and suspicion. Amen.

Four significant truths I witnessed in my intellectual and spiritual journey

During this journey, I witnessed the following truths:

First truth

KNOW, O FRIEND, that indifference to the True Owner, the All-Glorified and Majestic, causes people to claim absolute independence and ownership of their self. Such a mistaken belief leads one to imagine a realm of personal dominion. Then, after comparing other people and material causes to themselves, they share the rest of God's property or dominion among them. However, the Almighty has given us a (human) ego for a totally different purpose: to allow us to measure or compare Divinity's Attributes so that we may comprehend them.[42] But we abuse our powers or faculties, attempt to oppose the Divine Commandments, and contend against the Creator's Destiny and Decree.

O you who are accompanying me in my journey! This truth has become manifest to me in all its dimensions, as follows:

---

42 For example, a person equipped with the limited powers of sight, hearing, and learning may conclude that the Creator must be All-Seeing, All-Hearing, and All-Knowing. One's poverty, helplessness, and mortality may lead one to discover that the Creator is Absolutely Wealthy, Powerful, and Permanent. (Tr.)

People can learn subtle truths, particularly abstract ones, through comparison, and infinite things can be perceived by imagining limits to them. So the human ego, rooted in each one of us through the "water" of indifference [to the True Owner of creation], was given to us to serve only as a point of comparison by which we can perceive the Attributes of the Creator, Who has no partners, and none to contend against Him in His Sovereignty, Lordship, or Divinity.

The ego does not own itself or its body. Its body is not something found on the way, the result of chance, or self-formed. Rather, it is an extremely complex, intricate, and amazing Divine machine or factory in which the Pen of Divine Power continuously works in the hand of Destiny and Decree.

O SELFHOOD! Give up such a false claim. Submit the "property" (the body) to its Owner, and be a reliable trustee in fulfilling your responsibility toward the body with which you have been entrusted. When people claim ownership of even one particle, they begin to share God's property with fellow beings and then with material causes. [Herein lie the roots of many kinds of associating partners with God in the creation and rule of the universe.]

O SELFHOOD! People do not own themselves. They do not make or create their bodies. Material causes cannot claim to own them either. How can people make their own bodies, seeing that basically they do not differ from sheep? [People and sheep are made of the same elements and do not have the least part in creating themselves.] How can a sheep claim it has made its body? There is a close affinity between a sheep and a pomegranate. How can a pomegranate's dye make its seeds? How can a fruit placed at the top of a tree create the tree? If a sheep can make itself, if a pomegranate can create its tree, then a human being can own him/herself.

Each creature proclaims: "I was made, in accordance with precise measures, by an All-Knowing, All-Wise, All-Hearing, and All-Seeing One." Material causes are blind, deaf, and lifeless. Their intermingling only increases their blindness and deafness. Preparing a certain medicine requires proficiency in the relevant medical sciences and pharmacology, and accurate knowledge of the ingredients and the amounts needed. If these are all placed on a roof and a wind blows them down and then mixes them, can the required medicine be formed by itself or chance?

Materialists and naturalists attribute creation to itself, causes, or nature. If a given medicine can create itself in the circumstances outlined above, one can claim that creation is either self-created or the product of chance and causes. But the beginning of creation and the origin of things and life are awesome questions to be answered. Thus attributing creation to someone or something other than an All-Knowing, All-Wise, and All-Powerful Creator with an absolute Will is sheer, arrogant folly.

Second truth

Know, O evil-commanding soul, that each person has a world particular to himself or herself, one which is very spacious and founded upon personal aspirations, relationships, and needs. Its main pillar is the individual's life. However, this pillar is weakened by time, events, and diseases. In other words, it is unsound and subject to decay and sudden or gradual collapse. The human body is not long-lasting, for it is not composed of iron or rock, but of flesh, bones and blood, all of which are ready to disintegrate at any time. Its decomposition means the destruction of that individual's world.

Look at the past—a large grave containing the ruined worlds of the dead; the future is a grave waiting to be filled. All of us stand between two large graves: yesterday became my father's grave, and tomorrow will be mine. Although the world we live in is one, it contains as many worlds as the number of the people living in it. One's death means the end of one's world.

Third truth

This world and its pleasures are a heavy burden. No one (except the corrupt in spirit) is contented with it. Rather than suffering from dependence on almost the whole universe, being needy of all means and causes, and appealing to contending deaf, dumb, and blind masters, people should seek refuge in a single, All-Hearing, and All-Seeing Master. If they place their trust in Him, He is enough for them.

Fourth truth

Know, O ego, that the scientific inventions woven around your head, the lines of conscious artistry connected to you, and the things put in your hands stretched out in neediness all demonstrate that your Creator, Maker, and Helper hears your sighs of destitution and your cries for help. Having mercy on you, He gratifies all your needs. Seeing that the Creator and Maker answers your tiniest cells' calls for help, why should He—the All-Hearing, All-Seeing—not answer your call for help?

O spacious cell called ego or selfhood and built up of lesser cells. Say: "O God! O Lord! O my Creator! O my Fashioner! O my Owner! O my Master! O my Guardian! Yours is the dominion of all things and to You is all praise! I am a guest in this body, Your property that You have entrusted to me."

O selfhood! Why do you claim to own that which you will never own? Give up this false claim that throws you into acute pain. Consider the emotions of pity and affection, which are among the spirit's exhilarating embellishments: If they were left to your pretended ownership, they would harm and torment the spirit.

For example, the misfortune and calamities striking you or others would cause you to remain in continual pain and go so far as to blame Destiny for them. However, when you see a soldier who has lost his horse or whose residence has been burnt down by mistake working directly under a king, you do not feel much pity for the soldier. If you consider that both the horse and residence belong to the king, you will see that their disappearance does not cause a significant decrease in his property. Nor does the soldier worry about it—indeed, inasmuch as he is poor, it is highly probable that out of pity the king will compensate his losses with something better. In the same way, God is the All-Compassionate and always treats His servants with utmost compassion.[43] Therefore, compassion for creatures as creatures of God exhilarates the spirit. By contrast, pity arising from supposing that everything owns itself continually suffocates and distresses the spirit.

One with a sound viewpoint based on belief in Divine Unity sees every living being's body as resembling a hired captain on a king's ship being controlled by that king, who controls his property as he wills. This viewpoint does not allow one to see an ant or a honeybee as contending with attacking causes. Rather, according to it, the ant controls an earthly "vehicle" while the oth-

---

43 The best analogy applicable to certain aspects of the relation with God and the creation is that between a monarch and his subjects. Since many immaterial truths, especially those pertaining to the Divine Being, are abstract and difficult to understand, Divine Scriptures usually use parables, metaphors, similes, and analogies. For example, God is sometimes introduced like a monarch or king, having a throne and armies. Another reason why Said Nursi used such analogies may be that he wrote this book in the 1910s, when there was still a sultanate in Turkey. (Tr.)

er controls an "aircraft," the reins of which are in the hands of the Power of an All-Powerful One. Causes do not have much weight in the sight of either animal, which depend on the True Owner (of all things).

By saying: *Surely we are God's and surely we are returning to Him* (2:156), when struck by misfortune, one means: All property is God's and I am under His command, journeying to Him. My relation with my body, which is His property, is like that of a soldier holding something belonging to the king. When robbers attack him, he states: "I am responsible for guarding this property entrusted to me. However, I am unable to guard it now. Like this property, I also belong to the king and am going to him." When those with such a viewpoint see a fellow struck with misfortune or suffer personal misfortune, they are relieved of continual distress. Otherwise, they are constantly weighed down with pain and distress.

Second chapter

This is about *Subhan Allah* [the phrase glorifying God].

In the Name of God, the All-Merciful, the All-Compassionate.

- Glory be to God, the Absolutely Powerful through the Power essential to His being God, Absolutely Wealthy and free of powerlessness and need.
- Glory be to God, the Absolutely Perfect in His Being, Attributes and acts, and has no fault or defect. His works' perfections point to His acts' perfection, which points to His Names' perfection. His Names' perfection indicate His Attributes' perfection, which testifies to His Essence's perfection. All perfection and beauty in the universe are a shadow of His Perfection and Beauty. All people of spiritual experience and discovery, as well as those who unveil hidden truths in creation, agree that creation is a shadow of the Necessarily Existent Being's lights.
- Glory be to God, the One and Single. He has no partners in His dominion, for the work's unity points to its doer's unity; in His being Lord and Sustainer, as indicated by the Pen's unity ["writing" on the "page" of time and space]; and in His Divinity, as Divinity requires absolute independence and being unique and peerless.
- Glory be to God, the All-Powerful and beginningless, without helpers and ministers, as such finite contingencies would put limits on the infinite, perfect Power.
- Glory be to God, eternal and beginningless, without like or equal.

- Glory be to God, the Necessarily Existent One, Who is free of necessities pertaining to contingencies.
- Glory be to God, *for Whom is the highest comparison in the heavens and earth,*[44] and He is All-Mighty, All-Wise, and has no qualities attributed to Him by those with false beliefs. He has no defect, for faults and defects are particular to contingent mortals. As God is the Necessarily Existent Being, how could they be attributed to Him?
- Glory be to the Perpetual, Eternal One Who does not change or alter, for these characteristics are particular to contingent, created beings and contrary to His absolutely necessary Existence and Oneness.
- Glory be to the Creator of creation and space Who has no division and is not contained in space, for that is incompatible with the absolute independence essential to the Divine Being.
- Glory be to the Eternal, Permanent One Who has no beginning or end.
- Glory be to the Necessarily Existent Being, free of and exempt from whatever is not fitting for Him, such as incarnation and union.[45] What relation can soil or something made of soil have with the Lord of all those who claim lordship? Being limited means being dominated, and saying that God begets something means placing limits on Him. He is absolutely free of and exempt from such mistaken beliefs and conceptions.
- Glory be to God, Whom all angels and all that is in the heavens and on Earth glorify through what the Pen of Destiny has inscribed on their foreheads.

Third chapter

This is about *al-hamdu lillah* [the phrase praising God].

In the Name of God, the All-Merciful, the All-Compassionate.

- All praise be to God, Whom all creatures and creations praise and exalt either verbally or in the languages of their lives and being, by manifest-

[44] Since God Almighty is absolutely infinite, we cannot perceive His Essence. Therefore, to give us some knowledge and understanding of His Attributes, He usually speaks in parables, similitudes, or comparisons. (Tr.)

[45] Incarnation is the belief that God assumes a human body. Union is the belief that a human being can unite with God in spirit, thus becoming a god in human form. Islam absolutely rejects such beliefs. (Tr.)

ing His Attributes of Perfection. In their entirety and in the languages of their having a beginning and being contingent, and of their need, destitution, and purposes they serve, they praise His Majesty.

In the languages of their displayed artistry, orderliness, balance, firmness, and perfection, and in their acts of worship and glorification, they recite His Attributes of Majesty and affirm that He is God, the Necessarily Existent, Beginningless, Perpetual, Eternal, One and Single, Peerless, Eternally-Besought-of-All, All-Mighty, All-Compelling, All-Great, and All-Overwhelming.

They praise Him with His Attributes of Beauty and Grace, saying that He is our Creator, All-Merciful, All-Compassionate, All-Providing, All-Munificent, All-Generous, All-Loving, All-Diffusing (of blessings), All-Gracious, All-Subtle, All-Favoring, and All-Beautiful.

They mention Him with His Attributes of Perfection, saying that He is Our Creator and Owner, All-Living, Self-Subsistent, All-Sustaining, All-Knowing, All-Wise, All-Powerful, All-Willing, All-Hearing, All-Seeing, All-Speaking, and All-Witnessing. They also recite His Beautiful Names manifested in the universe.[46]

- All praise be to God, Whomthe universe praises, glorifies, and exalts Him by showing His Attributes of Perfection. With all its chapters, sections, pages, lines, sentences, and letters, and with the purposes it serves and the artistry and design it displays, this greatest book (the universe) is a whole in itself. Everything and everyone in it are mirrors reflecting the "lightning" of His Attributes of Majesty, the "flashes" of His Attributes of Grace and Beauty, the "gleams" of His Attributes of Perfection, the "rays" of His Beautiful Names.
- All praise be to God for the existence, which is pure good, He bestows on us; for the blessing of life, by which existence is perfected; and for the blessing of belief, the essence of true life and by which life attains perfection.

---

[46] In one respect, God has two kinds of Attributes and Names: those of Majesty and those of Grace. The Names All-Overwhelming, All-Compelling, All-Powerful, and the like belong to the first group; the Names All-Generous, All-Merciful, All-Compassionate, All-Providing, and the like belong to the second. Such events as death, storms, and calamities are, ultimately, the results of the Names of Majesty's manifestations, without excluding human free will in the events in which we are involved. Such events as life, instances of happiness, provision of living beings, and springtime are manifestations of the Names of Grace. (Tr.)

- All praise be to God for the light of belief that removes darkness and illuminates the outer world as well as our inner worlds. Belief is a source of light that consists of the six lights (the six pillars of belief), from which originate the Eternal Sovereign's rays of knowledge.
- All praise be to God for belief in God, for this delivers the spirit from the darkness of annihilation, the feeling of utter desolation in the universe, seeing all things in existence as singing dirges, and from innumerable other destructive sentiments.
- All praise be to God for the light of belief, which shows us Refuge, Favor, Munificence, Love, Pity, and Compassion. Belief unveils eternal life, displays its brilliance, and brings us good tidings of eternal happiness. It offers us a support and source of help, teaches us on Whom we should rely and from Whom we should seek help, and lifts the veil of lamentation from the face of the mercy enveloping creation. Belief also removes the pains of separation from lawful pleasures by comparing the two worlds, and enables the continuation of favors and blessings by showing the everlasting tree of favors.

  The light of belief shows the true nature of all things and states thought to be controversial, strange, dead, and fearful, and makes it clear that they are all friendly, familiar, living, and amicable. This light embraces all worlds and this realm and the next, which are replete with the gifts of Mercy for believers. Thus believers must say: "All praise be to God for whatever He has created," and approve of and be satisfied only with Him as Lord and Master. They must set their hearts on Him as the only One worthy of worship and love, and the object or goal of life.
- All praise be to the Lord of the worlds for His "mercy" for the worlds, which is our master Muhammad. Through him and his Messengership, the lights of the conception of Divinity, which had been extinguished under the thick veil of corrupted philosophies and religions, were rekindled and acquired stability and constancy. Through his Messengership, that which pleases the Lord of the worlds became clear to humanity, and through him humanity has been guided to belief, which is the light of creation and existence.
- All praise be to God for the blessing of Islam, which contains whatever pleases the Lord of the worlds. Islam shows us what pleases Him and

what our Lord, the Lord of the worlds and the Lord of the heavens and Earth, wills and approves.

- All praise be to God for the light of belief, which derives strength from *In the Name of God, the All-Merciful, the All-Compassionate*. Those who praise should turn their attention from the bounty to the act of giving bounties so that they may perceive that the Bestower of bounties sees them, is nearer to them than they are to themselves, and makes Himself known through giving bounties and loved through favoring. When people become conscious of His seeking to make Himself known and loved, they feel compelled to be thankful to Him.

Fourth chapter

This is about *Allahu akbar* (the phrase exalting God).

First section

In the Name of God, the All-Merciful, the All-Compassionate.

- God is the All-Great, He is incomparably greater than all things, for He is the All-Powerful, Who is powerful over all things through His infinite Power. He creates everything, without exception, with the same ease: *Your creation and resurrection are but like (those of) a single soul* (31:28). He can create a giant star, a whole, and a species as easily as He can create a minute particle, a part, and an individual.
- God is the All-Great, for He is the All-Knowing, Who knows all things through the limitless knowledge essential to Him as the Divine Being. Nothing escapes Him, as He is present everywhere. The comprehensive wisdom, all-embracing favor, and all-encompassing consciousness; the decrees putting all things in exact order; and the fruitful ordinances and measurements, appointed hours, regular provision, mercy of universal diversity, firm and magnificent organization, and exact care, all of which are witnessed throughout the whole universe, testify to the Almighty's all-encompassing Knowledge: *Should He Who creates not know?* (67:14).
- God is the All-Great, for His Will includes all things. While there was infinite number of probabilities for the universe and its contents to assume a certain form, it was arranged in the present order according to exact measures. Like a tree with leaves, blossoms, and fruits, all well-

ordered creatures were created of simple, inanimate elements. All this bears witness to the Almighty's all-encompassing Will and demonstrates that whatever He wills is, and whatever He does not will is not.

- God is the All-Great, for He is the Eternal "Sun," and this universe shows only a shadow of His lights, manifestations of His Names, and imprints of His acts.
- God is the All-Great, He is incomparably greater than all things. He is the Eternal Sovereign. All worlds are at His disposal in absolute dependence on the order and measure He has established.
- God is the All-Great, for He is the Eternal Ruler. He ordered the universe through the laws of His usual way of acting, the prescripts of His Destiny and Decree, the precepts of His Will and Wisdom, the requirements of His Favor and Mercy, and the manifestations of His Names and Attributes. What we call laws (of nature) are but manifestations of His Knowledge, Command, and Will on all species.
- God is the All-Great, for He is the Eternal Maker, Who has created and founded this macrocosm (the universe) and this microcosm (humanity). His stamp is on the foreheads of both, nay, on each part of both.
- God is the All-Great, for He is the Eternal Designer. This universe consists of the lines of the "pen" of His Destiny and Decree, the designs of the "compasses" of His Wisdom, the fruits of the diffusion of His Mercy, the decorations of the "bright hand" of His Favoring, the flowers of the dispensations of His Munificence, and the rays of the manifestations of His Grace.
- God is the All-Great, for He is the Eternally Powerful. This universe consists of the miracles of His Power, which testify that He is powerful over all things. Nothing has been (or is) able to escape His Power's dominion, in relation to which a minute particle and the sun are the same.
- God is the All-Great, for He is the Creator, Originator, and Fashioner for Whom are the Beautiful Names. All heavenly objects are shining proofs of His Divinity and Grandeur, and radiating witnesses of His Lordship and Splendor.
- God is the All-Great, for He is the Creator of all things, the Provider of all living beings, the Bestower of bounties to all in need of bounty, the Merciful in both worlds. Our master Muhammad and Paradise are

works of His comprehensive Mercy. He is the Lord and Sustainer of all things, Who rears, trains, and maintains all things.

- God is the All-Great, for He is the Fashioner of all things, the One Who has ordered this world and controls all things.
- God is the All-Great, for He is exalted high above human comprehension, and absolutely free of incompetence and defect.
- God is the All-Great, for He is incomparably greater than all things, for He is the greatest, Most High, Most Beautiful, the Best because of Himself, and the Most Grand and Most Majestic by Himself.

A note

These blessed phrases—*Subhan Allah*, *al-hamdu lillah*, and *Allahu akbar*—are recited repeatedly after the daily Prayers to establish and confirm their meanings, which support each other, in our minds and hearts. For example, throw a stone into the center of a large pool and watch as larger circles are formed one after the other. Say, "Greater... greater... greater..." Using the same analogy, we recite *Subhan Allah*, *al-hamdu lillah*, and *Allahu akbar* repeatedly after the five daily Prayers to establish and confirm their meanings and to obtain the fruits expected of their recitation.

* * *

QUESTION: Why do we compare God with creatures by saying that *He is the Greatest*, as the literal meaning of *God is the All-Great*? What is the role of contingencies, and why do we say that the One of Necessary Existence is greater than them? Are there creators or all-compassionate beings other than the Almighty that force us to describe Him as the "Best of Creators" and the "All-Compassionate of the Compassionate?"

ANSWER: There is, indeed can be, none greater and more exalted, more beautiful or grander or majestic than He. God is essentially greater than whatever we can conceive of, is greater than all that is in our minds and hearts, and more important than our desires and aims. He is too great for the veil of creation to conceal.

"The Best of Creators" means that He is infinitely better than whatever minds can conceive of as having creativity due to reflections of the Attribute of Creativity. This is like saying the sun is more radiant than suns, implying that the sun itself is more radiant than its images in mirrors or mirror-like things. Sometimes, whether consciously or unconsciously, we may mistakenly attribute creativity to material causes or creatures. "God is the Best of Creators" means that He is the best as Creator without being veiled by causes, and so we must always turn to Him, without considering apparent material causes.

Such comparisons relate to us and the things we are related to; in essence they do not relate to the Almighty. For example, when we say to a private concerning his particular duty that "the king is better and grander," we mean the king's part of his duty is greater than those of his immediate superiors.

God is too great for minds to comprehend, and for incompetence and defect to touch. He is absolutely perfect in His Essence, Attributes, and acts.

Second section

This is about the ranks of *Allahu akbar* (God is the All-Great).

First rank

In the Name of God, the All-Merciful, the All-Compassionate.

> Say: "All praise be to God, Who has never taken to Himself a son, and Who has no partner in sovereignty. Nor (needs) He any guardian due to weakness and humiliation. Magnify Him with all magnificence." (18:111)

We believe and are at Your command. God is the All-Great, greater than all things in power and knowledge, for He is the Fashioner Who made humanity and the universe by His Power, and inscribed humanity and the universe with the "pen" of His Destiny. Like the microcosm (humanity), this macrocosm (the universe) is something made by His Power, "inscribed" by His Destiny. He has made it a "mosque," while making human beings worshippers in it. He has established the former as an abode, and the latter as a servant inhabiting it.

His Art in the universe has been manifested as a book, while His coloring of humanity has flourished as speech. His Power in the universe displays His Majesty, while His Mercy toward humanity arranges His provision. His Majesty in the universe bears witness that He is One, while His provision of humanity announces that He is Single. His stamp on the universe, both on it as a whole and on its parts, shows itself in apparent calmness in never-ending motion, while His seal on humanity is on each part of as well as the entire human body.

Look at His works, which are firm and well-ordered. There is absolute order despite absolute abundance, absolute measure and balance despite absolute speed, absolute firmness despite absolute facility, absolute beauty of art despite absolute heterogeneity, absolute harmony and correlation despite absolute distance, absolute distinction despite absolute compositeness, and absolute worth and value despite infinite economy. This obvious quality of existence bears witness for a sensible person, and compels an unbeliever to admit that existence belongs to One Absolutely Powerful, the absolutely All-Knowing.

Existence can be explained with absolute ease by attributing it to One Divine Being. If you try to explain it by attributing it to various origins, you encounter insurmountable barriers. If you attribute it to the One Divine Being, the whole universe will be as easy to create as a honeybee, and a honeybee will be as easy to create as a fruit. If, by contrast, you ascribe it to multiple origins, creating a honeybee will be as difficult as creating the universe, and creating a fruit will be as difficult as creating all trees in the universe.

This is because a single being, with a single movement, can produce an effect and deal with a whole. If that effect or treatment is expected of multiple beings, it will be obtained, if at all, only with extreme difficulty and after many controversies. Which is easier or more difficult: managing an army by a single commander or the soldiers themselves, constructing a building by a architect or the stones themselves, having planets revolve around a single sun or vice versa?

When existence is attributed to One Divine Being, the connection between existence and that Being becomes like a boundless power, and causes do not have to be of the same power. Also, the effect produced becomes great in proportion to the Being to Whom it is attributed. Otherwise each cause would have to be so infinitely powerful that it could create existence, and the effect produced would be proportional to its own size only.

When all things are attributed to One Divine Being, they do not have to be created from absolute non-existence, for creation means giving external, material existence to things that already exist in Divine Knowledge. It is like developing a form reflected in a mirror, putting in words the meaning in one's mind, or rubbing a substance to make letters written in invisible ink visible. However, if things are ascribed to themselves or their causes, they have to come into existence from absolute non-existence. This is impossible.

The ease with which One Divine Being does this makes the existence of things as easy as absolutely necessary; the difficulty in the latter is beyond measure. A living being's existence requires that the particles forming it, which are spread out in the soil, water, and air, should come together. Therefore each particle or atom would have to have universal knowledge and absolute will. Anything with such knowledge and will would be independent of and have no need for any partners. Nowhere in the universe has any sign of such things and partners been found. Creating the heavens and Earth requires a perfect, infinite power that has no partner. Otherwise, this power would have to be limited by a finite power, which is inconceivable. An infinite power does not need partners and is not obliged to admit them, even if they were to exist (they do not).

This Power has no partners, assistants, or ministers. Material causes are only a thin veil before the Eternal Power's operation, and have no creative effect in the existence of things. Human beings, the noblest cause and equipped with willpower, have only a very small part in those of their actions done through free will. If we do not have complete control over ourselves, despite our free will, how can animals, plants, and inanimate objects [and the lifeless, blind, and deaf laws that only have nominal existence] be partners with the Creator of the heavens and Earth in creating and controlling things?

Obviously, the "envelope" in which the King puts His gifts, the "handkerchief" in which He wraps His offerings, or the "soldier" by whom He sends His bounties cannot be partners with Him in His Kingdom. Nature and causes, which are like "soldiers" through whom the Absolute Sovereign sends His bounties to us, envelopes or chests in which He stores His offerings to us, handkerchiefs in which He wraps His gifts for us, cannot be partners with Him or means of creative effect in executing His commands.

Second rank

God is the All-Great, greater than all things in power and knowledge. He is the Creator, All-Knowing, Maker, All-Wise, All-Merciful, All-Compassionate. All earthly creatures and heavenly objects are the miracles of an All-Knowing Creator's Power. The multicolored and decorated plants and innumerable species of adorned animals distributed throughout the garden of Earth are the wonders of an All-Wise Maker's Art. Its smiling flowers and bedecked fruits are gifts of Mercy from an All-Merciful, All-Compassionate One.

Everything proclaims that their Creator, Fashioner, and Bestower of gifts is powerful over all things, knows everything, and encompasses all things in mercy and knowledge. In relation to His Power, everything without exception is equal. All past events are miracles of an All-Wise Maker's Art, and bear witness that that Maker is powerful over all future contingencies and that He can do whatever He wills in the future, for He is the All-Knowing Creator, All-Wise, and All-Mighty.

Glory be to Him Who has made the garden of Earth an exhibition of His Art, the assembling ground of His Creativity's products, a place where His Power and Wisdom are manifested, a garden where His Mercy blossoms, the field to be sown for Paradise, and a place where creatures come and depart in a continuous flux according to fixed measures.

Ornamented animals, bedecked birds, fruit-bearing trees, flowering plants—all are miracles of His Knowledge, marvels of His Art, gifts of His Generosity, and proofs of His Favor. Smiling flowers promising fruits, birds singing at dawn, raindrops splashing on flowers, a mother's compassion for her infant—all are instances of an All-Loving One making Himself known, an All-Merciful One making Himself loved, imprints of the Compassion of an All-Pitying One, and the pitying of a Most Kind One for jinn, humanity, spirit beings, angels, and animals.

Seeds, fruits, grains, and flowers are miracles of Wisdom, marvels of Art, gifts of Mercy, proofs of [Divine] Oneness, and witnesses of His Bountifulness in the Hereafter. They proclaim that their Creator is powerful over and knows all things, and that He encompasses all things in mercy, knowledge, creativity, sustaining, making, and fashioning.

In relation to His Attributes of creating, arranging, maintaining, making, and fashioning, the sun is like a seed, a star like a flower, and Earth like a grain. Seeds and fruits mirror [Divine] Unity in the realm of multiplicity, and are signs of Destiny and indications of Power. The source of multiplicity (the universe and its contents) is the realm of Unity. Multiplicity testifies to the Creator's Oneness in originating and fashioning, and ends in Unity pointing out the Maker's Wisdom in creating, sustaining, and maintaining.

As the universal view encompasses and considers all particulars, Wisdom manifests that the Creator of all things considers the particular. If the particular is, for example, a fruit, obviously it is the reason why the tree was created. We are the fruit of the universe, the Creator's most manifest purpose [in creating the universe]. The heart is like a seed or the nucleus [of a person], and the brightest mirror of the Maker of creation. Thus we are the universe's pivot upon which the wheel of creation turns, and for the sake of which the universe is continually destroyed and changed, transformed and renewed.

> God is the All-Greatest: O Great One! O God, You are One Whose Grandeur, Greatness, and Majesty cannot be grasped by intellects. All things announce in unison: There is no deity but He, continually seek: O Truth, and eternally say: O Living One!

Third rank

God is the the All-Great, greater than all things in power and knowledge. He is All-Powerful, All-Determining, All-Knowing, All-Wise, All-Fashioning, All-Munificent, All-Subtle and Favoring, All-Decorating, All-Loving, the One Making Himself Known, All-Merciful, All-Compassionate, All-Pitying, All-Beautiful, the One with Absolute Beauty and Perfection, and the Eternal Designer. The truths of the worlds (in whole and in parts) and of creation (in whole and in parts), and existence and maintenance all consist in the lines drawn by the "pen" of His Decree and Destiny according to a definite ordering, determining, knowledge, and wisdom, and in the designs made by the "compasses" of His Knowledge and Wisdom according to a definite art and fashion.

They consist of decorations made by the "bright hand" of His Art, Fashioning, Decorating, and Illustrating with favor and munificence; in the flowers of His Favoring, Munificence, Making Known, and Loving with mercy and bountifulness; and in the fruits of the overflowing spring of His Mercy, Bountifulness, Pitying, and Affection with grace and perfection. They also consist of the radiations of an everlasting Beauty and perpetual Perfection, as attested to by the fact that the mirrors [reflecting those truths—that is, all creatures] are mortal and the reflections disappear, while manifestations of Beauty are permanent and continue to confer bounties despite their recipients' mortality.

The mortality of mirrors and the decay of creatures, despite the perpetual manifestation [of Divine Names, Attributes, and acts] in utmost abundance, is a clear sign and convincing argument that the manifest Beauty and flowering Perfection do not belong to those on whom they are manifested. This is a most eloquent explanation and evident proof of the abstract Beauty and ever-renewed Benevolence, of the Necessarily Existent and the All-Loving, Permanent One.

A perfect work points to a perfect act. A perfect act indicates a perfect name and a perfect agent. A perfect name betokens a perfect attribute. A perfect attribute shows a perfect function or essential capacity. A perfect function or essential capacity demonstrates the perfection of the Being through what is befitting for that Being, Who is the Most Evident Truth.

Fourth rank

Exalted is His Majesty. God is the All-Great, for He is All-Just and the source of justice, the All-Judging, All-Ruling, and All-Wise. He founded the tree of this universe in "6 days" by the principles of His Will and Wisdom, divided it into branches by the prescripts of His Decree and Destiny, arranged it by the rules of His way of acting, decorated it by the precepts of His Favor and Mercy, and illuminated it through the manifestations of His Names and Attributes. His creation's orderliness and balance; His creatures' decorations; the similarity, correct proportions, mutual assistance and answering among them; and the firm, conscious artistry in all things Destiny has determined for each, according to its capacity, attest to this.

There is a comprehensive, all-inclusive wisdom in creation's ordering; a perfect favoring in equipping each thing with necessary parts and organs, as well as making it good-looking and well-proportioned; an all-encompassing mercy in gratifying each creature's needs; an all-inclusive provision in each creature's raising and breeding all these qualities in creation and the life conferred on each living thing or being to make it an exhibition of the Creator's manifestations; and the beauties granted to it for certain purposes show that the Creator is One.

Members of a species die but the species remains. Each feels innate love for its Creator, Whom it adores, and an attraction toward Him. Its coming into existence, formation and life, and the perfect functioning of its bodily parts, are amazing. All such qualities in creation also show that the Creator and the Lord is One.

Plants and animals are sustained and nursed, and produce wisely and for many sublime purposes. There is a perfect and purposeful order in changes occurring on Earth, and each thing has amazing, perfect artistry and beauty despite its coming into existence as if all at once. All of this demonstrates that the Creator and Ruler is One.

Innumerable living creatures in the universe need provision. Creation is very diverse, and so meeting the needs of each part of creation requires great diversity. No creature can meet its needs. Seeing that a single grape costs almost as much as the universe, for the co-operation of all elements (especially the sun, soil, water, and the vine) is required to produce it, it is clear that no creature can fulfill even one of its needs. But the needs of every creature are met just on time from unexpected sources. This universal, precise provision shows that the Creator and Provider is One.

Every creature is essentially weak and helpless. It has nothing of its own. Whatever it has in the name of strength and wealth is from the Creator. Its acknowledgement of its weakness and helplessness attracts Divine help. Therefore its strength lies in its weakness, and its power derives from its helplessness. Inanimate matter and substances are equipped and radiated with life and consciences. They undergo numerous changes during their life-history. Their neediness, their innate incapacity, is a prayer acceptable by God. All of this shows that the Creator is One, Immutable and Answerer of prayers.

A conscious, living being draws close to God through its supplications and acts of worship. Sincere, regular worship and supplications enable one to have deep insight and an "eye of the heart" by which one can penetrate into the meaning of things and events, and the Divine purposes in creation, and unveil some hidden truths in creation and pertaining to Divinity. Regular worship, prayer, and remembrance of God give one peace and tranquillity and make one a perfect human being, a best pattern of creation—all such qualities of creation and many others unmentioned are witnesses that this universe is managed by a single All-Wise One; sustained and raised by a single, All-Munificent Lord, One Besought-of-All; serves a single Master; and is at the disposal of a single Ruler. Also, the origin of creation is a single Power, the stamps of Whose Oneness appear on each of Its "missives," on each of Its "pages," and as abundantly as the number of those missives and pages.

Every flower and fruit, plant and tree, animal and rock, sand particle and stone is a manifest seal demonstrating that the One Who placed it is the "Inscriber" of this space, the land and sea, and all their contents. He is the Designer of the sun and moon on the page of the heavens. Exalted is the Majesty of that Designer. He is God the All-Great.

Whence the world sings in unison: *There is no deity but He.*

Fifth rank

God is the All-Great. He is the Creator, All-Powerful, Fashioner, and All-Seeing. All celestial bodies and pearl-like stars are proofs of His Divinity and Grandeur, witnesses of His Lordship and Might. They attest to and proclaim the splendor of His Lordship's Kingdom, the vastness of His Rule and Wisdom, and His Power's magnificence and greatness.

Do they not look at the heaven above them, how We have built it and decorated it? (50:6). Look at the sky and see the serene silence, purposeful motion, and magnificent glittering smile with its orderly creation and well-proportioned art. Its "lamp" shines for the changing of seasons, its "lantern" radiates for the world's illumination, its stars glitter for the worlds' decoration. All proclaims the boundless Sovereignty in the universe's organization and maintenance.

That All-Powerful Creator knows all things and has a Will so comprehensive that whatever He wills is, and whatever He does not will is not. He is powerful over all things by an absolute, all-encompassing Power essential to His Divine Being. Just as it is inconceivable for the sun to exist without light and heat, it is inconceivable for the God and Creator of the heavens to be without all-encompassing Knowledge and absolute Power. He knows all things by an all-encompassing Knowledge essential to His Divine Being. Nothing can escape this Knowledge, by virtue of Its relation with all things and Its penetrative capability and comprehensiveness.

Whatever is observed in creation (e.g., orderliness, balance, and harmony; all-inclusive wisdom, perfect favoring, well-established measures, well-arranged dispensation, fruitful decrees, appointed hours, regular provision, and pleasing care [given to all things]; and perfect, distinguishing measurement, order and firmness, and the absolute ease thereof) testifies to the all-encompassing Knowledge of the Knower of the Unseen and of all things. The verse: *Should He Who creates not know? He is the All-Subtle, the All-Aware* (67:14), points out that the existence of something requires knowing it. If the beauty of art in one's work points to one's consciousness to the extent of a small star's brightness on a pitch-dark night, humanity's creation indicates its Creator's Knowledge to the extent of the sun's splendor at noon.

As He knows all things, His Will encompasses all things. Nothing takes place without His Will. Power produces the effect, Knowledge distinguishes, and Will apportions and individualizes. This is how things come into existence. There are as many witnesses of the Almighty's Will as there are characteristics, attributes, and states of things.

Creating and fashioning each thing with the distinguishing character and attributes purposefully chosen for it out of innumerable alternatives and potentialities; forming each most delicately and with most sensitive measures in an infinitely diverse flux; creating diverse, well-formed living beings from simple, inanimate elements (e.g., creating humanity with its senses and all other systems and bodily organs from a sperm [and an egg], a bird and its bodily systems from an egg, a tree with all its parts from a seed) witness that everything is given its individual character and attributes by the Almighty's Will and Choice. Glory be to Him.

The correspondence in bodily structures and basic systems among a species' members shows that their Maker is One and Single. However, the fact that each one is unique demonstrates that that One and Single Maker does whatever He wills and judges however He wills. Exalted is His Majesty.

As the All-Knowing and All-Willing Creator has an all-encompassing Knowledge and all-inclusive Will, He has a perfect Power issuing from and essential to His Divine Being. That Power has no opposite, for that would require the agreement or combination of two opposites, which, by universal assent, is inconceivable. There can be no grades in that Power, so in relation to It, everything, without exception, is equal. This is because the Power is not material.

The transparency of the immaterial dimension of existence with which It deals, the interrelation among things, the exact balance in creation, the perfect order of existence, and the utmost obedience of existence to It testify to this.[47] The absolute order and harmony in creation, the absolute measuredness and distinctness observed in it, despite the speed and ease of creation and the created's infinite multiplicity, individualization, and diversity, also testify to this fact.

The One Who has that Power can create anything, without exception, with great ease because He is One and Single, and because of the necessity of His existence and being totally different from the created (He is unrestricted, indivisible, and uncontained by space). Nothing impedes Him; rather, whatever seems to be an impediment serves as a means of ease, although

47 These qualities are explained in the Second Aim of The Twenty-ninth Word. (Tr.)

He has no need for any help in conducting and executing His commands. He can do so because anything He creates, without exception, has the same quality of art as that seen in everything else. Whoever creates the latter creates the former. The One Who creates a seed, which is a small-scale copy of its tree into which the Creator has included the tree by the principles of His Knowledge, must undoubtedly be the Creator of the tree. It is not difficult for the Power That brings into existence the particulars to create the universals.

Just as the copy of the "Qur'an of wisdom" inscribed in an atom with ether particles has the same quality of beauty and art found in the copy of the "Qur'an of grandeur" written on the pages of the heavens in the ink of stars and suns, so creating a honeybee and an ant requires no less skill and artistry than creating a date palm. The art contained in a rose is not less than the art contained in a pearl-like star. While the utmost and perfect ease of creating things causes the misguided to confuse creation with self-formation, which requires accepting impossibilities and superstitions that contradict sound reasoning and judgment, it leads people of truth to the certainty that planets and minute particles are the same in relation to the Power of the Creator of the universe. Exalted is His Majesty, and sublime is His Name. There is no deity but He.

Sixth rank

God is the All-Great, greater than all things in power and knowledge. He is the All-Just, All-Wise, All-Powerful, All-Knowing, One, Single, and Eternal Sovereign. All worlds are at the disposal of His "Hands" of order and balance, arranging and measuring, Justice and Wisdom, and Knowledge and Power. They show His Oneness and Singleness. Nothing is excluded from His order and balance or His arranging and measuring, which are two "chapters" of the Manifest Record and the Manifest Book,[48] which,

[48] The Manifest Record and Manifest Book are explained in The Thirtieth Word: The Manifest Record and Manifest Book are repeated in several places in the Qur'an. Some interpreters maintain that the phrases are identical in meaning; others say they have different meaning and connotations. Although their explanations of the true meanings and contents differ, they agree that both describe Divine Knowledge. However, via the Qur'an's enlightenment, I have this conviction:

The Manifest Record, which looks more to the Unseen world than to the visible, material world, expresses one aspect of Divine Knowledge and Commands. Looking more to the past and future than to the present, it is a book of Divine Destiny that contains

in turn, are the titles to the Knowledge and Command of the All-Knowing and All-Wise, and the Power and Will of the All-Mighty and All-Compassionate. The order and balance in this Book, together with that Record, testify that all is at the All-Merciful's disposal, the All-Pitying's ordering, the All-Gracious' decorating, and the All-Ruling's measuring.

In sum: The manifestations of the Divine Names "the First" and "the Last" in creation refer to beginning and end, origin and issue, past and future, command and knowledge, and point to the Manifest Record. The manifes-

---

the origin, the roots and the seeds of things rather than their flourishing forms in their visible existence.

The origins, sources, and roots from which God Almighty shapes things with perfect order and art, show that they are arranged according to a book of the principles contained in Divine Knowledge. The seeds and fruits, which contain the indexes and programs of beings that will subsequently come into existence, constitute a miniature register of Divine Commands. For example, a seed is said to be the program and index according to which a whole tree may be formed. Moreover, it is the miniature embodiment of the Divine principles that cause the tree to come into existence and that determine this program and index. In short, the Manifest Record is an index and program of the Tree of Creation as a whole, which spreads its branches through the past, future, and the Unseen world. In this sense, it is a book of Divine Destiny or a register of its principles. Through these principles' dictates and demands, minute particles or atoms are used and managed to bring things into existence.

The Manifest Book looks more to the visible, material world than to the Unseen world, for it looks more to the present than to the past and future. It expresses Divine Power and Will, rather than Divine Knowledge and Commands or laws and principles of creation. If the Manifest Record is the book of the Divine Destiny, the Manifest Book is the book of Divine Power. The perfect art and orderliness in everything's essence and existence, attributes and functions, demonstrate that everything is given existence according to the laws of an effective will and the principles of an absolute power. Also, it is specifically formed and given an appointed measure and particular shape. Therefore, this shows that Divine Power and Will have a universal, comprehensive register of laws, a great book, according to which a particular form and substance is determined for each entity.

It is curious that the people of neglect, misguidance and [corrupt] philosophy, although they have felt the existence of God's Supreme Preserved or Guarded Tablet (*Lawhun Mahfuz*) and seen the manifestations and reflections of that book of Divine Wisdom and Will, have named it "nature," and thus made it completely meaningless. In reality, however, through the dictates of the Manifest Record (the decree and instruction of Divine Destiny), Divine Power uses particles or atoms to created or manifest the chain of beings, each link of which is His sign, on the metaphorical page of time (the Tablet of Effacement and Confirmation). This means that particles or atoms are set to move so that beings may be transferred from the Unseen world to the material, visible world; from (the Realm of) Knowledge to the (Realm of) Power. (Tr.)

tations of the Names "the Outward" and "the Inward" on things connected with God's Attribute of Creation point to the Manifest Book.

The universe is like a huge tree, and each world in it is also like a tree. The universe's creation and division into worlds and species may be likened to a tree. A tree has an origin (its seed) and an issue that carries on its task after its death (the seed in its fruit). Its beginning and end manifest "the First" and "the Last." Through its composition and the purposes it serves, the original seed is an index or code for the tree's formation. Thus it manifests "the First." The seeds in the tree's fruits manifest "the Last."

Seeds are like miniature chests containing the Pen of Destiny's inscribed index and code for forming new trees that exactly resemble the original one. A tree's exterior manifests the Name "the Outward." Through its perfect, well-ordered structure, decoration, and purposes it serves, it is like a perfectly beautiful dress made with perfect wisdom and favor to fit the tree. The tree's interior manifests the Name "the Inward." Through its perfect, amazing organization and the way it is fed, its interior is like an extraordinary machine or factory working in perfect order and balance.

The tree's beginning resembles an amazing code, its end an extraordinary index, and both point to the Manifest Record. Its exterior points to the Manifest Book, just as human memory indicates the Supreme Preserved Tablet. All trees' original seeds and fruits indicate the Manifest Record, and their exteriors and interiors symbolize the Manifest Book. Compare with a particular tree the "tree" of Earth with its past and future, the "tree" of the universe with its beginning and future, and the "tree" of a person with his or her ancestors and descendants.

Seventh rank

God is the All-Great, greater than all things in power and knowledge. He is the Creator, Opener, All-Acting, All-Knowing, Bestower of gifts, Distributor of Blessings, and Eternal "Sun."[49] All worlds and their contents are shadows of His lights, works of His acts, colors of the embroidery of His Names' manifestations, lines of the "pen" of His Destiny and Decree, and mirrors manifesting His Attributes of Beauty, Majesty, and Perfection. All of this is attested to by the Eternal Witness—the Almighty Himself—with

49 Using these Names to view the Divine acts and imprints behind creatures, one can move to the One called by these Names.

all His Books, Pages, or Scrolls; by creation's signs of and the Qur'an's verses; by Earth, with its manifestations of absolute riches and wealth despite its essential destitution and need; and by the Prophets, saints and purified, exacting scholars with enlightened intellects and illumined hearts, their investigations, spiritual discoveries and supplications, and the blessings with which they are favored.

All of the above, with utmost certainty, accept the testimony of creation's signs, the Qur'an's verses, and the testament of the heavenly Books and Pages containing the testimony of the Necessarily Existent One. All of these witnesses agree that all creatures are works of His Power, inscriptions of His Destiny, mirrors of His Names, and images of His lights.

Conclusion: Different experienced issues

KNOW, O FRIEND, that as long as I am alive I say, as did Mawlana Jalal al-Din al-Rumi, may God sanctify him, that: "I am a servant of the Qur'an as long as I am alive; I am the soil of the way of Muhammad, the Chosen One."

The Qur'an is the source of all intellectual and spiritual radiation. Whatever truth is in my books is found in it. Thus my books contain references to the Qur'an's miraculous nature. I mentioned about 40 of them in *The Words*. Here, I will include only one as a means of blessing for this book: Ponder these questions concerning a speech made or a word uttered: Who said it? To whom was it said? Why was it said? About what was it said?

A word derives its strength and beauty from its speaker and its audience, and why and when it was said. Some literary people wrongly believe that the occasion is the word's only source of beauty. However, the wording or words chosen to express a meaning are not the speech's body; they are its dress. The speech's apparent or superficial meaning is not its "spirit," but its body. A speech derives life from the speaker's intention and feelings, and so its spirit is the speaker's intended meaning. If the speech or words contain an order or prohibition, they have an authority proportionate to the speaker's power, which adds to their strength and sublimity.

There is a great difference between a non-authoritative order issuing from one [who cannot ensure compliance] and a forceful and powerful command from a determined authority. How different is the order: *O Earth, swallow up your water*, and *O heaven, withdraw (your rain)* (11:44) [which issued from the sole Sovereign of the universe] from supposedly human orders to lifeless elements: "O Earth, be still and come to a rest"; "O heaven, split asunder"; and "O world, destroy yourself and be built again for the Resurrection."

Consider the difference between the command "March!" issuing from an obeyed commander to a mighty obedient army, and that of a person whose orders are ignored. See the difference between the narration of the acts by their true doer, an authoritative commander, a maker who makes whatever he wishes, when he says: "I have done and I do such and such," and by one having no direct relation with the acts done. See the difference between real stars and their reflections, which have no real existence.

How different are the "angels" of the words spoken by the Creator of the sun and moon from our words. How different are the Qur'an's words—the "mothers of pearls" of guidance, belief, principles diffusing from the Supreme Throne of God, and which constitute the Eternal Speech containing knowledge, power, and will—from our hollow words. How different is a tree that has divided into parts, grown, blossomed, and borne fruit from any substance obtained from some of its fruits by changing their form, removing the nucleus of life, and mixing them with another element.[50]

The Qur'an is like a tree whose seeds have grown into principles of conduct, and from which Islam's world has been formed. Minds have derived ideas from it, and the exalted truths originating from it have become incontestable principles and branches of knowledge. If you take one truth, change it, remove its nucleus of life, decorate it as you wish, and then make your opinion a criterion by which to judge the Qur'an's verses, you may judge whether it is justifiable to compare the forms given to precious stones according to childish desires with those stones themselves.

I have personally experienced and observed that experiencing the Qur'an's beauty requires a sound, purified heart. A heart tainted with [spiritual diseases] can feel only what its diseases have soiled and muddied. The Qur'an's styles and the [human] heart are two corresponding mirrors that reflect each other.

A subtle point

Belief establishes brotherhood and affinity among all things. Thus one does not find strong feelings of greed, enmity, hatred, or desolation in believers'

50 In these lines, the difference between the Qur'an and human words or speeches are stressed through comparisons that might seem unfamiliar to the reader. (Tr.)

hearts. Believers see even the strongest enemy as brothers or sisters in humanity. Unbelief causes separation and alienation, which manifest in unbelievers as strong feelings of greed, enmity, self-preference, and self-reliance. Such feelings help them succeed in this life, for they see their virtues rewarded mostly here and now, whereas believers suffer the consequences of some of their shortcomings and sins. That is why the Prophet declared: "The world is a prison for a believer, but a paradise for an unbeliever."[51]

KNOW, O FRIEND, that if belief enters your heart, you become like a jewel worthy of eternity and Paradise. Unbelief, however, reduces you to a valueless, perishable stone devoid of most sublime feelings and virtues. Belief unveils the sound, pleasant kernel or essence within the perishable covering, and displays the supposed perishable foam as a radiant diamond. Unbelief shows the covering as the kernel, clings to it firmly, and reduces you from resembling a diamond to resembling a piece of glass, ice, or foam. This is what I have observed concerning belief and unbelief.

A point

I have observed that the more people are preoccupied with philosophy, the more their hearts suffer from spiritual disease. I also have observed that the greater this spiritual disease of the heart becomes, the more people are preoccupied with rational sciences. Spiritual diseases lead to preoccupation with rational sciences, and preoccupation with rational sciences gives rise to spiritual diseases.

I have also observed that the world has two aspects: Its first aspect is that outwardly it is partly and temporarily attractive but inwardly it is eternally horrible. Its second aspect is that outwardly it is partly horrible while inwardly eternally beautiful. The Qur'an draws attention to the second aspect, which relates to the Hereafter. The first aspect is connected with eternal annihilation, as opposed to eternal afterlife.

I also have observed that existence based on the human ego ends in non-existence, whereas self-annihilation or annihilation of the ego results in existence and leads to the Necessarily Existent Being. If you desire existence and find it, try to annihilate your ego.

---

51 Muslim, "Zuhd," no. 2959; Tirmidhi, "Zuhd," no. 2324; Ibn Maja, "Zuhd," no. 4113.

A subtle point

KNOW, O FRIEND, that I mentioned *intention* in the Introduction among the four attainments of my 40 years of age. Intention changes ordinary acts and customs into acts of worship. It is a penetrating and pervading spirit through which inanimate states and deeds acquire life and become "living" acts of worship. It is also through a special quality of intention that evil changes into virtue or good deeds. Intention is a "spirit" that causes ordinary deeds and customs to become "living" acts of worship. Its "soul" is sincerity or acting solely for God's sake. Salvation is found only in sincere actions done in His cause. Sincerity multiplies an action's worth, and through it one can reach Paradise with a little action and in a short life.

Purity of intention makes you continuously thankful to God, for worldly bounties and pleasures have two aspects. Their first aspect is that you confess that the bounties consumed are conferred by the "hand" of Mercy and Favor. Thus you pass from bounties to the Divine act of giving bounties, and the pleasure received therein increases. The second aspect is that you pursue pleasure only to gratify bodily desires. The Divine act of giving bounties is not recalled; rather, you concentrate on the bounty and pleasure themselves as something falling to your lot for nothing, and do not consider how or why they have been bestowed.

In the first case, the "spirit" lasts when its pleasure disappears. By thinking "the Bestower of bounties' mercy does not forget me," you feel an unbreakable connection with the Bestower of bounties. This is not true for the second aspect, however, for the "spirit" disappears when the pleasure is gone. But the pleasure's "smoke" remains—sins [arising from ingratitude and unlawful ways of obtaining and consuming bounties].

When viewed with the light of belief, lawful pleasures in the world and bounties in the Hereafter form a virtuous circle. The disappearance of pleasures or separation from bounties does not cause pain, for the pleasures of belief and thankfulness are permanent. But without belief, pleasures change into pain for the decay of pleasures; even thinking of their decay causes pain. Unbelief views each pleasure as an end in itself, and its disappearance causes pain.

A point

KNOW, O FRIEND, that attachment to material causes engenders humiliation and rejection. Consider this: Why are dogs, which should be considered blessed due to their many good qualities (notably their proverbial loyalty), considered ritually unclean? Why are other domestic animals (i.e., hens, cows, and cats) that feel no gratitude and loyalty in return for the good we do to them, considered blessed? This is because—provided it is not to backbite dogs and break their hearts—dogs are greedy and so attached to apparent causes that they cannot see the true Bestower of bounties. Thus they suppose the means to be truly effective [in procuring their food] and so suffer the stigma of ritual impurity as punishment for their blindness and indifference to the true Owner and Bestower of bounties.

Blessed animals do not recognize means and causes, or give them any value or importance. Cats ask for food and, when they get what they want, behave as if they do not know you or you do not know them. They feel no gratitude toward you. Instead, they thank the true Bestower of bounties by saying: "O Compassionate One, O Compassionate One." By disposition, they recognize their Creator and worship Him consciously or unconsciously.

A subtle point

If all things are not attributed to the Almighty, an infinite number of deities, all essentially opposite but simultaneously identical, must be recognized. Due to the interrelation of all things and the essential quality of divinity, their number would increase in proportion to the number of particles and compounds found in creation.

For example, a deity who creates a honeybee or a grape should be able to rule and influence all elements in the universe, as a honeybee or a grape is a miniature of creation. Furthermore, in existence there is no room for a divine being other than a Single Necessarily Existent One. If things are attributed to themselves, each minute particle would require to be a deity. Thus each stone in the Hagia Sophia's dome would be its own architect. The universe's testimony to its Single Creator is more manifest, radiant, clearer, and expressive than its testimony to its own existence. Even if the universe's existence is denied, the existence of the One, Who is powerful over all things, cannot be denied.

A point

Heedless and misguided people derive the law of causality from the coming together of causes and the series of creation in producing a result, and then attribute creativity to that law. However, this requires accepting an endless series of impossibilities, in addition to realizing that no indication of the Creator's supposed partner has ever been found. Rather, everything's structure and art unveil an infinite power belonging to an All-Powerful, Necessarily Existent One. Given this, how can one believe or even think that the All-Powerful Creator has a partner?

A subtle point

The letter *nun* [meaning we] in *na'budu* [we worship] has a universal meaning. While reciting *na'budu*, people praying consciously in a congregation and in awareness of its meaning and significance regard Earth as a mosque in which all believers are standing in line to worship God. They see themselves as members of this huge community. By virtue of the consensus of all Prophets and saints on *there is no deity but God*, and because all individuals in the congregation recite the same words, believers can view time as a circle of reciters led by the Leader of the Prophets.

With the Prophets sitting on the right (representing the past) and the saints on the left (representing the future), the whole circle mentions God and recites His Names so loudly that those who listen can hear this recitation. Those with a keener hearing and sight can hear all creatures reciting God's Names, and see themselves in this universal circle of recitation.

A point

KNOW, O FRIEND, that loving all else besides God has two aspects. The first is that one loves God and thus loves those whom God loves. Love of God does not diminish this love, but rather increases it. The second is that one loves the means [to attain love of God], and uses this love to reach love of God. Such love has many kinds. However, a strong, attractive means may hinder one from advancing. Even if one attains love of God, it will be defective.

A subtle point

KNOW, O FRIEND, that as declared in: *There is not a moving creature in Earth but its provision depends on God* (11:6), God provides for all creatures. This provision is of two types: absolutely necessary and superfluous. God has undertaken to provide what is absolutely necessary. Superfluous needs become necessary through the misuse of one's will, as well as bad habits and customs. Such provision is not included in the provision God has undertaken in the verse mentioned above. Whoever reflects on eggplants ("fish" of the land) and fish ("eggplants" of the sea), on how the Creative Power makes them all fleshy and how their provision comes to them abundantly from sources unknown to them, surely understands that there is no need to feel anxiety about vital provision and so blame the All-Providing One.

A point

KNOW, O FRIEND, that misfortunes experienced by innocent children and animals contain reasons that people usually fail to notice. For example, Divine laws of nature and life are principles of Divine Will applied not only to intellectual beings; creatures without reason are also "obliged" to obey them by virtue of their disposition. Those laws also appeal to the heart, feelings, and senses. A child may be considered mature in some senses or feelings. A child's feelings may even be more perfect and alert than an adult's reason. While an adult's reason might not prevent him or her from oppressing an orphan, the compassion of his or her child who watches this oppression may drive that child to tears.

That being so, if children do not heed their feeling of compassion or pity and kill a honeybee to indulge an impulse, they will be punished. For example, a female leopard feels great affection for its young and is protective of its mate. However, when these feelings do not prevent it from killing a young gazelle, it may become the target of a hunter's bullet. Is this not what it deserves, for its lawful food is the carcasses of other animals?

[Like us,] animals do not own themselves and cannot behave as they wish. The universe's true Owner, the One of Majesty and Favor, is the Owner and sole Ruler of creation, including all living beings, and disposes of them in His Realm of Dominion however He wills. He does whatever He wills, and *is not to be questioned concerning what He does. Rather, they are to be questioned* (21:23).

* * *

Addendum

In the Name of God, the All-Merciful, the All-Compassionate.

All praise to God, the Lord of the worlds. Blessings and peace be upon our master Muhammad and all of his Family and Companions.

Symbol

KNOW, O FRIEND, that it is commendable [for believers] to perform each daily Prayer at the beginning of its time and imagine themselves before the Ka'ba. They imagine believers standing in Prayer around the Ka'ba as concentric circles, the first being the nearest to the Ka'ba and the last encircling the Muslim world. They feel a strong yearning to join the others wholeheartedly. After joining, this huge community's consensus and unity become a decisive proof for the truth of all meanings and causes contained in the Prayer.

For example, when those praying say: "All praise be to God," it is as if all believers praying in the mosque of Earth reply: "I agree. You say the truth." All doubt and suspicion disappear from their hearts. Each sense and faculty derives belief and a pleasure unique to itself, and such questions as *Why?* and *How?* cannot become obstacles. The huge congregation of pious, God-conscious believers is formed when the Prayer begins. Due to its uniform acts and recitations, regional time differences do not prevent such an imagination.

Wherever praying believers are, they turn to the Ka'ba. While imagining the Ka'ba in front of them and the community of believers standing in concentric circles around it, praying believers should not become distracted with this image. Rather, keep it simple. How do they know that Destiny, which neglects nothing, does not record every act and recitation of those orderly, blessed lines on the pages of the World of Representations or Immaterial Forms, in which all things are preserved eternally?

Symbol

KNOW, O FRIEND, that I have observed during my journeying in the "layers of darkness" that the Prophet's sayings and practices, as well as the principles of Islamic law, are like stars that guide us among innumerable dark and misleading ways. Deviating from the Prophet's way or Tradition [the Sunna] makes one a plaything of devils, an object of illusion and suspicion, a target of fear, and a mountain of unbearable burdens. Deliverance from such things comes only from following the Sunna.

I have also observed that the Sunna's principles are like ropes hanging down from heaven. Whoever holds fast to even a part of them can be elevated. Whoever opposes them and relies on their own or even public reason is like one who desires to obtain the means of traveling through the heavens' spheres in earthly vehicles and is ridiculed like Pharaoh, who said: *O Haman. Build for me a tower to obtain the means [of traveling] in the heavens* (40:36).

Symbol

KNOW, O FRIEND, that the soul contains an important, obscure knot that causes something to give birth to its opposite, and by which the soul regards what is against it as in its favor.

For example, the sun puts out its "hand" to you and either caresses or slaps you. But you cannot put out your hand to it and influence it. It is nearer to you than yourself, despite its great distance from you. If you think your distance from it is so great that it cannot exert any influence on you, or so near to you that you can affect it, you are mistaken. Likewise, if the carnal soul views its Creator as distant, despite His being nearer to it than itself, it is misguided.

When the carnal soul encounters a great reward, it says: "If only I had done the same. If only I had behaved that way." However, when it comes across a terrible punishment, it consoles itself by ignoring or denying it.

The acts of the Almighty are, first of all, concerned with Him, not with the carnal soul and its narrow mind. The "wheel" of creation does not revolve according to the carnal soul's fancies, and it did not witness His creation of the universe. Surely, Imam Rabbani told the truth: "The gifts of the Sovereign can be borne only by those qualified for them."

Symbol

KNOW, O FRIEND, that the One Who decorated your head beautifully and embellished it with sight sees you better than you do. The Maker Who embellished your head with eyes, ears, and a tongue sees and hears you better than yourself, is nearer to you than yourself, and is more compassionate to you than yourself.

Symbol

KNOW, O FRIEND, that the prayers of those in great difficulty and under severe hardship produce great results. They cause the mightiest and greatest thing to be subjected to the weakest and smallest one. For example, a roaring sea may subside in answer to the prayer of a broken-hearted infant on a piece of wood floating on its surface. This means that the One Who answers prayers has absolute authority over all things and is Lord of creation.

Symbol

KNOW, O FRIEND, that one important disease of a misguided human selfhood is that it seeks the whole's splendor in each part, and a king's glory in a private. Not finding it, it rejects the whole or the king. For example, it seeks to see all of the sun's manifestations when it is reflected in a bubble, and when it cannot, refuses to accept that the image belongs to the sun.

The sun's oneness does not require that its manifestations be one. A thing pointing to something else does not have to contain that something else. A thing describing something else with certain qualifications does not have to have the same qualifications. A minute, transparent object points to the sun and displays some of its qualities; a beehive exhibits the All-Wise Maker's Attributes.

Symbol

KNOW, O FRIEND, that following the way of unbelief is like walking on ice or underground, and therefore repugnant and very difficult for one inclined to follow it. One with a careless, imitative view cannot discern this difficulty. Following the way of belief, however, is like traveling on smooth earth under a light. It is essentially attractive, and therefore very easy for one inclined to follow it.

For example, if you want your six sides to benefit from the sun, either you expose your whole body to the sun by turning around and lying down, or have the sun come down to your level and turn around you. The first alternative illustrates the ease associated with belief in God's Oneness; the second shows the difficulty associated with unbelief.

QUESTION: That being the case, why do so many people follow unbelief and reject belief?

ANSWER: Almost no one consciously follows unbelief. Rather, unbelief sticks to and dirties a person because of the apparent attractiveness of one's bodily desires. Somebody who follows belief knowingly and consciously has belief established in their heart.

Symbol

KNOW, O FRIEND, that it makes no difference if a spoken word is heard by an individual or millions of people. In relation to the Eternal Power, there is no difference between an individual and a species.

Symbol

KNOW, O FRIEND, that the Qur'an is infinitely comprehensive in meaning, encompasses all levels of understanding, and considers its audience's feelings. For example, its words can be understood by ordinary people, for they are, after all, the absolute majority and the first to be addressed. Although this is one of the Qur'an's perfections, carnal souls are misguided by it, for they seek the most exalted styles and most balanced ways of expressing in the simplest manner necessary for the topics discussed and the audience's level. They make the style, which naturally should consider the audience's feelings and level, a criterion and an "observatory" to see and judge the Speaker—the Almighty. This is why they go far astray.

Symbol

The world has three facets. The first relates to God's Names. With respect to its second facet, the world is the arable field of the Hereafter. These two facets are beautiful. The third facet relates directly and exclusively to the world itself, and is where people gratify their bodily desires and seek to meet the needs of this transient worldly life.

I am forced to wear a body that is essentially lifeless. Today is my coffin. Between yesterday and tomorrow, which are the graves of my father and "his son," I am pressed between two dead bodies and graves. But be aware that, with respect to its facet as the arable field of the Hereafter, the world and viewing it with the light of belief give the spiritual pleasures of Paradise. How can one be pleased with the third facet and delight in it?

Symbol

KNOW, O FRIEND, that your body is like a publicly owned rifle or horse entrusted to a soldier. Just as the soldier is responsible for the rifle or horse, you are charged with preserving your own trust—your body.

KNOW, O FRIEND, that I say this because my carnal soul was proud of having virtues. I told it: "You own nothing." It replied: "Then I do not care for what I do not own of the body." I said: "You should not fall behind a fly [in caring for your body]. Look at how the fly cleans its wings with its legs, and wipes its eyes with its hand." Glory be to Him Who has inspired the fly to do so, and made it an instructor that silenced my soul.

Symbol

KNOW, O FRIEND, that error and deviation are one result of confusing the decrees and acts of the Divine Name "the Inward" with those of "the Outward," and expecting from the former what one should expect from the latter. One also confuses the necessities of Divine Power with those of Divine Wisdom, and seeks to see in the former what one should seek to see in the latter.

Confusing the requirements of the realm where the law of causality has a certain role in God's acts with those of belief in His absolute Unity, and the acts and ways of Divine Power's manifestation with the manifestations of Divine Existence or other Divine Attributes, and trying to find the former's rules and laws in the latter cause error and deviation. For example, your birth and growth in this world is gradual, but in the mirrors of the intermediate realms between this material realm and purely spiritual realms—as in dreams, for example—it is all at once. This is so because Divine Attributes vary in manifesting themselves, and creation and manifestation differ from each other.

Symbol

KNOW, O FRIEND, that Islam is a universal mercy. Islam enables even unbelievers to find some happiness in their worldly lives and ensures that their pleasure does not change into endless pain. Islam changes absolute unbelief and denial, which cause despair and pain, into doubt and hesitation. Influenced by its clear announcements, unbelievers may come to regard eternal life as probable. This relieves them from suffocating pain [arising from the thought of eternal extinction or punishment] and, since they are not convinced of eternal life, they consider themselves free of its obligations. Such people are like ostriches, camel-like birds that when told to fly reply: "I'm a camel, not a bird." But when told to carry a burden, they answer like a camel: "I'm a bird, not a camel."

Deluded by Satan, [paradoxically, with false hopes of salvation in the Hereafter while denying eternal life to be free of religious obligations], unbelievers and transgressors [of the Divine rules of conduct] find a superficial happiness, in contrast to atheists and sincere believers.

Symbol

KNOW, O FRIEND, that the ego, in order to maintain the dominion it claims in its own realm, does not wish to admit or conceive of something proceeding from itself as less valuable than that created by the Creator's Power. As long as the ego does not regard itself as the least creature or as nothing in essence, one cannot avoid denying the Creator's Attributes or associating partners with God secretly.

Symbol

KNOW, O FRIEND, that the ego, out of indolence toward its duties, wishes that no one watches it and tries to remain hidden. It considers the non-existence of the Owner of all things and seeks absolute freedom. First it desires, then considers, and thereafter conceives. It now begins to believe in the non-existence of an Owner and Ruler above itself, and finally abandons its belief. However, if it knew what great, consuming suffering and unbearable pain are under the freedom and ease it aspires to and the irresponsibility it seeks, it would flee and keep away from them, repent of them or die.

Symbol

Things differ according to their points of support. For example, a private connected with and supported by a great, powerful sovereign can do what a king cannot do. Thus this private is "seven degrees" greater than one who normally is "seventy degrees" greater than him. This is why a mosquito appointed by the Eternal Power defeated a most powerful and obstinate king.[52] With the permission of God Almighty, the Splitter of grains and

[52] This refers to the mosquito that entered Nimrod's body through one of his nostrils, thereby causing death of this tyrant who had cast Prophet Abraham into the fire. (Tr.)

seeds, a seed contains whatever a huge palm tree needs. Factories built in an area the size of nine villages cannot manufacture what that tree needs.

Know, O friend, that the difference between the Qur'an's way (which I followed in "The Drop") and that of the classical believing philosophers is this: I dig the ground wherever I am and water emerges. Philosophers try to open canals through the universe and lay pipes to provide water. They even go to the Divine Throne. Since they attach great importance to material causes, they should have millions of guards along the pipe's path to protect it from attack and destruction. What the Qur'an has taught me is like the Staff of Moses: Wherever I strike with it, even if I am on a rock, the water of life gushes forth. I do not feel compelled to make a long journey beyond the world and protect very long pipes from breaking or destruction. The saying: "In each thing is a sign demonstrating that He is One," clarifies this point.

Symbol

The human ego or carnal soul [the source of all defect and lust] is essentially blind. As long as it continues to exist [without being disciplined], even if it is only as small as a gnat's wing, it remains a veil covering the truth. Since it concentrates on its own existence [and tends to appropriate for itself whatever the Creator gives it and seeks to deny a supreme dominant power over itself], when it sees a defect in one stone of a large castle built of stones of decisive proofs [of that Power's existence], it denies the castle's existence. From this, one can get an idea of the ego's ignorance arising from its attachment to its own existence.

Symbol

O ego! You know that what belongs to you of yourself is miniscule, if indeed it really belongs to you at all! So put on that small, weak part that is your free will, as much as you can bear. Do not load your consciousness, as weak as a hair, with "huge rocks." Do not put anything upon what does not belong to you, except with its Owner's permission.

When you act heedlessly on your own behalf, do not overstep your limits. The field of your movement is as narrow as a hair. When you act on behalf of the Lord of all dominion, load yourself with whatever you see, provided it is according to His orders and Will and not according to your own will. You should learn His permission and Will from His Law—the Shari'a.

Symbol

O SEEKERS OF FAME AND REPUTATION! You can lend an ear to me: Fame is identical with show and ostentation, and it is poisonous honey that kills the heart. Only those who wish to be slaves to human beings seek it. If it happens to you, say: *Surely we belong to God and are returning to Him* (2:156).

To conclude:

- Consider anything other than God only on account of God Almighty.
- Good intention and correct viewpoint change even evil acts into good ones.
- The importance of: *I am not the owner or master of myself; death is inevitable; my Lord is One*; and *the human ego is a black dot, a point of comparison [to know and recognize God]*.
- Prophet Muhammad and the Qur'an are the most articulate proofs of Divine Existence and Oneness. Islam, other revealed religions, and every facet of life and order in the universe show God's Existence and Unity.
- Despair, self-admiration, vanity, and suspicion are four diseases of heart.
- Four significant truths witnessed by Said Nursi, and reflections on *Glory be to God, All praise be to God*, and *God is the All-Great*.
- The Qur'an from the viewpoint of questions about a speech or a word: Who said it? To whom was it said? Why was it said? About what was it said?
- Belief establishes brotherhood and affinity, and does not allow strong greed, enmity, hatred, or desolation to enter a believer's heart. Unbelief causes separation and alienation, making such people full of greed, enmity, self-preference, and self-reliance. As a result, unbelievers can succeed in this life, as they see the reward of their virtues mostly in the world, whereas believers suffer the consequences of some shortcomings and sins.
- Preoccupation with philosophy increases spiritual disease in the heart. The more one's heart increases in spiritual disease, the more one is preoccupied with rational sciences.
- Intention changes ordinary acts and customs into acts of worship.
- Attachment to material causes results in humiliation and rejection.
- The universal significance of the letter *nun* [meaning *we*] in *na'budu* [we worship].
- Why misfortunes that overtake innocent children and animals are usually not noticed by people.
- It is commendable [for a believer] to pray at the beginning of the Prayer's time and imagine the Ka'ba in front of him or her.

- The Prophet's sayings, practices, and confirmations (Sunna) and the principles of Islamic law guide and elevate us.
- The soul contains an important but obscure knot that causes something to give birth to its opposite, and that causes the soul to see what is really for it as being against it.
- The One Who decorated your head and embellished it with the power of sight sees you better than you do.
- The prayers of those in great difficulty and severe hardship produce great results.
- A misguided human selfhood mistakenly seeks the splendor of a whole in each part.
- Following unbelief is like walking on ice or underground, and thus very difficult for those who follow it.
- In relation to the Eternal Power, there is no difference between an individual and a species.
- The Qur'an is infinitely comprehensive in meaning, encompasses all levels of understanding, and considers the feelings of all whom it addresses.
- The world has three facets. These are related to the Names of God Almighty, the Hereafter, and this world.
- Confusing the decrees and acts of the Divine Name "the Inward" with those of "the Outward," and expecting from the former what one should expect from the latter, is a source of error.
- Islam is a universal mercy and enables even unbelievers to find some happiness in their worldly lives.
- To maintain the dominion it claims in its own realm, the human ego does not wish to admit or conceive of something proceeding from itself as less valuable than that created by the Creator's Power.
- The human ego, not wishing to be overseen, seeks to remain hidden.
- Things differ according to their points of support.
- The difference between the Qur'an's way (and that followed in "The Drop") and that of classical believing philosophers.
- The human ego or carnal soul is essentially blind. As long as it continues to exist [without being disciplined], even if it is as small as a gnat's wing, it blinds itself to the sun of truth.
- Fame is identical with show and ostentation, and kills the heart. One who seeks it becomes a slave to others.

The Fifth Treatise

The Fifth Treatise

A bubble from the ocean of the Qur'an

My Lord is Munificent. He buys His property from you, preserves it on your behalf, and gives in return a great price for it.

In the Name of God, the All-Merciful, the All-Compassionate.

All praise be to the Lord of the worlds. Peace and blessings be on our master Muhammad, his Family, and Companions.

KNOW, O BELIEVERS, THAT WHEN BELIEVERS PRAY AND RECITE GOD'S Names, for example, saying: "I bear witness that there is no deity but God," or "Muhammad is the Messenger of God," or "All praise be to God," they have made a claim, announced a cause and conviction, and declared a conclusion. At that very moment, hundreds of millions testify to the truthfulness of their cause, and they feel as if innumerable past believers had said and confirmed the same words.

Moreover, whatever testifies to Islam's truth, confirms its essentials or judgments, and supports it with proofs and witnesses affirms believers in their cause and strengthens their conviction and conclusion. These pronouncements receive innumerable blessings and gifts, and countless rewards pour down in return for them. They are surrounded by an attractive halo of meaning and an enlivening, inspiring spirit formed of the spiritual ecstasy radiating from the community of believers, and the showers of light emitted by the hearts of those believing in the Unity of God who absorb the water of life from the fountains of these blessed words.

KNOW, O FRIEND, that One who affirms something is preferred to one who negates it, for negation is self-restricted whereas affirmation is not limited to a single source or means. One thousand negations equal a single negation. In the case of one thousand affirmations, however, each affirmation is as strong as all affirmations.

Assume that several people look for the crescent moon [to establish whether the holy month of Ramadan has begun] through different windows. Since each person saw it through his or her own window and all confirm each other, one affirmation is as strong as all affirmations. But what if someone cannot see the crescent because there is no window, the observer has weak eyes, has not looked, and so on? Such a negation is restricted to that particular individual. His or her denial of the crescent's appearance does not negate its existence, for one such denial does not support the other denials. Thus each denial is restricted to the one who denies.

This subtle point reveals the following truth: Even if the whole world of misguidance and unbelief denies one issue of belief, the resulting denial would be like that of a single person who, raising a defective argument, finds it confined only to himself or herself. In matters of belief, however, on which all guided people agree and thus confirm each other, the argument presented by one person is as strong as that presented by all believers.

KNOW, O FRIEND, that a strong building's parts or stones support each other and derive strength from the whole. As each unit supports the other, all individual weaknesses are removed. It is as if the whole building helps each part. Knowing the properties of each branch and fruit of a tree depends on knowing the whole tree, as each provides knowledge for the whole. It is as if each part is a window through which to look at another part, and serves as a standard to know the whole. In this way, each radiation and subject matter of belief and Islam is supported by the whole, and can be made clearer and more understandable in parallel with the whole. The more belief and Islam branch out, the more we are convinced of each part's truth.

Despite this fact, the carnal soul and Satan tend toward the opposite way: One part's weakness serves as a pretext to consider the whole as weak.

KNOW, O FRIEND, that each part of the universe serves as a unit of comparison through which one can see all of its other parts' possible existence. Conversely, its parts also serve as units of comparison through which one can see each part's possible existence.

KNOW, O FRIEND, that the least part of a very great whole needs [for its being] whatever the whole needs [for its being]. Whatever a tree needs a fruit also needs. So the Creator of the fruit, rather, of its smallest individual cells, is the Creator of the tree, and (by the same token) of Earth, all its contents, and the whole Tree of Creation.

KNOW, O FRIEND, [that to understand the difference between belief and unbelief and like matters, consider this comparison:] The two halves of this issue are infinitely far from each other and each, like a seed, has flourished and grown into an elaborate tree. [After the evidence of its growth] no one should doubt that issue's uniqueness and authenticity. One can doubt the seeds' nature when they are underground. But after each has grown into a tree and yielded fruit, no doubt can remain, for everything has been made clear. An apple tree cannot be produced by a bitter gourd seed, unless one engages in self-deception or can change apples into gourds.

Prophethood is like a seed from which the tree of Islam, as well as its branches and fruits, has grown. The Qur'an is a sun that has yielded the fruits of the planets of Islam's eleven pillars.[53] [Is it still possible to doubt that seed's authenticity and soundness after seeing all its invaluable fruits?]

KNOW, O FRIEND, that an egg hatches and a peacock chick or another young bird emerges. The chick or young bird grows into a beautiful peacock or another beautiful bird. A tree grows from a seed, stretches its branches high into the sky, and yields fruit. If you seek the beauty and qualities of a peacock or another bird in the eggshell, or the tree with all its branches and leaves, flowers and fruits, in the seed, you will deceive or make fool of yourself.

If we view our Prophet superficially and in the light of what history books say about his early life, we will be unable to perceive him, appreciate his worth, and recognize his character fully. However, Islam and its world civilization have flourished because of him. We should regard historical and biographical accounts as a thin cover that have to be torn apart to show him as the seed and founder of this civilization. His merely human dimension should be seen as the shell of a seed from which the blessed tree of Prophet Muhammad has grown, a tree watered by Divine blessings and flourishing forever by the help of Divine favor. We should not cling to his human qualities and states or his early life, but rather should search out the

---

53 That is, the six pillars of belief and five pillars of Islamic life. (Tr.)

degree of greatness he attained [as a Prophet whose message has embraced a considerable part of the world, been the source of a magnificent civilization, and has the potential to embrace the whole world in the future].

Those who study his character with an attitude of doubt or curiosity cannot distinguish whether he is a subject or an object, a source or a mirror, a letter (which draws attention to someone else– God) or a word (which has a meaning in itself and so attracts attention to itself), and what is essential to or inherent in the Divine Being and what is disseminated or manifested by Him. The Prophet is purely a created servant of God Almighty, and the one most advanced in worshipping and servanthood to Him. We must view him as the object of Divine manifestations. All of his perfections are from the Almighty.

Nothing can be its own source or origin. But even the tiniest particle can contain, like a mirror [reflecting the sun], the stars. However, those who do not understand the reality of things see each thing in respect of itself, instead of in respect of that thing's true origin, and mistakenly think of the Divine art as nature.

KNOW, O FRIEND, that prayer or supplication contain the meanings of belief in One God and worship. Those who pray should be convinced that the One to Whom they pray hears, knows, and can fulfill their desires and needs. This requires believing that the One prayed to knows and has power over all things.

KNOW, O FRIEND, that the sun—the lamp of the world—can enter and illuminate a gnat's eye via manifestation. However, a flame produced by lighting a match cannot do this, for its flame would blind the eye. In the same way, a minute particle can manifest the Names of the Eternal "Sun," even though it contains nothing truly effective and operative in creation.

WHY, O SELFHOOD, do you remain obstinate, conceited, and proud, when in reality you are weak and impotent, destitute and abject? A tiny microbe can defeat you completely.

KNOW, O FRIEND, that this shows how weak and impotent you really are when left to your own devices and before the Creator's Power and Grandeur: If you try to traverse your memory, said to be the size of a mustard grain, this tiny grain will stretch into the distance like a vast uncrossable desert. If you cannot travel across your own memory, how can you travel through the whole [of your mind]? If, with respect to your mind, your memory resembles a boundless desert, your mind resembles a bottomless ocean. Glory be to Him Who has made the grain [of memory] like a world for the mind, and the world like a grain for it.

KNOW, O FRIEND, that people unjustly attribute the fruits of a group's action to one person, and assume that he or she has produced them. This mistake leads to a kind of secret association of partners with God, for such an assumption is based on one's belief that the individual in question has enough power to create something. The gods and goddesses of the ancient Greeks and other pagan peoples arose from such mistakes.

KNOW, O FRIEND, that individuals are surrounded by concentric circles: one's clothes and body, native town, Earth, the visible world, and so on. Except for the first one, they have no part in or influence on any circle. In fact, they are affected by the circles, as they can benefit from them materially and spiritually. If they try to interfere with them, they only cause the related benefits to decrease.

KNOW, O FRIEND, that those who recite God's Names, whether consciously or not, receive many benefits. Humanity is a very interesting creation. Each individual is a uniform being composed of many parts, simultaneously simple and complex, having organs, limbs, systems, senses, feelings, and faculties. Each of those have their own pains and pleasures, along with others related to and coming from the whole body. There is a swift, mutual helping and support among them. By virtue of this uniqueness, those who follow the way of servanthood to God will be rewarded, especially in the Hereafter, with all pleasures, blessings, and perfections [acquired by or allotted to their parts, organs, limbs, systems, senses, feelings, and faculties.] But if they follow the way of egoism, they will be the target of pain, suffering, and torment. A toothache is different from an earache, the pleasure of the eyes is different from that of the tongue, and the pleasure and pain originating in touch, imagination, reason, and the heart differ from each other.

KNOW, O FRIEND, that not defining the time of death is a clear proof of its being definite in the Originator's Knowledge. Had it been made definite [for each individual], supposing it to be dependent on a "natural" law, people would have thought that it is undefined within the Divine Knowledge. Since it is not defined for us, they cannot suppose that it is undefined [within the Divine Knowledge].

KNOW, O FRIEND, that regular recitation of certain Divine Names is a mark or sign of Islam, for the signs of Islam are too exalted for the "hand" of ostentation and hypocrisy to reach.

KNOW, O FRIEND, that repeating the formula of Divine Unity—*there is no deity but God*—isolates the heart from [inner] relations with [whatever separates one from God] and false objects of worship. For the one who recites this formula has many faculties and senses, each of which should be convinced of the Divine Unity and absolutely isolated from polytheistic attitudes particular to itself.

KNOW, O FRIEND, that it makes no difference whether you send as a gift the reward of reciting, say, *Surat al-Fatiha*, to one person or millions of people, as there is no difference between one person and millions in hearing a spoken word. Immaterial things multiply or spread very rapidly, without one copy thereof hindering any other, like a light reflected in one or in millions of mirrors.

KNOW, O FRIEND, that calling blessings and peace upon the Prophet is like answering the Bestower of bounties' invitation, Who spreads His blessings freely and has laid the table of His bounties on him whom He honored with Ascension. When you ask blessings and peace upon the Prophet and mention a (good) attribute of his, concentrate and reflect on the one you praise so that you may grow in zeal to call peace and blessings on him over and over again.

O RELIGIOUS SCHOLARS. Do not be upset with people's indifference to your knowledge and the small amount they pay you. Worldly payment comes in proportion to need, not personal merit, which will be given in the Hereafter. You are not allowed to sell your personal merit, at a small price, for this world's illusory provisions.

O WRITERS AND PUBLIC SPEAKERS who address people through the media. Be humble [before people] and freely announce and repent of your defects. You have no right to feel self-pride and publicize what is against the marks or signs of Islam. Who has allowed you to do so? Who has given you the right to spread groundless doubt about Islam, and spread misguidance throughout the nation and among the Muslim community? Do you think that the nation is misguided like you? No one can see or show others as deviated. Who gave you permission to suspect that the Muslim community has deviated from the marks of Islam? Publishing what most believers do not accept is calling to deviation, and one who publishes such material calls to deviation.

KNOW, O FRIEND, that since unbelief is the opposite of belief, unbelievers are hostile to believers. Thus the love of unbelievers [because of their unbelief], with whom it is impossible to establish friendship, is useless. The Qur'an condemns unbelievers and their unbelieving ancestors to Hell's eternal punishment. O people of the Qur'an, do not expect them to love and help you. Say: *God is sufficient for us. What a good guardian and good helper He is.*

KNOW, O FRIEND, that the difference between the civilization of unbelievers and that of (true) believers is this: The former is barbarism disguised as civilization, outwardly glittering but inwardly hideous, apparently pleasing but in reality frightening. As for the civilization of believers, its inside is more exalted than its outside. It is more perfect in meaning than in appearance. It is composed of friendliness, love, and mutual helping, for the believers' belief in and affirmation of Divine Unity causes them to see brotherhood among everything that exists, as well as friendship and loving among it parts, particularly among human beings, and more particularly among believers. They see brotherhood in the origin, and union in the end. [In other words, all things issue from a single origin and, after dividing like a tree's branches, come together in the end.]

Unbelievers see all things as hostile, alien to, and separated from one another. They even see this hostility among fellow unbelievers, since they consider brotherhood only a point of meeting between two lines of disunity or separation. One line extends eternally into the past, and the other eternally into the future. They only feel a strong (and very temporary) brotherhood at times of national zeal or racial passion. However, in reality such apparent love for a brother or sister is really no more than love for himself or herself. Any acceptable humanitarian aspects and spiritual virtues of the unbelievers' civilization are either borrowings from Islamic civilization, leftovers from the revealed religions, or are owed to the guidance of the Qur'an [being in the world].

O YOU WHO DESIRE *IJTIHAD* (using deductive reasoning to establish new religious precedents in Islamic law), the door to *ijtihad* is open. But you can pass through it only in certain cases:

One: When winter gales blow and small holes must be covered, how can doors be opened? When unacceptable acts are done freely, when innovations opposed to the spirit of the Religion flood in, and when destructive thoughts attack it from all sides, is it reasonable or permissible to destroy the "wall" by making breaches in it?

Two: Islam's essentials cannot be subjected to *ijtihad*, for they are like nourishment or sustenance for Muslims. When they are neglected or rejected, as they are today, we must strive to revive them and apply them in our daily life. If the need arises, *ijtihad* may be applied in secondary theoretical matters, which earlier scholars made spacious enough to meet future (and unknown) needs.

Three: Every time has its own demands. Today, these are politics and securing [the necessities of] worldly life. However, in the centuries following that of the Prophet, inferring from the Qur'an that which please the Creator of the universe and securing eternal happiness was in demand. Since at that time people's minds, hearts, and spirits were concentrated on those items, many people learned, consciously or unconsciously, from the prevailing circumstances, events, and conversations. It was as if everything served to teach and prepare them for *ijtihad*, so that the fuel of their minds ignited even if they were not lit with the "match" of special study. When they turned to *ijtihad*, this meant light upon light for them.

But today, minds and hearts are confused. [Because of modern life's disorienting complexity] people cannot concentrate on one subject, and modern trends of thought and politics dominate minds. Thus, someone as smart as Sufyan ibn Uyayna[54] needs to spend at least ten times as much time as Sufyan needed to be able to perform *ijtihad*. When Sufyan, at the age of puberty, started to study for *ijtihad*, he was like a match ready to ignite. His modern counterparts are far away from *ijtihad*, for they are deeply grounded [and bounded] in modern, non-religious sciences and hardened by them to the degree of their preoccupation with them.

Four: The desire to perform *ijtihad* by expanding the sphere of Islamic secondary matters in order to attain higher degrees of piety and follow Islam's

54 Sufyan ibn Uyayna (726-814), one of the greatest scholars of Islamic history, was well-versed in *hadith* and *fiqh*. He met more than 80 scholars belonging to the generation following the Companions. He narrated *hadith* from Zuhri, Ibn Munkadir, Ibn al-Zinad, A'mash, and others. Imam al-Shafi'i, Shu'ba, Ibn Ishaq, Ibn Jurayh, Yahya ibn Kathir, and others narrated from him. He was a very pious scholar. (Ed.)

essentials more strictly causes perfection. However, if one does not follow Islam's pillars and prefers the world over the Hereafter, such desire leans toward destruction insofar as it is really an attempt to cast off religious responsibilities.

Five: Islam holds that the benefit derived from a religious obligation is the reason why someone wants to fulfill it. In other words, it was not legislated because of the benefit to be derived. But that is exactly the view held by modern people. The modern view first considers worldly happiness; the Shari'a first considers the person's eternal happiness and then one's worldly life in proportion to its being the means of acquiring eternal happiness. Furthermore, many modern "needs" have become "necessities" only because people have abused their free will and followed unlawful tendencies. Therefore, their "necessity" cannot be put forward for new dispensations and making unlawful things lawful. This is the same principle whereby a drunk, who has become intoxicated by his or her own free will, cannot plead drunkenness as an excuse for criminal conduct. Any *ijtihad* done in such a context will be "earthly," not "heavenly." And any addition or amendment to the laws of the Creator of the heavens and Earth, and ruling of His servants without His authority, must be rejected.

O ONE ENVELOPED BY HEEDLESSNESS and naturalism, and thus "blind" and "deaf," a "worshipper" of material causes in the darkness of imagining nature as the origin of existence. I will explain to you one of the 55 "languages" spoken by each minute particle and compound of the universe to witness the Almighty's necessary Existence and His Unity in His Divinity and Lordship.

Consider this: Creation must be attributed either to creatures themselves and causes or to the One, Necessarily Existent Being. Due to defective reasoning, you may find it hard to attribute all things to the Necessarily Existent Being. But, because no cause can give existence to any creature, attributing their existence to self-creation or material causes is illogical and cannot be accepted. What is supposed in the first alternative is certain in the second.

Furthermore, while there is only one supposed difficulty in attributing creation to a Single, Necessarily Existent Being, the obvious impossibility in attributing it to creatures themselves or causes are as many as the number of parts in the universe. For example, if a honeybee is not attributed to a Single, Necessarily Existent Being, everything in the heavens and Earth would have to take part in its coming into existence because the honeybee is related, in one way or another, with all parts of the world. Also, creating multiple things from a single source is far easier than creating a single thing from numerous sources, all of which contradict each other, are deaf and blind, and whose coming together increases their deafness and blindness.

If the supposed difficulty in attributing things to a Single Being is only as great as a minute particle, that same difficulty will be as large as a mountain when creatures are attributed to themselves or to causes. With one movement, a single being can produce a result and give a form or order to multiple things. But multiple things cannot produce the same result even with many movements, and can give the same form or order only after exerting great effort and difficulty. For example, a commander can command many soldiers very easily; however, soldiers can do so only with great difficulty or not at all. Innumerable drops come from a single water faucet.

The one supposed difficulty in the former case becomes innumerable impossibilities in the second. Some of these impossibilities are as follows:

- Since the perfect artistry and design observed in things requires all-encompassing knowledge, absolute sight, perfect power, and all-inclusive will, each particle should have the attributes of the Necessarily Existent Being.
- If things are not attributed to a Single, Necessarily Existent Being, divinity must be attributed to each thing. This means that we associate partners with the Divine Being in His Divinity and Necessary Existence, which should be absolutely free from having partners.
- If we do not attribute a dome to a builder, then its faultless construction, which could not occur by chance, would require each of its stones to be as knowledgeable and skillful as an engineer. Like those stones, if things are not attributed to a Single Being, an item's particles or atoms should be consciously dominant over and dominated by each other and by the thing itself.
- Since the absolute balance, solidarity, mutual helping, and correlation observed in the universe require a comprehensive consciousness and an absolute power of seeing, each particle forming things and causes should have this degree of consciousness and knowledge and power of seeing. If things are attributed to themselves, they or even each parti-

cle forming them should have these attributes. If they are attributed to causes, each cause should have them.

Many other such impossibilities and false conceptions arise if the existence of a Single, Necessarily Existent Being is not accepted as the originator of all things.

When things are attributed to their true Lord, Who necessarily exists and is One, particles and compounds become like raindrops reflecting the sun's images. They come into existence by the rays of the manifestations of Divine Power, which is absolute, luminous, comprehensive, eternal and infinite, and based on—rather including—the eternal, infinite Knowledge and Will. It is the Power to Which the miracles of creatures testify, and of which a single ray is more radiant and penetrating than the sun, as sunlight can be hindered, refracted, divided, and scattered in the world of multiplicity—the (material) world where things exist separately and in abundance. This Power's smallest manifestation is greater than the greatest material cause, as a partial manifestation of something luminous has the properties of the whole, even in the world of multiplicity—like the sun being "contained" in the smallest piece of glass.

The difference between attributing things to themselves or causes and to the One, Necessarily Existent Being is like that between the sun's image reflected in a raindrop and claiming that that image is the sun. Could anyone believe such a claim? By contrast, the eternal Divine Power easily penetrates all things. In relation to It, everything that exists, without exception, is the same. Such Power is essential and intrinsic to the Divine Being Himself, eternal and infinite, and therefore can have no opposite, degrees, limitations, or impotence.

To understand this point more clearly through comparisons from the sphere of contingencies and multiplicity, consider the following:

In respect to receiving the sun's manifestations in the form of images, pieces of glass, oceans, and planets are the same because of their transparency and the sun's luminosity. In respect to reflecting the light of a lamp located in the center, the smallest mirror in the smallest circle (around that center) and all mirrors in the largest circle are the same because of their *reciprocating* or *facing-each-other position*. Since something *is immaterial*, large numbers of things can benefit from that thing simultaneously—as from a source of light, for example—without one hindering the other. For example, in hearing a word uttered, one and thousands are the same, for it can be heard by thousands of people at the same time without one preventing the other.

[There is a very precise *balance* or *measurement* in the universe. To understand such preciseness,] consider a balance so large and sensitive that walnut-sized or mountain-sized things could be weighed with the same exactness. Suppose we weigh a pair of things, whether as big and heavy as two suns or as small and light as two walnuts. If a walnut is put on either scale, the scales would be worlds apart from each other due to the balance's sensitivity. Due to the exact *orderliness* and *interconnection* among things, a child could start and then steer a huge vessel or a toy ship with the same ease. Due to *obedience*, a commander could move a huge army as easily as one private by ordering: "March!"

Since the main existence of things lies in their inner incorporeal dimension, and a species does not receive its nature from its physical composition, all members of a species, without exception, have the same nature. Thus, because of such essential properties of things or basic characteristics of existence, everything, in relation to Divine Power, is the same. There are no exceptions.

The inner dimension of existence [its essential dimension, for the outer visible, material forms are shells and transient] is *immaterial* and *transparent*. The *faces* of whatever exists *are turned toward* Divine Power, Which is incorporeal and of pure light. There is an infinitely precise *balance* in existence, and all things are infinitely *well-ordered and interconnected* with each other. All particles *obey* "enthusiastically" the Divine laws and orders of creation, which may be summed up in the word: *Be!* As the Necessarily Existent Being is absolutely *free of corporeality* and detached from corporeal things, it is equally easy for Divine Power to resurrect a fly and Earth, to create a honeybee and the heavens and Earth, to originate a minute particle and the sun.

Actually, this ease is so visible and tangible that it does not need proof [for example, the apparently dry, dead wood of vines or palm trees produces clusters of grapes or dates]. Divine Power is such that if Its acts are attributed to causes or themselves, innumerable difficulties arise. This Power, on the other hand, penetrates the inner, transparent dimensions of things or their archetypes—which constitute the essence of their existence in Divine Knowledge—even through such small openings as the eye of a needle, and manifests on them by Its creativity.

In sum, what we see concerning how Divine Power creates things demonstrates:

One: Means and apparent causes are veils to preserve the Divine Power's dignity [in the eyes of people] in Its dealing with the corporeal aspects of things.[55]

Two: Things that are transparent in both their outer and inner aspects (e.g., life, existence, and light) have no veils (means and causes) placed between them and Divine Power.

Three: Divine Power deals with all things easily. It creates a huge fig tree from its dust particle-sized seed, and hangs a cluster of grapes from a thread-like stem. The existence of the Owner of that eternal Power is more manifest than the existence of the universe. Each creature testifies to its own existence in a few ways, whereas it bears witness to its Maker's existence in many observable, intelligible, and rational ways. No creature, even with the help of all heavenly and earthly causes, could produce its like. In the art they contain and the skill needed to make them, the fig tree's seed is the same as the tree itself, and a human being is the same as Earth. So, the Power Who originates the seed and humanity easily creates the tree and Earth.

O YOU WHO GO ASTRAY by not attributing things to the One Necessarily Existent Being. You see how impossible it is to attribute existence to itself or to causes. The mental and spiritual anguish of such an effort will end only when you flee and submit to the One Necessarily Existent Being, by Whose Power alone the existence of all things can be explained. Referring to His Will clarifies all ambiguities, and remembering Him and depending on His Name brings peace and tranquillity to hearts and minds.

KNOW, O FRIEND, that the area where your heart and mind move cannot be encompassed. Although you sometimes travel within a minute particle, float in a drop, and imprison yourself in a dot, you actually put the whole world before your eyes and include all creation in your intellect, aspiring to see the Necessarily Existent Being. Sometimes you become small-

---

55 Unable to see the true wisdom behind this Power's sending misfortune and dealing with things and events that seem to be lowly and insignificant, people may blame the Divine Being. To save them from such mistakes, God acts behind causes in the visible, material world.

er than a minute particle or greater than the heavens, or you enter a drop or include everything that exists.

KNOW, O FRIEND, that the gifts God has ordained that humanity attain or make use of come with conditions. Some of these conditions are established by God, while others pertain to human beings themselves. For example, light, air, food, and speech are God's gifts, and how much we benefit from them depends upon our respective organs' soundness and health. All senses and organs have been created by God Almighty; our role is to keep them sound and healthy. Do not suppose that they come to us by chance and that, as a result, we can own and control them as we wish. They come to us by the Will of the One Who bestows them on us; we keep them working by our own will, and use them according to the will of the One Who grants them.

KNOW, O FRIEND, that things are not more ordered and sound in their beginning than in their end. Their outward appearances and forms are not more beautiful in art and more exalted in wisdom than their insides. Do you suppose that such things are left to chance? Do you not see that the flower of a tree and its fruit display more wisdom than the seed and its shoot? The Maker is He Who is First and Last, Outward and Inward, and Who knows all things.

KNOW, O FRIEND, that the Qur'an's miraculous eloquence saves it from corruption. One cannot confuse its words with the words of any person, regardless his or her identity or command of Arabic. One cannot put on the "dress" of the Qur'an, as was done with the other revealed books and eventually led to their corruption.

KNOW, O FRIEND, that the repetition of: *Which of the blessings of your Lord do you deny?* in *Surat al-Rahman* at the end of the revealed verses pointing to diverse "natural" phenomena—each is a sign of Divine Existence and Oneness. It indicates that humanity's and the jinns' disobedience [to God's commands], rebelliousness, and ingratitude arise mainly from their blindness to the Divine act of bestowing bounties and their heedlessness of the One Who bestows. Therefore, they attribute bounties to causes and chance and deny God's blessings. Given this, believers must say *In the Name of God, the All-Merciful, the All-Compassionate* when they begin to use or consume a bounty. This means that it is from God and is taken in His

Name and for His sake, not for the sake of means and causes. To Him belongs all praise and gratitude.

KNOW, O YOU WHO ARE EXPOSED to Satan's whisperings, involuntary thoughts and suggestions arising from your heart and carnal soul, and obscene scenes and imaginations when you try to consider and reflect on Divine truths. Obscene and malicious images pass before your eyes, making you tremble when you look at the "Sun" of truths. It is as if your imagination fouls your hands when you stretch them to glorify God, and your carnal soul soils your eyes when you fix them on God's praise and extolling.

When reflected on things you hold sacred, such dirt causes you to suffer and draws your attention to them more closely. Do not suffer on account of them, and do not ponder them to be saved from this state, for they are harmful only when you consider them as such and concentrate on them. Look at the sun and its light, the sky and its stars, a garden and its flowers through the holes of a dirt-stained garment. The dirt does not affect what you see. Unintentional thoughts and suggestions are like certain insects and bees: If you struggle with them to protect yourself, they will crowd and pester you more; if you ignore them, they will leave you alone.

KNOW, O FRIEND WHO, ALTHOUGH PREOCCUPIED with philosophy and preferring reason to Revelation, nevertheless comments on Revelation. You corrupt it, for your use of reason, self-pride, and deep attachment to philosophy prevent you from understanding it. Once I thought as you think now. But then I saw a high, brilliant castle whose floors are connected to the ceiling of the heavens. From its windows are hung different ropes, some of which are close to Earth. Whoever overcomes the carnal soul and holds tightly to a rope can rise to the highest stations. I have seen people who, lost in self-pride and heedless of these ropes, try to rise on things piled under their feet. After rising a little, they fall. How can these things help them rise?

I have seen others who, relying on their egos, drive nails into the castle's walls and try to climb up by them. However, they also fall and break their necks. And so on. Whatever abilities and intellectual faculties people possess have been given to them to use according to their capacities and to enable them to rise to the ropes, not to the stations. When used properly, your reason can lead you only to the ropes, while you can rise by Revelation. Whoever relies on God finds Him sufficient.

KNOW, O FRIEND WHO WONDERS about the triumph of the sinful over the pious, and the supremacy of the wicked over the righteous in this worldly life. In a vision I saw a castle that contained many pavilions. Their inhabitants varied in beauty and exaltedness, glory and luster. The one sitting in the center resembled the king. Below him down to the portal were rooms whose residents varied in rank and distinction. A servant stood by the door, and a fawning dog lay in front of the door. Then I saw another castle with a glittering front. In wonder, I looked into it and saw the king playing with the dog in front of the portal. The women, dressed immodestly, were joking with the children. Important tasks were left undone, as the duties or functions of the dog, children, and servants of the lowest degree seemed to have acquired prominence. The residents were busy with shameful things. However glittering, fortified, and magnificent its appearance, in reality the castle was dark and wretched.[56]

I see humanity, an individual, and my carnal self as castles. Those who live in castles have infinitely different degrees or ranks [in knowledge, morality, and values.] What modern, civilized people call "progress" is, in fact, falling and degeneration. What they call "acquiring and holding power" is vulgarization and loss of value. What they call "being awake," "revival," and "enlightenment" is deepening in the sleep of heedlessness. What they call "politeness" is show and hypocrisy, cleverness and Satanic intriguing, and humanity being metamorphosed into beasts.

Due to their God-given radiating faculties being together with their dark souls, some graceful and attractive scenes may appear in these fallen, rebellious people. But for the pious believers obeying God Almighty, their carnal souls represent the sorrowful-looking dog in front of the door. They use their God-given faculties not to gratify lowly desires and fancies, but to guide people back to the purpose of their creation. If God Almighty loves a servant, He does not make him or her love the world's beauty; rather, when necessary, He uses misfortune to make that servant despise them.

---

56 The first castle represents a believer who, although dull and not glittering in appearance, is in reality happy and brilliant, whose faculties (heart, intellect, senses, and organs) function according to the Creator's will. The second castle represents a modern unbeliever who, glittering and happy in appearance, is unhappy and uses his or her faculties, senses, and organs only for the world's temporary pleasures. (Tr.)

What a pity that this corrupt civilization has developed attractive devices and charming toys that fascinate those who live in the castle and who are, like moths attracted by light, drawn to burning fires.

KNOW, O WRETCHED, SINFUL SAID. Why this self-conceit, heedlessness, and indifference [to God's blessings]? Do you not see that your free will is as weak as a hair, your power less than a minute particle, your life as temporary as a flash of light, your consciousness as dull as a dim and decaying ray of light, your time as short as a passing moment, and your space the size of a grave? Yet your impotence is endless, your needs are infinite, your poverty is boundless, and your ambitions are limitless. Should such a person rely on what is in his or her hands and depend on his or her self, or should he or she rely on God, All-Merciful, All-Compassionate? Among the wrappings of His Mercy and chests of His bounties are light-filled and light-diffusing suns and fruit-bearing trees, and among the streams rising from the source of His blessings and the floods of His Mercy are water and light.

KNOW, O FRIEND WHO REGARDS the conclusion as too great to be supported by the evidence provided. Each truth of belief is corroborated, supported, and strengthened by every other truth, which indicates the truth of Islam and each of its parts. These innumerable evidences, witnesses, and signs of the truth of Islam and of belief corroborate the truth of each and set the seal of approval on it, for while the negation or rejection of many equals that of one, as explained earlier, the confirmation of one is strengthened by the confirmation of many.

KNOW, O FRIEND, that intense love causes one to deny the thing loved. This is also true for intense fear, excessive greatness, and comprehensive reason. Intense love for that which may not be attained can lead to denying the thing loved, intense fear may cause one to deny that which one fears, and greatness beyond the grasp of reason may be denied by that reason.

KNOW, O FRIEND, that the seed of unbelief potentially bears Hell, just as a mustard plant is contained in its seed. Likewise, belief potentially bears the seed of Paradise, just as a palm tree is contained in its seed. It is normal for a mustard seed to grow into a mustard plant, and a palm seed to grow into a palm tree. In the same way, misguidance leads to Hell and guidance leads to Paradise.

KNOW, O FRIEND, that if a seed is pierced in the heart, it cannot grow [into a tree] so that it becomes "proud" of itself. Similarly, when your ego's hard grain is pierced with the rays and burning "flames" of your regular recitation of the Divine Name, it cannot grow and become strengthened to be proud of itself, like Pharaoh, by heedlessly relying on human accomplishment and rebelling against the All-Compelling and Overwhelming Lord of the heavens and Earth. Naqshbandi saints have opened up the heart's grain and found a short way to ignite the rocky mountain of ego and smash the head of the conceited soul with the "drill" of silently reciting God's Names. The loud recitation of those Names destroys the idol of (philosophical) naturalism.

KNOW, O FRIEND, that even in the remotest, largest, and most delicate spheres of multiplicity [the corporeal spheres where things exist separately and in abundance], the imprints of wisdom, care, and making firm and perfect are observed clearly. Look at the remotest ends of your body's skin. See how the Pen of Divine Power has inscribed lines and designs pointing to the meanings in its possessor's spirit on the pages of your body's forehead, face, and palms. The invisible, immaterial copy of your life-history is hung around your neck and points to your destiny. This inscription [which indicates one's destiny] has no opening through which blind chance or any similar agent [like causality] can pass.

KNOW, O FRIEND who is fond of this worldly life. You think that the purpose of life and of whatever the Eternal Power has entrusted to humanity and living beings—such as wonderful systems and extraordinary faculties—is only to maintain this fleeting life and secure its continuance. But you are wrong. If the purpose of life is its continuance, then the most manifest, clearest, and radiant proofs of wisdom, favoring, and orderliness, as well as the absolute lack of futility observed throughout the universe and witnessed by its overall order would represent the most astonishing futility and wastefulness, purposelessness, and chaos [since everything perishes].

What comes to you from the fruits and purposes of life is proportionate to your part in owning and controlling your life. The other purposes and fruits pertain to the Bestower of life. Humanity is only the object of His Names' manifestations. God will display His Mercy's colors and radiations in the greatest degree in Paradise, which will consist of fruits growing from the seeds of this life.

Your relation with your life is like that between a steersman and the royal ship he steers. The steersman places his hands on those instruments that move and steer the ship. His share of the ship's uses and income is proportionate to his relation with the ship and the service he renders—perhaps one in thousands. This relation between you and the ship of your existence and life is the same, and your share from the uses and purposes of your life is also only one in thousands. Moreover, you have not even earned this part by your words or deeds.

KNOW, O MY HEART, that the world's pleasure and beauty, in the absence of knowledge about our Creator, Owner, and Lord, are no more than a hell, even if they were as great as those of Paradise. This is my experience and observation. With His knowledge, a blessing like compassion becomes so pleasing and sweet that it may make one indifferent to whatever is in the world, even to Paradise.

KNOW, O MY HEART, that whatever happens here has two aspects: One pertains to this world, the carnal soul, and our worldly desires and fancies; the other pertains to the Hereafter. With respect to the worldly aspect, the greatest, most important, and most established affair is the smallest, most insignificant and fleeting in itself. So do not worry or grieve about it, nor consider it important.

KNOW, O MY HEART, that no one is more stupid and ignorant than one who sees the sun's image in a transient, tiny object, or its manifestation on a flower as color, and then demands that that image or color be exactly like those of the original—the light and heat-diffusing lamp on the world's ceiling that enjoys the central position in the solar system and makes the planets revolve around it. Furthermore, when what is seen in the tiny object or the flower "disappears," due to their restricted and defective view, they deny the existence of the sun at midday, even if all that exists, without exception, testifies to it in broad daylight.

Such people confuse a shadowy existence formed through manifestation or reflection, according to what Destiny has determined, with the main, substantial existence. They see the sun's image in a transparent object and ask: "Is the sun so little? Where are its amazing heat and other properties?" And so on.

Within such objections is a mistaken wish to take hold of a brand of the sun's fire, to touch or influence it. They fail to understand that "nearness" to the sun does not mean or necessitate that they can influence it by their acts.[57] Further, seeing that the smallest things are made surprisingly firm, with astonishing care and pleasing art and for significant purposes, they derive a mistaken analogy: Their Maker must have exerted great (and unnecessary) effort in making them. So they ask: "Why has the Wise Maker expended such great labor upon this gnat? What value does it have?"

O YOU WHO THINK LIKE A SOPHIST. *God's is the highest comparison, and for Him the highest of examples and similitudes should be coined.* God is the Creator and Guardian of all things. Bear the following in mind so that you can consider this matter clearly:

First point: On account of what it bears [from His Attributes], everything indicates the Almighty in His Lordship's perfection. Whatever that thing has [of good] is from Him; it [i.e., that good] cannot be ascribed to it as its own [good].

Second point: Everything contains doors opened on the Almighty's Light. If one door appears to be closed, it does not mean that all others are closed. Rather, one open door means that all doors are open.

Third point: Destiny, a reflection of God's all-encompassing Knowledge, has determined for each thing a specific, fitting character out of the radiations of God's absolutely luminous Names.

Fourth point: When He wills a thing, His command is but to say to it "Be!" and it is (36:82); *Your creation and resurrection are but like (those of) a single soul* (31:28). Attributing things to themselves or to possible causes requires that we accept all kinds of impossibilities arising from such a mistaken judgment.

KNOW, O FRIEND, that the Qur'an explains many truths through parables and comparisons, for its abstract Divine truths can be presented only in limited, concrete forms in this [material] sphere of contingencies. A contingent being considers these concrete, contingent forms and contemplates, in their light, acts issuing from the sphere of Absolute Necessity (the sphere of Divinity).

---

57 To believe in God, some people desire to see God Himself or witness His Being in every thing and event with naked eyes, to "touch" Him or exert some influence on Him. They cannot see that their nearness to the sun and being within the scope of its direct influence is not due to themselves, but to the sun's manifestation of its lights and heat. So, God is nearer to Us than ourselves by His manifestations of His Names and Attributes, such as Knowledge, Will, Power, Grace, Bestowing Life, and Nourishing. But those heedless of Him cannot understand this reality and try to deny His existence on the pretext that they cannot see Him or touch Him. (Tr.)

KNOW, O FRIEND, that the heart has the same meaning for you as the Divine Throne has for the universe. Your heart is your being's "outer dimension," and you are your being's "inner dimension" in your heart. In the sphere of the Divine Name "the Outward," the Divine Throne encompasses all things. In the sphere of the Divine Name "the Inward," It is like the heart of creation. In the sphere of the Name "the First," It is pointed to by: *His Throne was upon the water* (11:7). In the Divine Name "the Last," it is symbolized by: *The ceiling of Paradise is God's Throne.*[58] The Divine Throne has the qualities of being first and last, outer and inner, issuing from: *He is the First and the Last, the Outer and the Inner* (57:3).[59]

KNOW, O FRIEND, that helplessness gives rise to entreating, and need causes praying.

> O Lord, O Creator, O Owner! I entreat You and pray to You because I am needy. I take shelter in You through my prayer because I am destitute. My helplessness is my means of imploring You and asking You for help. My weakness is my treasure. My ambition and pain are my capital. Your Beloved —the Prophet, upon him be peace and blessings— and Your Mercy are my intercessors. Pardon me, forgive my sins, and have mercy on me, O God, O All-Merciful, O All-Compassionate!

A supplication

O Lord! I looked in all six directions for a cure for my pain. Alas, I found none. I looked to past time on my right to find solace, but yesterday appeared in the form of my father's grave. I looked to the future on the left, and found no cure. Rather, tomorrow appeared in the form of my grave. I looked at the present day, and saw it like a coffin carrying my desperately struggling corpse. I raised my head and saw that my corpse was looking down at me. I lowered my head and saw that the dust of my bones underfoot had mixed with the dust of my first creation. Turning away from that direction, I looked behind and saw a temporary world with no foundation revolving in valleys of nothingness and the darkness of non-existence. Since I saw

58 A saying of the Prophet related by Ibn Maja and Ibn 'Asakir. *Jami' al-Saghir*, no. 3116.

59 The Divine Throne's truth and real identity is unknown. Its (symbolical) relationship with creation may be seen as an immaterial center through which God's commands are conveyed or conducted throughout the universe. For example, in one respect, water is regarded as the Throne of Mercy (the conductor of God's Mercy), and soil as the conductor of life. (Tr.)

no good from that direction either, I cast my eye ahead. I saw that the door of my grave stood open at the end of my way, behind which the highway leading to eternity caught my eyes from afar. What I have is but an insignificant free will lacking power and having only a short range that cannot penetrate the past or discern the future. The arena where the willpower is active is brief present time and the passing present instant. Despite all my destitution and helplessness, the "pen" of Your Power has inscribed infinite desire and ambition extending to eternity in my nature.

The sphere of need is as extensive as the eye reaches. In fact, wherever the imagination goes, the sphere of need extends that far, whereas the extent of my power reaches no further than my arm. My desire and need are infinite, whereas my capital is as little and insignificant as an atom. So, what does that insignificant willpower signify in the face of this need that is so great that it encompasses the universe?

However, O Lord, I give up my free will on Your way, and abandon my ego so that Your absolute Mercy may help and support me. One who finds the boundless sea of Mercy does not rely on his or her own free will, which is no more than a drop from a mirage.

O Lord, this passing life is but a sleep; this life too flies like the wind. O my wretched soul, fond of living and desirous of a long life. Awaken and come to your senses! Your Creator is He in Whose hand is all life and existence. His is all existence, and He bestows life and existence. So, sacrifice your self in His way to gain permanence, for a negation negated is an affirmation. Thus if our non-being is negated (in favor of being), our being finds true existence.

> O God, O All-Generous and Munificent! Grant to me a life and place from Your Presence. Make me of limitless value in Your sight, for surely You are the All-Preserver, the All-Protector.

An Address to the Parliament[60]

In the Name of God, the All-Merciful, the All-Compassionate.

Surely, the Prayer is obligatory for believers at fixed hours.

O members of Parliament, you will be resurrected for a mighty day. O soldiers of Islam. O supreme advisory council of the nation. Please listen to

60 This address was made to the Turkish Parliament on January 19, 1923, just following Turkish National War.

the advice of this humble person on a matter [of the highest importance]. The advice is offered in ten sections.

FIRST: The extraordinary Divine blessing contained in this victory requires thanksgiving so that it may last. If a blessing is not returned with thanksgiving, it disappears. Now that you have saved the Qur'an from the enemy's attacks, with God's help, obey its clearest, most decisive injunctions, such as the Prescribed Prayer, so that its blessings may come to you constantly.

SECOND: You have given joy to the Muslim world and won its love and favorable inclination. Nevertheless, this can endure only if you fulfill Islam's commandments, which demonstrate that Turkey is Muslim. Muslims love you because of your being Muslims.

THIRD: You have commanded the soldiers of Islam, who have been martyred or survived, and who may be regarded as saints. Thus, you are expected to obey the Qur'an so that you may be in the company of those illustrious persons in the other world. Otherwise, although you hold a position of authority here, you will have to beg an ordinary soldier for light in the other. For all of its fame and honor, this base world is not so worthwhile that it can suffice you and be an end for you.

FOURTH: Even if they themselves are not observant, Muslims still want their leaders to be pious. The first question the people in southeastern Turkey ask their officials is whether they pray. If they do, the people trust them. If they do not, the people condemn them, even if they are eminent officials. Once the tribes of Bayt al-Shabab rebelled against their officials. When I asked them why they did so, they answered: "Our governor does not pray and drinks alcohol. How can we obey such an irreligious person?" These people admitted that they did not pray. Moreover, they were robbers.

FIFTH: Most Prophets appeared in the East, while most philosophers emerged in the West. This is a sign of Destiny showing that the main impulse for progress in the East is religion and the "heart," not reason and philosophy. You have awakened the East. Now, direct it in its proper and suitable course so that your efforts will not be in vain or of temporary, superficial use only.

SIXTH: The Western powers, which are hostile to you and to Islam, have used—and are still using—your neglect and indifference to the Religion. Others who likewise exploit your neglect of the Religion harm you and Islam as much as your enemies do. For the sake of Islam's well-being and the nation's security and prosperity, renounce this neglect and resume your religious duties. Do you not see that, despite their extraordinary resolution and steadfastness and causing some degree of awakening among Muslims, the followers of the Union and Progress Party were despised and hated by the people because they appeared indifferent to and careless in practicing Islam? If Muslims living in other countries showed them respect, they did so because they did not witness this neglect.

SEVENTH: The world of unbelief has been fighting the Muslim world for centuries with all its power. Its technological facilities, civilization, philosophy, sciences, and missionary organizations finally established material and military superiority over the Muslim world. However, it has not triumphed over Islam. All deviant religious groups within the state have long been despised and remained negligible factions. Islam has preserved its firmness and fortitude through the adherence [of the many] to the way of the Prophet, and this has preserved our internal cohesion and unity. Given this, an irreligious movement originating from the corrupt elements of European civilization cannot be allowed to arise and grow through heedlessness. Revolutionary, important accomplishments in the Muslim world are possible only if the pillars of Islam are obeyed, otherwise not. Even if some achievements have been witnessed, they are not lasting.

EIGHTH: The corrupt elements of European civilization, which have caused indifference to the Religion, are on the verge of decline. A new Qur'anic civilization is about to appear. At such a time, it is not possible to achieve what is good by ignoring Islam. As to realizing negative, destructive trends, the world of Islam has suffered so much damage that it does not need them.

NINTH: Those who appreciate your services and the victory you won in this national war, who love you from the bottom of their hearts, are the believing majority of this country. In particular, the common people are strong Muslims who sincerely love and support you, appreciate your sacrifices, and feel indebted to you. They present you a vast, very great power that has been awakened. For the benefit of Islam, you must build a connection with them and rely on them by obeying the Qur'an. Otherwise, since it runs against the well-being of Islam and Muslims to prefer a fortunate, deviant minority that wholeheartedly imitates the West over the Muslim masses, the Muslim world will turn away from you and seek help from others.

TENTH: Only one who is tired of living tries to follow a way that is 90 percent certain to lead to perdition. There is a 99 percent chance of salvation in the Prescribed Prayers, an indispensable obligation of Islam that takes only an hour to perform. There can come, at most, 1 percent of worldly harm from praying, whereas there is a 99 percent chance of harm in not obeying Islam. I wonder what excuse can be given for neglecting or ignoring the Islamic obligations, for doing so is certain to harm one both in this world and the next. How do religious and national zeal allow it?

People imitate this group of Muslim soldiers, the members of Parliament, in their acts. People either imitate or criticize their leaders' defects and shortcomings. Whichever they do, it causes harm. This means that the rights of God on the leaders also contain the rights of people on them. Some follow the suggestions of their carnal souls and whims and fancies whispered by Satan. They do not listen to a clear message on which the whole Muslim community always has agreed, and do not heed the countless proofs for its truth, beneficial nature, and warnings about neglecting it. Such people cannot be expected to realize good, significant accomplishments.

This mighty revolution should be based on sound foundations. By virtue of the power it enjoys, the collective person of this honored Parliament has assumed the meaning and function of the governing body. It should not fail to assume the function of the Office of Religious Affairs by fulfilling and making the people fulfill those principles of Islam that show whether a country is Muslim or not. This Parliament should satisfy the religious need of the people who, while needing four things for life, feel the need for the Religion at least five times a day. They have not been debased by modern civilization's seductive pleasures, and have not forgotten their spiritual need. They will accept your appointment to the Office of Religious Affairs and give wholehearted support. Any support and power that do not originate in and depend on the Parliament will cause internal discord and rift, which is contrary to the Qur'anic commandment: *Hold fast, all together, to the rope of God* (3:103).

This is the time to be a united community and establish a collective consciousness. The collective personality originating in the community is firm and better able to enforce the Shari'a's commandments. One who assumes the burden of conducting religious affairs can fulfill its requirements only by depending on the collective person [represented in the Parliament for the people]. If this collective person is upright, the services provided will be much better and more extensive than those of a single individual. But if it is corrupt, the corruption will be greater and more extensive.

Whatever good or bad one person does is generally limited [in its effects], whereas a community's good or bad is boundless. By causing evil and corruption within the country, do not destroy the good and merit you obtained by fighting the external enemy. You well know that your external enemies and adversaries wish to destroy Islam's main pillars. Therefore, you are obliged to restore and preserve them so that you will not be unconsciously abetting the enemy's conscious will. Neglect and apathy in practicing Islam's main commandments demonstrate the nation's weakness, and that weakness does not stop the nation's enemies from attacking; rather, it encourages them.

God is sufficient for us and how good a Guardian He is. What a good Lord and what a good Helper.

Addendum

In the Name of God, the All-Merciful, the All-Compassionate.

Praise be to God Who is infinitely exalted above having a like both in His Essence and Attributes. He is the Creator. That macro-cosmos (the universe) is His creation, and this micro-cosmos (humanity) is His invention. That (the universe) is His construction, and this (humanity) is His building. That is His work of art, and this is His painting. That is His design and this is His adornment. That is His mercy and this is His bounty. That is His power and this is His wisdom. That is His grandeur and this is His Lordship. That is His creature and this is His fashioning. That is His kingdom and this is His servant. That is His place of worship and this is His worshipping servant. On the sides of both, nay, on each part of both, is a stamp showing that whatever exists is His property.

O God, O One sustaining Earth and heavens! Be witness and let those bearing Your Throne and Your angels be witnesses—together with the witnessing of all Your Prophets, saints, signs, verses (in the Books You sent), and all creation—that You are God, there is no deity but You, One, without partner. Forgive us. We turn to You in repentance and bear witness that Muhammad is Your servant and Messenger whom You sent as a mercy for all worlds. O God, bestow Your blessings on him as befits the reverence he deserves and Your mercy of which he is worthy, and on all his Family and Companions.

KNOW, O FRIEND, that your body and what maintains it have been bestowed on you by God. You do not own them, and so cannot control them as you wish. You can control what has been given to you only if He consents, just as a guest cannot waste or dispose of something belonging to the host without the latter's approval.

KNOW, O FRIEND who regards the Resurrection as impossible or improbable. Can you not see the innumerable instances of small-scale resurrection, assembling, and destruction happening in front of your eyes? When you see the annual death and revival of each fruit-bearing or blossoming tree, how can you regard the world's ultimate destruction and reconstruction as improbable?

If you want direct confirmation of this, stand under an apricot or mulberry tree at the end of spring and summer. See how their sweet and lively fruits are re-created and re-presented. These fresh, pleasant, and enjoyable fruits smiling at your face are almost identical with those that died last year. If they had souls like human beings, they would be the actual fruits that died last year.

Reflect on the fact that although the tree is made of dried wood and has complex, narrow capillary tubes through which food reaches its blossoms and fruits, its head suddenly becomes a dazzling "world." For a careful observer, this displays the meaning of: *When the graves are overturned [to bring forth their contents]* (82:4). Nothing is difficult for the Power that produces such sweet, pleasant blossoms, leaves, and fruit from a dried tree.

KNOW, O FRIEND, that each *sura* contains a summary of the entire Qur'an, as well as the purposes and narratives of other *suras*. Thus those who can recite only a short *sura*, not the whole of it due to some valid excuse, may enjoy the reward for reciting all of it. By virtue of this gleam of miraculousness, a single *sura* substitutes for the entire Qur'an.

KNOW, O FRIEND, that one who controls multiple things does not have to be among them or in direct, physical contact with them. This is even more the case if the one dispensing these things has a different nature than what he controls, or if one is not a contingent, corporeal entity. To enforce his command, a commander does not always have to be among his soldiers personally; rather, his command is usually enforced through his orders and decrees. If command were left to the soldiers, each soldier would have to act as commander and commanded, which would require the ability to command. The All-Glorious One, despite His infinite grandeur and lack of need to be among us or in physical contact with us, controls us as He wills. Like the sun, the All-Glorious One is nearer to us than ourselves, and we are far distant from Him.

KNOW, O FRIEND, that like a tree ending in its fruit, by virtue of a part including the whole's properties [and the unity of the origin or Originator], multiple things result in unity. A single whole thing becomes like the whole species, and a part becomes like the whole of that of which it is a part. For example, since each particle of sunlight diffused throughout space contains the sun's image, each vibrating particle of sunlight become as if a tiny sun due to its uninterrupted connection with the sun. The Names of the Eternal Light of Lights are manifested in a similar way. Each manifestation is seen on an individual and on the whole species.

KNOW, O YOU WHO ARE SATISFIED AND CONTENT with the world. You are like one who rolls down from the top of a high castle. After this, the castle rolls down in a flood coursing down a steep mountain, and the mountain collapses into the depths of Earth via earthquakes.

The castle of life collapses, and the "plane" of your lifespan flies with lightning speed. Soon you will be wrapped in your white shroud and buried. The stream of time turns its wheels with horrifying speed, and the "ship" of Earth floats like clouds. If, while traveling on a fast-moving train, you stretch your hand out to grasp thorny flowers alongside the railways and the thorns tear your hands, can you blame anybody other than yourself? Do not covet or reach for the world's pleasures, for if the pain of separation tears your heart when you grasp them, you will get a small idea of what will happen at the time of final separation.

O EVIL-COMMANDING SOUL, worship whomever you wish and claim whatever you wish. As for me, I worship only Him Who has created me and subjected to me everything that exists (other than Him). I ask help only of He Who conducts me on the "plane" of life moving through the "space" of Destiny and has subjected to me the "spaceship" among the planets. I ask help only of He Who makes me mount the "train" of time traveling with the speed of lightning through the tunnel opened up under the mountain of life toward the gate of the grave along the way to eternity. Sitting on it with His permission, I recall Him in the compartment of this day connected to both yesterday and tomorrow.

I call and ask help only of He Who can stop the wheel of Destiny, which apparently moves the ship of Earth, and stop the movement of time by reuniting the sun and the moon. I ask help only of He Who, by transforming this Earth into another Earth, can steady this changing world rolling down from the summits of existence into the depths of the valleys of decay. My ambition and aims are connected with all things. My ambitions are related to time's passage and Earth's movement. I also feel a deep connection with the joys and sorrows of all beings, particularly of humanity and especially with the righteous ones in the heavens and on Earth.

So I worship only He Who is aware of my heart's most secret thoughts and satisfies its least ambition and inclination. By destroying the world and changing it into the Hereafter, He realizes the desire of my intellect and imagination, namely, to establish eternal happiness for humanity. His "Hand" reaches the tiniest particle and the largest sun at the same instant, and nothing is too big for His Power to encompass. He is such that your pain changes into pleasure if you know Him, and that without Him science results in sheer fantasy and conjecture, and philosophy in fallacy.

Without His light, existence changes into non-existence, lights into layers of darkness, living creatures into dead things, pleasure into pain and sin, and beloved ones (indeed all things) into enemies. Without Him, permanence becomes a disaster, perfection goes for nothing, life is wasted and becomes a torment, intellect becomes a means of suffering and misery, and ambition becomes pain.

Those who submit to God's will and pursue His good pleasure are served by everything; those who disobey God find everything turned against them. This is also true for those who admit all that exists, without exception, belongs to Him and is His property. He has created you surrounded by circles of need and equipped you with devices that allow you, if you rely on your will and power, to satisfy only those needs in the smallest circle. Some of your other needs are related to an enormous circle stretching from the infinite past to the infinite future, and between Earth's center and the Throne of God. To satisfy these needs, He has equipped you with prayer or supplication: *Say: "My Lord will not be concerned for you, were it not for your supplication"* (25:77). An infant calls its parents to provide what it cannot reach, and servants pray to their Lord for what they cannot [obtain or overcome].

KNOW, O FRIEND, that the perfect art in everything and its firm structure come from the unity [of origin], which does not allow division and disintegration and cannot be prevented from manifestation. If this were not so, there would be disharmony and disorder in existence. For example, the sun, one and single, exists in whatever it touches with its light, from a transparent, minute particle to an ocean. And yet its reflection or manifestation in one thing does not prevent it from being manifested in another.

If this is true for the sun, a contingent, contained, inanimate physical object, a "drop" shining by the manifestation of a ray of the Divine Name "the Light," it is even more true for the Ever-Existing Sun, Eternal Sovereign, Necessarily Existent and Permanently Self-Subsistent, the One and Single, Ever-Living, All-Powerful, Eternally-Besought-of-All. The encompassing light's unity points to oneness; the sun's existence, with all its properties in individual things and wholes, parts and particles through the manifestation of its light, implies unity.

KNOW, O FRIEND, that among the most truthful witnesses of Divine Oneness are the following:

- The unity or miraculously harmonious organization in everything, from the particles of your eye's cells to the universe.
- The perfectly firm structure everything has according to its capacity, as determined by Divine Decree and Destiny.
- The absolute ease of creating and building things, which shows that the Creator's Existence is infinitely more deeply rooted and established than that of the created.

KNOW, O FRIEND, that Earth gives and sells you its produce for an extremely cheap price. If what it gives belonged to it or was produced by material causes, you could not buy a single pomegranate, for you would have to pay for what it had received from the soil, trees, fields, the sun, and air.

Your Maker shows the utmost care in [creating] everything, even grains, making them infinitely firm and furnishing them most elaborately. He also includes in it that which is necessary with perfect consciousness and wisest skill, equipping it with subtleties of color, nourishment, and fragrance to attract customers. He creates with ease, and does not require physical contact with it. If the One Who created these things were not the same as He Who has created everything in existence with such great ease, creating them all with the same relation to His Power, these things then would not have the perfect quality that they now possess.

Since it has been created so firmly and artistically, and in such abundance, those things could not have been created only to satisfy some animate beings' temporary pleasure and particular desire. If that were true, it would require that their Creator be—God forbid such a thought—without conscience, will, knowledge, choice, and perfection. However, the perfect, conscious, wise, and purposeful art in everything contradicts such a hypothesis.

The Necessarily Existent Being is All-Powerful, All-Willing, All-Knowing, All-Wise, and has absolute dominion over everything. *When He wills a thing, His command is but to say to it "Be!" and it is* (36:82); *Your creation and resurrection is but like [those of] a single soul* (31:28). He has placed in each creature instances of wisdom and purposes connected not only with the benefits of its customers but also, and more than them, with the manifestations of His Names and the meaning of His acts as God Almighty.

Such a universal banquet could not have been prepared by a blind power; the floods of fruits and other products could not be the result of chance and coincidence. The particular form, color, smell, and taste assigned to each thing for certain purposes, and the services that each consciously renders, rejects the intervention of blind chance and coincidence. On the contrary, their abundance and cheapness, the ease of creating them individually and as a species, their firm structure, and (despite their infinite variety) their formation out of only a few substances, all testify to the absolute generosity of the absolutely Generous, Wise and Powerful One.

Glory be to Him Who has combined infinite, absolute generosity with infinite wisdom and economy. Glory be to Him Who has put the unrestricted, absolute free-giving within the limits of a perfect order, a sensitive balance or measure, and an absolute justice. This order, balance, and justice are such that an elephant must protect itself against a fly, and haughty, too-conceited people must fight against the little "spear" of a mosquito:

> O humanity! A parable is set forth, so listen to it: Surely, those whom you invoke, apart from God, will never create a fly even if they combine together for the purpose. And if the fly takes something from them, they cannot rescue it from it. Hence, weak are both the seeker and the sought. (22:73)

And the fury of a sea and the rage of storms subside, and the severity of coldness diminishes, through a silent supplication of a broken-hearted child and the child is carried to safety: *Is He not the One Who answers the oppressed one when he supplicates Him and takes away [his] ills?* (27:62). The One Who hears a heart beating and is aware of whatever occurs to it answers him and directs the movements of the sun and moon.

KNOW, O FRIEND who ascribes everything to the law of causality. Creating a cause and making it the cause of an effect, furnishing it with the equipment necessary for the effect to come into being, is not an easier, more perfect and wonderful act than creating the effect with the command: "*Be!*" issuing from Him in relation to Whom everything that exists is the same.

KNOW, O MY HEART, that the suffering, decay, and death you see filling the world consist of similar things coming to the world and going, and events of birth and death occurring over and over again. In each separation and decay, however, believers find the pleasure of renewal instead of the pain of decline and disappearance. Believe and find security and satisfaction. Submit yourself to Him and find peace and happiness.

KNOW, O FRIEND, that racism is a combination of heedlessness, ignorance, misguidance, ostentation, and wrongdoing that support and strengthen one another. Racists make a fetish of their race. We seek refuge in God from such deviation. As for the zeal for Islam, it is a bright light coming from belief.

KNOW, O FRIEND who disputes with heretics, agnostics, and imitators of Western atheists. You are in a great danger, for if you are not perfectly purified and fully convinced of the truths of belief and Islam, you may be drawn gradually and unconsciously to your opponents. You cannot trust your evil-commanding soul in objective reasoning, for a seed of criticism and fault-finding begins to grow within a just disputant who temporarily accepts an opponent's ideas as true to find answers to them. Gradually, the disputant begins to behave like the opponent's deputy. Taking advantage of this, Satan occupies that person's mind and tries to make that seed grow and bear fruit. However, if you have a pure intention [in disputing], when you feel that you have begun to behave like your opponent's deputy, immediately struggle against your greatest enemy within you and humbly seek God's forgiveness.

SUPPOSE, O FRIEND, that a wonderful palace is being built and decorated for a mighty king. Whoever sees the instruments used and the workers employed, but without knowing their underlying purpose, will conclude that the workers are working not on their own behalf but on that of their employer and for a certain purpose. Look at the animate and inanimate beings employed in the universe for numerous noble and subtle aims and purposes, many of which even the smartest scholars cannot perceive. Ponder the exquisiteness that flowers display to make themselves loved by those who look at them. You will be convinced that flowers, like other beings, are charged by the All-Munificent, All-Wise One with serving His guests on Earth and making Him loved.

Do flowers have the feelings and animals the consciousness necessary to perceive the purposes for the design, decoration, and graces of generosity they are made to display? No. Rather, they make the All-Munificent Lord known and loved by His conscious servants, His guests.

KNOW O ILL-MEANING, EVIL-COMMANDING SOUL! You demand to see what is necessary for all grades of existence in a single grade, and what is needed by all senses in a single sense. You seek to experience all of the pleasures that your feelings, faculties, and senses enable you to experience separately. You seek to see the rays of all Divine Beautiful Names in each Name, the splendor of the Creator in each creature, and to find the real, manifested meaning of everything in its reflection in the mind. Rather, seek to find in each thing what it deserves and can encompass so that you are not exposed to evil suggestions and thoughts about the Creator.

KNOW, O FRIEND, that when you have a high opinion of yourself, consider those greater than you. When you see things that are smaller than you, like insects, consider your body's cells and concentrate on one of them. You will see that even a fly is greater than you. However, this should not lead you to despise the wisdom, mercy, favoring, and perfect art in you; rather, when you see the same innumerable bounties conferred on you, consider the extent of your need and weakness, and the purposes for those bounties so that you should not despise them.

Does it lessen your need for an eye that all animals have eyes? Does it reduce a particular bounty's inclusiveness and purpose? No. Rather, it intensifies the need for it and increases its inclusiveness.

KNOW, O FRIEND, that there are innumerable purposes for every living creature's life. Only one is concerned with the living creature itself, while those concerned with the Bestower of life are proportionate to His limitless

Ownership. No member of creation, however great, has the right to boast to those less than it. Although there is nothing useless and purposeless in creation, some people who consider everything with respect to their own interests and wishes may regard that which is irrelevant to their own use as futile and purposeless. Due to its duty to make Earth prosperous in the Name of God, the universal table spread on Earth is a gift to humanity, provided it fulfills this responsibility. This table does not belong to and is not spread for the sole use of humanity.

KNOW, O FRIEND, that if one whispers to you: "You are but an animal among countless others. The ant is your brother, and the bee is your sister. How can you have a relation with the One Who rolls up the heavens like a scroll rolled up for books? The whole Earth is His handful on the Day of Resurrection, and the heavens will be rolled up in His Right Hand," reply: "My admission of impotence, poverty, and insignificance before Him, together with my recognition and conviction of Him, becomes a mirror to show me His Power, Wealth, and Dignity. Thus I have progressed from being an animal to being a human being. The perfection of His Grandeur and the comprehensiveness of His Power require that He should hear my call and see my needs, and that His sustaining Earth and heavens should not prevent Him from sustaining me and directing my affairs."

God's concern with insignificant-seeming things and events does not contradict His Grandeur. Rather, if He did not concern Himself with them, His Lordship's Grandeur would be lacking. Do you not see that every bubble, drop of water, and piece of glass, however small, contains the sun's image? If it could speak, it would say: "The sun belongs to me. It is in me or accompanies me." Those drops, pieces, planets, or seas do not hinder one another from having a relation with the sun, nor does the sun's greatness prevent those relations. Rather, the more we know the Almighty and are aware of our poverty and insignificance before Him, the nearer we are to Him. How good is the position of those who remember their poverty and impotence before Him to Whose Wealth and Power, Dignity and Grandeur there are no limits.

Glory be to Him Who has included limitless kindness in limitless grandeur and boundless tenderness in boundless majesty, Who has combined infinite nearness with infinite distance and established brotherhood between minute particles and suns, and Who manifests His Power by combining opposites.

Sustaining and directing Earth and heavens does not prevent Him from sustaining insects. Sustaining and administering does not hinder Him from creating even the smallest animals, whether on land or in the sea. Violent winds and furious seas do not distract Him from providing His perfect kindness and goodness to every creature, without exception, regardless of size, location, or any other factor.

Mercy appears smilingly amidst the sea's fury and behind its stern, frowning face. While it roars: "O All-Mighty God, All-Majestic, All-Great! Glory be to You, how grand You are!," that little creature responds by calling silently: "O All-Subtle and Gracious God, All-Munificent, All-Providing, All-Compassionate. How gracious is Your favoring." In these two types of calling God by His Names and glorifying Him are a gentle, gracious splendor and a splendid grace and gentleness, as well as an exalted type of worshipping the One, Single and Eternally-Besought-of-All.

KNOW, O FRIEND, that after acquiring the necessary knowledge of belief, you must do good and righteous deeds. For, following belief, the Qur'an declares: *Those who do good, righteous deeds*.

This short life suffices only for doing what is most important and necessary. Science and technology are necessary insofar as they help satisfy essential needs, human progress (both intellectual and spiritual), and human prosperity in both worlds. If they cause dissipation and sedition, they are harmful.

> O God, O Most Compassionate of the Compassionate. Have mercy on Muhammad's community, and illumine its people's hearts with the light of belief and the Qur'an. Brighten the proof of the Qur'an, and exalt Islam. Amen.

To conclude:

- Believers who say: "I bear witness that there is no deity but God," "Muhammad is the Messenger of God," or "All praise be to God" have made a claim, announced a cause and conviction, and declared a conclusion.
- Each radiation of belief and Islam is supported by the whole.
- Each part of the whole, regardless of size, needs [for its being] whatever the whole needs [for its being].
- The Prophethood of Muhammad, upon him be peace and blessings, is like a seed from which the blossoming, fruit-laden tree of Islam has grown.

- History's account of the Prophet's life represents only the shell of the seed from which the blessed tree of Prophet Muhammad has grown.
- A minute particle can manifest only the Names of the Eternal "Sun," for it has no truly effective and operative ability to create anything.
- Attributing the fruit of a group's work to one person leads to associating partners with God, for the underlying assumption is that the person in question produced those fruits.
- Serving God leads to reward, especially in the Hereafter, while serving the ego leads to pain and suffering.
- Leaving the time of death undefined shows that it has been defined in the Originator's Knowledge.
- Calling blessings and peace upon the Prophet is like answering the invitation of the Bestower of bounties Who spreads His blessings freely.
- The difference between the civilization of unbelievers and that of (true) believers.
- *Ijtihad* is allowed, but not in all circumstances.
- One of the 55 "languages" that witnesses the Almighty's necessary Existence and His Unity in His Divinity and Lordship.
- The area where your mind and heart move is too spacious to be encompassed.
- God's gifts have conditions.
- The Qur'an's miraculousness saves it from corruption.
- Our disobedience, rebelliousness, and ingratitude mostly arise from our blindness to the Divine act of bestowing bounties and indifference to the One Who bestows.
- Satan's whisperings and involuntary thoughts and suggestions arising from the heart and carnal soul should be ignored.
- Philosophers who criticize Islam, and why unbelievers sometimes beat the believers in this world.
- Intense love causes one to deny the thing loved.
- The seed of unbelief potentially bears Hell.
- Your relation with your life is like the relation between a steersman and the royal ship that he steers.
- Do not confuse a shadowy existence formed through manifestation or reflection according to what Destiny has determined, with the main, substantial existence.
- The Qur'an explains many truths through parables and comparisons, for this makes the abstract Divine truths easily understandable.

- The heart has the same meaning for you as the Divine Throne.
- A supplication.
- An address to the Turkish Parliament.
- Your body and what maintains it do not belong to you, so you cannot control them as you wish.
- Each *sura* of the Qur'an contains a summary of the whole Qur'an.
- Those who submit to God's will and pursue His pleasure are served by everything; those who disobey God find that everything turns against them.
- If you had to pay for what Earth, with His permission, freely gives you, you would not be able to buy even a piece of fruit.
- *When He wills a thing, His command is but to say to it: "Be!" and it is* (36:82); and *Your creation and resurrection is but like [those of] a single soul* (31:28).
- Racism is a combination of heedlessness, ignorance, misguidance, ostentation and wrongdoing, which support and give strength to each other.
- Debating with heretics, agnostics, and imitators of Western atheists.
- When you have a high opinion of yourself, consider those greater than you.
- There are innumerable purposes for the life of every living creature.
- Your admission of impotence, poverty, and insignificance before God, together with your recognition and conviction of Him, becomes a mirror to show His Power, Wealth, and Dignity.
- After acquiring the necessary knowledge about belief, a believer must do good and righteous deeds.

The Sixth Treatise

The Sixth Treatise

A grain contained by a fruit in the garden of the Qur'an

The grain says:
I am a tree branch laden with the fruits of Divine Unity,
or a drop from the sea full of the pearls of praise unto Him.

In the Name of God, the All-Merciful, the All-Compassionate.

Praise be to God for Islam and the perfection of belief. May God's blessings and peace be upon Muhammad, the center of the circle of Islam and the source of the lights of belief, and on all his Family and Companions so long as days and nights continue and the sun and moon move in their courses.

KNOW, O FRIEND, THAT IF YOU SEE THE UNIVERSE AS A GREAT BOOK, you will see the light of Muhammad as the ink with which the Author of that book has written it. If you see the universe as a tree, you will see his light as originally its seed and consequently its fruit. If you see the universe as an animate being, you will see his light as its spirit. If you see the universe as a macro-human, you will see his light as its intellect. If you see the universe as a flower garden, you will see his light as its nightingale.

If you see the universe as a lofty, richly decorated castle with many rooms and apartments displaying the splendor of the Eternal Sovereign's sovereignty, the marvels of His Glory, the beautiful manifestations of His Grace, and the wonderful designs of His Art, you will see the light of the

Prophet Muhammad as a spectator. He first views them on His behalf and then announces: "O people. Come and look at these pleasant sights. Hasten to receive your share in them—love, amazement, refreshment, appreciation, enlightenment, reflection, and many other lofty things." He shows all these to them; he observes them and has others observe them. As he himself is amazed by them, he causes others to be amazed by them. He loves their Owner and makes Him loved by others. As he is illumined through them, he has others illumined. He benefits from them and makes others benefit.

KNOW, O FRIEND, that humanity is the fruit of the Tree of Creation. A fruit is a tree's most perfect part and the farthest from the roots. It also is the most comprehensive of those parts and has the properties of the whole tree. There must be one human being from whom the All-Powerful One grew this Tree of Creation. The Creator made that individual the tree's fruit, and then, as the All-Merciful One, made this illustrious fruit the seed of the tree of Islam, the lamp of its world, the sun of its system. That illustrious person is the Prophet Muhammad, upon him be peace and blessings.

What is necessary for a tree is also necessary for its seed. The tree being so large and the seed so small does not require that the tiny seed should be exempt from this rule. There is a grain also within humanity. If humanity had been a fruit, this grain would have been its seed. This grain is the heart.

Due to the variety of human needs, human beings have relations with all species and individual parts of creation. Due to the intensity of their need and poverty, they have connections with all lights of the Divine Beautiful Names. It is as if they have as many needs as there are parts of creation. People have world-filling adversities and hostilities, and are satisfied only with one who can make them independent of, and protect them from, everything.

Like a map, an index, or a sample, each person can include or represent all of creation. They have a seed that only accepts the One, the Single. They are content only with what is eternal and perpetual. This seed is the grain of the heart, which is to be watered by Islam and receive light from belief. If, in the soil of servanthood and purity of intention, it is watered by Islam and awakened to life by belief, it grows into such an illustrious spiritual tree that it becomes its corporeal body's spirit. If it is not watered, it remains a dried seed having to burn in fire until it acquires the quality of light.

The seed contains very subtle, delicate things like nerves, each of which, if it germinates properly, fulfills an important duty. Also, the grain of the heart has inactive servants that, when activated and developed with the life of the heart, travel through the gardens of the universe like birds. Consequently, this grain expands to the degree that one says: "Praise be to God for all His creatures, for all of them are bounties conferred on me." (This grain expands to the degree that), for example, imagination, the heart's weakest and feeblest servant, is burdened with a strange duty. Through it, human beings, who are confined in a narrow place, enter an exhilarating garden and, while praying in the remotest eastern or western corner, put their heads under the Black Stone of the Ka'ba, entrusting to it their testifying (to God's being their Lord).

Grain is threshed on the threshing-ground and preserved. In the same manner, the Plain of Resurrection is the ground awaiting humanity, the fruit of creation, [to separate the grain from the chaff].

KNOW, O FRIEND, that everyone has a particular world identical with the outer world, except that its center is that particular individual and not the sun. Its keys are in that person's hands, and are connected with his or her senses and faculties. This world takes its color from the individual and, based on this same individual, is either prosperous and beautiful or ugly, illumined or dark. Just as a garden's reflection and the changes it displays depend on the mirror, every person's world depends on its owner's views and characteristics. Your small bodily size is not an excuse for the insignificance of your sins. A negligible amount of darkness or hardness in your heart may extinguish all the stars of your particular world.

KNOW, O FRIEND, that for 30 years I have struggled against two "rebels": the ego within human beings, and nature in the outer world. I have seen the former as a shadowy mirror reflecting Someone Else. Nevertheless, humanity views it as having an independent existence, showing itself, and therefore becoming an unbending tyrant in rebellion against its Creator.

I have seen nature as a work of Divine Art, a painting of the All-Merciful. However, due to their viewing it heedless [of the Creator], materialists regard it as a deity, as self-originated and existing by itself, and as an excuse for ingratitude. This has resulted in unbelief.

Thanks be to God and praise be to Him, for by the help of the One, Eternally-Besought-of-All and by the enlightenment of the glorious Qur'an, my struggle has ended in the death of these two rebels, the smashing of these two idols. As discussed in many other sections in this book, a work of Divine

Art, a collection of the Divine laws of creation and operation of the universe, has appeared behind the veil of nature. Ego has broken into pieces, and behind it has emerged the One like Whom there is nothing. Exalted is His Majesty.

KNOW, O EGO, that there are nine things of whose nature and consequences you are unaware:

First: Your body is like a fresh, pleasant, and enjoyable fruit in summer, but dried and rotten in winter.

Second: Your animal quality. See how quickly decay and death come to animals.

Third: Your human quality, which vacillates between extinction and purification, decay and permanence. Preserve that which is inclined to remain forever through constant remembrance of the Everlasting One.

Fourth: Your short and limited lifespan, which lasts only until the hour appointed for it, is neither antedated nor postponed. So do not grieve for it, be anxious about it, or burden it with worldly ambitions that cannot be achieved while you are alive.

Fifth: Your material existence is in the Hand of the True Owner of all things, Who cares for it much more than you do. If you interfere in it without His permission, you will harm it. Do you not see how avarice brings despair and disappointment, how insistence on sleeping causes sleeplessness and restlessness?

Sixth: The misfortunes befalling you are not really bitter, for they disappear quickly. The pleasure of their disappearance is followed by fortune. Besides, they cause you to turn from what is fleeting to what is permanent through the All-Permanent One.

Seventh: You are a guest wherever you are. Guests do not set their hearts upon what does not concern them or accompany them on their trip. You will depart from here soon, and from this town—you will either go out of it or be buried in it. You will leave this transient world or be expelled from it. So abandon and renounce it, with honor and dignity, before you are expelled in humiliation.

Eighth: You should sacrifice your material existence to the One Who has given it to you, for He buys it for a very high price. Make haste to sell it, rather, to sacrifice it. For, first of all, it goes away for nothing. Second, it belongs to Him and will ultimately be returned to Him. Third, your reliance on it causes you to fall into non-existence, for your existence is a door opened onto Him. If you open that door through renunciation, you will find permanent existence. Fourth, if you cling to it, only a point-sized part of it remains in your hand and you will be enveloped by a thick darkness of "non-existence." If you blow off that part, the lights of existence will surround you.

Ninth: Worldly pleasure or enjoyment. Whatever Destiny has for you will come to you, so do not worry about it. Sensible people do not set their hearts upon fleeting things. However your own particular world ends, you should renounce worldly pleasure. If it ends in happiness, you can attain happiness by renouncing pleasure. If it ends in misery, how can one waiting to be hanged get pleasure from decorated gallows? Even unbelievers who think they are headed for absolute non-existence—I seek refuge with God from such a supposition!—should renounce worldly pleasure, for the continual disappearance of such pleasure brings a continual feeling of the pain of the absolute non-existence they suppose to follow death. Such pain is much more acute than the pleasure they find in life.

KNOW, O FRIEND, that your likeness, when stricken with a misfortune thrown by Destiny, is that of sheep trying to enter a public pasture. The shepherd seeks to turn them aside by throwing stones at them. The sheep struck by the stones turn back, as if saying: "We are under the shepherd's command. He knows us better than ourselves, so we must return."

Know, O my soul, you are not more astray than the sheep. When stricken with misfortune, say: "We belong to God and are bound to return to Him."

KNOW, O FRIEND, that out of innumerable evidences that the heart was not created to be occupied primarily with worldly affairs, heed the following: When the heart is attached to something, it becomes strongly attached. It sets upon it too zealously and, seeking permanence and eternity, is completely lost. When the heart stretches out its "hand" to grasp it, it tries to get as much as possible. However, it can only get that which is no bigger than a hair, or nothing at all. This is because the heart is the mirror reflecting the Eternally-Besought-of-All. It does not admit an idol carved out of stone, for that stone breaks it. A lover mostly suffers at the beloved's hand, because the beloved unconsciously rejects what does not belong to him or her, as the lover is not worthy to reside in the beloved's heart.

KNOW, O FRIEND, that a heavenly table was sent along with the Qur'an. On it, people can find whatever their intellectual appetites need. The food is arranged in a certain order. First is the food for ordinary people, who form the great majority of humanity. For example, their share in: *The heavens and Earth were at first one piece, then We parted them* (21:30) is: There was no relationship between the heavens and Earth. The heavens were clean and without clouds, unable to send rain, while Earth was dried and barren. Then, by the Almighty's Will and permission, a relationship (a contract) was established between them. So when the heavens gave birth to rain, Earth began to bring forth its produce. The part of the verse just following the sentences above, *and We have made every living thing from water*, alludes to this.

The meaning inferred by those with a higher level of understanding is: The sun and planets were separated from the matter that was created from the light of the Chief of all creation (the Prophet Muhammad) and [that matter] could assume any shape, like dough. This is indicated by the hadith: "What God created first is my light."[61]

Consider: *Were we then worn out by the first creation? Yet they are in doubt about a new creation* (50:15). From this verse, ordinary people understand that those who cannot admit the Resurrection affirm their creation, which they ought to recognize as much more astonishing. They regard the Resurrection as improbable, although it will be easier. Beyond this level of understanding lies a bright evidence for the perfect ease of the Resurrection: O deniers of the Resurrection. You are revived and resurrected many times in your life, nay, annually, nay, daily. Like changing clothes in the morning and evening, you put on and then discard your bodies daily.

KNOW, O FRIEND, how foolish the human ego or selfhood is. It sees in itself the imprints, traces, and signs of an absolutely Free, All-Wise Lord's making, sustaining, and administering, and discerns that this is true of all other individual beings, species, and kinds as a universal, all-encompassing rule. It therefore must be convinced of this as an undeniable reality confirmed by creation. Yet the foolish ego deceives itself by seeing such an overall and universal manifestation of the Divine Beautiful Names, which also are manifested on it, as a sign of (Divine) neglect of it and a veil under which it can hide from [the Lord's] watching and inspection. These manifestations' uni-

61 Al-'Ajluni, *Khasf al-Khafa'*, 1:205.

versality and intensity lead it to suppose that no one is watching it. Even Satan is ashamed of such a sophistry.

KNOW, O DISTRESSED, RESTLESS SOUL. Like the sun's rising in the morning and setting in the evening, whatever happens to you and all your conditions has been predetermined by the Pen of Destiny and inscribed on your forehead. Your distress and depression will only increase if you critisize destiny; this will be no different from striking your head against an anvil wilfully. One who cannot penetrate the regions and depths of the heavens and Earth must consent willingly to the Lordship of the One Who created everything and decreed its destiny.

KNOW, O FRIEND, that if the maker of a thing were within it, he or she would be of the same nature as it, and there would have to be as many makers as the things made. For example, look at this book. It is written with one pen, but printed by using all letters of the alphabet. [Or someone types it by pressing many keys on a typewriter.] The designs or embroideries in a work of art are not made by that work, a tree's fruits are not made by that tree, and a page's letters are not produced by that page. Otherwise, order would be destroyed and everything would descend to chaos. But we see that there is a perfect order and stability in the creation, for everything is inscribed by the Pen of the Divine Power on the lines of Destiny.

KNOW, O FRIEND, that intellect, which comprehends the universe and goes so far beyond it, is sometimes drowned in a drop, disappears in an atom, is lost in a hair, and restricts existence to what it is lost in, wishing to include all that it comprehends in that which has swallowed it.

If you had the power to possess and control this material domain, if it really belonged to you, your fear and anxiety about maintaining it would make it very hard for you to benefit from it. However, the All-Munificent Bestower of bounties agrees to provide whatever you need. All you have to do is to eat from the table of His favors and thank Him. Thanking Him will cause Him to increase His favors upon you, for it means seeing the act of favoring or giving bounties. Seeing this act removes the grief arising from the bounties' disappearance, for this disappearance is not eternal. Like fruits eaten this year being succeeded by new ones next year, it means departing to make room for something new. Thus, it gives you the delight of ever-renewed pleasure. Their latest call: *All praise be to God, the Lord of the worlds* (10:10), indicates that praising is itself a pleasure. Praising means that you see the tree of [Divine] favoring in the favor of fruits. It removes the pain arising from the thought of their disappearance, and becomes the pleasure itself.

KNOW, O FRIEND, that information provided by materialistic science and philosophy about the outer world cannot always be free of doubt and error. But information based on one's sound conscience is mostly free of doubt and trouble. So look from your inner world, your conscience, toward the outer world if you want to avoid error.

KNOW, O FRIEND, that as this civilization has made the world into a small town, people know and hear from one another through the media, help each other to commit sins, and pursue what does not benefit them. This leads them to sin and thickens their heedlessness [of belief and religious life]. Only a mighty effort and struggle can rend this veil. This civilization has made innumerable openings to the world in our souls. Only God's special mercy can close them.

KNOW, O FRIEND, that a minute, transparent particle contains the sun's image, although it cannot hold two particles of its own size and nature. Raindrops [and bubbles on an ocean's face] shine with the sun's images. Similarly, the universe's constituent particles and compounds can receive the manifestations of the luminous, absolute, and eternal Divine Power, accompanied by the eternal, infinite Divine Knowledge and Will. A constituent particle of a cell in your eye cannot be the origin of the power, consciousness, and will that it needs to fulfill its functions in your veins, arteries, and nervous system, and in your powers of seeing, hearing, thinking, and describing.

This perfect and astounding art, this fully decorated and orderly design, and this profound and subtle wisdom can be explained in two ways. Either each of the universe's constituent particles and compounds is the origin of the perfect, absolute, and all-encompassing attributes [such as power and will, knowledge and consciousness], or each is an object receiving and reflecting the radiations of the Eternal "Sun," which actually has all such attributes.

The first alternative has as many impossibilities as the number of the universe's particles and compounds. Accepting it means that a bee can carry the Ararat and Suphan mountains on its wings,[62] and that the Nile and Euphrates rivers can flow from a gnat's eyes. But in reality, every particle cannot bear whatever is beyond its power and so testifies that there is no creator, sustainer, upbringer and administrator, no owner, self-subsistent, or

62 Ararat and Suphan are two mountains in eastern Turkey. (Tr.)

deity save God. The universe's particles and compounds announce in different tongues and bear witness in different ways:

> Our expressions differ, but You are always the One of the same Beauty;
> so whatever exists points to that All-Beautiful "Face."

Every letter of the Book of the Universe points to its own existence only in one way and in its capacity of being a letter, while it indicates its Writer and Artist in numerous ways. It sings a long poem of praise in the tongue of the Names manifested on it.

> Reflect upon the lines of the [Book of the] Universe,
> for they are letters to you from the Highest Realm.

KNOW, O FRIEND, that many "mirrors" reflect the Divine manifestations: glass, water, air, the World of Representations or Immaterial Forms, the spirit, the intellect, imagination, time, and many other things that we do not know. The reflections of solid, material things are dead, separated, or disconnected from themselves. They do not have the essential characteristics of their originals and therefore are not identical with them. This is indicated when their pictures are taken: They are seen only with their outer, physical forms.

The reflections of luminous things, however, are connected to their originals and bear their characteristics or attributes. [Although not exactly identical with their originals,] they are not other than them either. If the Creator had made the sun's heat its soul, its light, its consciousness, and the sun's colors in its light its senses, it would have spoken to you through the "heart" of the mirror in your hand. It would be like talking to you through your telephone or your heart's "mirror." For, according to its capacity, the sun's image in the mirror would have had the heat of life, the light of consciousness, and the colors of senses. Due to this fact, the Prophet, who is luminous in identity, becomes aware of all blessings called upon himself at the same moment. This is a key to many mysterious truths.

KNOW, O FRIEND, that *Glory be to God* and *Praise be to God* describe the Almighty with His Attributes of Majesty and Grace. *Glory be to God* implies your contingent nature and distance from God, the Necessarily Existent One, the High and Grand. *Praise be to God* implies His nearness to you and His creatures with His Mercy and Grace. Consider: The sun is near to you, its heat and light reach you, and it has a certain control over you by its

Creator's leave. Thus it functions as a mirror to manifest the Divine Name "the Light" and as a receptacle of His bounties of heat and light. But you are very far from it and can do nothing to it. If affects you, but you cannot influence on it.

Similarly, God is near to us so that we praise Him, and we are distant from Him so that we glorify Him. Praise Him, for He is near to you with His Mercy. Glorify Him, for you are distant from Him. Do not confuse His nearness to you with your distance from Him, lest you become bewildered. If you do not confuse these two things, consider His nearness from the viewpoint of your distance and your distance from the viewpoint of His nearness. Then, combine these two considerations and say: "Glory be to God with His praise."

KNOW, O FRIEND who strives for the world. Renounce the world for the following four reasons:

First: It goes swiftly and decays. The pain arising from decay and separation remove the pleasure of attainment of, or union with, something subject to decay.

Second: Only pain and grief are left after pleasure.

Third: The grave, which waits for you and toward which you travel, is the door to the other world. It does not accept your ornaments of the world as gifts, for in the other world they will change into error and sin.

Fourth: [To understand the difference between this world and the Hereafter, reflect on] the difference between staying for an hour among enemies and vermin and among your most beloved friends and elders for years. The Lord of earthly and spiritual dominion calls you to abandon that hour of pleasure so that you may have perfect comfort and satisfaction in the company of your beloved ones in those years. So answer His call before you are sent to Him fettered.

All glory be to God, how great are His Mercy and Favor toward humanity. He buys the property that He has entrusted to us for a very high price, and preserves it permanently for us. If we claim ownership of it and do not sell it to God, we are exposed to great calamity and misfortune, as our power is so small and insufficient that we cannot preserve and carry it. If we try to carry it, it will prove too heavy for us to carry. It will disappear swiftly and go for nothing, leaving to us only our sins.

KNOW, O FRIEND, that it is as if the following couplet were said about me:

My eyes were in sleep during the night of my youth;
They woke up only when it was the morning of old age.

What I regarded as the greatest wakefulness in my youth was in fact the deepest sleep. So what modernists describe as enlightenment and wakefulness must resemble my youthful wakefulness. They are like people who dream that they wake up and tell it to others, when in reality they only have entered a deeper state of sleep. How can such people, resembling the dead, wake up those who are awake? How can sleeping people make themselves heard from behind the thick veils of sleep?

O sleeping ones who think they are awake. Do not approach modern, corrupted people by making concessions and trying to resemble them in religion. You cannot build a bridge or fill up the valley between them and us in such a manner. The distance between believers and unbelievers is too great to remove, and the intervening valley is too deep to fill up. (If you try to do so,) probably you will join them or greatly deviate from the Right Path.

KNOW, O FRIEND, that there is the seed of unbelief in the essence of sins, especially frequently committed ones, for such sins make people indifferent and become addictions that only abandonment can cure. Such people hope that there will be no punishment for their sins, and so unconsciously look for an excuse to believe in the non-existence of torment in the eternal world. This continues until they deny the abode of punishment. As the shame arising from sinning is not followed by remorse and asking forgiveness from God, sinners begin to deny that their sins are really sins, and then begin to deny the existence of those—like guarding angels—who oversee them and are aware of their sins. Due to this intense shame, they hope that there will be no reckoning in the other world. When they encounter even a false argument for its non-existence, they take it as a strong proof and deny the final reckoning. Consequently, their hearts become even darker. May God save us from such a consequence! Amen.

KNOW, O FRIEND, that there are about 40 kinds of radiations belonging to the Qur'an's miraculousness. The following are only some of the many aspects of its eloquence:

It has a pure, genuine fluency and is free of all defects in wording and meaning. Its sentences and paragraphs, which corroborate one another, have a firm solidarity and are perfectly proportional. Although revealed in parts over 23 years on different occasions, the sciences of rhetorical style and semantics testify that the cohesion and accord among its verses and purposes are so firm that it is as if the Qur'an had been revealed all at once. Although many parts of it came to answer different questions, it contains no contradiction in meaning, and there is such agreement and harmony among those parts that it is as if it had come as the answer to only one question.

It came to explain and judge vastly different events, but its order is such that it could have been revealed to judge only one event. In the Qur'an, God speaks in styles suited for all levels of understanding. It came down, first of all, to the Prophet, in his different moods. However, its parts show such smoothness and correspondence that it could have been revealed when he was always in the same mood. Although it addresses all peoples of all times, it speaks so smoothly and fluently, so orderly and clearly, that it seems to address only one level of understanding. (It speaks in such a way that) each group of people whom it addresses thinks that it addresses them directly and primarily.

The Qur'an guides everyone and enables them to attain guidance, but is so balanced, orderly, and straightforward that it is as if it pursued a single purpose. However, it primarily has four or five purposes: Divine Unity, Prophethood, Resurrection, justice, and worship or devotion to God in belief and one's daily life. Since the Qur'an concentrates primarily on Divine Unity, it is perfectly coherent and harmonious, consistent and orderly.

Whoever has eyes will see that the Qur'an has an eye seeing all of creation like a single, clear page. It repeats itself to establish its purposes in minds and hearts, and repeatedly narrates stories of certain Prophets to reinforce its warnings and lessons. However, its repetitions do not tire or spoil its listeners' taste for it. Like musk giving more scent as it is worn away, the more the Qur'an repeats a subject, the more it exudes perfume and the more "breaths of the All-Merciful" are diffused from it.

The more you read it, if you have good taste and a sound heart, the more delight you find in it, for it nourishes the heart and gives health and strength to the spirit. Such essential bodily nourishment as air, water, and bread does not displease when taken repeatedly; rather, the body needs them all the time. We need air at every instant, water a few times a day, and food at least once a day. We also need light. Since we need these basic nourishments all the time, taking them repeatedly gives us ever-renewed pleasure instead of boredom. Similarly, the Qur'an meets all the intellectual and spiritual needs of human life. We need some of its elements, like *He ... God* at every instant, for they refresh our spirit; some like *In the Name of God* every hour; and still some others daily, according to the degree of our need for it. So, the Qur'an contains repetitions in accordance with the need felt for it by the heart.

For example, since *He ... God* or *In the Name of God* is like fresh air that refreshes the body and gives oxygen to the blood, it must be repeated all the time. Each time the Qur'an mentions the same event, it does so from a different perspective and thus points to certain universal principles. For instance, the phrases and sentences used to tell Moses' story are more beneficial to us than his staff, and their benefits are not limited to a certain time and people.

In sum: The Qur'an is a book of recitation of Divine Names, reflection, legislation, knowledge, truths, and law; a cure for what is in human hearts; and a pure guidance and mercy for believers.

KNOW, O FRIEND, that human beings have a very strange nature: Through heedlessness, they confuse the functions of their physical senses and organs, and of their intellectual and spiritual faculties. They are like those who, because of the nearness between their eyes and hands, try to grasp whatever they can see. Unaware of the difference between what is Divine and what is human, [as they see both side by side, even mixed, in their being and in the outer world], they try, in their vanity, to interfere with God's control of the universe, even though they can do nothing by themselves.

Although there is not much physical difference between people, the difference in their natures is as immense as that as seen between an atom and the sun and "the sun of suns." Fish and birds have great physical differences, but in their being "animals" they are almost the same. As for human beings, they stand at the top central point of the "cone of existence," and everything that exists has the same distance from them. This is because their faculties or powers—lusts, anger, intellect, and so on—are not restricted. Egotism and vanity reduce them to the lowest ranks, while abandoning these two things and worshipping and serving God elevates them to the highest ranks, to the degree of being "the sun of suns" like Prophet Muhammad, upon him be peace and blessings.

KNOW, O FRIEND, that the Eternal One does not allow things to pass into absolute non-existence. Even things that decay swiftly or disappear, like spoken words and momentary ideas, are preserved. However, they may assume different forms according to where they are preserved. It is as if things are charged with preserving a thing either in its exact form and nature or with one aspect only. Although scientists have discovered this reality, they still do not comprehend it perfectly. They continue to attribute, mistakenly, such chemical processes as combination, composition, and dissolution to things themselves and thus ascribe eternity to matter. But matter cannot be eternal, for God Almighty dissolves, compounds, and composes things, and He creates and makes them die. He acts as He wills, and ordains and judges as He wills.

O WRETCHED SAID! The grave is a door—inside it is mercy and happiness; outside it lie suffering and wretchedness. Almost all of your loved ones and friends dwell on the other side of this door. Is it not time for you to want to join them and their world? Purify yourself [of your sins]; otherwise they will be disgusted with you.

If you were told that Imam Rabbani Ahmad al-Faruqi, may God bless him, was living in India, surely you would leave your homeland and risk all to visit him. But there are thousands of stars called Ahmad round the "sun" mentioned as Ahmad in the Bible, Ahyad in the Torah, and Muhammad in the Qur'an. And there are millions called Muhammad. All are inside the door of the grave, enveloped by the mercy of God. Therefore always bear in mind the following principles:

If you are a good servant wholly submitted to God, everything is subjugated to you. If you have not submitted to God, everything is hostile to you. Everything is preordained, so be satisfied with what comes to you so that you may be at rest. Otherwise you are exposed to suffering after suffering. Your life and body belong to God but have been entrusted to you. However, He wills to buy them from you to preserve them for you permanently. If they are left with you, they will go for nothing. You need Him in every respect and under all circumstances. You are surrounded on all sides and being driven to the grave awaiting you. The heart does not derive pure pleasure from what is impermanent. You are decaying, as is your world and the world of all other people.

The universe will be stripped of its present cloth and dressed in another garment, as if it were a huge clock whose hands have finally reached the appointed hour. So do not attach importance to your works and traces to be left in this fleeting world and which will not benefit you in the Hereafter.

Do not view His disposition of creation with mercy and favoring from the perspective of your smallness and distance from Him and of His Grandeur and Might. [In other words, do not think that creation's distance and insignificance, in relation to Him, prevent Him from treating it with favor and mercy, and do not ask why He should condescend to favor you and meet your needs.] This type of His relation with creation requires you to glorify Him, as He deserves.

Do not view His Attributes of Majesty from the perspective of His nearness to creation and enveloping it with His Knowledge and Mercy, and of your being His creature included in His favoring and munificence. This will cause suspicion and misconception [about His Might and Grandeur] to attack you.

> Glory be to Him Who cannot be comprehended by minds and intellects, and praise be to Him Whose Mercy encompasses all things. There is no deity save He, One, and He has no partners. His is the dominion of all things and all praise is His; He gives life and causes to die. In His hand is all good, and He is powerful over all things.

KNOW, O FRIEND, that when people with "living" hearts turn their attention to the universe, they see mighty, comprehensive affairs beyond their understanding and are astonished. To find a cure for this pain of astonishment, like a thirsty person hurrying to sweet water, they cannot help but utter: "Glory be to God." They see the subtlety of Divine Favoring and experience the pleasure that compels them to express delight. They desire more pleasure by discerning the act of favoring in the bounties they consume, and also discerning the Bestower of bounties in the act of favoring. Then like one who has discovered a buried treasure, they are relieved by saying: "All praise be to God."

When they see strange and remarkable creatures that they cannot describe, the desire to know the truth about them occupies their minds, and they find relief only in saying: "God is the All-Great." That is, their Creator is incomparably and immeasurably great, and can create and govern them with ease. Such people are like those who are greatly astounded at the moon's rotating or frightened when a mountain rises out of the ground during an earthquake. They are saved from the "burden" of astonishment and fright by putting them on the "ship" of the All-Powerful, All-Strong, All-Firm.

KNOW, O FRIEND, that your sins and evil cannot harm God; they only harm you. For example, God has no partners. Your ascribing a partner to Him does not affect His perfect, absolute sovereignty and rule over the universe. This only hurts you, for it will lead you to destruction.

KNOW, O FRIEND, that whoever relies on God finds that God is sufficient for him or her. *So, say: God is sufficient for me, what an excellent guardian He is.*

First: God is absolutely perfect. Absolute perfection is loved for its own sake, and great things are sacrificed for it.

Second: Since He is loved for His own sake, He is the true beloved, and love requires sacrifice.

Third: He is the Necessarily Existent One. In His nearness originate the lights of existence, while absence from Him brings the darkness of extinction or non-existence, and causes the human soul incurable pain by extinguishing its aspirations.

Fourth: He is the refuge of the human spirit suffocated within material existence's narrow confines, suffering from the world's deceit, crushed by the pain arising from its affection for creation.

Fifth: He is the Everlasting, by Whom things become permanent and without Whom things decay and are extinguished, which cause grief and sorrow. Without Him pain accumulates in the human spirit, whereas light pours from everywhere over one who finds and trusts in Him.

Sixth: He is the sole Owner of existence. He wants to bear your burdens of life and bodily existence that He has entrusted to you, as you cannot carry them and suffer if you think you own them. If you desire their permanence and His continued favoring, do not be grieved when He takes them from you. Bubbles containing the sun's images do not grieve when they disappear, and gladly sacrifice their apparent forms for the renewal of the sun's reflections. Fruits do not grieve when they are separated from their tree, and seeds do not grieve over the fruit's disintegration in the ground, for its disintegration means the growth of a new tree that will yield many fruits. You are also a fruit, an embodiment, of His favoring.

Seventh: He is the All-Wealthy and Bestower of wealth, and in His Hand are the keys to everything. If you become His sincere servant and then look at the universe, you will see your Master's sovereignty and magnificence and find relief. You will come to view the universe as if it were your property that you own without trouble, and the disappearance of which would not grieve you. A sincere servant of the King who is annihilated in His love becomes proud of whatever belongs to Him.

Eighth: He is the Lord of all Messengers and Prophets, saints and God-conscious people, all of whom are happy in His mercy. If you have a sound, uncorrupted heart, your knowledge of their happiness must give you happiness and pleasure.

KNOW, O FRIEND, that if your intellect is sound, you should not rejoice or grieve, be angry or complain, about anything you gain or lose here, for this world is decaying, as is your own world and you. You are not [created] to stay here permanently, nor are you made of iron or wood so that you can stay longer. You are made of ever-renewed flesh and blood and delicate limbs, and are vulnerable to everything. One part or component of you breaks, another freezes, and still another dissolves through its atoms' disintegration. The dawn of old age has broken on your head and has covered half of your head like a white shroud. The diseases visiting and intending to dwell in you are forerunners of death and destroyers of [this life's] pleasures. Eternal life is before you. Although your comfort and happiness in the Hereafter depend on what you do here, your avarice is so great that you think you can stay here forever. Awake before the throes of death awaken you.

KNOW, O FRIEND, that when you turn to the Almighty supposing that He is One known and recognized, He will become unknown and unrecognized, for your supposition is based on a commonplace, imitative knowledge about Him. In most cases, such knowledge has nothing to do with truth. The meaning it conveys to your mind is far from explaining the absolute Divine Attributes. But if you turn to the Almighty, accepting Him as One existent but unknown, then rays of true knowledge of Him will be revealed and the all-encompassing, absolute Divine Attributes manifested in the universe will appear in the light of this knowledge.

KNOW, O FRIEND, that it is enough for you, as a limitless source of pride, that you have a Master, an Owner, One powerful over all things. He is such a Powerful One that on Doomsday the heavens will be rolled up in His "Right Hand" and Earth will be His handful. He brings up, trains, and sustains you with a caring and compassion much more perfect than that of your parents. You are like a drop in the sea, the sea is like a point in the known part of the universe, and that part is like a minute particle among His huge creatures. He is the Light of Lights, the Knower of all secrets.

If a king is not occupied with his kingdom's affairs, it is not because he is too great but because he cannot do so. By contrast, due to the Eternal Sovereign's grandeur, He inscribes His Divinity's signs on the page of the sky with the pen of His making in the ink of pearl-like stars. At the same time, He inscribes His Lordship's signs on the page of the eye's pupil with the same pen in the ink of atoms.

Glory be to Him for Whose Divinity and Grandeur all heavenly objects and pearl-like planets are bright proofs, and for Whose Lordship all those smiling, luminous stars are rays of witnesses.

KNOW, O FRIEND, that like the seven-colored light, Divine Beautiful Names contain, imply, testify to, are the result of, and are reflected in one another. They may be recited simultaneously as if they were both the analogies and the conclusions reached through them, or both the arguments and the conclusions reached through them. Each Greatest Name contains all other Names to the greatest degree. Some may reach the light of the Greatest Name via some other Name or Names, and what the Greatest Name is differs according to one who tries to discover and reach it. God knows the truth.

A supplication

O God, I do not care if I lose both lives—this one and the next—or if the universe becomes mine, as you are my Lord, my Creator, and my God, and I am one created and made by You. Despite my rebelliousness and remoteness from other connections of grace, I have a connection to You, which is my being Your creature. I entreat in the tongue of this connection.

O my Creator, Lord, Provider, Owner, Fashioner, and my God. For the sake of Your Beautiful Names and Your Greatest Name; Your wise Criterion (the Qur'an) and your Noble Beloved (Prophet Muhammad, upon him be peace and blessings), Your eternal Speech, and Your Greatest Throne; and for thousands and thousands of *Say: "He is God, the One,"* have mercy on me, O God, All-Merciful, All-Pitying, All-Bounteous, Supreme Ruler.

Forgive me, O All-Forgiving, All-Covering [of sins], All-Relenting, Free-Giving. Pardon me, O All-Loving, All-Clement, All-Pardoning, All-Excusing. Favor me with Your kindness and gentleness, O All-Kind, All-Aware, All-Hearing, All-Seeing. Overlook my faults, O All-Forbearing, All-Knowing, All-Munificent, All-Compassionate. Guide us to the Straight Path, O Lord, Eternally-Besought-of-All, All-Guiding. Always favor me with Your grace and generosity, O

Originator, Everlasting, All-Just, He. Enliven my heart and [illuminate] my grave with the light of belief and the Qur'an, O Light, Ultimate Truth, All-Living, Self-Subsistent and All-Subsisting, Master of All Domains, One Having Majesty and Benevolence, First and Last, Outward and Inward, All-Strong, All-Powerful, my Master, Forgiving, Most Merciful of the Merciful.

For the sake of Your Greatest Name in the Qur'an and Prophet Muhammad, upon him be peace and blessings, who is the greatest embodiment of the meaning You have given to the creation, I ask you to open through these Beautiful Names windows through which the lights of Your Greatest Name may come into my heart while in this world and to my spirit while in my grave. Let this page be the ceiling of my grave, and these Names the windows through which the rays of the sun of truth pour into my spirit.

O God, I desire an everlasting tongue with which to call upon You until the Last Day. Accept these lines as a perpetual substitute for my mortal tongue. O God, bestow peace and blessings on our master Muhammad, upon him be peace and blessings, in a way by which You will save us from all misfortune and calamity, meet all our needs, purify us of all our evil, and forgive us all our sins and faults.

O God Who answers all prayers. Accept from me at each moment during my life and after my life unlimited blessings and peace on our master Muhammad and on His Family, Companions, helpers, and followers. Increase these callings of blessings to the number of my breaths I take in and out during my life, and forgive me and have mercy on me for the sake of each calling of blessing, and for the sake of Your Mercy, O Most Merciful of the Merciful. Amen.

Addendum

KNOW, O FRIEND, that I am compelled to unveil something very important through my works. I do not know if I have discovered it already or if it will appear in the future, or if I am only a means for someone else to discover and reach it.

There is no power and strength save with God. God is enough for us, and what a good guardian He is. O God, take us out of the world as martyrs and believers.

In the Name of God, the All-Merciful, the All-Compassionate.

I offer unlimited praise to God for the blessing of belief and Islam, and unlimited thanks to Him for each of His bounties in all circum-

> stances. Peace and blessings be upon the prince of pure saints and the good of human beings—the chosen Prophet, Muhammad—and on his purified Family and Companions, each of which is a luminous, guiding star, as long as nights and days continue.

KNOW, O FRIEND, that there are conditions special to each station. Those traveling to God should adopt an attitude particular to each station, rank, and veil that they either pass by or through, and to each state they are to experience. Whoever confuses these [with one another] makes mistakes. They would be like those who hear a horse neighing in a village and then, hearing a nightingale singing in a town, confuse the two animals with each other or expect the nightingale to neigh like a horse.

KNOW, O FRIEND, that one reason why you see worldly life as beautiful is the preceding illustrious, great persons shining as stars of guidance in the "mirror" of the world. The future is the mirror of the past. The past, already mixed into the intermediate realm between this world and the next, leaves its form in the mirror of the future, and in history and people's memories. The resulting love you feel for these people is like the following parable: On the road, someone finds a huge mirror in which he sees images of his friends and beloved ones who have emigrated to "the east" (death). But in the mirror, they appear to have gone to the west. Terrified of the east, he retreats and runs toward "the west." If the veil of unawareness and heedlessness is lifted from his face, he will see himself running in a vast desert toward a mirage and torment, not toward a source of sweet water.

KNOW, O FRIEND, that one aspect of the Qur'an's greatness and most truthful evidence of its truth is as follows: It contains whatever is necessary for complete confirmation of Divine Unity and its varieties—Unity in Essence, Attributes, Names, and Acts—and observes the balance among all exalted Divine truths. It comprehends whatever is required by the Divine Beautiful Names, preserves the proportion among them, and encompasses the essential qualities of Lordship and Divinity with perfect balance.

This quality of the Qur'an is not found in the products of any human mind, whether a saint penetrating the inner dimension of existence, an illuminist philosopher (Ishraqi) with insight into the inner side of things and events, or a perfect, purified scholar seeing into the Unseen. They cannot comprehend the absolute truth with their limited views, but only can observe an aspect of it. In their attempt to grasp it, they handle it in some extreme, unjust ways that destroy this balance and remove this perfect proportionality.

Such people are like divers gathering treasure on the sea floor. Some find a large diamond and conclude that the treasure consists of only that kind of diamond. When they hear that others have found other gems, they think that those gems are to be set in their diamond. Still others find a round ruby or a square amber. Each group supposes that the treasure consists of what it has found and that the other gems are to be added to it. If this were true, the balance and proportionality would be destroyed, and the groups would make false or unacceptable comments on (or even deny) what the others had found. Whoever uses the Sunna's criteria to examine the works of illuminist philosophers and of spiritual masters based on their particular findings and observations will agree with me.

The Qur'an is also a diver—but a diver with an open eye that sees the whole treasure and describes it exactly as it is, without going to extremes, neglecting anything, or destroying the balance and proportion among its parts. For example, it contains whatever is necessary to describe God Almighty's Grandeur, such as:

> The whole earth is His handful on Doomsday, and the heavens will be rolled up in His Right Hand. (39:67)
>
> On that day We will roll up the heavens as written scrolls are rolled up. (21:104)
>
> He fashions you in the wombs as He wills. (3:6)
>
> There is no moving creature but He has grasped it by the forelock. (11:56)
>
> He has created the heavens and Earth. (6:73)
>
> He creates you and whatever you do. (38:96)
>
> He revives Earth. (30:50)
>
> Your Lord has inspired the bee. (16:68)
>
> The sun, the moon, and the stars are all susbervient by His command. (7:54)
>
> Have they not seen the birds above them flying in lines with their wings spread out and alighting [with their wings] closed? None save the All-Merciful One sustains them. He is the Seer of all things. (67:19)

He inscribes the page of the heavens with stars and suns like inscribing the wing of a bee with its cells and particles.

> His Seat embraces the heavens and Earth. (2:255)
>
> He is with you wherever you may be. (57:4)
>
> He is the First and the Last, the Outward and the Inward, and He knows all things. (57:3)

(Deviant) sects appeared because their leaders, who "set out" into existence's inner dimension, turned back halfway in reliance on their findings. They obtained something and lost many things.

KNOW, O FRIEND, that the Qur'an mentions seven heavens. Its mentioning the heaven of the world in *We decorated the heaven of the world* (41:12) and the world as the opposite of the Hereafter, points to the fact that the remaining six heavens are related to the worlds of the Hereafter, from the intermediate world of the grave to Paradise. The heaven that we see with its stars is the heaven of the world. However, God knows best.

KNOW, O FRIEND, that you were created from "non-existence." Then, your Originator favored you by elevating you from the lowest level of existence to the level of being a Muslim human being. Whatever you received and whatever happened between your first movement and your present state is a favor of God on you. From each favor, a fruit and a color is attached to you. You are like a necklace or a cluster on which the "beads" or "grains" of favor have been strung, an index of the Almighty's favors. Existence requires a cause; non-existence does not. You will be asked how you attained so many favors while obtaining a full, perfect existence from the level of being a particle to death, how you deserved them, and whether you thanked [God] for them. No one asks a stone why it has not become a tree, or a tree why it has not become a person.

O SAID, YOU WRETCHED, ARROGANT CREATURE! You are a point in the middle of the series of creatures. You have been distinguished with infinite favor, and are responsible for giving thanks for each of them. As for the favors conferred on those above you, they are not for you. You will not be questioned about what you cannot attain, just as a particle has no right to sigh, saying: "Alas! Why did I not become a sun?" or a bee to complain to its Creator: "I wished you had created me as a fruit-bearing date-palm."

KNOW, O EGO, that your refusal to give everything its due and burden it only with what it can bear is one reason why you perish and why you are led to perdition, deviation, and humiliation. You burden a soldier with an army's requirements. You want to see the sun, with all its grandeur and planets, in its image, in a drop's eye, or on a flower's face. In truth, a drop or a flower describes the sun to you [each according to its capacity of reflection], but they do not have its qualities.

KNOW, O FRIEND, that the ownership and dominion of all things belong to Him. He owns your body, which He has entrusted to you. There is no benefit in worrying about it, and no good in what is not permanent. Avoid trying to do what you cannot do. You are destined to die, and death resulting in life is better than life resulting in death.

KNOW, O FRIEND, that while the image of something reflected in a mirror is not identical with the thing itself, it is not other than that either. The image is at once both identical to and other than the real thing. As the image is the form of the "meaning" reflected, it is identical with the thing. What is true of the thing is also true of the image. However, as the image only consists of the thing's form reflected in a mirror, it is other than the thing. Given this, although it is not identical with the thing itself, it is not something other than the thing. Similarly, what is reflected in the mirror of the mind, since it is the form of the meaning, is something known. But since it is the description of the thing reflected, it is knowledge.

KNOW, O FRIEND, that many worlds are situated in existence without one preventing the other. If on a pitch-dark night you enter a room with walls made of glass and illuminated with an electric lamp, first you will see numerous illuminated places in the walls, and the town itself being reflected and illuminated. You can change or alter these reflected images. You also will notice that the lamp is nearest to the remotest of the reflected lamps, as it is the original of all the reflected lamps. This is how part of this grain-sized existence can contain a whole world of reflected existence.

All these qualities are true of many other things, even of the Necessary Existence and the world of contingencies, which are shadows of the lights of the One Whose existence is absolutely necessary. Although the existence of the world of contingencies is illusory by itself, it has stability by the command of the Almighty and is seen and sensed by the creation of the Necessarily Existent One.

KNOW, O FRIEND, that this domain of existence must have One Who created and owns it. In addition, the Owner must make Himself known to humanity, who can perceive this domain's beauty [and understand that it is] testifying to the Owner's perfection. Humanity, who has been made a ruler on Earth (its cradle), which was leveled and prepared for human dwelling, controls Earth and its ceiling (heaven). In addition, despite human weakness and smallness, as testified to by our strange and wonderful human disposition, we are the noblest of creatures. Also, among the causes [that God uses to veil His acts and free disposing], humanity is the most comprehensive and influential when it comes to choice and free decision. So, the Owner sends the one [Prophet Muhammad] who will make the Owner known to those inhabitants of His domain who are unaware of Him, and inform them of what is pleasing to Him and what He demands from them.

KNOW, O FRIEND, that all your feelings and faculties, even those of supposition and imagination, finally are compelled to agree on and take refuge in truth. Falsehood can find no room in them. They affirm that the universe cannot be different from how the Qur'an describes it.

KNOW, O FRIEND, that there is no collision and repulsion between the worlds of light, heat, air, electricity, and gravitation and those of ether, ideas or immaterial forms, and the intermediate world of the grave. They exist together with you wherever you are, without one preventing and being mixed with the other. Similarly, although much more spacious or larger than this narrow world, many of the unseen worlds can exist together. Also, air and water do not prevent us from journeying, from going [on or through it], just as glass does not stop light from passing through it, and a solid object does not hinder the penetration of X-rays, the intellect's light, and an angel's spirit. Iron cannot block heat's permeation and electricity's conduction. Nothing can stop gravity's penetration, the spirit's movement, and the intellect's light. Likewise, this solid, material world does not stop or prevent spirit beings from circulating, jinn from moving around, Satan from infiltrating and penetrating, and angels from journeying.

KNOW, O FRIEND, that the light and those things made of light are like an eye, a lamp, and the sun. It is equal to them [to encompass with their manifestations] whether they are one or many, part or whole. Look at the sun, and see how planets, oceans, bubbles, drops, dewdrops, raindrops, or glass contain and reflect its images simultaneously and with great ease. The disposition of the Book of the Universe by the Eternal Sun, the Light of Lights, is similar. He writes all its chapters, sections, paragraphs, lines, sentences, words, and letters at once and with absolute ease. He declares: *Your creation and resurrection are like but (those of) a single soul* (30:28).

KNOW, O FRIEND, that one who reflects upon the motions of tiniest component particles of things and how they fulfill their purpose(s) in life becomes convinced that there is One Who orders them: "Stop and be settled!" It is like the casting-mold ordering the melting gold in a firm manner: "Do not flow! Be fixed and stable within the borders of the mold made for a particular purpose!" What commands the tiniest component particles of things is the Encompassing Knowledge that manifests Itself as Destiny—the power destining, determining, and ordaining. Destiny becomes a fixed measure or amount, and the measure becomes a mold.

KNOW, O FRIEND, that just as the Qur'an's verses interpret each other, the parts of the Book of the Universe also interpret each other. Just as the corporeal world truly needs the sun from which the lights of the Almighty's favorings diffuse upon it, so the spiritual world needs the sun of Prophethood to diffuse the lights of the Almighty's compassion upon it. The Prophethood of Ahmad—Muhammad— is as manifest, clear, and certain as the sun at noon [on a clear summer day]. Does daytime need any evidence?

KNOW, O FRIEND, that the purposes of something's life do not concern only its life, benefit, and perfection. They are related to that thing in one respect only, but are related to the Bestower of life in infinite respects. The realization of the thing's inherent purpose takes a long time, while the purposes relating to the Bestower of life are realized instantly. By reflecting the manifestations of His Most Beautiful Names, a living thing fulfills instantly its function of praising its Creator with all His Attributes of Perfection, Grace, and Majesty.

KNOW, O FRIEND, that each person is like a species of other beings, for each one has a past and a future. [Since all human cells are renewed every 6 months,] everyone's two individual forms depart every year, but only after depositing in that person all of their pain, sin, ambition, and so on. It is as if human beings are all-inclusive individuals.

Also, their intellectual capacity and comprehensive thoughts, feelings, and emotions make each individual like a species. As an individual and as a species, they are responsible for improving the world in accordance with God's commands [which we call vicegerency] and being the pivot around which their particular world and the whole world rotate. Their conscious concern with all parts of creation, as well as the disposal of many plant and animal species and of elements, cause each person to be like a species.

Furthermore, a believer's prayer for all inhabitants of the heavens and Earth shows that he or she becomes like a world or its center through belief. Consider what occurs in animal and plant species every year in the name of death, revival, and renewal. Look at the imprints and traces of God's Mercy manifested every year in the fruits renewed or recruited with their almost identical successors, and at the resurrection of many insect and vermin species with perfect ease. The same thing happens in every person. Through all these "verses" of creation, the Book of the Universe indicates the world's overall destruction upon humanity and humanity's resurrection, a fact that the Qur'an points to with its verses of Revelation. I have mentioned rational arguments for the Resurrection in the Tenth Word and the Twenty-ninth Word.[63]

KNOW, O FRIEND, that each melody of the Qur'an assumes a new attitude and mood according to the level of the audience it is guiding. Try to assume the mood of the intermediaries ranging from Gabriel, who brought it to the Prophet, to the one from whom you hear it directly. While listening to its recitation, try to hear it as if you were listening to the Prophet reciting it at the summit of Prophethood to all people and other beings. Then assume the manner of Gabriel while he recites it to the Prophet, on the "highest horizon." Finally, try to hear it as if you were listening to it from behind 70,000 veils from the Eternally Speaking One, Who speaks to the Prophet at "the distance of two bows' length."[64]

KNOW, O FRIEND, that your share of consciousness and knowledge is proportional to your share in your existence, for there is no waste in existence, cause is proportionate to effect, and power to result. When your share in your existence is compared to that of the One Who created you, it is like a hair compared to a thick rope, a fiber compared to clothes. When your consciousness and knowledge of yourself is compared to your Creator's knowledge and sight of you, they are a firefly's light at midday. You are in the dark-

63 Said Nursi, *The Words*, The Light, Inc., New Jersey: 2005.

64 "The distance of two bows' length" is mentioned in Qur'an 53:9 to express the Prophet's nearness to God during his Ascension. It is metaphorical. (Tr.)

ness of indifference, and the night of nature or naturalism shows you your light as if it is a piercing star.

KNOW, O FRIEND, that between God's acts is a proportion, and between His works is a similarity. His Names are reflected on one another, His Attributes are intermixed, and His Essential Qualities are commingled with one another. However, each has a particular attitude and way of manifestation and operation, with the others dependent on and subordinate to it. In the sphere of one's manifestation and operation, rule and consequence are not attributed to others, nor should others' imprints and works be sought from that one. So when you look at inanimate objects, first consider His Power and Grandeur, and then you will see the other Names' manifestations as subordinate to these. When you look at animals, first consider the Names that are most manifested on them. He created and established a measure for all things.

KNOW, O FRIEND, that *There is no force and strength save with God* has a relation or concern with each stage you undergo during your creation, from the stage of being a component of elements in nature to that of being a believing human being. In connection with each stage and [for the satisfaction of] each sense and faculty, you have different needs and expectations and suffer different pains:

> *There is no force* to bring forth from non-existence *and no strength* to give existence, save with God.
>
> *There is no force* to save from decay *and no strength* to give permanence, save with God.
>
> *There is no force* to cause harm *and no strength* to give benefit, save with God.
>
> *There is no force* to protect one from misfortune *and no strength* to meet needs, save with God.
>
> *There is no force* to enable one to resist sin *and no strength* to enable one to continue his or her worship of and obedience to Him, save with God.
>
> *There is no force* to save one from pain and torment *and no strength* to bestow bounties, save with God.
>
> *There is no force* to save one from evil *and no strength* to earn grace and do good, save with God.
>
> *There is no force* to enable one to endure pain *and no strength* to enable one to attain his or her ambitions, save with God.
>
> *There is no force* to remove the veil of darkness *and no strength* to send illuminating lights, save with God, the High, the Grand.

KNOW, O FRIEND, that whoever trusts God and relies upon Him, *He is sufficient for him* [to protect against evil and attain all good].

> *God is sufficient for us and what a good Guardian He is,* for He is our owner and the owner of all things. Therefore, if we submit ourselves to Him, it will be as if everything is in our possession.
>
> *God is sufficient for us and what a good Guardian He is,* for He is the Absolutely Perfect One, and perfection is loved by Him. It is worth being sacrificed for the sake of that perfection.
>
> *God is sufficient for us and what a good Guardian He is,* for He is the All-Majestic and All-Beautiful One having absolute perfection. Beauty is loved by Him and, for the sake of the zeal and ecstasy produced by the renewals that His Beauty's manifestations bring about, we die smiling and are revived rejoicing.
>
> *God is sufficient for us and what a good Guardian He is,* for He is the Necessarily Existent One, Who gives existence to all things. Our knowledge of the absolute necessity of His existence makes everything that exists (except God) subservient to us and bestows on us eternal existence. Our ignorance or denial of His necessary Existence leaves us enveloped by the darkness of non-existence.
>
> *God is sufficient for us and what a good Guardian He is,* for He is Everlasting and Eternal, uncontained by time and space. *All things are perishable except His "Face"* (28:88).
>
> *God is sufficient for us and what a good Guardian He is,* for the world is transient and life is ephemeral.
>
> *God is sufficient for us and what a good Guardian He is,* for without Him, all pleasure in the world changes into pain. By turning to Him and connecting with His Mercy, one is saved from the pain of being mortal, and fleeting pleasures gain permanence.
>
> *God is sufficient for us and what a good Guardian He is,* for one receives the lights of existence through Him, while without Him one falls into the darkness of non-existence.
>
> *God is sufficient for us and what a good Guardian He is,* for if we recognize Him and refer our needs and complaints to Him, He satisfies them. If we turn to causes and refer our needs and complaints to them—although causes are blind and deaf, and cannot see or hear us—we are confused and lost. We are like one who, although allowed to refer complaints directly to the king who can answer them instantly, instead asks the whole population of the country, one by one, for help.

KNOW, O FRIEND, that among the Qur'an's miraculous subtleties and evidence that it is an all-encompassing mercy for creation are the following: Just as each one of us has his or her own world within this world, we also have a Qur'an that addresses our individual temperaments, educates us, cures us of our [spiritual] diseases, and answers our intellectual quests.

Among the Qur'an's merits of guidance are the following:

There is a perfect coherence, consistency, and connection among its verses, which enables each person to select specific verses for guidance and to cure personal spiritual diseases. This is what scholars and spiritual guides belonging to different schools do. Although the Qur'an was revealed in parts and on different occasions, its verses are arranged, like the beads of a necklace, in perfect harmony and coherence. Its division into verses and chapters does not cause discord and disunity, and does not distract readers from its main purposes. Its transition to other verses or groups of verses causes no disruption. Most of its verses are subtly interlinked with one another so that they can be mentioned together or gathered together to form, for example, a compilation of supplications.

The verses of *Surat al-Ikhlas* corroborate one another, as they are both arguments for one another and conclusions to be reached from those arguments.[65] Similarly, because of its verses' interrelation and comprehensive meaning, there are innumerable Qur'ans within the single Qur'an, and a book is formed around each of its truths.

> O God, Revealer of the Qur'an, for the sake of the Qur'an, make the Qur'an my intimate friend during my life and following my death, and a light in my heart and my grave.
>
> There is no deity but God. Muhammad is His Messenger.

An addendum to the addendum

In the Name of God, the All-Merciful, the All-Compassionate.

All praise be to God, the All-Merciful, among the greatest fruits of the sacred tree of Whose Mercy are our master Muhammad and Paradise, both hanging down to this world and the next. He is the All-Powerful One. All these ever-renewed, spectacular creatures and heavenly objects

65 *Surat al-Ikhlas*: "Say: "He is God, (He is) One. God is the Eternally-Besought-of-All. He begets not, nor was He begotten. There is none comparable to Him." (112:1-4). For its verses corroborating one another and being both arguments for one another and conclusions to be reached from those arguments, see Said Nursi, *The Words*, The Light, Inc., New Jersey: 2005, pp. 393-394.

are witnesses of His Lordship. These multicolored plants and diverse animals in the garden of Earth are marvels of His Art and evidence of His Divinity. These lustrous flowers and, with all their leaves, blossoms and fruits, these fruit-bearing trees are miracles of His Power and proofs of His Mercy. All testify that He is powerful over all things.

Past events are miracles of His Power indicating that He can make their likes in the future. Nothing that has happened or will happen is beyond His Power's decree. In relation to Him, the tiniest particles and the largest suns are the same. He is the Evident Truth, One, Single. In their various tongues, the universe's particles and components point to His absolute Beauty and say:

Though we differ in expressing, You have the same Beauty;
Whatever exists [in the universe] points to that Beauty.

With all its chapters, sections, paragraphs, sentences, words, and letters, the Book of the Universe reads the signs of His absolute necessary Existence and Unity, and its lines announce:

Reflect upon the lines of the [Book of the] Universe,
for they are letters to you from the Highest Realm.

Peace and blessings be upon our master Muhammad and on all his Family and Companions.

O REBELLIOUS SAID, look at yourself instead of what is not for you. What are you? What is your value? What do you rely on? You are an embodiment of impotence and neediness, for whatever you have is conferred on you by God. And yet you sleep and believe yourself to be awake.

Your body is impotent, and your need is its spirit that incites it to move. With all that you have, you are an embodiment of God's favoring. Your life passes in sleep. Alas! I have drowned in a drop that has become an ocean swallowing me. I am lost in a moment that has become like an eternity for me. I imagine that this flash of life is a shining sun that will never set.

O WRETCHED SAID, your capital is only about $60, of which you have already spent $45 to satisfy your worldly needs.[66] You have forgotten and neglected your "house," and your property has become a debt for you to pay and a fire. As for the remaining $15, it is doubtful whether you will be able

---

[66] The author uses $60 to refer to a person's normal lifespan, and $45 to refer to his age when he wrote this book. (Tr.)

to spend a part of it, or any of it at all. Whatever you spend of it, spend it on your permanent house. Let one third of it, at least, be a light for you. Your ignorance and loss are great, for you have spent most of your capital on this passing life, and so what remains for your eternal abode is insignificant. You are a heedless traveler, for you have departed already from your home and town and are about to step out of this transient world.

KNOW, O FRIEND, that those who say: "Things are formed by themselves," "Causes have brought it about," or "Nature requires it [to be so]" cause much confusion, for such statements are false. You exist. So, according to the first statement, you are your own creature. According to the second one, [material] causes have brought you about. According to the last one, some unconscious, deaf, and blind laws or forces [attributed to nature] or lifeless things called "nature" required your existence. But the truth is that you are a creature of God, the Almighty.

As for the first statement, things cannot be formed by themselves, because each particle or atom forming your body would have to have an eye to see your whole body and all of creation, as well as consciousness [to be aware of all requirements of life and existence]. Your perfect composition, the perfection of art in you, requires this, for all particles of existence are in vital and substantial relations with each other and with all creation.

To print a book, a printing house must have as many iron letters or keys as needed to print it. If you made yourself, you must contain as many molds as the number of atoms in you, for they are in conscious relation and communication with one another. Your composition is uniform, meaning that all parts are in close interrelation with each other. Therefore, like the stones forming an arch or a dome, all your atoms or building blocks should be both dominant over and dominated by one another. They also should be like the manifestations of the Names and Attributes of the One Who rolls up the heavens like a scroll rolled up for books—both opposite and complementary to each other.

Causes cannot create anything by themselves. For example, if bottles containing medical ingredients fall off the shelf and become mixed on the floor, would the desired medicine be produced? Using the same analogy, could you be formed by chance or random causes? How could innumerable deaf, blind, and unconscious causes come together and create something that has perfect order? By coming together they only increase in deafness and blindness. Each human being is a perfect work of art [intelligent, conscious, and equipped with endless and extremely complex feelings, senses, and faculties, and feeling infinite need]. How can that which is deaf, blind, and unconscious bestow hearing, sight, and consciousness on something else?

Assume that innumerable causes come together in a most orderly fashion and in exact measure to create a cell in your eye. With the same amount of effort, then, the universe's basic parts or elements, including huge heavenly objects, should be able to assemble themselves in your palm or in each of your cells. Why? Because if you work in a house, this means the house contains you. All of the universe's parts and contents are related to humanity. So if causes created you, the entire universe should be able to operate within each of your body's parts and be contained by one of your cells. This is a most inconceivable sophistry.

Nature cannot create because it is something supposed to exist, a name given by those who do not know the real facts of the matter. However, in its true meaning, it is a Divine art, a painting by the All-Merciful.

"Natural forces" are only manifestations of the Power of the All-Merciful, All-Knowing, All-Aware, All-Willing. "Chance" is only a mistaken supposition put forward by those who are unaware of or deny the Single Maker. In many of my treatises included in this book, I have argued that this wonderful art [that constitutes the essence of what they call nature] is really the work of the Power of the All-Aware, All-Seeing, having all the attributes of Perfection.

Could something restricted, solid, inanimate, whose existence or non-existence is equally possible (meaning that one must prefer its existence and create it), have woven the universe's garment? Could a gnat have participated in weaving these perfectly designed and adorned garments in which those words are dressed? The only explanation for your existence and that of creation is that everything that has been created is a creature of an Eternal Maker, and that they all testify to this fact. Among these witnesses is the visible, corporeal universe, with all its particles and compounds, that testifies to Him in 55 tongues (explained in the Fourth Treatise.)

There are other witnesses: the Qur'an and all other revealed Books; the writings of saints and believers in God's Existence and Unity; all that exists and happens in the universe; the lord of creation and all other Prophets, saints, and angels: Prophet Muhammad; humanity and jinn with all their "natural" needs; and God—all of these testify that *there is no deity but He* (3:18).

KNOW, O FRIEND, that the falsehood of attributing creation to things themselves, nature, or causes can be explained through the example of a fruit-bearing tree. If you attribute this tree to God, the One and Single, you attribute it to its seed and to the laws of germination, creation, and growth issuing from the Necessarily Existent Being, the One and Single, and on which that seed depends. The tree is dependent on the laws issuing from a Single Creator because of the ease coming from the Oneness of Him Who governs its germination, growth, and life. It is just as easy for that Single Creator to grow that seed into a large coconut palm bearing countless fruits or into a very small one with only a few fruits.

But if you attribute a tree to itself, causes, or nature, then each fruit, blossom, leaf, branch, and twig on it would need whatever the whole tree does, for each part is an epitome of a whole. Thus, whatever is needed by the whole is needed by each part.

Consider these two alternatives. The first one, which is done by God with perfect ease, makes creation necessary and inevitable, whereas the second one is so unbelievably difficult that it renders the creation of anything inconceivable.

In short: If you attribute creation to things themselves, you must accept that every cell of your body can encompass the universe. If you attribute creation to material causes, you must affirm that every cell is like a room in which all causes operating in the universe are included, for all cells are the same and display the same structure. This uniformity leads you to unity in diversity, to the interrelatedness seen in the universe, and therefore to the Maker's Unity. Something unified, displaying uniformity, and composed of countless interrelated parts in a basic relationship with each other could not have been created by more than one Creator. How can a cell in which even a gnat's two wings cannot be included contain the many material, bodily causes needed for it to function?

Something having external existence is more established, stable, and fixed than something having only an ideal existence. A tiny particle of the former can contain a mountain of the latter. [For example, a mountain's reflection can fit into a small mirror. Since whatever exists is contingent, its existence or non-existence was equally possible. Its coming into existence was the result of a preference by One having the absolute authority of preference, the One with an absolutely necessary existence without which nothing could exist. Therefore,] that Necessary Existence is more established, stable, and fixed than all material existence. It is the Real Existence, and so cannot be contained by contingent existence.

Contingent things—whatever exists other than the Necessarily Existent One—are reflected in the mirror of the Eternal, all-encompassing Knowledge; their real existence consists in their existence in that Knowledge. They come into material existence through the manifestation of the lights of Necessary Existence, and thus show the Necessarily Existent One's existence. Their material existence in the corporeal world, the result of their transference from the all-encompassing sphere of Knowledge, can never be of the same essence and quality, or of the same existential degree, as that of Real Existence.

KNOW, O FRIEND, that solid, material, and corporeal things are acted on and affected by immaterial things or things of light. Look at sunlight and a mountain. The former comes from the sky and operates on Earth freely, while the latter, despite its huge size, can do nothing and has no effect on its environment. The subtler and more composed of light something is, the more effective and active it is; the more material and solid something is, the more susceptible it is to being acted upon and affected. We can conclude from this that the Creator of causes and effects is He Who is the Light of Lights: *Nothing is like Him, He is the All-Hearing, the All-Seeing* (42:11). *Vision comprehends Him not, but He comprehends all vision. He is the All-Subtle, the All-Aware* (6:103).

KNOW, O FRIEND, that reflecting [on creation and God's signs in the universe] is like light, for it removes or melts your frozen heedlessness to and unawareness of [God]. Being careful and attentive is like fire, for it burns your "dried rubbish" of doubt and suspicion [about Him]. However, when you reflect on yourself (and on your inner world, feelings, emotions, faculties, and conscience), reflect deeply, as the Divine Name "the Inward" wants you to do so. The perfection of art is seen in its details and ramifications.

When you reflect on the outer world, do so briefly and superficially, for you only need to understand the foundations upon which it is based. This is what the Name "the Outward" requires, for the splendor of art becomes more evident and more dazzling when looked on and examined as a whole.

The outer world is very spacious and has no shores. If you dive into it, you may drown.

If you go deep in your inner world but make a brief and fast journey in the outer world, you can approach unity. Individual parts acquire wholeness, compounds become composites, and composites become unified. From this unity issues the light of conviction of unity. If you only make a brief and superficial examination of your inner world while going into detail during your travels in the outer world, the diversity of things will engender confusion and doubt. This will strengthen your ego and ingrain heedlessness in you, developments that will make you incline to naturalism and, eventually, away from the diversity of things and to misguidance. O God, do not include us among the misguided! Amen.

KNOW, O FRIEND, that it is narrated that when people move [with greed], their provision stops. When they stop [showing greed], their provision moves. This explains a profound truth. Trees do not move, and their provision comes to them. Animals move with greed, and their provision is motionless on the stems of plants. With its diverse colors and smells, a plant invites hungry animals to itself and rouses them to move toward it.

KNOW, O FRIEND, that human beings are strange creatures. They heedlessly abandon a great good if they think it might harm them even in a small way. But when it comes to true guidance proven by thousands of proofs, they abandon it due to a slight doubt and embrace misguidance. If we are so cautious that we abandon a thing that might harm us only marginally, why do we embrace that which will cause us great harm in the Hereafter?

KNOW, O FRIEND, that the human soul has endless need and suffers endless pain. It has an appetite for endless pleasure and nourishes endless ambition. Even compassion may cause endless pain for a misguided soul [because of its unbelief in God and its distrust in His Destiny and true Compassion]. So you cannot ask: "Am I so valuable and worth so much that God will destroy this world and then rebuild it to judge me therein?"

O MISGUIDED, DOUBTFUL ONE! Do not be deceived here. The pleasure you find in this world depends on a misleading argument. Those who doubt the afterlife's existence, who fear being mortal and facing eternal extinction, may seek relief in the probability that there is eternal happiness in the other world. However, when they feel obliged to do religious duties, they seek relief in the probability that there is no other world and that they will not be called to account for what they did in this world. Through such ways they seek to escape both kinds of pain. But soon the problem is solved and the truth unveiled: The first alternative throws them immediately into accumulated pain, and the second alternative causes them to encounter Hell's torments.

They try to console themselves by thinking: "The coming calamity [death and the punishment to follow] will embrace most people. Since I will be like everyone else, why should I care?" However when death approaches, their pain increases proportionally to the number of the afflicted. In addition to their own pain, they feel that of their relatives and friends. Since people feel innate relations with other people, the misfortune's generality causes their own pain to increase.

Do not think that what you taste in heedlessness and doubt is real pleasure, for in reality they contain severe and accumulated pain that will attack you all at once and appear as the torments of Hell. If you want this pain to be transformed into renewed pleasure, and that fire into light, give up conceit and prostrate before God in humility five times a day. Be so humble before God that the "table" of the Qur'an should descend with the light and gifts of belief. Continue to reflect on its verses and "natural" phenomena, and engage in regular worship, so that the veil of doubt and heedlessness may burn away, the sweet taste of being saved from the bitterness of misguidance may emerge, and the pleasure of supplicating to God Almighty arise.

KNOW, O FRIEND, that servanthood to God Almighty requires submission. You cannot test God [whether He will fulfill His promise]. The Lord has the right to test His servant, not the servant his Lord.

KNOW, O FRIEND, that the spheres of the Divine Names "the Inward" and "the Outward" are both within and face each other. Those who limit themselves to the latter, seeking Him only in nature, eventually associate partners with God by attributing creativity and creative effect to causes and nature. Those seeking to reach Him only in the light of the former eventually attribute division and union [with certain human beings] to God.

The sun's images in transparent things carry the sun's attributes, and thus may lead one who cannot distinguish between the real and the reflected image to consider each image as the sun itself. Similarly, one seeking to reach God only in the light of the Divine Name "the Inward" may confuse

God's manifestations in oneself, heart, and other inner senses and faculties with God Himself. This may lead people to see themselves as incarnations of God.

Those who limit themselves to the Name "the Outward" and those who restrict themselves to the Name "the Inward" are like those who, respectively, follow a superficial interpretation of the Qur'an and reject the Sunna, and those who follow only an esoteric interpretation of Islam. They forget that Islam is the middle, straight way.

> O Revealer of the Qur'an, for the sake of the Qur'an, guide us to the middle, straight way. Amen. Amen. Amen.

To conclude:

- Humanity is the fruit of the Tree of Creation, and therefore its most perfect and comprehensive part.
- Everyone has a particular world within this world. In its center is the individual who "owns" it.
- My struggle against my ego and nature in the outer world.
- Nine things of which the ego is unaware.
- When Destiny allows misfortune to reach you, you are like a sheep that must be prevented from entering a public pasture.
- Your heart was not created to be preoccupied with worldly affairs.
- The Qur'an can satisfy everyone's intellectual appetite.
- Everything that will happen to you has been predetermined by Destiny.
- If you were responsible for maintaining this material domain, you would be so distressed that you hardly could benefit from it.
- A minute transparent particle contains the sun's image, even though it cannot hold two particles of its own size and nature. Similarly, all constituent particles and compounds in the universe receive manifestations of the luminous, absolute Divine Power, accompanied by Divine Knowledge and Will.
- *Glory be to God* implies the servant's contingent nature and distance from God. *Praise be to God* implies God's nearness to the servant and His creatures with His Mercy and Grace.
- God, from His Mercy and Favor, buys the property (our existence) He has entrusted to us for a high price so that it may be preserved permanently.
- Sins, especially frequent ones, contain seeds of unbelief.
- The miraculousness of the Qur'an has about 40 different radiations.

- The Eternal One does not let that which is considered essential pass into absolute non-existence.
- The grave is a door. On this side are suffering and wretchedness; on the other side are mercy and happiness.
- Your sins and evil harm only you, not God.
- Whoever relies on God, God is enough for him or her.
- Do not rejoice at or grieve over, or be angry at or complain about, what you gain or lose in this transitory world.
- If you turn to the Almighty supposing that He is One known and recognized, He will become unknown and unrecognized. If you turn to Him accepting that He is One, existent but unknown, the rays of true knowledge of Him will be revealed to you.
- The fact that you have a Master, an Owner, One powerful over all things, is a source of limitless pride.
- Like light containing seven colors, Divine Beautiful Names contain and imply one another.
- A supplication.
- Each spiritual station has specific conditions attached to it.
- An aspect of the Qur'an's greatness and the most truthful evidence of its truth.
- Your ego may be one cause of your perishing, deviation, and humiliation.
- A reflected image is not identical with that thing itself, but it also is not something other than that thing.
- Many worlds are situated in existence. One does not prevent the other.
- There is no collision and repulsion between the worlds of light, heat, air, electricity, and gravitation and also those of ether, ideas or immaterial forms, and the intermediate world of the grave.
- Just as Qur'anic verses interpret each other, the parts of the Book of the Universe interpret each other.
- Each person is like a species of other beings.
- The Qur'an's recitation assumes, for each of its melodies, a new attitude and mood according its audience's intellectual and spiritual level.
- Your share in your consciousness and knowledge is proportional to your share in your existence.
- Between God's acts there is a proportion, and between His works there is a similarity. One Name and Attribute has a particular way of manifestation on a particular thing, with the others dependent on and subordinate to it.

- *There is no force and strength save with God* has a relation or concern with each stage of your creation.
- Subtleties of the Qur'an's miraculousness and evidence that it is an all-encompassing mercy for creation.
- Look at yourself. What are you? What is your value? What do you rely on?
- The meaning of such false assertions as: "Things are formed by themselves," "Causes have brought it about," and "Nature requires it [to be so]."
- Why attributing creation to things themselves, nature, or causes is mistaken.
- Reflection removes your indifference to and unawareness of [God]. When you reflect on your inner world, do so deeply. When you reflect on the outer world, do so briefly and superficially.
- When you move [with greed], your provision stops. When you stop [showing greed], your provision moves.
- You abandon a great good out of fear that it may harm you in a very small way. So, why do you abandon true guidance, although there are thousands of proofs for its truth, and adopt misguidance carrying limitless harm?
- The spheres of the Divine Names "the Inward" and "the Outward" are both within and face each other. Those who limit themselves to the latter eventually associate partners with God, while those seeking to reach Him only in the light of the former eventually attribute division and union [with certain human beings] to God.

The Seventh Treatise

The Seventh Treatise

A flower from the garden of the Qur'an

Every living creature is like a regular soldier who works on behalf of the king and in his name. You are mistaken if you think you are your own lord, for you are subject to perishing.

The absolute order and balance observed in the universe are two of the principles of the All-Merciful, and two chapters from the Manifest Book and the Book of the Universe. The Qur'an expounds or translates these two books, the index of the two chapters, and the concise summary of the two principles.

In the Name of God, the All-Merciful, the All-Compassionate.

All praise be to God, the All-Wise Ruler Who has ordered and organized this universe with the laws of His way of acting, and has given it a certain shape and form with the principles of His Decree and Destiny. He has built it with the rules of His Will and Wisdom, decorated it with the standards of His Favoring and Mercy, and illuminated it with the manifestations of His Names and Attributes. He is the All-Powerful, Self-Subsistent and Everlasting.

This universe, with all its outer and inner features and properties, contents, decorations, and beauty, is no more than the lines of the Pen of His Decree and Destiny. It is the designs of the compasses of His Knowledge and Wisdom, the decorations of the "Bright Hand" of His Art and Favoring. The universe consists of the flower gardens of His Bountifulness and Munificence, the fruits of His gushing Mercy and Benevolence, and the gleams of the manifestations of His Absolute Beauty, Grace and Perfection. Exalted is His Masjesty.

Praise be to Him to the number of all the particles in the whole universe multiplied by themselves.

O One Who has manifested all those wonderful creatures through His Names' lightning-like manifestation. O One in relation to Whose Power the minutest particles and planets are the same (in creation and direction). O One Who has inscribed all those adorned worlds according to the measures of the Manifest Record—the source of the order and balance.

Before every pause and start by which all particles and compounds of the universe start moving, we offer You the testimony of belief: We testify that there is no deitş but You—You are One, without partner. We testify that Muhammad is Your servant and Messenger, whom You sent as a mercy for all worlds.

O God, bestow peace and blessings on him, and his Family and Companions, to the number of the Qur'an's letters. By your permission, it takes on forms in the mirrors of air molecules during their recitation by every reciter, from the first day of its revelation to the Day of Resurrection.

O WRETCHED SAID! YOUR LIVELIHOOD REACHES YOU THROUGH either another's choice or without the intervention of any free (human) choice. In the latter case, it comes in God's Name and for His sake. Receive it and eat it saying God's Name and thanking Him alone. If something comes to you through choice, only receive and eat it if God's Name has been invoked. When you are given something to eat, remember or consider its real Owner and direct your attention to Him—as alluded to in: *Eat not of that on which God's Name is not mentioned* (6:121).

However, if they give it and you have to receive it, invoke God's Name on it and consider the One Who has bestowed it on that person (who gives it to you) and on you. Consider the act of bestowing in what is bestowed, and the real Bestower in the act of bestowing. Such consideration means giving thanks. Then, thank the person through whom that thing has reached you, as it has come to you through him or her. But beware, O my heart, that you first consider the real Bestower.

In short, mention God's Name twice on that which comes to you through someone else, and once on that which comes to you through no one. Do not take the means for a real cause. If you get something through someone's action, you suppose that that particular action is the real reason why it came to you. But such a view is mistaken. If you think a thing is absent due to the absence of some other thing, act, or person, you ascribe its existence to the existence of that thing, act, or person. But according to God's way of acting, the absence of even one condition, part, or cause necessary for a thing's existence results in that thing's absence, for its existence depends on the existence of all conditions, parts, or causes. So, can one entrusted with opening and closing the main valve of the irrigation canals that water a garden's flowers claim that he or she is the real maker and owner of those plants? This helps us to understand the extent of our unawareness and forgetfulness of the real Maker, Owner, and Director, and of associating partners with Him unknowingly.

BEWARE, O MY HEART, that you do not ascribe any work or product resulting from a group's effort to yourself or to the group's representative, leader, or guide. Doing so is a grave error that will cause you to feel a false and awful self-conceit, arrogance, and egotism. It opens the door to associating partners with God unknowingly, for the means is taken for the doer, with the result that you seek and appeal to the means, asking the "doorman" for what belongs to the "king."

BEWARE, O MY HEART. Whenever a certain effusion of spiritual radiance and ecstasy reaches you through someone, do not think that he or she is its source, for he or she is nothing more than a means of reflecting [like a mirror] what is manifested in him or her. However, your devotion to that person causes you to imagine that what flows to your heart from the Director of Hearts is first received by your spiritual guide and then reflected to you consciously. You resemble those who focus on a piece of glass and, after a certain period of concentration, begin to travel in the World of Representations or Immaterial Forms, see some marvels, and think that they really appear or are manifested in the mirror. Such a view is mistaken.

KNOW, O SEEKER OF HELP from [material or natural] causes. You have chosen the wrong source and are making a wrong appeal, just like one who considers gaining weight to be a sign of good health when in reality it is due to an illness.

Imagine that you see a palace being built of different marvelous jewels. But some can be found only in China, others only in Morocco or Yemen, and still some others only in Siberia. Would you not say that only one who dominates the whole world, who can have anything he wants brought to him whenever he wants it, can build that palace?

Each living thing is like a building, and each animal is like a Divine palace. Humanity is the most beautiful and wonderful palace [its jewels—particles or atoms—are gathered from many worlds: the Supreme Preserved Tablet, the worlds of spirits and immaterial forms, and from the worlds of air, water, earth, light, and fire]. Human needs are infinite, and human desires encompass the heavens and Earth. As human beings have connections with everything in this world and the Hereafter, they have no right to pray and worship that which is not the One Who dominates Earth and heavens and holds the reins of the world and the Hereafter.

KNOW, O MY HEART, that the stupidest people are those who do not recognize the sun while seeing its image in a mirror, but rather love the mirror and seek to preserve it so that they can hold onto the sun permanently. If only they understood that the sun does not perish or disappear when the mirror does, they would direct their love only to the sun itself. A reflection does not depend on the mirror for its permanence; rather, the mirror's permanence depends on it, whereas the original object is self-subsistent. The permanence of the mirror's "liveliness" and its shining [with the sun in it] are possible only through the permanence of the sun's manifestations and the mirror's facing the sun. Your heart is like that mirror, and the love of permanence implanted in your nature must be directed only to what is manifested in it. So, say: "O Everlasting One, You are the Everlasting," and turn to Him so that you may become permanent. Then let mortality do as it wishes, for we do not mind whatever befalls us.

KNOW, O FRIEND, that the All-Wise Creator has implanted within human nature a strange characteristic: Since the world cannot contain you, you frequently utter, as if in a suffocating dungeon, a sound of disgust. Yet something as small as a mustard seed, a cell, a memory, or a minute of time so absorbs you that you are lost in it and passionately attracted to it. The Creator has given you such faculties that some of them would not be satisfied even if they could swallow the world. Some others are bored even with microscopic particles and cannot tolerate even a hair out of place. You know that your eye cannot work properly if there is a hair in it.

So be alert and careful of what you do so that you will not ruin yourself and your most subtle faculties. An (unlawful) morsel or a word, an (illicit) glance, beckoning, or kiss can ruin you. Everything has an aspect of non-existence that can ruin and swallow you. Look at the mirror in your hand, and see how the sky and its stars are contained in it. See how the

Ultimate Truth inscribes most of your acts or deeds and even most of your life in your mustard seed-sized memory.[67] Glory be to Him, the All-Powerful, the Self-Subsistent.

Know, O friend, that your private world is a grave-like, narrow place. But since its "walls" are made of "glass," you see it as spacious. With respect to this worldly life's material dimension, the past has finished and the future does not exist. However, as your world's two mirror-like walls face each other, they come together at the point of your present time and make it difficult for you to distinguish between what is real and what is reflected [in them]. The "line" of your present extends into [your past and future] and becomes an area. When misfortune moves you, you strike your head against the walls, suffer disappointment, and lose sleep. You see your world as narrower than a grave and a bridge, and your life moves faster than a river and even lightning.

KNOW, O ONE WHO WANTS TO SEE the witnesses of the manifestations of the Divine Name the All-Recording and Preserving. This Name is referred to in: *Whoever does an atom's weight of good shall see it, and whoever does an atom's weight of evil shall see it* (99:7-8) and *Not an atom's weight in Earth and in heaven escapes your Lord, nor is there anything smaller or greater, but it is in a Manifest Book* (10:61).

Know, O one who wants to see them in the Book of the Universe's sheets, inscribed according to the Manifest Book's standards.[68] Take a handful of flower and tree seeds, which, despite being different species are so similar that you cannot distinguish between them, and bury them together in darkness—the darkness of simple, lifeless-seeming soil. Then, sprinkle on them water—water that has no measure and standards to know and distinguish them. It just goes wherever you sprinkle it. Look at them in the spring, the time of the yearly resurrection when nature comes to life again.

---

67 The writer uses "most," not "all," because humanity is forgetful. (Tr.)

68 The Manifest Record signifies one aspect of Divine Knowledge and Commands in which everything has an essential, archetypal existence. It is an index and program of the Tree of Creation, a book of Divine Destiny, a register of Divine laws operative in the creation and life of the universe and its content. The Manifest Book signifies Divine Power and Will. Everything is given existence according to that Will's law and that Power's principles. Through the Manifest Record's dictates, that is through Divine Destiny's decree and instruction, Divine Power employs particles to create beings or manifest them on the "page" of time. For a more detailed explanation, see footnote 36. (Tr.)

See how those mingled seeds resembling one another obey the orders of creation given by the All-Wise Creator (by producing various flowers and trees) to manifest the perfection of His Wisdom, Knowledge, Will, Purpose, Discernment, and Consciousness. Do you not see that these flowers have been adorned for you and smile at you, making them loved by you? Do you not see that these fruits sharpening your appetite invite you to themselves and sacrifice themselves to you?

This handful of seeds has changed by the Creator's will into a Paradise-like garden full of various flowers and trees. Can you see in it any error or defect? *Then look again! Can you see any rifts?* (67:3). The All-Preserving One has given each seed exactly and completely what was passed on to it from its parent's property. The One Who does this is He Who will destroy and rebuild the universe on the Last Day. The perfect recording and preserving seen here, even in trifling, perishable things, is an undeniable evidence for the recording and preservation of important things, whose effects extend into eternity. The deeds and works of those honored with ruling Earth according to Divine laws—the good and evil deeds of the servants of the One, the Single, of those who assumed the Supreme Trust—are recorded. *Does humanity think that it will be left to its own devices, uncontrolled, without purpose?* (75:36). Humanity will not be left to its own devices, for all people journey to eternity, where they account for their deeds and words.

This is only one of the infinite number of examples or analogies of the Divine act of recording and preserving. Glory be to Him, the All-Preserving, All-Controlling, All-Witnessing, All-Reckoning.

KNOW, O HEEDLESS SAID! Do not set your heart on what will abandon you when both it and this world are destroyed. How can you set your heart on what will leave you when you die, on what will not accompany you on your journey to the intermediate world of the grave? How can you count on what will abandon you in one or two years, debiting your account with its sins, and on what forsakes you at the very moment you have obtained it?

Have no care for what will not accompany you on your journey to eternity, what perishes during the world's tumults and convulsions, the continuously changing conditions of the intermediate world of the grave, and the Hereafter's revolutions. Do you not see that something in you is pleased only with eternity and the Eternal, that it turns only to Him and lowers itself only before Him? This is the king of your faculties. Obey it, for it obeys the command of its All-Wise Creator.

KNOW, O MY FRIEND, that I saw myself in a dream telling people: "It is a Qur'anic principle that you must not consider anything other than Him, the Glorious One, as greater than you and so begin to worship it. Nor must you consider yourself greater than anything and so claim absolute dominion over it. That which is other than Him is equal to anything else in its distance from being the Object of Worship and in respect of its being a created thing."

KNOW, O HEEDLESS SAID! You look around and, believing the world to be stable and perpetual, think you are stable and perpetual. Therefore the world's final destruction scares you, as though you would live until that destruction. But this is not true, for you and your own world are decaying every moment. Due to this illusion, you are like one who holds a mirror reflecting a mansion, a town, or a garden. The least movement or change of the mirror causes a tumult in that reflected image with which the person is so content. Their apparent, seeming permanence does not benefit you, for your share is only what the mirror reflects. Consider your mirror and how both it and the reflection can perish at any moment. Do not burden it with what it cannot bear.

KNOW, O FRIEND, that the All-Wise Creator usually revives that which is of great value. That is, He does not let those valuable things perish permanently through the changes of seasons, years, and centuries; rather, He continually returns them to life. When you look at the types of resurrection occurring daily, yearly, and every century, you see this established, regular law. Scientists agree that humanity is the most perfect fruit of the Tree of Creation and has the greatest importance and value. As each person is like a species of other living beings, each person will be resurrected on Judgment Day with his or her exact identity and body, title and form.

KNOW, O IGNORANT, ARROGANT SOUL, that every station or position has many different shadows. How can a shadow be equal to the original? How can one who sees the king's throne reflected in water or dreams of sitting upon it think that he or she is the king or equal to the king? How can one who sees stars reflected in a pool and imagines himself or herself to be in the sky be like one who journeys among or above stars? Those who rely on personal intellect and knowledge while traveling in the inner dimension of existence are in perilous arrogance, for although their station is only a shadow of the original, they are proud of their knowledge. They attribute it to themselves, seeing themselves as comparable with that station's real owner. They make a serious mistake and, due to their conceit, begin to say in ingratitude: "This has been given to me because of my knowledge." But this is only a means to test them.

KNOW, O FRIEND, that the conclusive phrases or sentences usually coming at the end of Qur'anic verses have connections with the actual verses, as well as with the subject matter being discussed, the *sura*, and the entire Qur'an. They connect the verses with one another, causing one to recollect and consider them. Do not judge what is stated therein only by the meanings of the verses in which they are found, nor seek their grandeur only where they are mentioned.

For example: *Thus We detail the signs and Revelations* (7:174); *We make recurring explanations in this Qur'an* (17:41); *We coined for humanity in the Qur'an all kinds of similitudes* (30:58); *Surely, God is All-Dignified, All-Wise* (9:58); *Surely, God is All-Knowing, All-Powerful* (16:70); *that You may reflect* (51:49); *that You may deserve God's protection* (2:183) and similar verses have eyes looking at most of the Qur'anic verses, most of God's signs of creation, and the general conditions and affairs of human life and characteristics. These concluding phrases or sentences, which seal and confirm the verses, draw the reader's attention from the mingled and detailed particular affairs to universal and inclusive laws and truths, and toward higher aims and purposes.

KNOW, O MY HEART, that Satan deceives you by calling to your attention that which is infinitely abundant in order to diminish the value of the bounties conferred on you. To save yourself from this deception, consider how needy and unable you are to meet even your own needs. Reflect upon the purposive wisdom in the bounties you are given, and the purposeful act of giving bounties. Meditate on the boundless manifestations of Divine Power, Knowledge, and Will, on the purposes for your existence, and on its consequences with respect to the One Who has given you existence, the One Who owns the All-Beautiful Names.

Satan also deceives you through your egotism and formidable conceit. He calls small creatures and vermin to your attention, asking: "What is the use of creating such short-lived things?" thereby implying that life's purpose lies in life itself and derives its value from perpetuity. This argument suggests that creating short-lived creatures is meaningless, and thus causes you to reduce the value of the mercy, favoring, and perfect artistry in what you observe. This, in turn, causes you to forget or even deny the Maker. Respond to Satan's deception by showing him heaven with its stars, and Earth with its animate creatures. Compared with you, their huge size will awaken you. Look at your own cells, and see how marvelous they are and how wonderfully they fulfill their tasks. See what vital tasks your white and red blood corpuscles perform while you are alive. Look at the subtle faculties springing from your heart.

KNOW, O EUROPE! There are two of you: One that, benefiting from the religion of Jesus and Islamic civilization, has made human life more comfortable through its inventions; and another one that, based on naturalistic and materialistic philosophy, opposes the revealed religions. The evil of the latter surpasses the good of the former, and is the cause of most human wretchedness and suffering. I now address this second Europe:

You have taken in your right hand the dark, deviating philosophy and in your left hand the corrupt, harmful civilization. And then you claim that humanity's happiness lies in them. I wish your hands were broken, and your two offerings will cause you to die.

O spreader of unbelief and ingratitude! Can one with a corrupt conscience and mental and spiritual illnesses be happy with rich clothes and worldly possessions? For one disappointed or disillusioned by the non-fulfillment of even one expectation, sweetness turns sour, pleasure changes into pain, and the world becomes narrow. How can one exposed to your evil, whose heart and spirit have been stricken with your misguidance and left frustrated and distressed, find happiness with what you offer? Can one be described as happy when his or her body is in a deceiving, fleeting paradisiacal state while his or her spirit and heart are in hellish torment?

Listen, O intriguing and corrupting spirit, to what I tell you. You have brought many perils and troubles upon humanity. Consider the following parable: There are two roads before us. We choose one and begin to walk. At every step helpless people are attacked by thugs who rob them of everything, destroy their houses, and beat them so savagely that even heaven weeps for them. Wherever we look we see the same scene, filled with the oppressors' shouts and the oppresseds' cries and lamentations. Since we feel pain when others are in pain, our conscience cannot bear such injustice and lamentation. So, those who see such events and cannot prevent them lose hope and abandon all human feelings. No longer concerned with others' destruction—so long as they remain safe—they surrender to the utmost degree of savagery.

O Europe! You have used your genius to bring humanity to this hellish state as a "gift" and then, seeing that this illness is incurable, you offer people charming amusements and fancies as a cure to anaesthetize them. However, your cure will kill you.

Taking the other road, we see something quite different: At every station, place, and town, soldiers perform their duties. Now and then the king's officials come, take the weapons and other belongings lent to them by the government, and give them their discharge papers. The soldiers are pleased, although outwardly they look sad, for now they can return to their king. If the officials meet a recruit who does not know them, that recruit tells them: "I am the king's soldier and in his service. My final destination is with him. If he has sent you here, welcome. If not, stay away, for no matter how many of you there are I will fight with you (not for myself) to preserve my lord's trust and protect his royal dignity and honor."

Thus we constantly see new troops concentrated or mobilized with joy and praises of the king (birth) while many others are discharged with contentment and glorify the king (death). The Qur'an offers humanity a gift. If people respect it and use it as a guide, they will enter this second road. *Then no fear shall come upon them, neither shall they grieve* (10:62).

O Europe! You assume that all living creatures are their own lords, work in their own name and for their own pleasure, that their only aim in life is to survive. Do you not see the universal mutual helping among them, as established by their Creator? Plants help animals, and animals help humanity. But you see this as conflict and contention, and preach that life consists of conflict. Glory be to God! How can this be true? Can you not see that the particles or atoms of all foods help nourish the body's cells? This mutual assistance results from everything obeying the order of a Munificent Lord, and proves that no living creature is the lord of itself.

Moreover, this is so because humanity, among all living agents, is the most honorable, as it is endowed with free choice and a wider field of activity. Despite this, our part even in our daily acts is miniscule. If this most honorable creature, one endowed with free will and the widest field of activity, has so little part in its own ownership and lordship, to what degree can other animate and lifeless things claim lordship over themselves?

O Europe! You have fallen into such error because your genius has caused you to forget your Lord—the Creator of everything. As a result, this illusion of your true nature has caused you to attribute all things and acts to (material) causes, and to share what belongs to God with false "claimants" to divinity. This compels all living beings to struggle with innumerable aversions and hostilities to satisfy their endless needs through an atom's weight of power, a hair's capacity of will, a single gleam's light of consciousness, and a tiny sparkle of life. Whatever they have (in the name of power and will, consciousness and life) cannot satisfy even one of their needs. When misfortune visits them, they seek help from deaf and blind causes. But *the appeals of unbelievers are futile* (13:14).

Your dark and darkening genius has changed humanity's day into a night illuminated with false, illusory lights. Students of your genius see every living being as the wretched people we saw along the first way, attacked by darkness from all sides. They see the world as an abode of lamentation, and all voices in it as wailings over death and groans of orphans.

Students completely educated by your genius become Pharaohs and tyrants who adore the meanest things and are attached to every beneficial means, as if they were their lords. They are apparently refractory, but so humble themselves for the sake of pleasures that they even kiss Satan's feet for the meanest benefit. They appear to be very powerful, but as they have no point of support (in their inner worlds), they are in reality infinitely weak. Your students seek only to satisfy their stomachs and private parts, or to benefit their tribes or races (not in the tribe's name but in that of personal interest, greed, and conceit). They love only themselves and sacrifice everything for it.

Sincere students of the Qur'an, however, are servants who do not lower themselves even before the greatest creature or interest, even if it be Paradise. They are mild and gentle, but only humble themselves before their Creator and with His permission. They are poor, but the richest of all through what their Munificent Lord has stored in them; weak, but the strongest of all through their Master's strength, Whose power is infinite. Let alone seeking this fleeting world as their aim in life, they do not seek even to enter Paradise, and are not pleased with it. [Their aim is to obtain the good pleasure of their Lord only, and Paradise in only a reward.]

Consider the degree of difference between these two groups' objectives. Students of the Qur'an see even the greatest things, such as the Supreme Throne of God and the sun, as helpless in themselves, dutiful, and subjugated. Their spirits have a very strong relation with all pious inhabitants of the heavens and Earth, and they pray for them as sincerely as they pray for their own families.

Consider their qualities: Those in the first group flee from even their own family members to pursue their own interest; those in the second group regard all servants of God as family members. The Qur'an gives its students all particles in the universe to use as prayer beads to glorify God. In place of the 99-bead rosary, it gives them all the atomic chains in the universe to mention their Lord to an infinite degree.

Look at such saintly students of that Divine Revelation as 'Abd al-Qadir al-Jilani, al-Rufa'i,[69] or al-Shadhili, and see how they used everything in the universe to glorify, mention, and praise God to an infinite degree. They saw their actions as small, and so stretched their hands to what is infinite and referred to knowledge of the Knower of the Unseen. Look at these people. Although defeated by a microbe and driven to distress and despair by the least grief and anxiety, see to what exalted ranks they rise, to what extent their faculties are developed by the Qur'an's enlightening guidance. Such people regard the world and its contents as insufficient to say their beads, and belittle Paradise as the aim of their praise and glorification. Despite this, they do not consider themselves greater and more virtuous than the least of God's creatures.

The Qur'an guides humanity. O humanity, what you hold in your hand is a trust and belongs to the Owner (of all things), Who has power over and knows everything. He pities you and is munificent. He buys from you His property that He entrusted to you, to preserve it on your behalf so that you will not lose it. He gives you a very great price in return. Like a soldier, you have responsibilities and certain duties, so act in His Name and for His sake. He provides you with whatever you need and protects you against whatever you cannot overcome.

The purpose of life is to reflect the manifestations of His Names and Essential Qualities. When misfortune visits you, say: "We are God's and in

69 Ahmad ibn 'Ali ibn Yahya al-Rufa'i (1120-84), founder of the Rufa'iya Sufi order, is one of the most renowned and celebrated saints of Islam. (Tr.)

His service. If you have come with His permission, welcome. We are returning unto Him and desire a vision of Him. He will free us from life's duties and difficulties whenever He wills. If, O misfortune, this will happen through your hand, it is alright. However, if He has allowed you to come to test my truthfulness to His trust, but has not allowed me to submit myself to you, then I will never submit His trust—the life He has given me."

This is the reality of the two ways. But people vary in guidance and misguidance, and heedlessness has many degrees. The degree of heedlessness that has caught the "civilized" has made its people insensible to acute pain. However, increased scientific sensitivity and the warning of death may yet rend this veil of heedlessness asunder.

O YOUNG PEOPLE, especially those in Muslim lands! After you have suffered such misfortune at the hands of this second Europe, will you still follow its debaucheries and ideas and unconsciously join its ranks? Does this not contradict your claim of patriotism, as it means despising devotion to "national" values and ridiculing the nation? May God guide us and you to the Straight Path.

KNOW, O FRIEND shaken by the great numbers of unbelievers and their shared denial of some truths of belief. Value is not judged by quantity. If a man or a woman cannot remain human, they turn into devilish animals. As they advance in animalistic greed and appetites, like many of those who deny the Religion, they increase in bestiality. In the same way, you see that this world contains far more (real) animals than human beings, although human beings are God's vicegerents. [This shows that value lies in quality, not quantity.] Moreover, denial is a negation, but two people who affirm are preferred to 1,000 people who negate.

What is an unbeliever? They are people who do not believe in religion, a species created to improve material life in this world and the Fire (in the other). They may serve as a means of comparison in understanding the degrees of the Almighty's blessings upon believers. They agree on denying the Truth, but their agreement has no weight, for denial, even if in the form of affirmation, is negation, repudiation, rejection, ignorance, and acceptance of non-existence.

For example, if all but two people in Istanbul rejected the sighting of the crescent moon (at the beginning of Ramadan), and those two state that they have seen it, their testimony is preferred, for they support each other. In other words, two affirmations are considered stronger than any number of negations. Affirmation relates to the reality or fact itself, whereas negation depends on the one who negates. If a thick cloud makes it impossible for all people, except a few, to see the sun, can we say that the sun is not there? Of course not, for those who cannot see it will say: "I cannot see the sun," not "The sun does not exist."

Those who negate or deny the truths or essentials of belief offer similar excuses. But as their denials do not corroborate one another, they do not support one another. Such agreement is like coming together to go through a narrow hole; it is useless and has no weight or value.

KNOW, O YOU WHO URGE MUSLIMS to strive for worldly life and material progress. Be careful, for some of the ropes connecting them to the Religion are thin. Take care that they are not broken and that their social life is not greatly harmed, for unlike unbelievers, apostates go completely bad and cause corruption. Unlike followers of other revealed religions living among Muslims, people who commit major sins openly and without shame are treated like traitors. Their testimony is not accepted in court, for their consciences are guilty and corrupt.

Do not be deceived by the great numbers of such transgressors, for they are not pleased with their transgression. Without seeking transgression, they have found themselves in it. Almost all transgressors want to be pious and devout Muslims, to see their superiors as pious and righteous. Do you think that Muslims never love the world and need awakening, that they forget their share here? It is not so; rather, greed has intensified and caused believers to lose.

Also, many factors invite people to the world: one's carnal soul, needs, passions, desires, Satan, bad friends like you, the sweetness of immediate profit, and the like, while those inviting to the Hereafter are few. Patriotic feelings and efforts should add to the few. Do you think that our poverty comes from our ascetic tendencies? No! Do you not see that the Magians, Buddhists, and others subjected to Europe's assaults and domination are poorer than us? Do you not see that the Muslims have more than they need to make ends meet and live well enough, but that it is usurped and swindled from them by Westerners?

If you expect that following their civilization will lead to better rule and security in your country, you are mistaken, for controlling and governing a hundred transgressors with bad morals and weak, shaken belief is harder than doing the same with thousands of pious believers. Muslims do not need to be urged to strive greedily for the world. What they need is a good organization of labor, arrangement of working hours, profitable cooperation, and internal security. These are possible only through awareness of God and piety.

KNOW, O FRIEND, that out of His perfect Mercy, the Ultimate Truth has included part of the reward for service in serving, and part of the reward for action in acting. Thus even lifeless creatures obey God's commands of creation and operation of the universe with perfect zeal and pleasure. By doing so, they reflect the manifestations of the Names of the Light of Lights. A minute seed buried in the ground, for example, turns to the sun with its pure heart and, by making its heart the sun's throne, smiles at your face. Suppose that minute particles and compounds have consciousness, like the above-mentioned seed developing from a very simple object to one of flourishing and illumination. They take pleasure from receiving and reflecting the manifestations of the Names of the One of absolute Majesty, Beauty, and Perfection, and thereby realize a great development through obeying the Creator's commands.

Look at how your senses and organs enable you and humanity as a whole to survive. They take so much pleasure in serving that they are tormented if they can no longer serve. See how much pleasure animals get from fulfilling their duties. Do you not see that the rooster prefers hens to itself and calls them to eat the food it happens to find? It is understood from its manner that it does so with zeal, pleasure, and pride. Also, look at the hen leading its chicks. Like other mothers, it leaves them only when they can take care of themselves. This shows that the hen does this not for its own sake or perfection, but for the sake of Him Who employs it and, out of His Mercy, gives it pleasure in fulfilling its task.

Look at plants and trees obeying their Creator's commands. Their adornment and scent display their zeal, and their sacrifice of themselves for their sprouts and fruits shows that their pleasure lies in obeying those commands. It is as if they ask the purest sustenance from the door of Mercy and, with their Lord's permission, feed their fruits with it. A fig tree feeds on mud but supplies its figs with pure milk taken from the treasury of Mercy; a pomegranate tree drinks water but offers its fruits pure sherbet given to it by its Lord. Look at the seeds in the ground and see how, like a prisoner in a very narrow dungeon who earnestly desires to go out to a garden, they are zealous to grow and send shoots into the air.

This Divine law prevalent throughout the universe shows that an inactive thing gets more tired than an active, ever-renewed one, for while the former complains about the slowness of time and its life, the latter is full of thanks. Comfort lies in fighting with troubles and difficulties, while trouble lies in sitting idly.

When you look at lifeless things, you see that the potentiality in them moves in order to be realized. It is almost as if they feel pleasure in that movement. Do you not see how a drop of water opens its heart enthusiastically when its Originator commands it to do so? Despite its weakness and tenderness, when it hears its Lord command: "O water! Turn into ice and expand," it "feels" such intense zeal that it can crack hard iron.

All movement and effort in the universe, without exception, depend on the law of Destiny and are determined and controlled by Divine Power. They manifest themselves by the Divine command of creation containing Knowledge, Will, and even Power. Each particle or atom, compound, and living creature is like a soldier who has relations with all appropriate military spheres and duties. For example, a particle in one cell of your eye has relations with your eye, your facial nerves, your body's veins, and so on as necessary. So, in the tongue of its essential impotence to perform the duties with which it is charged in the order of the universe and the maintenance of the balance, everything testifies to the necessary Existence of the All-Powerful One.

Order and balance are two important, subtle "chapters" of the visible Book of the Universe. How, for example, could a particle or a bee read that Book in the hands of the One Who will roll up the heavens as rolling up a scroll? Although itself an individual, every thing bears witness to the Unity of the Necessarily Existent-Being, the Ultimate Truth, the Glorified through its relations with all other compounds and duties, and through its position with respect to all parts of those compounds.

The All-Wise Creator determined for everything, specific to it and according to its needs, principles out of the two chapters—order and balance—of the visible Book of the Universe. When it acts according to those principles, it acts, even though unconsciously, in compliance with the laws of that book.

For example, when a gnat comes to the world, it immediately attacks a person's face with its stinger to get the water of life for itself. Who taught it this art of fighting? If I were in its place, I would have been able to learn it only after a long period of instruction and many trials. The same is true for all other animals and plants, for the absolutely Generous One has given each one a "guidebook" written in the ink of pleasure and need. See how He has included the secrets of the two chapters of the visible Book of the Universe in the "guidebook" inserted in the head of, for example, a bee. The key to these secrets is the pleasure particular to the bee charged with certain tasks.

Based on what has been said already, you can draw a significant message, one of many, through belief out of: *My Mercy embraces all things* (7:156); *There is nothing that does not glorify Him with praise, but you do not understand their praising* (17:44); and *When He wills a thing, His command is bu to say to it: "Be!" and it is. Glory be to Him in Whose Hand is the dominion of all things, and unto Him you are returning* (36:82-83).

KNOW, O ONE WHO CALLS Muslims to the world. You are wrong. Do you think that the essential purpose of one's life is restricted to material progress, scientific and technological development, earning a livelihood, and other things connected with worldly life? The Lord and Ruler of creation, the One Who says: "*Be!*" says a word confirmed by existence, creation, realities, and the feelings and faculties included in human nature: *I have not created jinn and humanity except to worship Me* (51:56), and *There is not a moving creature that bears its own provision, but God provides for it and you* (29:60). Do you think that the One Who has made you and continually renews your body needs what you make in His Kingdom and your help in His disposal? Do you not see that even the most sophisticated thing you can make can never be equal in art and creation to a date palm, a bee, an eye, or a tongue?

Know, O heedless one, that it is inconceivable that the One Who created you does not know what happens to you while you move through social conditions and worldly circumstances. Whatever your beliefs and thoughts are, even if you are an atheist and a materialist, you must accept that there is a creative act, an art and a disposal in a sperm or an egg, a grain or a seed. Is it rational for you to think that whoever or whatever places a tree's ingredients in its seed is unaware of the world of trees and of all its conditions and relations with other worlds? Or that the One Who splits the seed and makes it grow into a young plant and then into an elaborate tree does not see and observe the one who plants and then benefits from it, and its relations with animals, its environment, and what is happening in that environment?

Is it rational for you to imagine that the One Who forms and shapes the egg to hatch, and equips it with the tools needed by birds, does not see the bird's conditions, world, and the species with which it has close relations? Is it conceivable that the Creator, the One Who created humanity, does not see humanity's world, conditions, and events, although He created humanity from a seed and a fertilized egg through several stages (e.g., a clot suspended, tissue, bones, flesh, and another creation), gave it life and a form displaying artistry that can belong only to one with boundless knowledge, sight, and wisdom, and equipped it with the tools necessary to relate with most species and worlds? Or that He does not know humanity's periods and the worlds in which people move with their bodies, feelings, spirit, intellect, imagination, and all other faculties that enable them to observe worlds and discern truths?

O heedless one! Do you think you are exempt from the intervention of the One Who stretches pomegranates to your hand by tree branches, and melons and watermelons by fiber-like stems, grown and prepared for you? Your heedlessness causes you to assume that the Maker of a melon is unaware of its eater. Your blindness causes you to imagine that the Maker of a pomegranate is unaware of what He does for those who eat it and are astonished at the artistry it displays, proclaiming: "Glory be to Him Who has formed and shaped me. How beautifully He has formed me"; for those who reflect on its beauty proclaiming: *So blessed be God, the Best of Creators* (23:14); and for those who think about its firm, perfect structure proclaiming: *Should He not know, Who creates? He is the All-Subtle, the All-Aware* (67:14). Or do you think that the One Who sends those fruits to satisfy our needs does not see and know us, or that He Who has scattered before us and throughout our world domesticated and other animals for our benefit does not observe us?

KNOW, O YOU WHO RELY on yourself, causes, and the world. You resemble a firefly that relies on its light and changes daylight with night, or a private who sees that his king favors and is kind to all people and even animals, but then says to himself: "What value do I have that will cause him to show me special consideration? Since my heart needs an affectionate, beloved one to protect and support me, I should find another protector and supporter." So he sets out to do so without considering the law. They tell him:

> Don't you know that the king's treasury can meet all your needs and those of all other soldiers? What is in your hand and in the hands of

> those to whom you appeal cannot meet even your smallest need, for you are surrounded by innumerable enemies and endless ambition. The king's law doesn't exclude you; rather, it includes everyone. Even if you were the only soldier, you would receive the same treatment as if the king were especially concerned with you, as his law encompasses all equally. Moreover, if the king is saintly and can be present in many places at once, he will not be unaware of your needs even for a moment. Each being's needs are met appropriately, which shows that the king sees you in his overall favoring, is aware of each being, and is interested in the needs of the general public. He is like the sun, which illuminates every object and is seen in every transparent object while giving light to the world; or like the perfect, universal order prevailing in each thing amidst the apparent confusion arising from things being intermixed with each other.

In short, your Creator and Owner is infinitely more compassionate, munificent, and affectionate to you than any other friend or beloved could be. He knows your secrets and can meet your demands, even the greatest and most secret ones. So trust only Him.

KNOW, O FRIEND, that the Book of the Universe (the Book of Power) is inscribed according to the measures of the Manifest Book (the Book of Destiny), which is like a lined paper placed under the former to be written in exact measures. The universal order and balance, two chapters of these two books and a line of connection between them, attest to this. They are also two titles of the two Grasps of the All-Merciful. All wet and dry things (everything) are included in the Manifest Book's two chapters.

The Qur'an, issuing from the Divine Attribute of Speech, translates the books of the Seen and Unseen, the books of Power, and of Knowledge and Destiny. It is the index of the two chapters, and the concise expression of the two Grasps. One principle of these three books issuing from the three Divine Attributes of Knowledge, Power, and Speech is that every living creature, indeed every thing, is like a regular soldier or servant entrusted with special duties. They work for the sake and in the name of the Sovereign Who owns them—not for their own sake, ownership, or pleasure, but for the sake of the pleasure lying in fulfilling their duties. Whoever assumes and claims that they own themselves is subject to perishing, being torn to pieces.

KNOW, O FRIEND, that the heavens are made without any visible rift. Their Maker is so mighty and dignified, glorified and great, that He easily created everything in its exact place. Nothing can escape His kingdom. Members of a species, such as fish and flies, are found mingled with one another, which shows that the Creator of one species and of all species is the same One. His is the kingdom and praise, creation and command, and judgment. There is no deity but He.

KNOW, O FRIEND, that the Prophet Muhammad, upon him be peace and blessings, and his Prophethood are the best, the epitome of the perfection and good shared by humanity. His way and Religion are the most perfect expression of absolute happiness and pure beauty. We see in his creation superior perfection, articulate truth, distinguished good, and radiant beauty. Right and truth are found on the Prophet's side; misguidance, illusion, and extinction on the opposite side. Out of the countless beauties and virtues that the Prophet brought, look at only this: The hearts and tongues of all believers in God's Unity are united on many occasions, such as the five daily Prayers and the Friday congregational and festival day Prayers. At these times, each believer responds to the illustrious and majestic address of the Eternal Object of Worship with the sounds of the hearts of all believers, and their supplications and recitations. This vast agreement and encompassing solidarity are like the entire Earth speaking and praying, fulfilling the order: "Perform the Prayer correctly," which issued in all its awe from above the seven heavens.

By executing this order and participating in the huge congregation of praying believers, weak and helpless human beings, despite their being like a minute particle amidst those worlds, become servants loved by the Creator of Earth and heavens. They are honored with ruling on Earth in His Name, and become the head of all animate beings as well as the final purpose for the universe's creation. If, as in the Unseen world, those countless exalters of God would say: "God is the All-Great" at the same moment during and after the festival's congregational Prayer, it would be equal to Earth's exaltation—if it exalted as humanity does.

It would be as if Earth shook mightily on the festive day, exalting God with all its spheres and mountains, saying: "God is the the Great" with its mouth of Makka, with the sincerity of its heart of *qibla*—the Ka'ba. The words coming out of its caves—the mouths of believers scattered throughout it, rather, throughout the intermediate world and the heavens—would rise in waves. May the Glory of Him Who has created Earth and made it like a cradle and a place of prostration for His servants be exalted and glorified.

KNOW, O ONE WHO WOULD LIKE TO SEE and reach the light of knowledge of the Ultimate Truth through arguments and evidence, through His signs and witnesses. Do not meddle with what happens around you by objecting. Do not approach what occurs to you with suspicion. Rather, extend your hands to seize the light appearing to you. Isolate yourself from the conditions of heedlessness, open yourself to those lights' coming, and turn to them wholeheartedly.

It is my experience that there are three categories of witnesses and evidences of knowledge of God. First, those that are like water. You can feel and see them, but cannot hold them with your hands. Free yourself from random thoughts, and be absorbed in them with all your being. Do not regard them with criticism or an inquisitive manner, for they flow away and are not pleased with such actions.

Second, those that are like air. You can feel them, but cannot see or seize them. Expose your face, mouth, and spirit to those breezes of Mercy. Breathe them in by your spirit, rather than responding to them with your hands stretched out to seize them. Discard your criticism and suspicion, otherwise they disappear. It is not the hands in which these witnesses and evidences can be held.

Third, those that are like light. You can see them, but cannot touch or receive them. Turn to them with the eyes of your insight and expose your heart to them. Light can be seized and hunted only with light [the light of the heart and insight]. Do not extend your hand to it ambitiously, or measure it with material tools, for this will cause it to hide (but not extinguish) itself. It is not pleased with material or physical confinements, restrictions, and solid owners.

LOOK, O FRIEND, at the degree of the Qur'an's mercy and affection for ordinary people. See how it respects and considers their simple understanding. It reiterates the clear signs inscribed on the foreheads of the heavens and Earth, and makes them easy to read, such as the creation of the heavens and Earth, sending down rain from heaven, and reviving the soil (each spring). Ordinary people can barely discern what is written in small, delicate letters. Consider the purity and eloquence of the Qur'anic expressions, how they relate to humanity what the Power has written on the sheets of the universe. It is as if the Qur'an is the recitation of the universe, its order and harmony, and the pronouncement of its Composer and His acts. Listen with a wakeful heart to such *suras* as the Tiding (78) and verses like: *Say: "O God! The Lord of Sovereignty..."* (3:26)

KNOW that although they should be kept secret, I write my heart's supplications to my Lord. I expect the Almighty, out of His Mercy, to accept the speech of my book after death silences my tongue.

> O Merciful Lord, Munificent God! My life and youth have passed in misuse of my willpower. What is left is only painful and humiliating sin, devastating and deviating pain and trouble, and annoying, paralyzing anxiety. With this heavy burden, diseased heart, and ashamed face, like my ancestors, beloved ones, relatives, and contemporaries, with utmost speed and out of my free will I am approaching the door of the grave, the house of loneliness on the way to eternity after separation from this transient, fleeting abode, which is subject to waning, and unpitying and deceiving for those who, like me, follow their carnal, evil-commanding souls.
>
> O Compassionate, Munificent Lord! The appointed hour is at hand. I have put on my shroud, laid down in my coffin, bid farewell to my friends, and headed for my grave. I am crying at the door of Your Mercy: "Help! Help, O All-Affectionate, All-Bounteous One! Save me from the shame of rebellion!" Ah! I am in my shroud, standing beside my grave and, raising my head toward the door of Your Mercy, crying: "Help! Help, O All-Merciful, All-Affectionate One! Deliver me from the heavy burden of rebellion!" Ah! I am in my shroud, lying in my grave. Those who saw me off have left me. I am expecting Your forgiveness, seeing that there is no shelter and refuge except in You. I am crying: "Help! Help (me) against the narrowness of this place, the loneliness my rebellion has caused, and the ugliness of my face because of sin! O All-Merciful, All-Affectionate, All-Bounteous, All-Requiter (of good and evil), save me from the company of sins and rebellion."
>
> O God! Your Mercy is my refuge and my means to reach You. I complain of my anguish and sorrow unto You. O Munificent Creator, Compassionate Lord, Master, Guardian! Your impotent, heedless, ignorant, diseased, abject, sinful, old, wretched, and fugitive creature, Your work of art and Your servant has returned to Your door after 40 years, sheltering in Your Mercy, acknowledging his sin and error, addicted to illusion and ailments, and supplicating to You in utmost humility. If You admit him, forgive and pity him, for that is what is expected of You, the Most Compassionate of the Compassionate. Otherwise, what other door is there to be sought save Yours?

> You are the Lord to be sought and the Truth to be worshipped. There is no deity save You alone, Who has no partner.

In conclusion, I bear witness that there is no deity but God, and I bear witness that Muhammad is the Messenger of God.

Addendum

> In the Name of God, the All-Merciful, the All-Compassionate.
>
> All praise be to God for His favoring us with the Qur'an, and for His mercy manifested by sending the master of creation, Muhammad, upon him and his Family be peace and blessings.

KNOW, O FRIEND, that the All-Wise Creator has made the plant and animal kingdoms—particularly the small ones—one of the broadest arenas for displaying His Power and manifesting His Attributes in the greatest abundance, and one of the fields containing most of the "mirrors" reflecting His Names. He has done this for certain wise, lofty purposes, some of which are as follows:

Vegetables or plants serve as seeds for Earth, and animals are fruits of the world. A seed is a miniature tree, and its fruit is its miniature index. Whatever is manifested in a tree is manifested in the seed and the fruit. The purpose for existence and life is to receive and reflect the manifestations of the Names of the All-Majestic and Beautiful One of absolute Perfection. Divine Favoring manifests itself through the elaboration and reproduction of plants and animals, especially with their most delicate parts and individual members. This is most suitable to the eternal Wisdom.

It is narrated that Prophet Moses complained to God about the abundance of gnats attacking him and asked: "What is the wisdom of creating so many of them?" God revealed that: "The gnat asks: 'Why have you created human beings, who are so large? They are unaware and heedless of You. If you had made their heads of gnats, [in return for each,] You would have had tens of thousands of those praising, mentioning, and glorifying You, and displaying Your Names' manifestations and Your art's embroideries through their tongues and disposition.'" True! While the invisible Qur'an inscribed in the ink of stars on the sheets of the heavens shows you the signs of creation's grandeur and splendor, the Qur'an inscribed in the ink of subatomic particles or the atoms in your eye reads the signs of Knowledge and Wisdom.

The former says: "Glory be to Him. How splendid are His Essential Qualities," while the latter says: "Glory be to Him. How delicate is His Wisdom, how subtle His Art." Although both Qur'ans have the same value and significance, since observers and watchers derive no benefit from multiplying the large one, multiplying the small one is of great importance to those numberless angels and jinn, people and others who study it and reflect on it. When it is multiplied, it will not remain the same, single book; rather, it will be a book of endless variations containing different uses and meanings, one that has increased greatly in beauty and purity of expression. Furthermore, when many chapters of the small Qur'an and its copies are inserted in some of the letters of the large one, the small Qur'an excels the large one to the degree of its smallness.

Another wise purpose for creating many animals and plants is that the most perfect Divine manifestation is that God manifests Himself with all His Names focused on a single being. Art becomes most perfect when the greatest thing, with all of its embroideries, is inserted in the smallest. The seed and fruit with respect to the tree, the plant and animal with respect to Earth, humanity and the Prophet with respect to the universe, and the heart and innermost human sense or faculty with respect to humanity—these are essential, compact samples receiving and reflecting all of the Names manifested on the originals growing from them.

For example, a fruit, part of the tree (which represents the whole) points to Unity—the manifestation of Divine Names on all fruits and trees. However, being a sample of the tree (containing whatever is in the tree) and the tree representing the total growing from it and resulting in it, a fruit indicates Divine Oneness—the manifestation of Divine Names as focused on the fruit.[70]

---

[70] The manifestation of Oneness (*Ahadiya*) and Unity (*Wahidiya*), part (*juz'*) and whole (kull); sample, particular, or individual (juz'i); and total (kulli) are important points requiring explanation. For example, an arm, a leg, or a head is part of one's body, the body being the whole. But that person is a sample or individual representing humanity, whereas humanity is the total. Whatever is in the whole is not found in the part, just as whatever is in a person is not found in his or her arm, leg, or head. But whatever is in the total is found in the sample. The Divine Names manifested on the whole (a person) are not to be sought in a part, but the Names manifested on the total (humanity) are manifested on the sample (a person). The Divine Names' manifestation on the total or the whole is called *tajalli-i wahidiya* (manifestation of Unity), while Their manifestation on the total, as focused on the part or individual, is called *tajalli-i ahadiya* (manifestation of Oneness). (Tr.)

For example, the sunlight illuminating the world in daytime is a manifestation of Unity (*Wahidiya*), while the sun's image reflected in each transparent object is an example or analogy for the manifestation of Oneness (*Ahadiya*). When you see the sun in your mirror as having taken on the mirror's color and attributes and then see it in other mirrors, you understand and witness what Oneness or Unity means. It is the same (and only) sun manifested in all mirrors that announces: "We speak in different tongues, but Your Beauty is one and the same."

Whatever exists points to that Beauty. We understand from this that the All-Wise Creator, with glorified Wisdom and delicate Art, turns with His subtle Power, complete Favoring, perfect Mercy, and sensitive Wisdom from creation to Earth, and then, in succession, to living beings, humanity, and one's heart; from humanity to its heart; and finally to the heart of creation and its seed from which the universe, as well as its illustrious fruit, the final purpose for its creation, and the embodiment of the Creator's love and Mercy, was created. That exalted, noblest, pure, unblemished heart is Muhammad, our master and the master of creation, upon him be peace and blessings to the number of the Tree of Creation's fruits.

KNOW, O ONE WHO THINKS that some creatures exist in nature overabundantly and in vain. Creation's perfect order and balance refute this, for the order is a design interwoven by the *raison d'être* of all parts, particulars or individuals, and details in creation. One cannot observe the purposes of all details of a palace, nor neglect the main purpose of why it was built. Since the main purpose is considered while building it with all its parts, the secondary purposes expected of the details are thus observed. Listen:

There are subtle purposes behind everything related with the All-Living, Self-Subsistent Owner in proportion to His Ownership and disposal, and the extent of His Names' manifestation on that thing. The purposes related to the thing itself are also in proportion to its life and existence.

Everything has been entrusted with a goal in life, which is studied by intelligent beings. If one cannot discern it, others can. There are many ways of benefiting from each thing. *God has uncountable hosts. None knows the hosts of your Lord but He* (74:31). Innumerable beings focus their attentive gaze on all things that exist. Among them are angels glorifying and exalting God, jinn observing creation in amazement and reflecting on it, and spirit beings extolling God and proclaiming His Unity, for whom the solidity of things does not conceal what is in them and who can observe many things at once. Above all, the Maker of all things looks on the works of His Art. Many awake and enlightened believers, as well as many animals moved by their perceptions, also look on God's works of art.

QUESTION: The signs in the Book of the Universe point to the existence of non-human creatures who gaze on and study them in amazement and reflection and then glorify God. Which line indicates this?

ANSWER: The *order* on the line of *balance* in the page of *wisdom* indicates it. When you enter a theater where a play is being performed, you see many marvels that amaze the audience, as well as pleasing melodies and many types of charms in which minds and imaginations take pleasure. There are also many other things that give pleasure to your innumerable faculties, feelings, and senses. Then you look at the spectators' hall and see only a few paralyzed, deaf, and blind children. You will conclude that behind the veils hanging in front of the walls are various intelligent beings with different tastes and temperaments who have come for innocent amusement and are pleased with and want to see every novelty in the play. They see you and the play from where you cannot see them.

If you understand this comparison, look at those creatures and their world. You see "carpets" spread, "couches" raised, "raiments" worn, and "sheets" unrolled. There are flowers and fresh fruits inviting living, needy beings to themselves with their color, taste and smell, and appealing to those who understand such things with their design, decoration, and art. Plants climb straight up their stalks to fulfill their duty of creation, and animals stand on their legs to do their duty of worship. Most of these creatures are not conscious of the astonishing, pure beauty and excellent faculties lodged in their creation, for they are for other creatures who can see and hear.

Despite this attractive majesty, charming adornment, kinds of favoring, things and events arousing curiosity to know and feelings of love for the One behind them; despite all undertakings, intentions and decisions, self-ornamentation, smiles, beckonings, and flirtations; and despite many similar attractions and charms that almost start to talk and tell their meanings, it appears that only two kinds of intelligent, living beings of understanding can appreciate all of this: humanity and jinn. However, most of them are heedless and are like deaf and blind children with paralyzed minds in the darkness of materialism and naturalism. This shows that apart from humanity and jinn, the universe is full of beings with spirit who reflect on existence and glorify God: *The seven heavens and Earth, and whoever is in them, glorify Him; there is nothing that does glorify Him with praise but you do not understand their glorification* (17:44).

KNOW, O FRIEND, that the vaster the control of Divine Power in particulars is, and the more numerous those similar to them are, the greater the favoring on an individual. Do not say: "I am a drop in an ocean to be forgotten because of the ocean's vastness." No! Rather, as the ocean testifies, you are under the protection of the firm order prevailing, with all its strength, in all the things like you in proportion to the expanse of your environment. For the smaller, more concealed, and more strictly surrounded a thing is, the greater care it is given and the less neglected and more protected it is against the interference of others and the tricks of those who believe in coincidence. It becomes more favored as a created thing. The center is more guarded against assault, the seed is under greater protection against the tricks of those who believe in coincidence and the harassment of storms, and the seed is given greater care.

O HUMANITY! You are Earth's seed and Earth is the universe's egg. This is why the Qur'an frequently mentions the creation of the heavens and Earth together, and means by this the creation of all things.

KNOW, O FRIEND, that favoring's perfection comes through wisdom's perfection (favoring can be perfect if wisdom is perfect), wisdom's perfection comes through order's perfection, and order's perfection is through the perfection of balance or measure. One example is the five human senses, which the Creator created so that people could sense the features and qualities of all fruits, flowers, sounds, smells, and so on. This is why the sense of taste has so many delicate, well-ordered pieces, which equal the varieties of all fruits, food, and drink. The sense of hearing can receive and distinguish among innumerable sounds. Compare with these the other external senses and the more numerous and richer inner ones. This comprehensive nature has made human beings what they are: able to receive and reflect endless kinds of manifestations of the Creator's Names and taste endlessly varieties of His bounties.

Human beings are like a telephone switchboard that has a central key to make connections within a city. Each person has a central sense to taste all of God's bounties, as well as special keys attached to his or her head and faculties to experience the pleasure of receiving and reflecting all His manifestations. Use those keys in accordance with the Shari'a's guidelines to please your Originator.

How people use these keys determine to what degree they will experience Paradise's pleasures. Although the promise that *you will be together with the one you love in Paradise* brings the highest and lowest together in the same place, (your experiencing these depend on how and to what extent you used your senses, feelings, and faculties in this world).[71]

KNOW, O FRIEND, that the apparent confusion and commingled state of things does not mean that they are playthings of chance. Rather, they are the most delicate embroideries of the general design of the Book of the Universe. However, that design cannot be easily discerned with a superficial, untrained look at reflections in the mirror of illusion. Do you not see that commingled seeds of different plants scattered at random display a perfect order when they grow? The Pen of Destiny puts them in that amazing order.

KNOW, O FRIEND, that a decisive proof that Prophet Muhammad, upon him be peace and blessings, is the seal of Prophets is that he so extended the Religion's bounds in all respects that no one can imagine a more comprehensive and perfect order. For example, concerning Divine Unity and Lordship, he says: *In His Hand is the dominion of all things* (36:83); *He grasps everything by the forelock* (11:56); *The heavens are rolled up in His Right Hand* (39:67); *He forms you in the wombs as He wills* (3:6); *He is the First and the Last, the Outward and the Inward; and He has perfect knowledge of all things* (57:6); *You will not unless God wills* (76:30); and *We are nearer to him than his jugular vein* (50:16).

Also, the Religion revealed to Prophet Muhammad, upon him be peace and blessings, decrees that all things are equal and obey their Creator's commands, Who does not share their qualities or needs. What Islam teaches about the Resurrection and Divine Unity cannot be surpassed. So it is in every other respect, for it is already complete and perfect, and therefore deserves to be eternal, to continue until the Last Day.

KNOW, O FRIEND, that moved by the environment's touching appearance, I cried. The tears I shed are as follows:

---

71 Bukhari, "Adab," 96; Muslim, no. 2640.

I am mortal, but I do not want the mortal.
I am impotent, so I do not desire the impotent.
I surrendered my spirit to the All-Merciful One,
so I desire none else.
I want only One Who will remain my friend forever.
I am but an insignificant particle,
but I desire an everlasting sun.
I am nothing in essence,
but I wish for the whole of creation.

* * *

Do not invite me to the world;
I came and found it evil and mortal.
Heedlessness was a veil;
I saw the light of Truth concealed.
All things, the whole of creation,
I saw were mortal and full of harm.
Existence, indeed I put it on.
Alas! It was non-existence; I suffered much.
As to life, I experienced it;
I saw it was torment within torment.
Intellect became pure retribution;
I saw permanence to be tribulation.
Life was like a wind, it passed in whims;
I saw perfection to be pure loss.
Deeds were only for show;
I saw ambition to be pure pain.
Union was in fact separation;
I saw the cure to be the ailment.
These lights became darkness;
I saw these friends to be orphans.
These voices were announcements of death;
I saw the living to be dead.
Knowledge changed into whim;
I saw in science thousands of ailments.
Pleasure became unmixed pain;
I saw existence to be compounded non-existence.
I have found the True Beloved;
Ah! I suffered much pain because of separation.

I have finally found God:

(You would never be able to find Him
save only by renouncing worldly things.)

With this light I have found Paradise in the world;
The dead have started to be revived.
I have seen that voices are glorifications
of God and recitations of His Names.
Things have become familiar.
Pleasure lies in suffering and pain.
Life has become a mirror reflecting the lights of the Truth.
Permanence, I have seen, lies in self-annihilation.
All particles recite God's Names.
Everything bears witness to the Truth.
In everything there is a sign
Pointing to the fact that He is One.

* * *

O YOU WHO THINK that the world's pleasure and happiness lie in heedlessness and ignoring religion's restrictions. I once tested my carnal soul. I saw myself on a bridge between two mountain peaks, under which was a deep valley. There was darkness everywhere. I looked right (into the past) and saw only frightening levels of darkness. I looked left (into the future) and again saw only terrifying darkness. I looked down and saw a deep, bottomless precipice. I looked up and saw dark, deaf, and mute clouds sending down sorrow and grief, despair and harm. Afterwards I looked ahead and saw, amidst darkness, the most malicious demons and scorpions, lions and wolves with teeth ready to tear. When I looked back, I saw neither help nor helper.

While hopeless and tired of being tested, Divine guidance helped me. I saw the moon of Islam rise over creatures, and the sun of the Qur'an illuminate all sides. I saw the bridge (of life) as a road extending between the Glorified One's bounties and the All-Merciful's Paradise. To my right extended gardens (of the past) full of the flowers of the righteous and illustrious fruits of Prophets and saints, under which flowed rivers of time carrying them to eternity.

To my left were gardens where the flowers of hope and expectation opened by the Mercy of the All-Affectionate, All-Bounteous. Above me hovered clouds of mercy sending down the water of life profusely. In the middle of these clouds, the sun was smiling with the light of guidance and eternal happiness. In the fields extending in front of me were my brothers and sisters, friends, and tame animals that the darkness of misguidance had showed me as wild, harmful beasts.

To understand this vision, read the verse: *God is the protecting friend of those who believe. He brings them out of the levels of darkness into the light. As to the unbelievers, their protecting friends are those leading unbelief and rebellion. They bring them out of the light into the levels of darkness* (2:257).

> O Light of Lights. For the sake of Your Name the Light, bring us from the levels of darkness into the light.. Amen.

KNOW, O WRETCHED SAID! You are like a silly child sitting on the seashore, who cries without stopping when bubbles reflecting the sun disappear. The child cries as each bubble pops, thinking that the sun's smiling image reflected in it will be lost forever. The child cries as the bubbles become turbid and unpleasant with the mixture of solid things, and does not look up until he or she understands that all these reflections are manifestations of the sunlight renewed on the sea's surface, the waves' cheeks, in the drops' eyes.

The sun does not disappear when the mirror reflecting it does so. Therefore, the disappearance of some bubbles and their images must not engender any painful decay or distressing separation. With its radiant face and beauty and the perfection of its majesty, the perpetual sun's manifestations in the multiplicity of the mirrors (where it is reflected) are renewed continuously. The mirrors and other objects receiving the sun's manifestations fulfill their tasks cheerfully and, when they complete their tasks, hide smilingly.

You sit on the shore of the ocean of life and cry over the setting of beings of perfection, beauty and grace, and the decay of the fruits of Divine blessing when their time is finished. You think that beauty belongs to the beautiful things and fruit to trees. Storms of chance blow and snatch them away, and you think they disappear into the darkness of eternal non-existence. But, remember that the One Who illuminated the things you love with the light of beauty is also He Who illuminated all flowers in the garden of the universe, and stirs the hearts of loving nightingales toward them.

O WRETCHED ONE! How much longer will you cry because the fruit in your hand has disappeared? Consider the continual bounty of the Splitter of the Grain and Seed by maintaining the tree of those fruits. If that tree stops yielding fruit, consider the extent of His favoring throughout the world, where innumerable trees of the same kind are found. If there is a shortage of fruit this year, consider the extent of His favoring renewed with the renewal of seasons and years. Then consider the extent of His favoring continuing in the World of Represantations or Immaterial Forms, and in the Intermediate World with the likes of what you see in this world. Finally, consider the extent of His most vast, eternal sphere of the Hereafter, where you will find the likes of what you have made friends with in this world's garden.

If you think about bounties but are indifferent to the act of bestowing them, your only choice is to weep. See the act of bestowing and its continuance in the bounties themselves. In the act of bestowing, see the Bestower together with His comprehensive pouring out of His bounties freely and the perfection of His Mercy. Smile with gratitude to Him, and be relieved by His graciousness.

When your eyes and heart weep over the loss of decaying beautiful things, consider the multiplicity and vastness of the spheres one within the other containing all that you love. The pleasure of their renewal in their likes will cause you to forget the pain of separation. All those spheres are mirrors that reflect the manifestations of the shadows of the lights belonging to the Beauty of the All-Majestic, Munificent One, Eternal, Perpetual, Self-Subsistent, Permanent, Who has no beginning or end, and does not change in any way.

What is reflected in the mirror is not owned by the mirror, so there is no reason for you to weep over it if the mirror ceases to exist. Detach your attention from the world and turn to the mirror of your heart so that you may see the Sun of Beauty and come to know that whatever you see and love in the world is a sign of Him.

Among the signs of His Grace and Beauty is that He decorated the heavens with lamps and Earth with flowers. Among the signs of His Grace is that He created humanity in the best pattern and of the fairest stature, and wrote the Book of the Universe in the most marvelous letters. Among the signs of His Excellence is that He made the Prophets' spirits shining and brilliant, illuminated the saints' inner senses, and decorated the hearts of those knowing Him with the lights of His Beauty.

KNOW, O HAUGHTY EGO, possessor of absolute impotence and poverty, confined within so many limitations and restrictions. There is no comparison between you and Him, Who has limitless Power and Wealth, Whose Names and Attributes are unrestricted. All creation is in His Power's grasp, and the heavens are rolled up in His "Right Hand." No particle moves without His permission. He has no partner in His Sovereignty and Divinity, and no one can contend with Him in His dominion and Lordship. There is no deity but He.

If you were to enter into partnership with your Creator in His Lordship, there would have to be a comparable relationship between you and Him. But there is not, nor can there ever be, such a relationship. How can a gnat weave those richly decorated garments for those worlds according to each one's size? Your duty is to be a worshipping servant, for therein lies the perfection of your potential. Servanthood is based on and flourishes by humility and acknowledgment of one's being nothing before God. It begins with this acknowledgment and ends in being a beloved of God, which yields the fruit of being loved by God. As servanthood is the opposite of Lordship and Sovereignty, there can be no comparison between them. You are loved by God and deserve His Mercy based on your awareness of your distance from His Lordship and Sovereignty.

Like a black page showing the letters written on it in light, servanthood reflects and shows Lordship through contrast. The blacker a page is, the more clearly and radiantly it shows Lordship. The more conscious beings are of their nothingness before God, the more radiantly and apparently they reflect the manifestations of the Necessarily Existent Being's Existence. There is no deity but He.

KNOW, O one who fancies that some Prophetic sayings exaggerate the virtues of religious deeds. Some narrations say that whoever does certain virtuous deeds will receive as much reward as that of all humanity and jinn. Some say that such narrations only seek to encourage people to do them; others say that they show how meritorious these deeds are. However, what is true in this matter is that it is possible to gain the promised reward if certain conditions are met. It is enough to establish their truth that some, but not all, who do such deeds may gain the promised reward—not whenever they perform them, but only in certain circumstances.

Such narrations convey the idea of potential reward in such deeds. However, the reward cannot be obtained by everyone or whenever those deeds are done, as gaining it requires utmost sincerity and God's acceptance. Also, any reward comes from His overflowing Grace and Munificence, and the servant will feel infinite need for reward in the everlasting abode. Thus, a servant cannot comprehend what is given by Him Whose overflowing generosity to such infinitely needy servants has no limit.

God's generosity, when considered from the viewpoint of God Himself, denotes infinity and so is beyond the servant's knowledge. For example, it is narrated that whoever recites a particular supplication will be given a reward equal to that given to Moses and Aaron. The reward given for reading a certain verse does not increase, in your limited view, in this limited world. However, when approached with respect to God's infinite generosity, the reward promised depends on the intention's sincerity or purity and its being acceptable by God. Also, the comparison in the narration expresses quantity, not quality. A drop containing the sun's image can say to the sea: "Your face is not vaster than my eye in receiving the sun's light and its colors."

The reward promised in the Prophetic sayings in question relates to the World of Unconditioned Existence. A minute particle of that world can contain a world from this material realm, just as the smallest piece of glass can contain the heavens. Sometimes, one easily opens a treasury of Mercy with a good word in a blessed, "auspicious" state. People (look at everything through their own mirrors, and) tend to judge the absolute and universal by their partial, individual criteria. However, true knowledge is with the Knower of the Unseen and the Converter of hearts.[72]

To conclude:

- Your livelihood comes to you either as a result of some other's choice or without the intervention of any human free choice.

---

72 Another point the writer mentions in this respect is: The reward promised in such narrations also should be considered from the viewpoint of our imagining. Imagine a primitive, uncultured person who has never seen the king and thus is unaware of his kingdom's splendor. This person imagines a lord in a village and, with his narrow experience, thinks of the king as a bit greater than that lord. Among the tribes living in the East there were once people who used to say: "Our lord knows what the Sultan does, while he cooks his bulgur soup in a saucepan over the fire." In other words, they imagined the Sultan as someone greater than an ordinary man, who cooked his own soup. If someone were to say to one of these people, "If you do this work for me today, I'll reward you with as much splendor as you think the Sultan has," he would be promising the man as much splendor as he cold imagine—namely, what the Sultan has. Thus, with our worldly views and narrow minds, we cannot think, even as much as the person in the example of the Sultan's lifestyle, of the actual rewards related to the Hereafter. What the Traditions in question state is to compare the unknown reward for a righteous of a believing servant of God. See Said Nursi, *The Words*, The Light, Inc., New Jersey: 2005, p., 368. (Tr.)

- Your need and desire are infinite, and so you have connections with everything in this world and the next.
- The stupidest person is one who, not recognizing the real sun, loves and tries to preserve the mirror in which it is reflected.
- The All-Wise Creator has implanted in human nature numerous faculties for specific purposes.
- The manifestations of the Divine Name the All-Recording and Preserving are pointed to in: *Whoever does an atom's weight of good shall see it, and whoever does an atom's weight of evil shall see it.*
- Why do you set your heart on temporary things that eventually will abandon you?
- It is a Qur'anic principle that you consider Him, the Glorious One, as greater than you and worthy of your worship. He has dominion over everything; you have dominion over nothing.
- Every human being will be resurrected on the Judgment Day with his or her exact identity and body, title and form.
- The phrases or sentences usually coming at the end of Qur'anic verses have connections with the verses themselves, the subject matter discussed, the *sura* and the whole Qur'an.
- Satan deceives you through your egotism and formidable conceit.
- There are two Europes. One has used the religion of Jesus and Islamic civilization to make our life more comfortable, while the other has used naturalism and materialism to bring about most of our suffering.
- Students of modern civilization and those of the Qur'an.
- Islamic and modern civilization.
- Why are there so many unbelievers?
- Those who call Muslims to the worldly life.
- Out of His perfect Mercy, God has included part of the reward of service in serving, and part of the reward of action in acting.
- Those who rely on themselves, causes, and the world.
- The Book of the Universe (the Book of Power) is inscribed according to the measures of the Manifest Book (the Book of Destiny), which is like a sheet of lined paper placed under the former to be written in exact measures.
- The Prophet and his Prophethood represent the highest level of human perfection and good.
- The three categories of witnesses and evidence of knowledge of God.

- The plant and animal kingdoms are among the broadest arenas for His Power's disposals and His Attributes' manifestations, and contain most of the "mirrors" reflecting His Names.
- The reason why there are sometimes "too many" members of a species.
- The vaster the disposal of Divine Power in particulars is, and the more in number those similar to them are, the greater the favoring on an individual.
- Favoring's perfection is through wisdom's perfection, wisdom's perfection is through order's perfection, and order's perfection is through the perfection of balance or measures. An example of this is the art found in the five human senses.
- Muhammad is the seal of Prophets because he so extended the bounds of religion that a more comprehensive or perfect one is impossible.
- The world of the misguided and that of the rightly guided.
- Those who think that pleasure and happiness in this world come from ignoring religious obligations.
- Your ego only possesses absolute impotence and poverty, and is confined within so many limitations and restrictions that it can do nothing.
- Why do some Prophetic sayings seem to exaggerate the virtues of religious deeds?

The Eighth Treatise

The Eighth Treatise

A spark from the rays of the Qur'an's guidance

O One for Whom is all dominion (over existence) and praise, bestow peace and blessings on the lord of humanity, whom You addressed as: "O *Prophet*" *(who has all qualities of Prophethood in the most perfect degree)* (8:64). He responded: "Here I am, at your service." His response reached even to the angels of the highest heavens. You ordered him: "Give good tidings and warn." He called: "O *humanity, worship your Lord*" (2:21). His call has echoed throughout time and space, and he has become *a bearer of good tidings and a warner* (2:119). He sees and bears witness to the truth of what he sees, calls to all generations of humanity across time and space, and has been heard in all times and places, so that the world has been filled with the Qur'an's call.

He has brought under his rule a considerable part of the world, which he has attracted to himself and the Qur'an by his perfect earnestness (attested to by his life and conduct) and his utmost trustworthiness and confidence in his Message (attested to by the simplicity of his life and his abstention from the world's pleasures.) He also attracted these people with his infinite conviction and peace of mind and heart (attested to by the strength of his principles and teaching), and with the perfection of his belief (attested to by the fact that he was the most advanced in servanthood to God and most careful in avoiding sins).

KNOW, O IGNORANT SOUL! There are as many doors opened toward God as there are parts of the (Book of the) Universe and its pages, and as there are compounds. How mistaken it is to assume that all doors are closed when only one is closed to you! You are like one who, not seeing a soldier in a town, concludes that the country has no king and so ignores his rules and instructions. In reality, the country is full of the king's soldiers, officials, and government offices.

KNOW, O FRIEND, that this proves that the inner existence is more perfect and excellent, vigorous in life, decorated, subtle, and better than whatever the outer existence displays in the name of life, consciousness, and perfection. All that is seen in the outer existence is only a sign of the inner existence's life, consciousness, and perfection. If the inner existence were lifeless, the outer existence could not display life and consciousness. Your stomach is much more orderly than your house, your skin more excellently woven than your clothes, and your memory better designed than your book. Compare with these examples the material and immaterial worlds, the visible and invisible worlds, and this world and the next. Your carnal and evil-commanding soul looks with the eye of fancy and desire, and thus sees the outer existence as animated and lovely and spread over the lifeless, dark, and dreadful inner existence.

KNOW, O FRIEND, that your face has features that distinguish you from all other people, past and future, although all human faces have the same main parts and structure. It is as if unity has manifested itself within multiplicity. While it shows the Maker's Oneness that all human faces have the same main parts and structure, the infinite differences that distinguish individuals indicate that the Maker is infinitely independent and Wise and has absolute free choice. This reality becomes more significant when people are considered individually. Such a wise distinguishing, fruitful differentiation, and beneficial distinction prove the purposeful choice of an All-independent, the will of an absolutely Willing, and the knowledge of an All-Knowing One.

All glory be to Him Who includes and inscribes endless features on the page of your face. Although they cannot be comprehended by reason and beheld with a superficial look, they are discerned through insight and can be perceived in detail by a careful look. Such purposely arranged and beneficial human differences and the correspondent similarity among members of the same species cannot be due to blind chance and coincidence. Rather, they are the art of an All-Hearing and All-Seeing, All-Knowing and All-

Wise One. There is no room for chance in such perfect multiplicity. It is not neglected and left to its own devices, but rather is the arena for the operation of an all-wise purpose and intention, an all-knowing free choice, and an all-hearing and seeing will. Thus there is no room for chance in God's domain. It belongs, with its "brother" of naturalism and "father" of associating partners with God, in the hell of non-existence and eternal annihilation. The verse: *Among His signs is the creation of the heavens and Earth and the variety of your tongues and colors* (30:22) points to the first and last levels of Divine Wisdom's manifestation.

KNOW, O FRIEND, that Satan whispers: "If a cow is a creature and design of the All-Knowing, Eternal Power, why is it such a poor animal? If the Pen of the Destiny of an All-Knowing One of absolute Will works under its skin and within its body, why is its outer skin (the apparent part of its body) so docile and ignorant, helpless and miserable?"

ANSWER: If the Eternal Power's Art did not clothe everything with what it needs, your donkey's ear would be more intelligent and skillful than you and your teachers, and the inside of your fingers would excel you in consciousness and willing. In addition, your fingers would have greater consciousness and willpower than your present consciousness and willpower. Everything has been given a certain capacity, together with a potential to expand and develop.

Moreover, Divine Destiny appoints a certain measure for everything and a receptacle according to that measure. This determines the capacity of that thing which is received from the absolute Source of everything. What is emitted from inside to outside is in accord with the will of that Source and the capacity of the thing, and in proportion to the need and its degree, and to the extent of the ability and according to the measure fixed by the Divine Names manifested on that thing. A cow is no exception; it is not the inside of another creature that determines its outside. One who expects all of the sun's qualities to be in its image reflected in a bubble is grossly deluded, for an image points to the original but does not possess all of the sun's qualities.

KNOW, O FRIEND, that you are a conscious work of art made with wisdom, one indicating the Maker's Attributes. Your being alive reflects the Wisdom that embroiders creation, the Knowledge with an absolute power of choice, and the Power that sees what you deserve. You are the fruit of a Mercy that hears the calls of your need, an embodiment of an act of the All-Willing that wills what your potential wills, and the favoring of an All-

Knowing that knows your demands. You are a form of shaping, measuring Destiny that is aware of how you were constructed. How can you exclude yourself from the general rule of creation, with your partial will and consciousness, and then compare the whole to the part? How can you be heedless of your Lord and Owner, Who owns and exerts lordship over everything? How can you imagine, despite the knowledge encompassing all creation, that there is no one watching you, One All-Hearing and All-Seeing, All-Knowing and All-Answering (the calls and prayers), All-Helping, Who hears your crying, sees your destitution, and knows your sins?

O WRETCHED SOUL! Why do you fancy that you are excluded from the sphere of Divine laws and wrong all other beings without attaching any importance to them, or feel constrained to bow before them or see yourself as responsible for managing them? You cannot bear such a burden. Abandon associating partners with God, which signifies your separation from the primordial nature He has given to creation, and enter the sphere of God's dominion, where you can find peace of mind and heart and become a respected brother or sister of all beings. Otherwise, you are like one charged with handling a steering wheel on a vessel carrying the king's goods. Instead of putting the load on the ship and steering the wheel lightly, such a person carries the load on his or her back. Anyone with a bit of intellect would say: "I travel on this vessel, so I must place my load near the goods of the king, my lord and administrator." In addition, O wretched soul, obtain rest and peace by placing the Islamic rules and principles on the vessel of the Muslim world's mind.

KNOW, O FRIEND, that the One Who created you also must have created the universe and its contents, for whatever is in you also exists in it. The One Who created you must be the Creator of all things, for the Creator of a melon is also the Creator of its seed, which is its miniature sample taken from and contained within it.

KNOW, O FRIEND, that as a restricted being, your body, lifetime, and power are all restricted. Do not waste your short, transient life on transient things; rather, spend it for what is permanent so that it may gain permanence. At most, your life here will last for 100 years, as if eating 100 dried dates. Without the tree that yields them, they give some benefit (but cause more hardship) only during your life. They are of no use to you after you die. If you seek the afterlife (and bury those dates in its soil) and water them with the Shari'a, you can obtain 100 marvelous date palms. One who sells

100 excellent date palms for 100 dried dates deserves only to be wood for the Fire.

KNOW, O FRIEND, that the carnal soul's belief that it is somehow excluded from the sphere of the manifestations of Destiny and Divine Attributes is the source of all illusion, doubt, and misguidance. This supposed exclusion leads the carnal soul to think that it is free of Divine rule. And so it excludes from God's Kingdom and His Power's control whatever it comes across in existence, which depends on Divine Destiny and is ruled by one or more Divine Names. Through forced analogies and interpretations that will make it the teacher of devils, the carnal soul reflects some of its states coming from associating partners with God to that innocent thing.

The carnal, evil-commanding soul resembles an ostrich—it sees that which is against it as for it. Or it is like the Sophists, who say to one of two people arguing with each other: "Your opponent's arguments reject you," and then turns to the other and says: "Your opponent's arguments invalidate yours. You are both wrong."

KNOW, O FRIEND, that the carnal soul supposes the other world to be an expansion of this one and seeks to continue its heedlessness. Thinking of the afterlife, although not convinced of its coming, it seeks relief from the terror of the world's annihilation and the pain of decline. Taking refuge in heedlessness or doubt (about the afterlife), it seeks to be saved from the troubles of working for the afterlife. It looks upon deceased generations as living but concealed from us and learns nothing from death. Under the illusion of implanting its worldly expectations in the afterlife's soil (using the afterlife as an excuse for clinging to worldly expectations) it thinks: "My expectations have two aspects: One relates to the world, which is impermanent and scatters like dust; the other relates to the afterlife, which is built on the same foundations as the world and its expansion." For example, knowledge has two aspects: one illumined, the other dark. The devilish carnal soul shows the illumined side and offers the dark one under its guise. By trying to convince people that knowledge will bear fruit in the Hereafter, it calls them to use it for worldly benefit. In short, the carnal soul is like an ostrich or a devilish Sophist.

KNOW, O FRIEND, that I am absolutely convinced that if God is not accepted as the Creator of all things, then He is not the Creator of anything. Creation is a complete entity (like an organism), all parts of which are interlinked and related. As there is no room for division, whatever we acknowledge with respect to something necessitates doing the same for everything. Also, the Creator is either One or endless in number. If there were not a true Creator, (for the same reasons as requiring His being the Creator of the universe), there would have to be an infinite number of true creators. [There cannot be many beings with the same infinite attributes, and it is impossible that there should be more than one infinite being.] This would necessitate accepting many strange ideas and the non-existence of unity in absolute terms. Eventually, this would lead to accepting the impossibility of a sole Creator's existence.

It is impossible for a being who gives light to be without light, who gives existence to be non-existent, and who makes the existence of something necessary to be unnecessary in existence. It is also inconceivable for a being who bestows knowledge to be without knowledge, who grants consciousness to be without consciousness, who gives willpower to be without willpower, and who gives perfection to be imperfect. Is it possible that one who shapes the eye and gives sight cannot see? All perfection shared by what has been created must originate in the Maker's Perfection.

KNOW, O FRIEND, that what a human soul desires most is permanence and perpetuity. If it does not deceive itself with an illusive permanence, it cannot find pleasure in anything. O soul demanding permanence, continue to mention the Everlasting One so that you may gain permanence. Be like a mirror reflecting His Light so that you may not be extinguished. Be a mother of His pearl so that you may be purified. Be a body for the breeze of His remembrance so that you may be eternally alive. Hold fast to a beam of one of His Name's rays so that you may not fall into the bottomless pit of non-existence. If a fruit is heedless of what sustains and maintains it, and thus is attracted to a foreign light smiling at its face, it is disconnected from its stem and falls to the ground.

O SOUL! Hold fast to Him Who sustains and maintains you, for 999 parts of your being are in His charge; only one has been entrusted to you. Place that one part in the vessel carrying His property and find peace. If you cannot create and maintain yourself, if your hands are too short to bring you any good, then all other people and more distant causes or agents are even more unable to take part in your creation and maintenance. Can you make your tongue, which is a tree of words, a pool of tastes, and an exchange of communication? If not, and you will never be able to do so, do not ascribe partners to God, for *that is a tremendous wrong* (31:13).

KNOW, O FRIEND, that the world is a Divine shop with all kinds of cloth, food, and drink, some of which are thick and solid and some, thin; some short-lived and some, perpetual; some in forms of kernels, some fluids, and some gaseous. Some are woven from nothing and created; others are fashioned through manifestations (of the relevant Divine Name or Names). (Most) philosophers have gone astray by seeing the existence of all as self-necessitated, and so confuse creating with fashioning.

KNOW, O FRIEND, that when associating partners with God in a veiled form arising from human egotism is solidified and condensed, it turns into associating material causes with God. [First of all, human ego sees itself as the originator and the real cause of its successes, or attributes its successes only to itself.] If this continues, it changes into attributing nothing to God with respect to its life. Beyond that, it changes—may God save us from such a state—into atheism.

KNOW, O FRIEND, that seeking light within darkness, by remaining under the carnal soul's influence and making that state one's nature, causes severe pain and shows disrespect to and defilement of light. Instead, leave darkness and look toward light once you are away from it, not from within it.

KNOW, O FRIEND, that humanity was created to open and unveil [the treasuries of Divine Names and Attributes], be a luminous sign [guiding to God], receive and reflect [Divine manifestations], be a light-giving moon reflecting Eternal Power, and a mirror for the manifestations of Eternal Beauty. Humanity has gained greater refinement and purity, and become more polished by undertaking the Trust refused by the heavens, Earth, and the mountains.

One requirement of undertaking this Trust is that people should be a unit of comparison to understand God's all-encompassing Attributes. The human ego, which becomes a dark point through heedlessness and associating partners with God, should be a switch to turn on those Attributes' lights. (Contrary to these essential functions), why and how do most people become veils and barriers? People are charged with opening; why and how do they close? They must illuminate; why and how do they darken? They must believe in God's Oneness; why and how do they associate partners with Him? They must view God through the observatory specially created for looking to Him, and acknowledge that His property and kingdom belong only to Him. Instead, viewing creation through the observatory of the human ego, people share His property among creatures, thus doing wrong and becoming ignorant.

KNOW, O SOUL, that if you please your Creator by abstaining from sin, obeying His commands, and doing righteous deeds, all that has been created also will be pleased. If the created are pleased with you on behalf of the Almighty, you will benefit; if they are pleased on behalf of themselves, there is no benefit, for they are impotent—just like you. Choosing the first alternative pleases your Lord; choosing the second causes you to associate partners with God. If you go to the capital to take care of some matter and please the king, your job will be done with great ease and you will gain the subjects' love. But if you expect your job to be done by those under the king's rule, many difficulties will be encountered, for all of them will have to be pleased and agree to fulfill your need. Moreover, even if this is accomplished, you still will have to obtain the king's permission, which depends on pleasing him.

KNOW, O FRIEND, that the Necessarily Existent Being does not resemble contingent things, which are absolutely dependent upon the Necessarily Existent Being for their existence, in His Essence, Attributes, and acts. For example, in His view there is no difference between near and far, few and many, small and large, individual and species, and part and whole. Unlike the contingent, He acts with ease, in no time, and does not busy Himself with anything. This is why the intellect cannot understand the nature of the Almighty's acts and goes so far as to deny the One Who does them.

A lion's teeth and claws show that it was made to tear; a melon's taste shows that it was made to be eaten. A human being's potential indicates that we were created to worship God. Our lofty spiritual dimension and longing for permanence and eternity point out that first we were created (in spirit) in a world more subtle and refined than this one, and then sent here to obtain the necessary equipment to return to our origin. As we are the fruit of the Tree of Creation, one person had to have been the seed of humanity from which the Maker grew the Tree of Creation. That seed only can be the most virtuous and greatest of the creation, upon whose identity all perfected people, nay, half of humanity—as creation has been painted in his spiritual color—have agreed: the master of all creation, Muhammad, upon him be peace and blessings.

Second part of the spark

In the Name of God, the All-Merciful, the All-Compassionate.

KNOW, O FRIEND, that God orders the heavens and Earth, and wraps night and day around the head of Earth, our cradle, like a lined turban. How could He entrust some sections of creation to some poor, contingent beings? Can that which is not the Lord of the Throne dispose of what is under the Supreme Throne? It cannot, for the Power has control and authority over all things, and leaves no room for outside intervention. Besides, the honor and dignity of His absolute authority and independence, as well as His will to be known and loved, do not allow others to be a veil (between Him and His creation) or a nominal means to attract God's servants to themselves.

Control over the whole and the part, of the species and the individual, occur simultaneously, one within and supporting the other. This activity cannot be shared between two agents, for the One Who ordered creation sustains, brings up, and directs humanity while simultaneously governing and conducting Earth. At the same time He conducts a species' affairs, He makes human cells and creates particles—the smallest parts of things—with the same Power He uses to control creation. He controls and manages by putting in order; He sustains, trains, and brings up by controlling and managing; and He disposes and creates by sustaining, training, and rearing. The sun cannot illuminate the ocean's face without simultaneously illuminating its bubbles' cheeks, its eyes' drops, and the pupils of the raindrops falling upon it.

That which is not the Power that wraps night and day around Earth cannot interfere even with a cell belonging to the smallest organ of any earthly inhabitant. The One Who made, fashioned, and ordered a fly's mind and a microbe's eye also has your actions recorded in a clear "notebook," and will call you to account for them.

KNOW, O FRIEND, that the absolute disposal, all-encompassing power, and all-seeing wisdom observed in every creature and particle—together with all they relate to and what happens around them—are clear evidences and manifest signs that the Maker of all things has no partner. There is no division, separation, or distribution in His Power. If a contingent being were the Maker, there would be division, separation, and sharing in his control and executing his power and will. Therefore, it is absolutely necessary that the Maker is One, and that His existence is Necessary. There is no limit to or division in His Power, which operates according to the measures of His Destiny and "writes" on Its lines.

KNOW, O FRIEND, that small animals are more intelligent, more sophisticated in structure, and more subtle in art than large ones. Despite this, their life is shorter and they seem to benefit from the world less than others. This clearly shows that the Maker can create everything with ease, and that He does not specially busy Himself with any of them. He only says: "*Be!*" and they are. Nothing can compel Him to do anything; He does what He wills and acts as He wills. There is no deity but He.

KNOW, O FRIEND, that the sun's image reflected in a bubble is both a part (of the bubble) and a tiny, individual sun bearing the real sun's attributes. These attributes give it the sun's identity, but not its nature. In short, it is neither the sun itself nor something other than the sun. The shares of all other things in the sun, that is, the sun's giving light and heat and color to the world, do not decrease the bubble's share, for it makes no difference to the bubble whether all other things exist or not. The bubble can say: "The sun belongs to me exclusively, is contained in me, and exists for me."

KNOW, O FRIEND, that what recedes from the vastest sphere of the Name "the Outward" and sees itself as almost nothing before It, comes near and restricts itself to the relative or real sphere of the Name "the Inward." In either case, *God surrounds them all* (85:20) through His Names and His Knowledge, Will, Power, and other Attributes. With their partial, limited minds lost in what they deal with, people viewing the Almighty's Grandeur and administration of the planets think it unlikely that He concerns Himself with creating, for example, a fly. People compare the absolutely Necessary One with the poor and contingent—a comparison provoked by Satan that causes people to despise small creatures.

This is a great injustice, for everything glorifies its Creator. Nothing lowers itself to accept as its lord anything or anyone other than the One for Whom this world is but one of His houses, the sun but one of His lanterns, and the stars but a few of His lamps, as if there were nothing living in the world save He. A large thing has no right to see itself as greater than a small one and feel pride therein, for like right being right without any difference between large and small, the existence of a small thing is just as valuable as that of a large thing.

KNOW, O FRIEND, that everything, from the sun of suns to the fruits of trees, when viewed carefully is chosen and distinguished among that which is infinite. Only the One, the manifestations of Whose Attributes are limitless, can control that which is infinite.

KNOW, O FRIEND, that all-encompassing provision does not exclude particular provision. God's bounties are not like rain or water, from which everyone can benefit without considering individual needs. Thus, individuals do not need to feel particular gratitude for them. Their needs are not like homemade pots to be filled with the Divine bounties they expect to pour in like rain. Rather, the real Bestower of bounties considers each individual comprehensively, makes a particular pot, and then fills it with His bounties. Just as giving thanks is incumbent on everyone for general favoring, it is incumbent on each individual for these particular bounties.

KNOW, O FRIEND, that most people do not give the proper respect due to the observed Book of the Universe and the Qur'an. Philosophers attribute to the Necessary Being a little part, a thin covering, a compound of nominal value, and then share the rest among causes—rather, among certain impossibilities and mere notions. *God destroy them! How they are perverted!* (9:30). However, one who believes in His Unity says: "Whatever exists belongs to Him, has come from Him, is returning to Him, and subsists by Him." Learned people, deceived by ideas and findings over time, wrong the Qur'an by ascribing only parts of the wording and meaning to the Lord of the Supreme Throne from that magnificent palace—the Qur'an. The rest of its firm foundations, well-established principles, golden building blocks, and blossoming trees they share among Earth's inhabitants.

Those who think that humanity has some control over what happens in the universe are sorely mistaken. They are like those who give only a few bubbles to the one who fills the ocean, or who ascribes the ocean's overflowing to a few bubbles. A truth-loving believer says: "Whatever is in the Qur'an is from God and belongs to Him." The Qur'an is interwoven in styles that consider each audience's level of understanding and temperament. Having come to us through 70,000 veils, it penetrates the depths of hearts and spirits, and spreads its blessings through all levels of human societies. Every era understands and knows it, every age acknowledges and accepts its perfection, every epoch makes friends with it and accepts it as its teacher, and every period needs and respects it to the degree it answers their specific needs. The Qur'an is not a superficial, shallow book; rather, it is a bottomless ocean, a shining sun, a profound guidance.

LOOK, O FRIEND, at water and air, how gentle and pervasive they are in creation. Glory be to Him Who provides and feeds both a microbe and an elephant. Look at the Owner of Power, how He makes food that both passes through a bee's throat and fills an elephant's mouth, which is not too big for a microbe's mouth nor so small that a rhinoceros disdains it. An audible word is received by an atom's ear and fills the sun's ear. That word is so multiplied that a cave is filled with it and echoes it back to you, yet it is not too big for the cells of a gnat's ear.

IMAGINE, O FRIEND, the Muslim world as a mosque at the times of daily Prayers, with Makka being the *mihrab* (where the imam stands), and the Ka'ba as the *mihrab*'s central point. Generations pray in this mosque, which is continuously filled with and emptied of successive generations.

O SAID! If you would find happiness and maintain your dignity, leave today with honor and dignity what will leave you tomorrow, causing you humiliation and misery. If you abandon the world, you will save yourself from its evils and inherit its good. If the world abandons you, you will be devoid of its good and reap its evil.

KNOW, O FRIEND, that modern civilization, which is corrupt, has opened a door to such an enormous, disgusting show and hypocrisy that, in the name of fame and reputation, hypocrisy rules the individual and the nation. The mass media make these "famous" people known to everyone, and, as modern concepts of history and recently written history books acclaim them, they urge others to follow them. The lives of individuals are sacrificed for racial considerations under the guise of nationalism.

KNOW, O FRIEND, that if people come together to make a sound unity, a community of women can acquire firm manliness, while a weak unity of men becomes woman-like. The Qur'anic phrases *women say* (12:30) [the original Arabic verb has the masculine form, while according to Arabic grammar it should have been feminine], and the *(male) Arabs of the desert say* (48:14) [the original Arabic verb has the feminine form], point to this. The united community of the weak is strong, while the disunited community of the powerful is weak.

KNOW, O FRIEND, that by rejecting devils and overcoming them, the doors of Paradise are opened.

KNOW, O FRIEND, that Divine Unity is one of the clearest proofs of Muhammad's Prophethood. Our master Muhammad, upon him be peace and blessings, raised the flag of Divine Unity above the heads of all beings and planted it at the peak of the universe. He also proclaimed Divine Unity, with all of its manifestations, to all beings and expounded what previous Prophets had left in an outlined and generalized form.

Third part of the spark

In the Name of God, the All-Merciful, the All-Compassionate.

KNOW, O FRIEND, that the decoration, perfection, beautiful spectacle, and majesty of Divine Lordship, as well as the splendor of Divinity, seen in the universe require an observer to observe them in amazement. When reflecting on them, such an observer must move from there to the Majesty of their Maker and Owner, and to His Power and Perfection. Human beings, despite their ignorance and tendency toward injustice, have so comprehensive a capacity that they can be considered samples of creation who have received a trust that can perceive and open the "hidden treasury." As our powers or faculties have not been restricted in creation, we may have a universal consciousness to understand the splendor of the eternal Sovereign's kingdom and His Divinity's magnificent beauty. Just as beauty demands the beholding of a lover (to see it), the Eternal Designer's Lordship requires the existence of those who will watch It in appreciation, amazement, and reflection. Such Lordship also necessitates permanent reflecting and bewildered observers to accompany what bewilders them on the way to eternity.

The One Who adorned the faces of flowers also created insects and birds to love them. He adorned the cheeks of beautiful things and created lovers who long for them, and made the world's face so ornate and attractive, its eyes shining with those smiling lamps. He embroidered the world with such excellent, perfect, and exceptional beauty that it arouses feelings of love for its Maker and curiosity to know Him. Such a Creator would not leave it without lovers to be amazed by it, those who would reflect, be fascinated, and aware of the value each beauty has. With his comprehensive nature, a perfect, universal person becomes the *raison d'être* of the universe's creation. Happiness and real pleasure lie in forsaking everything, including existence, for His sake. His existence is absolutely necessary. He is the absolutely Perfect One, the One of absolute Majesty, Grace, and Beauty.

May whatever I have, even my whole existence and whatever exists, be sacrificed for Him.

KNOW, O FRIEND, that just as correspondence and similarities among things point to the Maker's Oneness and Unity, orderly and purposeful dissimilarities and distinctions among them indicate that He is All-Wise, has absolute Will, and does as He wishes. For example, the similarity among human limbs and organs, particularly between pairs of organs, proves the Creator's Oneness. The essential dissimilarity among people, each being unique, is a clear sign that the Creator has absolute Will and Wisdom.

KNOW, O FRIEND, that humans are the most unjust of all beings. Due to their intense self-love, they value things according to how much benefit can be derived from them. They consider their fruits (as valuable) only to the degree they can benefit from them. They suppose that the aim of life is life itself, whereas every creature has wisdom, which is difficult for people to comprehend, relating to the Creator. Why should short-lived animate beings and fast-declining living organisms not be samples and examples, foundations and seeds for their wonderful likes in the intermediate worlds between this and the next, the material and the spiritual, and in the inner dimension of existence? Why should they not be manifestations or reflections and fruits in this world of the Divine Power's control in the World of the Unseen?

KNOW, O FRIEND, that just as the eye restricts itself to what it sees or what presents itself before it, the carnal, evil-commanding self denies the existence of what it does not see, even if it is clearly evident.

KNOW, O FRIEND, that through His Power's perfection, God subjugated all particles and compounds to His laws and commands of creation. He says to a gnat: "Be so!" and it becomes so, and says with the same ease to all animals: "Be of such features and forms, and with such length of life," and they are as they are ordered to be. The Power that took these heavenly objects in Its hand and arranged them, just as you have set gems on your mirror's frame, can do anything and allows nothing to interfere.

KNOW, O FRIEND, that a drop of water has the same nature as an ocean (both are water) and a river (both form from clouds). The sun's image in a drop has almost the same identity as the sun, and a minnow belongs to the same species as a shark (both are fish). A grain of wheat is the same as a heap of wheat. This is how the Divine Name manifested on the tiniest cell comes together on the thing on which It is manifested with the Name manifested on all creation. For example, the Name "All-Knowing" manifests Itself on a cell together with the Name "Creator," on a bee together with the Name "Fashioner," on a fruit together with the Name "Builder," and on an illness together with the Name "Healer." It is inconceivable for a Name with the broadest sphere of manifestation not to be manifested on the smallest thing.

KNOW, O FRIEND, that inertia, motionlessness, inactivity, and renewal mean a kind of death or non-existence for a contingent thing, for its life and survival depend on activity and constant renewal. Non-existence is pain and evil. Activity is a great pleasure, and renewal through change brings great good. Although there may be pain and sorrow in change and renewal, such pain and sorrow are good in many respects. Being the light of existence, life is refined through sorrow, purified through pain, and measured according to how it receives and reflects the Bestower of life's manifestations and qualities. Each life contains many aspects related to the Bestower of life, while a living thing itself has only one.

A bubble adorned with the sun's reflection cannot oppose the sun and demand something from it. Through belief, human beings, who are like bubbles in the ocean of existence, become like transparent, shining objects and glittering stars whose lamps are lit from the rays of the Eternal Sun.

KNOW, O FRIEND, that a builder builds a huge palace and furnishes it with whatever is necessary. He or she then builds and furnishes a smaller palace from the same material. Can one say that the builder's main aim is not to build a third, smaller palace, and that the purposes for its construction are not related to the builder? You, humanity, are that smaller palace, Earth is a palace, and so is the universe.

KNOW, O FRIEND, that God makes Himself known through His creatures and art, and loved through His Mercy, bounties, and provisions. He manifests almost all His Names for various reasons. Whoever understands perfectly why each Name manifests Itself and then explains it to others perfectly deserves to be addressed with the words: "But for you, I would not have created the worlds." He is such a firm, trustworthy bond between Earth and the heavens that Earth is connected to God's Supreme Throne by the rope woven in his heart. As a human being, he is the most honorable of creation; as a sample of humanity, he is the most perfect of living beings; and as an individual, he is the master and lord of the species honored with God's vicegerency on Earth. He is the master of the Messengers, leader of the pious, beloved of the Lord of the worlds—Muhammad, peace and blessings be upon him, and his Family and Companions until eternity.

Conclusion

Whatever is suffered for God is good. It is sweet even if apparently bitter, for it makes you taste the pleasure of supplicating and praying to Him. Ibn Sam'un[73] says: "Every speech unconcerned with Him is idle talk."

I am journeying to the Hereafter. I have so many sins that even several lifetimes would not be enough to ask forgiveness for them. Thus I entrust this task to my book. Alas! How pitiful, regrettable, and deplorable that I wasted my life, health, and youth in sin and rebellion for harmful, transient desires and fancies. What is left to my old age and ill health are sin and pain. With this heavy burden, dark face, and diseased heart I approach the door of the grave for an eternal separation from the transient world. How humiliated I will be when my Lord orders: "Drive all hypocrites to the Fire!"

O God! There is no shelter and refuge save
the door of Your Compassion.
O God! Your rebellious servant has come
acknowledging his sins, and he prays to You.
If You forgive him, this is what You love to do;
if You repel him, who else will have mercy on him?[74]
O God! I regret my sins and repent of them;
I am ashamed of my evil words and deeds.
Pour blessings into my heart from the world of holiness
so that fancies may be removed from my heart.
I ask You to open the door of Mercy
with the call of Mawlana:
O God! Repeatedly I call O God, O God!
And utter things for God on Your way.
O God! Guide me to the way leading to You;
I am astray, looking for the right way.
O God! I am not worthy of the highest floor of Paradise,
nor do I have strength to bear Hellfire.
Enable me to feel repentant of my sins
and ask forgiveness for them, and forgive me,
for You are the Forgiver of sins, however great they are.

---

[73] Abu al-Husayn Muhammad ibn Ahmad ibn Isma'il or Sam'un (913-97) was a Muslim ascetic from Baghdad renowned for his wisdom and wise sayings. (Tr.)

[74] Attributed to Ibrahim ibn Adham. (Tr.)

To conclude:

- There are as many doors opened toward God as there are parts of the (Book of the) Universe and its pages, and as many as there are compounds.
- The inner existence is superior to the outer existence in all aspects of life, consciousness, and perfection.
- Your unique facial features distinguish you from everyone else, although all faces have the same parts and structure. This shows that the Maker is infinitely independent and Wise and has absolute free choice.
- You are a conscious work of art made with wisdom, one indicating the Maker's Attributes.
- The One Who created you created the universe and its contents, for whatever is in you also exists in it.
- You are a restricted being, having a restricted body, lifetime, and power. So, do not waste your life on transient things.
- The carnal soul mistakenly thinks that it is excluded from the sphere of the manifestations of Destiny and Divine Attributes.
- One who gives light and existence and makes existence necessary must have these qualities, or else how could he give them?
- What a human soul desires most is permanence and perpetuity.
- Associating partners with God in a veiled form, due to human egotism, gradually turns into associating material causes as partners with God.
- Humanity was created to open and unveil (the treasuries of Divine Names and Attributes), be a luminous sign (guiding to God), receive and reflect (Divine manifestations), be a light-giving moon reflecting the Eternal Power, and be a mirror for the manifestations of Eternal Beauty.
- If you please your Creator by abstaining from sins, obeying His commands, and doing righteous deeds, you also will please the created.
- The Necessarily Existent Being does not resemble the contingent in His Essence, Attributes, or acts.
- A lion's teeth and claws show that it is expected to tear, a melon's delight shows that it is for eating, and human potential shows that humanity is to worship God.
- Small animals are more intelligent and sophisticated in structure, and subtler in art, than large ones.
- All-encompassing provision does not exclude specific, individual provision.

- Most human beings do not give the proper respect due to the observed Book of the Universe and the glorious book of the Qur'an when it is recited and heard.
- At the times of daily Prayers, imagine the Muslim world as a mosque, with Makka being the *mihrab* and the Ka'ba as the *mihrab*'s central point. This mosque, in which generations pray, is continuously filled with and emptied of successive generations.
- Leave today with honor and dignity what will leave you tomorrow.
- Modern civilization values corrupting hypocrisy, show, and fame.
- When coming together to forge a sound unity, a community of women can acquire firm manliness, while a weak unity of men becomes woman-like.
- Divine Unity is one of the clearest proofs of Muhammad's Prophethood.
- The Divine Lordship's decoration, perfection, beautiful spectacles, and majesty, as well as the Divinity's splendor, require observers to observe them in amazement.
- Just as the correspondence and similarities among things point to the Maker's Oneness and Unity, so do their orderly and purposeful dissimilarities and distinctions indicate that the Maker is All-Wise and has absolute Will, doing whatever He wills.
- Humans are the most unjust of all beings.
- Through His Power's perfection, God subjugated all particles and compounds to His laws and commands of creation.
- Inertia and motionlessness, inactivity and non-change mean a kind of death or non-existence for a contingent thing, for its life and survival depend on activity and constant renewal.
- God makes Himself known through His creatures and art, and loved through His Mercy, bounties, and provisions.
- Whatever is suffered for God is good, for it makes you taste the pleasure of supplicating and praying to Him.
- A supplication.

The
Ninth Treatise

The Ninth Treatise

A whiff from the breezes of the Qur'an's guidance

In the Name of God, the All-Merciful, the All-Compassionate.

Praise be to God, the Lord of the worlds, for His mercy to the worlds through the Messengership of Muhammad, the master of the Messengers, upon him, his Family, and Companions be peace and blessings.

KNOW, O FRIEND, THAT CREATION, WHETHER IN THIS WORLD OR THE World of the Unseen, testifies that *There is no deity but He*. This is required and displayed by the cooperation and solidarity among creation's parts. The pillars of creation and all structures testify that *There is no Lord but He*,[75] which is required and displayed by the similarity and correspondence among those pillars and structures.

All organs and limbs of all earthly beings testify that *There is no owner and master but He*, which is required and displayed by their having almost the same formation and functions. All parts of all plants and animals testify that *There is no director and organizer but He*, which is required and displayed by the mutual helping among those parts. All subdivisions of these same parts testify that *There is no trainer but He*, which is required and displayed by the correspondence among individual members of species. The fact that they have almost the same organs and structures shows the same Pen and

---

75 The Divine Name *al-Rabb*, usually translated as Lord, denotes God as One Who raises, brings up, sustains, educates, trains, and administers all things. (Tr.)

indicates that the Trainer is one. The diversity among countenances bears witness that the Inscriber is absolutely free, doing whatever He wills.

All cells forming these parts and organs testify that *There is no disposer but He*, and that disposal is possible only by His commands or laws of creation and operation. If the Disposer were not one and single, there would have to be infinite disposers who are absolutely equal in terms of qualities and opposites, independent and dependent, unrestricted and restricted, and so on. All atoms forming these cells testify that *There is no orderer but He*, as is required and displayed by the similarities and correspondence among atomic structures, working, and functions. And with all its particles, the main substance of creation—ether—testifies that *There is no deit- but He*, as is required and displayed by its simplicity, calmness, and immobility as well as by the speed it shows in fulfilling the Creator's orders.

KNOW, O FRIEND, that no one has the right to complain about and object to the Maker of the universe. If such a demand were to be satisfied, thousands of instances of wisdom having parts in the general order of creation (which rejects such a satisfaction) would have to be violated or sacrificed. *If truth had followed their caprices, the heavens, and Earth, and all those who live in them would certainly have gone to ruin* (23:71).

O COMPLAINING ONE! How can you object and make your caprices the standard for the universe's order, and your corrupt taste as the measure of Divine bounties? How do you know that what you see as a misfortune is not a blessing? Are you authorized to change the direction of creation's turning wheels to satisfy your trifling and worthless fancies? You can complain only to Him, not about Him, for what falls to your lot from Him is only a "grain" out of heaps of corn. One who is owned cannot be the owner. Know your place and do not overstep the limits of your authority.

KNOW, O FRIEND, that the one who operates in a cell operates in the whole body, for he must operate in a cell according to its relation with the body. The operation in a cell is under the command of the Creator of all things.

HOW, O FRIEND, can it befit the Wisdom and Attribute of Preserving of the One Who preserves the eggs of vermin and fish and the seeds of plants for wise, merciful purposes not to record and preserve your deeds? Those deeds are the seeds of trees that will yield their fruit in the Hereafter. This is especially true in our case, since we are the bearers of His trust and His vicegerents on Earth. Every living being has the strong desire and inclination to preserve its life. This, and the tendency in creation to reconcile opposites to continue life, point out that worldly existence will result in eternal permanence through the manifestation of the Names All-Living, All-Preserving, and Everlasting. They also allude to a fact determined by Divine Destiny: Each perishable, transitory thing has a vital, permanent point or aspect.

KNOW, O FRIEND, that the One Who preserves a fig tree's seed while it is changing into a fig, and does not allow it to rot in the ground so that it can grow into a fig tree—that All-Preserving and Protecting One Who protects all other plants and animals—will not neglect the deeds of humanity, His vicegerent on Earth.

KNOW, O FRIEND, that meaning's material existence (i.e., letters and words) may change and be effaced, but the meaning continues to exist. A covering may be rent, but its essence or kernel remains. Clothes are worn out but the body survives; the body is ruined but the spirit survives. The body gets old but ego remains young; multiplicity and the multiple are divided and decay, but unity and the unitary remain permanent. Matter dissolves but light endures. Despite its putting on different "bodies" and its numerous changes and different conditions, "meaning" endures from the beginning of its life to its end and maintains its unity (it does not change). This shows that it will pass over the "ditch" of death and, freed from its hooks and stripped of its body, continue on to eternity safe and sound. The strong tendency of material (temporary) things to remain and survive points out that such simple things as meaning, light, and spirit (inclined to permanence) will remain eternally.

KNOW, O FRIEND, that the grandeur of God's Divinity and Its dignity and absolute independence require that all things should be at His control. Your physically small size and some of your seemingly unimportant states do not necessitate your being excluded from this control. Your distance from Him does not mean His being distant from you. The insignificance of some of your attributes and of your existence; your imperfect character, mind, and life-style; and your ignorance with regard to the universal wisdom in your existence do not exempt you from this control. The Creator's greatness does not require excluding small things from His control, as greatness necessitates being encompassing in controlling and independent in creating.

KNOW, O FRIEND, that as material, solid things get larger, they lose their sensitivity to delicate, subtle things. But light, when it expands and spreads, begins to pervade and penetrate more deeply into hidden and subtle things. As light becomes more refined, like X-rays, it becomes more penetrating. If this is so with the dimensions of contingent existence, imagine how it is with the Light of Lights, Necessarily Existent and Single, Knower of all secrets and the hidden, and the Disposer of night and day. His greatness necessitates His being all-encompassing, penetrating, and pervasive.

KNOW AND SEE HOW the Qur'an considers ordinary people's level of understanding, as they are the absolute majority. When a matter can be explained in several ways, it chooses the one most suitable for its audience. If this were not so, the argument would be more abstruse than the conclusion.[76] The Qur'an mentions natural phenomena to deduce the Creator's Attributes. What is understandable to ordinary people is also more suitable for guidance.

For example, the Qur'an says: *And of His signs is the creation of the heavens and Earth and the differences of your tongues and colors* (30:22). Behind the difference of colors lies God's creation of people with distinguishing marks and countenances. The Qur'an also says: *There are signs [for God's Existence and Unity] in the creation of the heavens and Earth and the alternation of night and day* (3:190). Earth's rotation on its axis and revolution around the sun is revealed under the "sheet" of night and day.[77]

The Qur'an says: *(We have made) the mountains as pegs* (78:7). In this verse, Earth is likened to a ship (sailing in the ocean of space) or a tent fastened and made steady with pegs (mountains), which cause Earth's wrath to subside. Otherwise, *it would nearly burst with rage* (67:8) because of its inner convulsions. Earth also breathes through mountains. Without them, it would cleave apart, for it is by virtue of its mountains that Earth only quakes and then settles down. Mountains are reservoirs of water, filters for air, and protect land from the ocean's invasion. So, in a figurative meaning, mountains are pegs (pillars) of life.

---

76 For example, if the Qur'an, which guides people to Divine truths, described the subatomic world in the phraseology of modern science, earlier generations could not have understood it.

77 If it said: *There are signs [for God's Existence and Unity] in Earth's revolution around itself and sun, and night and day occurring thereby respectively*, it would have confused millions of people who lived before this discovery. (Tr.)

The Qur'an considers ordinary people first. For example, Islamic law recognizes the sighting of the crescent moon (to determine the beginning and end of Ramadan and the beginning of Dhu al-Hijja, the month of Hajj), rather than astronomical calculation, and also contains reiterations to establish and repetitions to confirm.

KNOW, O FRIEND, that the Qur'anic verses are far richer in meaning than poetic imagination and far superior in every possible way. The One Who speaks in the Qur'an describes His Essential Qualities and acts, whereas most poetry talks about others. The Qur'an is mostly extraordinary when describing the ordinary; poetry is mostly ordinary when talking about the extraordinary.

KNOW, O FRIEND, that the mirrors reflecting and the "pages" (of creation) bearing witness to God's Unity are infinite and multifarious, one within the other, and originate from the same center. Seeing one requires seeing the others; unveiling one enables one to enter into all of them. If you cannot see one, this never means that the others are veiled or non-existent. Despite this, the carnal, evil-commanding soul, instructed by Satan, denies what is essentially true and confirms what is essentially false.

KNOW, O FRIEND, that the one who writes the word writes the letter, the one who writes the line writes the page on which it appears, and the one who writes the page writes the book. Thus the Creator of an ant must be the Creator of all animal species, and the Creator of all animal species must be the Lord of the worlds. It is a sign of the absolute, all-encompassing Lordship that a word or even a book is inscribed in a large letter. A sea is a large letter, and trees are lines of the Book of the Universe. Earth is a point in the whole universe. The Creator writes (creates) the word "fish" in the letter of the sea, and some earthly, moving creatures in the lines of trees and animals in the point of Earth. One may think that a small ant would be neglected, but this is not true. Just as *Sura Ya Sin* can be written within its initial letters *Ya* and *Sin*, so are creatures written in their eggs or seeds.

KNOW, O FRIEND, that the resemblance among stars and suns shows that their Lord cannot be like or one of them. The Lord of one of them is the Lord of all of them and of all things. O people, if only you were just and fair-minded in respect of what you suffer from such creatures as fleas and gnats. While those fine, innocent creatures bear with a perfect submission your biting of all fruits and most animals, is it fair to retaliate for even the slightest thing they inflict upon you?

KNOW, O FRIEND, that a person is a community formed of responsible organs and limbs. Each outer and inner sense has a particular form of worship, as it may be rebellious or sinful due to misuse. Prostrating before that which is not God is misguidance, as is the imagination of poets prostrating themselves before and adoring all beauty that is not God and not for His sake. Such things lead the imagination to transgress [the limits established by God].

KNOW, O FRIEND, that one of the greatest causes of misguidance is the human tendency to regard something familiar as known because it is common and usual. However, this tendency may cause ignorance, for people do not reflect on such things, even though they are miracles of Divine Power. Rather, they pay attention to what they consider extraordinary because it is rare. This is like looking at the waves caused by wind, and the sea's shining with the sun's images, without considering the whole sea with all its animals and flora. Then people attempt to mention those waves or images, not the animals and flora, as the proofs of the grandeur of the sea's Owner and Maker.

KNOW, O FRIEND, that most of what we know about Earth and consider evident is based on a superficial familiarity, a veil spread over ignorance, and without foundation. Thus the Qur'an draws our attention to the usual and the ordinary. With its piercing expressions, it draws aside the veil of superficial familiarity to show that what we see as usual and ordinary is in fact extraordinary.

KNOW, O FRIEND, that the relationship and conversation between two things do not require their being equal or similar to each other. A raindrop and a blossom have a relationship and transaction with the sun. Human beings should never suppose that their smallness veils them from the favoring of the Creator of all things.

KNOW, O FRIEND, that the expansion of time for some saints should not be regarded as impossible. For example, Imam Sha'rani studied Ibn al-'Arabi's four-volume *Al-Futuhat al-Makkiya* (Makkan Conquests [Discoveries]) two-and-a-half times in a day.[78] This can be understood by the fol-

---

78 Imam Sha'rani, 'Abd al-Wahhab ibn Ahmad ibn 'Ali al-Hanafi (1493-1564) was an Egyptian Sufi scholar. His most famous works are *Al-Mizan al-Kubra'* (The Greatest Balance) and *Al-Anwar al-Qudsiya fi Ma'rifat Adab al-'Ubudiya* (Sacred Lights in Knowing the Matters of Servanthood). This ability was recorded at the end of *Al-Yawaqit wa al-Jawahir* ["Rubies and Other Kinds of Gems"]. (Tr.)

lowing examples: During a dream that lasts for a few seconds, you seem to have lived for a year. If you read the Qur'an during such a time, you could read it from beginning to end several times. Certain saints who can unveil what is hidden to other people experience such expansions of time while awake. They are as if acting in the sphere of the spirit, which is uncontained by time, and almost with its speed.

Motion is like time's body, or time is like motion's color, for whatever takes place in one takes place in the other. So, why should a saint whose bodily existence is dominated by his or her spirit not be able to move with the speed of the spirit or imagination?

Know, O friend, that some people cannot comprehend the consequences of Divine Unity, and their corrupt imagination cannot bear them. They try to reject the authentic, decisive proofs that establish Divine Unity and, arguing that such proofs cannot give such a tremendous result, try to undermine their authenticity. They do not know that belief supports and leads to consequence, the proof being only a window through which to look at it, or a brush to sweep away the (dust of) illusions on it. Besides, there are as many proofs for Divine Unity as there are specks of dust in deserts, raindrops, and waves in the ocean.

Know, O friend, that the One Who prepares melons and apples for you to eat knows better than you what you need to eat, and is aware of what pleases your conscience. Do the branches and stems of plants and trees know these things? Such means or causes of Divine bounties are only channels of Mercy and canals of bounties.

Second part of the whiff

In the Name of God, the All-Merciful, the All-Compassionate.

Glory be to God. How thin is the veil between the outer and inner, invisible dimensions of existence. And yet how great is the distance between them. How short, yet long, is the way between this world and the Hereafter. How fine, yet thick, is the veil between knowledge and ignorance. How transparent, yet dense, is the space between belief and unbelief. How short is the distance between servanthood to God and rebellion, despite their being as far apart as Paradise and Hell. How short is life, yet how great is ambition.

Likewise, between yesterday and today there is a thin veil that cannot prevent the spirit from passing and penetrating into yesterday and even beyond. For the body, however, this distance is so great that it would take a year to travel through it. The veils between the outer and inner dimensions of existence and between the world and the Hereafter are thin and transparent for people whose hearts and spirits are alive and awake, while they are extremely thick for those who obey their carnal souls and bodily desires.

Similarly, there is a fine interval between your night and day: your "eyelid." When you open the eye of your self, your night disappears and your day shines. But if you forget what you are, you fall into permanent night. When looking at the universe for the Almighty's sake, all that is seen becomes a (source of) knowledge; when doing so from heedlessness and material or natural causes, all that is seen as knowledge becomes sheer ignorance.

Between the illumination of the Aya Sofya (Hagia Sophia) and its being in thick darkness at night, there is a moment as short as switching the lights on or off. The flash of lightning and its disappearance occur almost simultaneously. The sky darkens and is cleared, in rapid succession, by a breeze of mercy. One who sees with the light of belief and belief in Divine Unity sees the universe as filled with light and friendship, mutual love and affection, and all things and beings in it as amiable, living brothers and sisters. But one who looks with unbelief sees all things and beings as dreadful corpses and strangers hostile to one another. Such a person also sees the universe in veils of darkness, and oneself in a deep sea covered by waves, above which are clouds. When he or see stretches out a hand, it is almost invisible.

The veil between a mirror's two faces is thinner than a leaf, but the difference between them is as great as that between east and west. With a movement of a finger, the mirror either smiles at you or makes your face completely dark. In the same way, our deeds have two "faces." Those done with the intention to please God provide you with a transparent face, in the depth of which numberless manifestations are reflected. The lack of such an intention shows a dark, opaque face that bears nothing in the name of truth.

While a dark face has no depth and contains nothing, as it only occupies enough space to show itself, a transparent face, because of its relation to the immaterial World of Representations or Immaterial Forms, can contain limitless huge things. In the same way, life has two faces: One relates to the world and is dark, narrow, and transient; the other relates to the Ultimate Truth and is transparent, broad, and permanent. The heedless carnal soul, under the influence of a devilish sophistry, wears the dark face but demands what is possible in the transparent face, such as seeking eternity.

KNOW, O FRIEND, that your ego holds the key of creation. Although creation's doors seem to be open, actually they are closed. God, the Ultimate Truth has entrusted humanity with a key that opens all of creation's doors and unveils the Creator's treasury. This key is your ego, which is an enigma. When you solve that enigma by knowing its nature, creation is opened to you.

God Almighty gave each person an ego, which serves as a unit of comparison, so they could understand the attributes of Divine Lordship. When you know what the ego is, you see it as fine and weak, like a conscious hair in the rope of your existence, like a thin stripe in the cloth of your nature, like an *alif* (the first Arabic letter) in your book. It also has two faces: One turned to good, a passive recipient (not the agent) of God's bounties and blessings; the other turned to evil and non-existence, and thinking itself an agent. It has an illusory nature and an imagined lordship and sovereignty. Its existence is so weak that it can bear nothing by itself. It is like a thermometer or a similar instrument that measures things and properties to know the Necessarily Existent Being's absolute, all-encompassing Attributes. You should be well aware of this and, becoming a referent of: *He has indeed prospered who purifies it* (91:9), should fulfill the Trust you have been given.

If you consider your ego a unit of comparison to comprehend the Creator's Attributes and Names, it becomes an eye for you to see what exists in the universe. In your ego, this information finds that which will confirm it and transform it into real knowledge. Then its claim of lordship or sovereignty and self-ownership ends, and it perceives its existence as illusory. But if you consider your ego independent and thereby breach the Trust, you will be among those referred to in: *And indeed he has ruined it who stunts and spoils it* (91:10), for it is the ego that the heavens, Earth, and mountains shrank from bearing. For such an ego is the source of associating partners with God, as well as of all evil and misguidance. If ego hides itself from you, it grows thick and swells until it swallows you and transforms you into an ego. It grows stronger with tribal and then racial fanaticism, until it becomes a devil contending against its Maker's command. Then it likens other people, things, and natural causes with itself, attributing self-ownership and sovereignty to each, and begins to associate partners with God. If you look at creation while in this state, everything is closed just when it seems to have opened, for your eyes return to your self and you see everything as colored by ego. The color of ego is associating partners with, or denying, God. Even if all horizons were filled with the most manifest signs (of the Creator's Existence and Unity), what remains in the ego would be a dark point covering all those signs.

An important matter

Ego has two faces, one represented by prophethood, the other by human philosophy.

The first face, the origin of pure servanthood to God, points only to God. With this face, ego has an illusory, dependent existence. Although it appears self-owning, it is owned and controlled by God. It has a supposed (not an established) reality, and serves as a measure, a unit of comparison, to understand the Creator's Attributes. This reality is seen by all Prophets, who submitted existence to God; affirmed and demonstrated that He has no partners in His Sovereignty, Lordship, and Divinity; and that He holds the keys of, and has absolute power over, all things. From this transparent face of ego, the All-Compassionate has grown a blessed tree of servanthood whose blessed branches, spread through the garden of the universe, hang with clusters of fruits of Messengers, Prophets, saints, and truth-seeking, pure scholars glittering in the darkness like stars.

The second face, based on philosophy, presents ego with an independent, self-owned existence pointing to itself. Philosophers say that ego has an established reality and that its duty is to become perfected through self-love. This has engendered many kinds of associating partners with God, especially the accursed tree of misguidance. Its branch of lust, which appreciates unjust might or force and physical beauty enamored of show, has given to humanity idols before which the misguided prostrate.[79] The branch of wrath has saddled humanity with Pharaohs and Nimrods, while that of reason has produced atheists and materialists. Philosophers attribute to God only a part of His kingdom, and attribute the rest to that which is not Him.

[79] Idols are both objects worshipped and idolized people, such as movie stars, sports personalities, singers,"heroes," and others. Ironically, people idolized by their admirers or followers must themselves bow before their admirers to preserve their status. (Tr.)

Although ego is essentially like air or vapor, the philosophers' mistaken view causes it to grow denser, becoming like fluid and then, due to superficial familiarity, like a solid thing. Heedlessness then causes it to become frozen, after which rebellion causes it to get stronger and swell until it swallows its owner. It becomes broader with tribal or racial attitudes and then, because of ascribing self-existence, ownership, and even creativity to other people and natural causes (as it ascribes the same to itself), ego starts to contend against its Creator's command. Some philosophers believe that natural causes have real effects in creation and the control of things, and attribute creativity to nature and chance. That is why they deny the Resurrection and accept that spirits or, as is the case with materialists, matter have no beginning. May God assail their perversity, for their conceit has made them playthings of devils, who have thrown them into the pits of misguidance.

Ego in the normo-cosmos (humanity) is the counterpart of nature in the macro-cosmos: Both have been attributed partnership with God and therefore deified. *Whoever denies false deities and believes in God has indeed taken hold of the most unbreakable handle. God is All-Hearing, All-Knowing* (2:256).

KNOW, O FRIEND, that good deeds acquire vitality through sincere intention, and are corrupted through show, ostentation, and hypocrisy. The feelings for and (natural) tendencies toward good ingrained in one's conscience lose their purity through conscious or purposeful intention. Intention is the life of deeds, while purposeful intention is the death of natural states. For example, the intention to be humble spoils humility, the intention to be great provokes contempt, the intention to have relief causes relief to disappear, and the intention to be sad decreases sadness.

KNOW, O FRIEND, that the law of growth operates in a tree. The tree's seed (its essence) is contained by the fruit and, unless somehow impeded, grows by eternal Favoring into the tree and again is placed in its fruit. The fruit is the tree's most valuable, esteemed, pleasant, important, and illustrious part, as it is the reason for the tree's existence. The universe is a tree, and its branches are such basic elements as earth, water, air, and fire. Its leaves are plants, its blossoms are animals, and its fruits are men and women.

The greatest, most radiant, illustrious, beautiful, noble, comprehensive, and beneficial fruit is Prophet Muhammad, the master of the Messengers, the leader of the pious, and the beloved of the Lord of the worlds. He made the Ascension and his eyes did not swerve. The moon split for him. The lizard, gazelle, wolf, camel, mountain, rock, pole, tree, and clod of earth spoke to him. From his fingers flowed water like the Spring of Kawthar. He is the most virtuous person, one carrying all truths of belief in his person. All manifestations of Divine Favoring reach creatures through him, and on him are concentrated all mysteries of God's Mercifulness.

He commands the "cavalry" of the Prophets and the pious ones faithful to their allegiance and promises, and is the most virtuous of all creatures. He bears the standard of the greatest glory through belief in and submission to Divine Unity, and owns the most esteemed and dignified rope through Islam. He witnesses eternal mysteries, observes the lights, and translates the tongues of those preceding him. He is the source of knowledge, forbearance, and wisdom. He attained servanthood's highest rank, was distinguished with the highest morality of the purest ranks, and is God's greatest friend and His most noble beloved. Upon him be the most meritorious blessings and peace so long as the heavens and Earth remain.

> Take my hand, O master of the Messengers. You are a desired and sought one, O manifest light of God's Munificence; I have no leader, no refuge, other than you. My proof is: "There is no deity but God, and Muhammad is God's Messenger."
>
> O God! I wish I had thousands of tongues with which to ask You for forgiveness until the Day of Judgment. O God! Substitute my treatise for those tongues asking for forgiveness and calling blessings upon the Prophet on my behalf forever.
>
> O God! Sins have made me dumb, and the abundance of my rebellion shames me. My great heedlessness causes me to lower my voice. I knock on the door of Your Mercy and cry at the door of Your Forgiveness with the tongue of my master and support, Shaykh 'Abd al-Qadir al-Jilani, may God bless him, and with his appeal, which is acceptable and familiar to the door-keeper:
>
> O One Whose Mercy embraces all things! O One in Whose Hand is the dominion of all things! O One Whom nothing can harm or benefit, Whom nothing can overcome and from Whom nothing can be hidden, Whom nothing tires or helps, Whom doing something can prevent from doing another thing simultaneously; and Whom nothing resembles nor baffles! Forgive me for whatever I do (that displeases You) so that You may not call me to account for anything (sinful) that I did.
>
> O One Who holds everything by the forelock and in Whose Hand are the keys of all things! O One Who is the First, before all things; the Last, after all things; the Outward, above all things; the

Inward, inmost of all things; One overwhelming all things! Forgive me for all things. You are powerful over all things. O One knowing, encompassing, seeing, beholding, overseeing, penetrating, and well aware of all things! Forgive me for all my sins and errors so that You may not call me to account for anything. You are powerful over all things.

O God! I take refuge in Your Majesty's might and Your Might's majesty, and in Your Sovereignty's power and Your Power's sovereignty, from losing my relation to You and lethal fancies. O Neighbor of those who seek Your neighborhood! Protect me from satanic lust, clean me of human dirt, and purify me through sincere love of Your Prophet Muhammad, upon him be peace and blessings, from the rust of heedlessness and fancies of ignorance.

(I ask this so) that I may be freed of my selfhood, my ego, and so that only what is for and with You, to and from You, may remain; and that I may be overwhelmed by Your favor in the ocean of Your Generosity. (May I be) among those made victorious by Your Sword, favored with Your gifts, and kept away by Your protection from engagements interrupting from You.

O Light of lights, Knower of secrets, Director of night and day. O Sovereign, Mighty, Overwhelming, Compassionate, Loving, Forgiving. O Knower of the Unseen, Turner of hearts and eyes, Veiler of defects (of His servants), Forgiver of sins! Forgive me and have mercy on him who is in insurmountable difficulty, to whom all doors are closed, who follows the path of the righteous with great difficulty, and whose days are spent in places of heedlessness, rebellion, and sin. O One Who answers when called! O One swift at reckoning! O Munificent and Bestower! Have mercy on him who has severe ills that are hard to cure, and who has small and weak means while stricken with grave misfortune! You are His refuge and his hope.

O God! I complain to You about my difficulties and affliction. O God! My need is my justification, and whatever I have in the name of means is only my lack of means and my helplessness. O God! One drop from the ocean of Your Grace makes me rich, and one droplet from the flood of Your Forgiveness suffices me.

O Loving! O Loving! O Loving! O Owner of the Supreme Throne! O Starter and Returner! O One doing whatever He wills! I ask You, for the sake of the Light of Your "Face" that fills all the columns of Your Throne, and Your Power with which You are powerful over all Your creatures, and Your Mercy that embraces all things. There is no deity but You, O Helper. I ask You to help me and forgive my sins and the blunders of my tongue during my life, for the sake of Your Mercy, O Most Merciful of the merciful! Amen. Amen. Amen.

O ONE WHO RECITES this cry of asking forgiveness! Recite it first on your behalf and then on my behalf for the sake of God. For I lie in my grave unable to do or say anything. I can speak only with your tongue through my book, so speak on my behalf only for the sake of God.

Third part of the whiff

In the Name of God, the All-Merciful, the All-Compassionate.

I ask God for help to continue on the way to Him. Glory be to Him Who makes the heavens speak with His praise and glorify with the words of the planets and other stars. O One Who makes Earth speak with His praise and glorify (Him) with the words of trees and plants, Who makes trees and plants speak with the words of flowers and fruits, Who makes flowers and fruits speak with the words of seeds and stones, and Who makes seeds and stones speak with the words of spikes and grains.

Glory be to You Whom light glorifies with praise in all its radiations, air with its winds, water with its rivers, Earth with its rocks, plants with their flowers, trees with their fruits, the atmosphere with its birds, clouds with their rain, and the sky with its moons.

Blessings and peace be upon our master Muhammad, the lamp of the Prophets, the moon of purified scholars, the star of saints, the sun of humanity and jinn, and the light of the east and the west, and upon his Family, the stars of guidance, and Companions, the lamps illuminating darkness.

KNOW, O ONE WHO finds it very hard to understand the meaning of: *We have made them* (stars) *missiles for devils* (67:5). In order to reach the sky of this verse, we need a ladder with seven steps.

First step: The heavens have inhabitants of their own called angels. Just as Earth, despite its insignificant size when compared with the heavens, is full of living, conscious beings, so the heavens, with their decorated castles of constellations, must be full of conscious beings particular to themselves.

The universe is richly adorned with beauty, design, and embroidery requiring the existence of beings to reflect on them with appreciation and amazement. Beauty is displayed only for its lover, as food is given only to the hungry. Humanity and jinn, due to their number or inability, cannot observe and reflect on all of the majestic beauty of existence, for this requires the existence of many kinds of angels and other spirit beings.

Second step: There is a close relationship and transaction between Earth and heavens. For example, light, heat, and similar blessings come from the heavens. This shows and requires that there is a way for humanity to ascend to the heavens, as realized by the Prophets, saints, and spirit beings (other than angels), by being stripped of their bodily weight.

Third step: The heavens' order, peace, and tranquility show that their inhabitants must not resemble those of Earth, where confusion and convulsion, conflict and testing prevail due to the intermixing of good and evil. The heavens' inhabitants are obedient, doing what they are ordered.

Fourth step: The Master of the Day of Reckoning and the Lord of the worlds has Names with different rulings and requiring different manifestations. For example, the Name requiring that angels be sent to fight unbelievers in the lines of the Prophet's Companions also requires the struggle between angels and devils, between the good of the heavens and the evil of Earth.

Fifth step: Evil spirit beings imitate good ones in their attempt to ascend to the heavens. The inhabitants of the heavens confront and repel them. The wisdom of the Divine Lordship's sovereignty requires that this heavenly contest have a sign in this visible, material world so that humanity, who has been told to watch and observe, can be informed of it. The best way of making this struggle known is to shoot stars or meteors from the high towers of constellations. Unlike all other cosmic events having many instances of wisdom, there is no wisdom proper to this event other than serving as a sign of this heavenly struggle—an instance of wisdom known and witnessed by all truth-seeking people.

Sixth step: The Qur'an seeks to guide people to truth and hold them back from rebellion with lofty styles and exalted analogies or comparisons. For example, consider: *O company of people and jinn, if you can penetrate the spheres of the heavens and Earth, then penetrate (them)! You will not penetrate them except with an authority* (55:33). The verse proclaims the helplessness of humanity and jinn before the kingdom of Divine Lordship's vastness and immensity, as if to say: "O humanity, helpless, poor, and tiny. How dare you rebel against a Sovereign Whom all suns and moons, stars and angels obey; who throws missiles as large as mountains, or even larger, at devils! How dare you rebel in the kingdom of a King among Whose soldiers are those who shoot in the face of enemies stars the size of your Earth as easily as you throw walnuts or hazelnuts!"

Seventh step: There are many kinds of stars, just as there are many kinds of angels and fish. Whatever shines in the heavens is called a star. Some glitter like jewels and adorn the heavens as fruits adorn a garden and fish a sea. There are others used to kill devils as a sign of the existence of the guards in the heavens who are on the alert, and obedient, and who refrain from mixing with the rebellious, or as a symbol of the law of struggle or contest prevailing in the heavens. God's is the perfect, most conclusive argument and the greatest wisdom.[80]

KNOW, O FRIEND, that many Qur'anic verses state that things are recorded before and during their physical existence, such as: *Nothing of wet or dry but (it is recorded) in a Manifest Book* (6:59). This is confirmed by the Book of the Universe's systems and compositions and its "verses," especially those of universal order and harmony, balance and fashioning, adornment and distinguishing.

---

80 Scientists have offered no acceptable reason for meteor showers, which occur almost every year. However, the Perseid meteor shower observed almost every year suggests that meteors are shot for certain, important purposes, for they surprise observers by showing great diversity. The observations made in 1993, for example, show that the structure of such showers remains poorly understood.

Preliminary data from European observers indicated that the rates gradually increased to ZHR of order 100 m/h between 20:00, 11 August and 01:00, 12 August. Observers in France reported a noticeable increase in rates after 00:30, 12 August, with the rate being about twice that of "normal." The rates continued to climb between 01:00 and 03:00. A preliminary ZHR of 200-250 was ascribed to this period. The rates appeared to reach a maximum between 03:00 and 03:30. The ZHR at maximum was estimated to be of the order of 500. Observations from the Canary Islands indicated that the rates began to decline after 04:00.

Higher than normal rates were reported from many observers in the U.S. and Japan. As Martin Beech commented in *Astronomy* (p. 11), the results clearly indicated that the shower did not behave as predicted. Speculation about a possible meteor storm proved incorrect. Another unexpected feature in 1993 was the high number of bright fireballs seen. Observers reported something like five times the normal level of Perseid fireballs on the night of 11/12 August. The Perseid shower once again showed how hard it is to predict meteor shower activity. (Tr.)

According to data given by the International Meteor Organization about the events of the 1993 shower (*Astronomy*, October 1993), the first results posted for the night of 11/12 August came from Japan. Up to 20:30 (all times UT), 11 August, the meteor rates were found to be normal. A zenithal hourly rate (ZHR) of 40 meteors per hour (m/h) was tentatively assigned to the shower at this time. (Tr.)

Other proofs are seeds, measures, and forms. Seeds are tiny cases holding that which Divine Destiny has measured, determined, and appointed. Divine Power builds according to Destiny's precise measures, and uses particles in that building. These measures are exact molds (pre-)existing in Divine Knowledge. Despite their being blind, deaf, and unconscious, particles move for the growth of things in exact measure. Without overstepping the limits determined for them, as if having very acute sight and hearing, they go and settle just where they must to produce great results like fruits.

As evidence of recording during the existence of things, all fruits, the result and consummation of trees and like rolls of paper on which their "deeds" have been recorded, display to witnesses what the trees have experienced. The seeds they contain are buried in soil and burst forth the following spring to grow into a new tree, demonstrating thereby the life of the previous tree.

Another evidence is the mustard seed-sized human memory, which is like a document copied out of our deeds' notebook by the Hand of Divine Power with the Pen of Destiny. This will be given to us at the Final Reckoning so that we may see what we did here. Memory also shows that behind this hustle and bustle, turmoil and decay, there are "permanent mirrors" on which the All-Powerful One records the pictures and identities of all decaying things. In addition, there are boards or tablets on which the All-Preserving, All-Knowing One copies the lives of transient things and writes their results.

KNOW, O FRIEND, that a clock is not stable, for its parts vibrate and move. So does the world, which is like a huge clock that also shakes and moves. Including time in its movement, night and day resemble the second hand, a year the minute hand, and a century the hour hand. Including space, atmosphere occurs and undergoes very swift changes and alterations, like the second hand; Earth's surface displays a continuous change of plants and animals through the cycle of life and death, like the minute hand; and Earth's interior exhibits, like the hour hand, great changes and convulsions. Like the hand pointing to days, the heavens become a vast scene of change with its bodies' movement, the appearance of comets and meteors, and the birth and death of stars.

The world or worldly life is based on these seven pillars—day and night, year and century, Earth, atmosphere, and the heavens. It serves as a scene where the Divine Names are manifested or operate, and where the Pen of Power and Destiny works continuously. It is in a continuous flow, like a river, and is fleeting, transient, and perishable. Nevertheless, the eye of heedlessness considers it permanent and perpetual, as stable with the eye fixed on nature and naturalism veiling the Hereafter.

Modern philosophy views the world or worldly life on behalf of itself and concentrates on its physical side with the modern materialistic–scientific attitude. This only makes the veil thicker and presents it as far more stable and perpetual. However, the Qur'an's verses "card" the world and make it like *carded wool* (101:5), make the veil transparent with their statements, melt it with their light and heat, smash its illusory permanence with its announcements [of death, the dreadful end of previous rebellious peoples and frightening events of afterlife] and disperse with their "thunderbolts" the heedlessness that engenders and breeds naturalism. The reality of the ever-shaking world recites in the tongue of its actual state: *When the Qur'an is recited, give ear to it and listen in silence so that you will find and be treated with mercy* (7:204).

KNOW, O FRIEND, that one factor that distinguishes us from animals is that we have relations with the past and the future and can comprehend both the inner and outer worlds. We can discover the apparent causes of events and know how to obtain a desired result. However, our greatest and most prominent duty, for which we have been equipped with very important faculties, is to glorify and praise God. We glorify the Maker with the tongues of the past, the present, and the future, and with the tongues of our inner and outer worlds. We praise the Lord and glorify Him for the past and present blessings and bounties He has bestowed, and which will be bestowed in the future, and for the blessings found in our inner and outer worlds. As we witness other creatures glorifying God, we extol the Maker of things by discerning the Names manifested in their creation and the purposes for their lives.

> Glory be to God, praised and glorified in amazement and appreciation, awe and love, Whose Holiness and exemption from defect are proclaimed, Whose Grandeur is beyond perception.

KNOW, O FRIEND, that God destines and decrees, executes His decrees and spares (forgives and withdraws His decree's execution). His decree yields to His sparing, as hard rock and soil yield to very thin, fiber-like roots, and as iron's resistance cracks in the face of ice. Sometimes the law of Destiny is not enacted because of His Decree, or a universal law that is the fate of a species or group is not enacted for a particular member. [For example, a helpless infant survives a calamity that caused great death and destruction.] This shows that the All-Glorified One is absolutely free in His acts, does whatever He wills, and decrees however He wills. What He gives cannot be prevented, and His decrees cannot be resisted.

The relation of sparing to executing decrees is like that of the decree to Destiny. Sparing means that something is exempted from the law of decree, just as a decree is sometimes exempted from the law of Destiny. Those who are aware of this relation cannot help but say: "O God! My good deeds are from Your sparing. I know that Your decree will eventually come. If You do not spare me, I will be among those who perish." Due to its inclination toward evil, the evil-commanding self deserves to perish.

KNOW, O FRIEND, that many Qur'anic verses end with Divine Names to bring Divine works to the reader's attention. At the end of its miraculous expressions, it concludes with the Divine Names, the true origins of those works, as in the verse: *He it is Who originates creation, then causes it to return again, and it is easier for Him. His is the highest comparison in the heavens and Earth. He is the All-Mighty, the All-Wise* (30:27).

The Qur'an unfolds the weavings of His Art before our eyes and then wraps them in Divine Names. It expounds Divine acts and then summarizes them with the Divine Names. It mentions and uses creatures to show the order, balance, and favoring. The Qur'an then offers the Divine Names, as if the creatures were "words" written by those Names. They give creatures their meaning, appoint their functions and purposes for their lives, thereby making them what they are. They act as the water of life giving life to them, the seeds from which they grow, or their concise summaries containing the information ingrained in their nature and according to which they act. The Qur'an also mentions particular, material, changeable things of certain qualities and then summarizes them with the Divine Names and their universal manifestations.

The Qur'an displays things growing freely and found in many places, and then places the stamp of unity on them to draw the reader's attention to their common points. It manifests the effects or results, together with their apparent causes, to show the great distance between causes and their results and that causes cannot be the real origin of results, as even the greatest cause cannot produce the smallest effect. It fills in the great gap between cause and effect with the relevant Divine Names. The Qur'an mentions the evil deeds of creatures and threatens them, and then consoles them by mentioning the Names containing mercy. It mentions particular purposes and then establishes them with the Names containing the universal laws ensuring those purposes.

KNOW, O FRIEND, that like love, one's perception of innate helplessness before God and acknowledging it is a way leading to God, a way even more direct and safer than that of love. Those initiates seeking to reach God by silent recitation prefer to purify their ten faculties (the heart, spirit, and other innermost ones); those seeking to reach God by loud recitation choose to purify their souls having seven kinds or levels (the carnal, evil-commanding soul; the soul resisted but still rebellious and accusing itself of its evil; the soul obedient and at rest; and the soul well-pleasing and pleased with God's decrees about it, etc.).

The way of helplessness consists of four steps, each of which is indicated by a Qur'anic verse:

> *Do not justify and hold yourselves as sinless.* (53:32)
>
> *Be not like those who forget God, and He therefore makes them forget their own selves.* (59:19)
>
> *Whatever good visits you is from God, and whatever evil befalls you is from yourself.* (4:79)
>
> *All things are perishable save His "Face," and good pleasure.* (28:88)

First step

Human beings love themselves on account of themselves. They restrict their love to themselves, praise themselves as if they were worthy of worship, strongly defend themselves, and consider themselves defect-free. Like those who deify their desire, they use their faculties, given to them to praise and glorify God, the True Worshipped One, to glorify themselves. Here, purification can be attained only by not considering oneself to be purified.

Second step

Human beings hold themselves back during times of hardship and rendering service, but consider themselves entitled to the first reward given when it is time to collect the fruits. Here, purification can be attained only by forgetting oneself when rewards are given.

Third step

Human beings should consider themselves as having only defects and insufficiency, helplessness and poverty. They should know that whatever good and beautiful they have are the Creator's blessings, which require praise and thanks. Here, purification comes through knowing that perfection lies in confessing imperfection, power in perceiving helplessness, and wealth in accepting essential poverty and inadequacy.

Fourth step

Human beings must perceive that, on account of their own selves, they are essentially non-existent and contingent, ephemeral and mortal—but only on account of being mirrors reflecting the Maker's Names, they exist, experience, and are experienced. Here, purification can be attained by perceiving that non-existence lies in seeing themselves as self-existent, existence in confessing essential non-existence, and in being totally convinced that only the Almighty deserves existence and all praise.

Those who follow the way of the Unity of Existence (*Wahdat al-Wujud*) regard the universe as actually non-existent. Those who follow the way of the Unity of the Witnessed (*Wahdat al-Shuhud*) confine all existence within the prison of absolute oblivion. What I have inferred from the way of the Qur'an requires neither denying nor ignoring the universe's actual existence, for it sees all things to show the Divine Names as mirrors reflecting them. It considers all existence on behalf of the Almighty, not on behalf of itself.

Each human being contains different spheres of existence and levels of creation—plant, animal, human, and being a believer. The first three are found in everyone; the fourth is found only in a believer.

The process of purification begins in the fourth level—that of belief—and continues downward to the plant one, where the most resistance is shown. During this treatment, which continues without interruption, people may confuse the levels and say: "Whatever is on Earth has been created solely for me." They err by thinking that humanity is restricted to being plant or animal, by considering the purposes for things' lives as restricted to his or her own benefit, and seeing them as valuable only to the degree that they benefit him or her. Therefore, they do not exchange a fragrant flower for Venus. [They are content with what is of little value since they are attached to the world. They cannot see what is beyond the world, which is much more valuable.]

KNOW, O FRIEND, that worship is the result and price of the bounties already given to humanity; it is not the means of any future, expected reward. O humanity, you have received your wages already, for He created you in the fairest form, as a pattern of existence, and made Himself known to you by bestowing belief on you.

By giving you a stomach, He has given you unlimited food and granted you life, which has made this visible, material world a table full of bounties for you. By giving you human selfhood, He has made the visible and invisible worlds a table filled with bounties. By bestowing belief on you, He has given you these tables plus others stored in the treasuries of His Names. By granting you His love, He has opened for you and bestowed on you indescribable bounties and blessings. Since you have received all of these already, you must serve Him. What He gives you after your service is purely from His Grace.

KNOW, O FRIEND, that the infinite abundance of the members of species, especially of small creatures and without the least defect in structure and with perfect orderliness, shows that the Maker's manifestations are unlimited, that He is absolutely different from all of them, and that all things are the same in relation to His Power and Necessary Existence. Such abundance and creation are the result and evidence of His Necessary Existence. The abundance of species pertains to His Majesty, while the firm and defect-free creation of members pertain to His Grace.

KNOW, O FRIEND, that the ease (or difficulty) with which something is made depends upon the maker's knowledge (ignorance) of it. This is especially true of small things with many tiny, delicate parts. The more knowledge the maker has of them, the easier they are to make. The absolute ease and swiftness observed in the creation of innumerable things in abundance and without defect show that their Maker has infinite knowledge. The verse: *Our command (or doing something) is but one (word) (and it is fulfilled) in the twinkling of an eye* (54:50) points to that ease.

KNOW, O FRIEND, that One who produces a delicately embroidered work of art and covers it with extremely delicate "garments" —like the derma and epidermis—woven of the same substance, hewing cavities in it to set different instruments so that its various parts can work close together, is its exclusive owner.

Similarly, the One Who most delicately creates innumerable varieties of species of almost the same simple things and clothes them in suitable garments, One Who includes them, especially animals that are miniature worlds, in the abdomens of worlds built to house those creatures that are their fruits or seeds—that One is One and Besought-of-All, manifesting Himself with all of His Names on each creature separately and on the worlds as a whole.

KNOW, O FRIEND, that just as a king's different titles designate his authority in governmental departments and state offices and among his subjects, and denote his duties of kingship as if he were present everywhere, so God, the One with the All-Beautiful Names, manifests Himself in the departments of His Sovereignty with His Names. One Name is dominant in a department, and the others are subordinate. He executes His Lordship by manifesting a Name particular to each level, as if that Name were particular only to that level. In His Lordship's levels, the All-Glorified One has essential controls corresponding to one another; in His Divinity's spheres, He has Names reflecting one another; in His Splendor's mirrors, He has different representations; in His Power's operations, He has varied titles; in His Attributes' manifestations, He has flowering ways of disclosing Himself; in His acting's modes, He has corresponding controls; and in His division of creatures into species, He has His Lordship's manifestations specified for each creature surrounded by manifestations on the species itself.

Prophet Muhammad, translator of the Eternal Tongue (the Qur'an), points to this reality in his *al-Jawshan al-Kabir* (The Great Armor) supplication. This supplication has 100 jewel box-like sections, each of which contains 10 gems of Divine Unity.[81] When the Almighty is called by one of them, the Name or Attribute mentioned is specified for Him exclusively. For example, when we call: "O Perpetual," we mean: "O One save Whom there is no perpetual in existence." As is narrated from the Prophet, the All-Glorified One has as many as 70,000 veils of light.[82] For an Existence penetrating all levels, Whose essential disposals correspond to one another, Whose Names reflect one another, Whose representations and titles are one within the other, Whose ways of making Itself near resemble one another, Whose ways of making Itself known support one another, Whose Lordship's

[81] Each section contains ten Names, each of which the writer likens to a jewel, so each section is like a box containing jewels. (Tr.)

[82] Tabarani, *Al-Mu'jam al-Kabir*, 2:580.

manifestations corroborate one another, and Whose Names' manifestations concentrated on a thing are encompassed by their manifestations on a group of things as a whole—it is necessary for one who knows that Existence by one of those Names, Attributes, or ways of manifestations mentioned to know It also by the others.

> Surely We have created humanity in the fairest creation. (95:4)

KNOW, O FRIEND, that it is a peculiarity of our comprehensive primordial nature that the All-Wise Creator included in that small object innumerable meters to measure what is endlessly stored in His Mercy, as well as countless faculties to understand the uncountable items in His All-Beautiful Names' treasuries.

Look at your 10 senses and see how they make you aware of the worlds of the things seen, heard, tasted, and so on. He has given you highly restricted attributes or powers of will, knowledge, and hearing, among others, to understand His encompassing Attributes and essential, all-embracing Qualities. He has knit your ego with as many fibers [feelings and desires, faculties and senses] as there are things in the worlds so that you may know your ego's nature. He has clothed your essential nature in as many garments as His Lordship's veils so that you may rend them and realize intellectual and spiritual progress. He has given you such an amazing faculty of perception that it travels in your mustard seed-sized memory without stopping, as if it were an infinitely vast world whose frontiers could not be reached. Sometimes that vast world becomes so narrow that your perception encompasses it; at other times, your perception, together with all spheres through which it travels and the books it studies, is, in turn, encompassed by that tiny memory. Glory be to Him Who makes it so small despite its infinite vastness.

This amazing nature causes great differences among people. One is lost in a particle; the world is lost in another. One opens a vast world of multiplicity with the key given to him or her and, straying, becomes lost and able to reach unity and belief in Divine Unity only with great difficulty. People also differ greatly in the way they follow on their spiritual journeying. Some advance easily and attain peace and unity; others are overcome by fancies and heedlessness and, completely lost in multiplicity (of things), forget unity. Those "civilized" people who consider corruption and regression to be progress, ignorance to be certified knowledge, and the deepest sleep to be fully awake are among the second group.

KNOW, O FRIEND, that the manifestation of Divine Unity (*Wahidiya*)—the manifestation of one or many Names on a whole—shows that the Divine Name manifested encompasses all things. The manifestation of Divine Oneness (*Ahadiya*)—the manifestation of many Names on a particular thing—points out that a living creature indicates all the Names relating to creation.

KNOW, O FRIEND, that groups, wholes, and species are objects of Divine Majesty's manifestation, and thus necessitate the absolute abundance in species, while most of the "mirrors" manifesting Grace are individual parts of these wholes or members of those groups and species. The beauty of individuals and the radiance of "mirrors," as well as their firmness in structure and orderliness, are due to that manifestation. Majesty arises from the manifestation of Divine Unity (*Wahidiya*), and Grace comes from the manifestation of Divine Oneness (*Ahadiya*). However, Grace also may arise from Majesty and Majesty from Grace. How beautiful is Majesty in the eye of Grace, and how beautiful is Grace in the eye of Majesty.

KNOW, O FRIEND, that "bejeweled" creatures are seen with the power of sight, and that the power of insight's inability to see the Creator is due to its blindness, inability to perceive the matter's importance, or the absence of necessary guidance. Denying the Creator would otherwise be much more ridiculous than denying the power of sight.

KNOW, O FRIEND, that seeds sown in a field cause the sower to protect them from the elements and from those who would harm them. Seeds thus function as an invisible wall around the field. In the same way, every plant and animal species is like a field sown and found throughout the world. It only allows the one who has "sown" it to assume control over it. All species, together and with their individual members, form such a strong wall that only the "sower" can assume control over them.

KNOW, O FRIEND, some people who want to see and display the beauty and splendor of their Paradise-like gardens, [according to the principle that things are better known through their opposites], randomly place in them some shapeless rocks, crooked statutes, and other things, and dig some caves here and there. Their order or harmony seem to lie in their disorder. However, one who studies these gardens concludes that their apparent disorder shows them as beautiful and orderly.

Similarly, (in the garden of Earth) the Hand of Control has scattered, seemingly at random, deserts, hills, and rocks of different sizes and shapes. In reality, the All-Wise Maker, All-Knowing Creator has added them purposefully to contribute to the general order and harmony of existence. Thorn-bearing trees and plants use their thorns to defend themselves against plant-eating animals.

Their amazing orderliness and delicate beauty is a sign that the All-Wise Maker has a special purpose for that apparent lack of orderliness, that things seemingly outside their species' general order have a different size and shape. Difference shows purpose and rejects chance. [Human facial differences are clear evidence of this.]

KNOW, O FRIEND, that humanity's comprehensive nature allows people to comprehend the salutations living beings offer to the Bestower of life. This factor distinguishes people from animals. As people perceive their own speech, they also perceive with the ear of belief all words spoken by living beings and inanimate objects to glorify their Creator. A deaf person can speak inwardly only to himself or herself, and each being can perceive the speech of its own inner self. However, only human beings can speak and perceive all sounds produced by all creatures, at the same time, as signs of the Divine Beautiful Names. Every other being's value is restricted to itself, whereas a believer is as valuable as all beings combined, for although an individual, he or she is like a species—even all species. God knows the truth.

KNOW, O FRIEND, that although the truth of something seems to consist in or be restricted to its outward aspect, there is a great distance between them. For example, an average person's belief in God's Unity involves attributing things only to the Almighty. This is a simple rejection of attributing anything to that which is not God. However, the belief of those who know the real meaning of Divine Unity involves attributing whatever they see and experience to the All-Glorified One. They see His stamp and notice His seal on everything. Such acknowledgment gives peace of mind and heart and prevents heedlessness.

KNOW, O FRIEND, that the wisdom in God's giving respite to unbelievers lost in the worldly life is that they unconsciously manifest various blessings of God by their labor and skill, and unknowingly arrange the beauty and excellence of the works of Divine Art to display to others. Just as a clock is not aware of telling time, unbelievers are not aware of their function.

KNOW, O FRIEND, that one receiving God's help can proceed from the outward to the truth without joining a spiritual order. I have seen in the Qur'an one way leading directly to truth without any such initiation, and another way leading to the attainment of desired (religious) sciences without studying instrumental sciences (such as logic, mathematics, and methodology). The all-embracing Divine Mercy is expected to grant the children of the present time—a time flowing too fast—a short, yet safe, way.

KNOW, O FRIEND, that a thing's existence and life are decisive proofs of its Creator's necessary Existence and Attributes, a radiant sign that the Creator is One to Whom all things belong, and that He holds all (material or natural) causes in His "Hand." In the same way, decay, death, and replacing things with their likes show the permanence of the Originator, Returner, Heir to all, and Reviver. They also show that He has no partners in creation, and that only He controls the inner selves of things.

KNOW, O FRIEND, that Life says: "There is no deity but He, the One," and denies that causes have any part in it. Death says: "There is no deity but He, having no partners at all," and denies that the inner selves of things have any part in it.

KNOW, O FRIEND, that one duty of human life is that it should witness living beings' praise to the Bestower of life, the worship of all things, and announce it as if it represented all of them and their tongue proclaiming their deeds to their Master.

KNOW, O FRIEND, that the Qur'an and Prophet Muhammad inform us of awesome matters, establish tremendous truths, and lay down immense foundations. For example, they prove and establish the Oneness of the One:

> We will roll up the heavens as written scrolls are rolled up. (21:104)
>
> Earth altogether shall be His handful on Doomsday, and the heavens shall be rolled up in His Right Hand. (39:67)
>
> The matter of the Hour is as a twinkling of the eye, or nearer. (16:77)
>
> The seven heavens and Earth and whoever is in them glorify Him. (17:44)
>
> He has created the heavens and Earth in six days. (7:54)

He revives Earth after its death (30:19), and during that revival, He resurrects countless plant and animal species, and "inscribes" them on the sheet of Earth, all mingled with (but unique from) one another. Humanity's resurrection on the Day of Judgment is not harder than this annual resurrection. Remember that far more flies are brought to life during one summer than the number of people who have lived, and will live, from the creation of Adam until the Last Day.

The Qur'an and Prophet Muhammad also say:

> God is the Creator of all things and He is Guardian over all things. His is the keys of the heavens and Earth. (39:62-63)
>
> He creates you and what you do. (37:96)
>
> He has prepared a painful torment. (33:8)
>
> Whoever does an atom's weight of evil shall see it. (99:8)

The Qur'an and Prophet Muhammad do not view the universe in the same way as modern scientists, philosophers, and other people. Rather, they instruct in the arts or provide a skill with which to know the Maker, Who holds all creatures in His Hand and controls them as He wills. They show the inner and outer dimensions of existence, together with the parts and what they mean for their Creator. They instruct through a book with all its meanings and connotations.

Modern scientists and philosophers describe creatures according to their literal meaning and according to what they perceive with their external senses, and not in the inner dimensions and meanings of creatures, of which they are unaware. Like a mind occupied with involuntary evil thoughts or Satan's whisperings, they occupy your mind with superficial issues and, without understanding their meaning, instruct you in their outward forms and the parts thereof. They instruct you in a bejeweled book ornamented with explanations of its letters' forms, structures, and positions with respect to one another.

You cannot judge the truths of the Qur'an and Prophet Muhammad by such standards, nor weigh them by their balances. Mountains fixed deeply in the ground are not weighed on the balances of jewels. The "earthly"—profane—principles of science and philosophy cannot appraise and confirm the Qur'an's and the Prophet's truths. Ignore critics of some small details of those truths, as they are misguided by modern science and philosophy.

O LONG-SUFFERING ONE! When a misfortune is sent to you, do not divide your patience by confronting both past and present misfortunes. Focus on the present one, for the painful past has joined with the remaining spiritual blessings and rewards they gained for you in the Hereafter. Do not use up your patience confronting possible future misfortune, for what the future brings depends on Divine Will. Use your patience for today, even for this hour. Reinforce it by smiling at misfortune and loving it so that it will join your patience and help you rely on your Owner, the All-Munificent, All-Compassionate, and All-Wise. When you do that, your weakest patience will suffice for the greatest misfortune.

KNOW, O FRIEND, that some people dismiss various Traditions as "exaggerated." In fact, such traditions contain valuable truths. For example, the Prophet is recorded to have said: "If the world had as much weight in the view of God as a gnat's wing, an unbeliever could not drink a sip of water from it."[83] This means that the world's external face manifesting in the mirror of your fleeting life has no more weight than the wing of a gnat from the eternal world, just as a grain of corn attaining permanence by growing into a plant is preferable to the amount of straw needed to fill a vast threshing field—for it can only blow away. Everyone has his or her own particular world. If this particular world is considered to point to its true Owner rather than to itself, and to the tillage of the Hereafter and the area where the Divine Beautiful Names are manifested, it gains a great value. Otherwise, with respect to its fleeting aspect, its value is less than that of a single grain.

KNOW, O FRIEND, that one demonstration that life is based upon mutual assistance, not upon conflict, is that dense soil and hard rocks allow a plant's delicate roots to penetrate them. Rocks crack their hardened hearts when touched by a plant's silk-like fingers, and soil opens its hard breast for the plants' veins. The universe's parts cooperate with its sun and moon for the benefit of animals, plants serve as food for animals, elements of sustenance compete to be sustenance for fruits; fruits are adorned to attract those needing provision, particles (of soil, air, and water) cooperate to be food for the body's cells, and so on. All of this is a decisive proof that life's general principle is mutual assistance. Conflict is only a particular, exceptional principle, notably among some wild animals.

---

83 Related by al-Tirmidhi, who judged it authentic, in *Al-Jami' al-Saghir*, no. 5168.

KNOW, O FRIEND, that the absolute, observable ease of things coming into existence is one of the clearest proofs of God's Unity, for everything, especially living things, requires for its existence that which is necessary for the whole to exist.[84] If there were more than one Creator, the existence of one thing would be as difficult as the existence of the whole universe.[85]

KNOW, O CARNAL, EVIL-COMMANDING SELF, that you deserve condemnation even for your most "noble" demand. You deeply desire the things of the Hereafter, but only to be relieved from the gloom of transience and find consolation for the pain of mortality. How can a king serve a mortal creature? You build an inn on columns of jewels you have taken from the royal castle, so that some animals may stay in it overnight. [You use the precious faculties given to you for the Hereafter to satisfy your carnal, fleeting desires.] You cause the castle to collapse on you, and eat the fruits of the everlasting Paradise in the illusory paradise of the world.

KNOW, O SOUL ENAMORED of itself and relying on its physical existence. You became content with a drop from an imaginary ocean of the water of life, with a weak radiance at night from the sun of a clear day. The relation between your physical existence with the manifestations of your Creator's Existence is like that of one soul with all creatures multiplied by the particles forming those creatures. Your existence points to itself only in that respect, while pointing to its Creator's existence in endless respects, as does every creature. His existence, when compared with yours, is as manifest as the greatness of the universe.

You love your selfhood because it is the source of your carnal pleasure, the center of your existence, the mine of your interests, and because it is

---

84 A cherry's existence requires the existence and cooperation of the sun and air, soil and water, and its tree's elements. The ease with which it comes into existence shows that a single Creator has absolute control over these factors. (Tr.)

85 Since the creation and control of all things requires infinite knowledge and power, the existence of more than one creator with infinite knowledge and power is inconceivable. There cannot be two infinities at the same time. Second, it is inconceivable that a different creator could create and dispose of a certain part of existence, and that these creators would cooperate among themselves. Such a situation would lead to disagreement, for independence is an essential quality of divinity. The result would be the disorder of existence. Also, the unity and interrelatedness in existence require that all supposed creators know and control all existence, which makes the existence of multiple creators with the same qualities unnecessary. So, associating partners with God is absolutely illogical and mistaken. (Tr.)

nearer to you than anything else. However, you confuse a dim, fleeting shadow with the very origin of all existence. If you love your selfhood for a transient pleasure, then you must love Him Who gives you infinite, eternal pleasure and creates everything that makes you happy. If your selfhood is the center of your existence, then your Lord is the One Who has given you that existence and maintains it, together with all those to whom your existence is related.

If your existence is the mine of your interests, then your Provider is He in Whose hand is all good. He is the Everlasting, Benevolent One, and with Him are all your benefits as well as the benefits of those who are beneficial to you. If your selfhood is nearer to you (than anything else), then Your Creator is still nearer. His "Hand" reaches what your selfhood cannot reach, and what is beyond the reach of its consciousness. So unite all your love now divided among creatures and, adding to it your love of your selfhood, direct it to the Almighty, the True Beloved One.

KNOW, O FRIEND, that what veils you from God and keeps you in heedlessness is seeing things and parts separately and attributing them to chance and causes. However, one who looks at the whole and universal with a comprehensive view cannot attribute even the least thing to the greatest cause. For example, you ascribe food to some causes. But when you see Earth's wilderness and utter destitution in winter followed by its being adorned and filled with varieties of food by the Divine Power, you will be convinced that the one who provides for you could be none other than the One Who provides for all living things by reviving Earth after its death.

For example, you ascribe the illumination of your house and your (intellectual and spiritual) enlightenment to some apparent causes and say: "*What has been given to me is because of certain knowledge that I have* (28:78)." However, when you see that your light comes from the light of daytime and that your enlightenment depends on the Source of all lights, you will be convinced that only He Who alternates day and night by moving the solar system, Who creates guidance and misguidance, and Who guides whomever He wills by sending down Scriptures can illuminate your body and enlighten your mind and heart.

KNOW, O HUMANITY, that some awesome issues compel every conscious being to pay attention to them. Among them are death, separation from all that you love and the world, your journeying to eternity through awful circumstances, and your complete impotence and poverty both here and in the Hereafter. How can you behave as if oblivious of and blind to such issues? You are like an ostrich that buries its head in the sand so as not to see the hunter. How much longer will you be absorbed in transient, perishable drops and pay no attention to fearful oceans?

KNOW, O FRIEND, that God makes it possible to solve the greatest ontological problems by one linguistic rule: The meaning related to the letter and the meaning related to the name.[86] This universe is a book; the creatures in it are its words. These words should be viewed only on their Inscriber's behalf, for their primary function is to serve as messages of the Lord manifesting His All-Beautiful Names. Considering creatures on behalf of themselves causes ignorance, ingratitude, and erroneous philosophy, while considering them on behalf of their Inscriber is the origin of knowledge, belief, and wisdom.

KNOW, O FRIEND, that God makes it possible to solve a tremendous matter pertaining to Divine Lordship via a rule of logic: the difference between a universal having particulars or individuals and a whole formed of parts.[87] The manifestation of His Grace and Oneness—manifesting His Names on a single thing—may be compared to the universal having particulars or individuals.[88] The manifestation of His Majesty and Unity—manifesting a Name on a group or a whole—may be compared to the whole formed of parts. The manifestations of Perfection and Grandeur encompass both. That is, Perfection in the view of Majesty is like the universal in the view of the whole, and the particular in the view of the part.

KNOW, O FRIEND, that the world is the Hereafter's "contents," and has a bearing upon the most important matters connected with it. For example, consider the pleasure you take in eating and drinking. The One Who, in this fleeting abode that gives no true pleasure, has given you senses and

86 A letter has no inherent meaning and so points to something else, such as the work of which it is a part and its author. A word, however, has a complete meaning in itself and so points primarily to itself. (Tr.)

87 Humanity has universality, and an individual human being is one specific or "particular" member of that universal entity as well as a whole entity formed of parts. A "particular" or individual carries all attributes of the species, while a part does not have all of the whole's attributes. (Tr.)

88 God has two general kinds of manifestation: His Grace (the origin of mercy, forgiveness, provision, and the like) and His Majesty (the origin of glory, awe, wrath, chastisement, and so on). (Tr.)

feelings, systems and organs, parts and instruments to taste these material bounties and sense His Names' manifestations on things pertaining to your physical existence—the Wise One Who has provided you with different senses—has certainly prepared for His guests everlasting feasts in palaces *underneath which rivers flow, and where they will remain forever* (5:119).

O FEARFUL, HELPLESS SAID! When you fear or love the created, fear becomes a pain and love an affliction. The one you fear has no mercy for you or does not listen to your requests. The one you love does not recognize you, despises you because of your love, avoids you, and abandons you despite your desire. Rather, fear and love your All-Munificent and Compassionate Creator so that your love may become an innocent, eternal happiness without pain or humiliation, and your fear an agreeable humbling by taking refuge in the bosom of Mercy, just as an infant's fear of its mother compels it to throw itself into her warm arms, where it finds pleasure.

KNOW, O FRIEND, that you are the Tree of Creation's fruit or seed. Although physically a weak, impotent, and small individual being, the All-Wise Maker has favored you with a universal disposition. By giving you life, He has freed you from the confines of an insignificant, individual existence and enabled you to travel throughout the visible world so that your very developed, inquiring senses may obtain their particular nourishments. By making you human, He has endowed you with a potential to flourish, like a tree growing from a seed. He has bestowed on you belief and Islam, and thereby enabled you to acquire a universal existence. By favoring you with knowledge and love of Him, He has made you like a comprehensive light. Now you must choose. If you attach yourself to the world and bodily desires, you will become a weak, humiliated individual. But if you use the instruments of your life, senses, and faculties on behalf of the greatest humanity (Islam), you will acquire a universal existence and become a central, illuminating lamp.

KNOW, O ONE WHO LOVES worldly things as much as your restricted physical existence allows. Since you spend your love away from its proper place (God), you are distressed. But if you love the One of Unity and other things on His behalf and with His leave, you will be saved from the distress and pain of separation (from what you love). You will be like one who, faithfully serving a ruler with relations to everyone in his country, hears with his lord's ears and sees with his lord's eyes all that happens as if he or she were there. By using the ruler's communicative systems, he or she hears all pleasant music and sees all beautiful scenes in the country.

KNOW, O ONE WHO SHOWS great curiosity about the moon and other planets. If you were told that someone has come from the moon to tell you about it, or to tell your future, you would give almost anything to hear his or her words. However, a man tells you about Him in the realm of Whose rule the moon is less than a moth flying around a light: It flies around the light among innumerable candles hanging from the ceiling of the house He has prepared for His guests. That man also tells you about eternity and eternal life, and fundamental truths and awesome matters, the least of which is more important than Earth's and moon's destruction.

Listen to the chapters of the Book he has brought, which begin with: *When the sun is folded up* (81:1), *When the heaven is rent asunder* (82:1), and others like them. He shows you a straight, leveled path leading to unity, and saves you from confusion in the twisted, crooked ways of misguidance. He extends the "firm handle," a chain of ascension, that keeps those who hold on to it from drowning in the darkness of things' bewildering multiplicity. He offers you the water of life (eternal life) from the pure source of belief so that you may be saved from the fire of separation from what you love. He informs you of what pleases your Creator—to Whose command the sun, moon, and stars are subjected and by Whose permission Earth was settled and stabilized—and what He commands you to do. He explains to you, an infinitely weak and poor creation, the communication and conversation of the King of Eternity, to Whose Power there is no limit.

Such being the truth, why not renounce your self to perceive the Qur'an's guidance, listen to the Messenger of the All-Merciful One, and welcome him with belief and submission. Love sincerely the one who has come with peace and salvation. Learn from him what our All-Affectionate Master, the All-Bounteous Owner, asks of us.

KNOW, O FRIEND, that We see the All-Wise Maker's perfect Wisdom, and witness that His acts are free from waste and futility. He weaves extensive, enduring, and precious "textiles" from lowly and very small things. His acts are purposeful. For example, He charges each bodily organ or part (especially those in the head) with very important duties. If a tiny organ were required to perform each duty entrusted to your head's organs, your head would be as big as Mount Sinai.

Look at the tongue. As one of its many important tasks, it inspects the bounties stored in the All-Merciful One's treasury, as well as all food and beverage prepared in His Power's kitchen. Its tasks are as many as the tastes of all foods. Does this purposeful activity not show that the Maker weaves (from the things moving in the flux of time) "textiles" for the Unseen and the Hereafter by moving the "shuttle" of day in order to produce day and night and change the seasons?

He does the same weaving in humanity, the index of the universe. He records and permanently preserves the minutes of each person's life in the "textiles" or on the "sheets" of memory, and uses death to transport living beings from this visible, narrow world to the unseen worlds of purity and permanence. We hear from the sources of Revelation that these minutes return to each individual either darkened with heedlessness and sin or illuminated with lamps of good deeds hanging from their links.

KNOW, O FRIEND, that the All-Beautiful, All-Wise Maker makes members of animal species, especially winged ones and fish, in different sizes, just as He does for angels and all other creatures. He makes the small a specimen of the large so that people will be guided to truth, reflect on His creation with ease, and read and understand His Power's missives. He also does this to display that Power's perfection and exhibit His two kinds of art, one originating in His Grace and the other in His Majesty.

Small things that are discerned only with difficulty usually remain unknown, and can be known only when "written" in "capital letters." Large things that are too huge to be seen and comprehended also remain unknown until they are "written" in relatively "small letters." Despite this, the carnal evil-commanding soul, taught by Satan, thinks that smallness results from weakness or defect in artistry, and so attributes them to deaf and blind causes. It likewise claims that huge things show a lack of wisdom and purpose, and are thus attributable to chance.[89]

KNOW, O FRIEND, that the almost infinite multiplicity of things and absolute abundance of provisions do not mean futility and contradict wisdom. If a thing, especially a living being, had only one purpose, this charge

---

[89] Throughout his book, Said Nursi draws attention to many intrigues of the human carnal soul and Satan. He does not mean that everyone is exposed to all of these intrigues. Rather, the carnal soul deceives some with some of them, and others with others. By drawing the attention to all the deceptive ways of Satan and the carnal soul, the author calls people to wake up and remain awake. (Tr.)

might be true. But each existent thing has innumerable purposes, tasks, and fruits. Your tongue has as many tasks as the number of hairs on your head. There are endless purposes for that abundance and, with respect to each thing's assigned tasks, there is no contradiction with wisdom. Although an army is mainly charged with guarding or defending borders, we have many troops, since an army also represents the government's authority, guards against internal conflict, and performs other services.

KNOW, O FRIEND, that a human artist can be seen with his or her works of art, but there are 70,000 veils between God and His works. If only you could view all creatures of God together at the same instant, the veils of darkness might be lifted, leaving only the veils of light, which is very difficult. However, the most direct and shortest way to reach that level of vision is within you; it can be found in the outer world only by intense love.

KNOW, O FRIEND, that each member of most of the reproducing plant and animal species seeks to spread over Earth as much as possible so that it can use Earth as a place of worship by manifesting its Creator's Names. Each worships its Creator, Who alone deserves worship, in its own way. Look at a melon and its seeds, fruit-bearing trees and their seeds, and fish and birds and their eggs. Since the world is too small for all of them to realize their "intention" fully, the all-encompassing Knowledge of the Knower of the seen and the Unseen, Who knows everything that happens regardless of when it happens, is expected to accept their intended worship.

KNOW, O FRIEND, that out of the purposes for things' existence, the Qur'an sometimes mentions those related to humanity. This does not mean, however, that humanity was created only for the purposes mentioned. Rather, it draws our attention to their benefits, to the order and harmony they display, and thus to their Maker's Names. We only pay attention to and prefer that which is related to us, even if it is microscopic, in preference to a "sun" with which we have no relation. For example: *And the moon: We have determined stations (phases) for it* (36:39), *that you might know the number of years and the reckoning* (10:5). This is only one of the moon's thousands of purposes, and it is mentioned because it is the most evident one for humanity.

KNOW, O FRIEND, that one of the inimitable stamps and seals particular to Him, and one of the most evident signs of the unity of boundless Power and endless Knowledge observed in the absolute authority over existence, as well as the absolute firmness and ease in its creation and maintenance, is that innumerable different things are created from a simple single thing. For example, soil is the main element for all kinds of plants to come into existence and be maintained. Moreover, all animal and human organs, as well as their flesh and bones, blood and tissues, are made from simple food. Glory be to Him Who has absolute power to make all things from a single thing and a single thing from all things.

KNOW, O FRIEND, that: *Or are We the sowers?* (56:64) contains a profound meaning. Just as you store some seeds to sow later, so does the Heir to all things, the Reviver, the Preserver, Who revives the soil after its death, records the results of all plants' "deeds," and preserves them for later sowing in many areas according to certain measures. Then, He causes them to produce leaves and blossom, as if each recited: *When the records are laid open* (81:10).

Consider how careful you are to preserve the seeds you will sow, and try to understand how perfectly the Absolute Preserver preserves innumerable delicate cases containing their parents' indexes, as determined by Destiny, from change and corruption, and distinguishes them from each other without confusion. Such preserving does not mean that you can do whatever you wish and then die for eternal rest. *Does humanity think that it will be left to roam at will* (75:36)? No! [He preserves your deeds, the seeds of your eternal life,] and you will be called to account for whatever you do in this world.

KNOW, O FRIEND, that humanity's particular attributes and essential qualities were given so that human beings could perceive the Creator's Essential Qualities and Attributes. To understand His destroying and rebuilding of the universe, and resurrecting everything that has died with all of His other disposals in the other world, consider His revival of soil in spring and its death in autumn and winter. This will give you an idea of the Supreme Resurrection and interpretation of such verses as: *When the sun is folded up* (81:1).

KNOW, O FRIEND, that Islam's essentials encompass everything, from the Owner's Greatest Names and Attributes and creation of the Supreme Throne, the heavens and Earth together with their angels, down to the occurrences in your heart. They also encompass all that is between the heavens and Earth.

* * *

In the Name of God, the All-Merciful, the All-Compassionate.

> Let not the life of the world delude you, nor let any deluder delude you in regard to God. (35:5)

KNOW, O ONE WHO INVITES Muslims to the worldly life, a plaything of sleep and sport, urging them to leave the lawful sufficient for them to satisfy their needs and desires for the forbidden, as well as some public marks of Islam or even the Religion itself. You resemble a drunk who cannot distinguish a wild, ravenous lion from a docile horse, a hangman's noose from a child's skipping rope, a gaping wound from an opening rose. You suppose the lion to be the horse; the noose to be the skipping rope, and the open wound a red rose. Despite this, you think that you are putting things right.

You resemble one who sees a person in a dreadful condition—a lion behind him waiting to attack, a gallows in front of him, and two grievous wounds on either side of his body. He has two kinds of medicine that will change the wounds into two red roses; two talismans (one in his tongue, the other in his heart) that will cause the lion to change into a horse that will carry him to the presence of his munificent master, who invites him to the abode of peace to feast. The hangman's noose dangling from the tree of decay and mortality will, by God's grace, carry him through continuously changing scenes to increase the pleasure taken in the renewal of their beauty, forms, and favors through the days and seasons, years and centuries.

You say: "Leave those talismans and medicine, and let's amuse ourselves." The person replies: "What I am allowed to do by preserving the talismans and medicine is enough for my pleasure, for only they bring true pleasure and happiness. Can you kill the lion of death that will die only in Paradise[90]; remove decay and mortality and so change Earth into something other than itself; heal my wound (of impotence) and so change my fleeting, perishable life into a permanent, everlasting one; and cure my other wound of poverty and destitution into perpetual richness? If you can, I will do as you say. Otherwise, leave me alone! You can deceive only other drunks who cannot distinguish between laughing and crying, permanence

---

[90] A Tradition says that on the Day of Judgment, death will appear as a ram and be slaughtered between Paradise and Hell. Thus, there will be no death in Paradise or Hell. *Sahih al-Muslim*, hadith no. 2849. Also recorded in *Sahih al-Bukhari*. (Tr.)

and transience, remedy and ailment, and deviation and guidance. God is sufficient for me. How good a Guardian He is, and how good a Helper.

KNOW, O FRIEND, that students of corrupt, misguided civilizations and philosophies are driven by greed and various passions. They invite Muslims to follow foreign traditions and customs, to abandon their public marks radiant with the light of Islam. Students of the Qur'an respond: "If you can remove decay and death from the world, and impotence and poverty from humanity, then you may be indifferent to the Religion and its public marks. Otherwise keep silent, for your words are no more than a fly's buzzing compared to the thunder-like cry of the four things mentioned above. The laws of creation and life, [as well as human psychology and sociology,] also proclaim the necessity of the Religion and of following its public marks." *When the Qur'an is recited, give ear to it and listen in silence so that you will find, and be treated with, mercy* (7:204).

The lion of the appointed hour of death is behind us, waiting. If you believe in the Qur'an, that lion will change into a horse, and separation [from those we love] will become a Buraq [a mount of the Unseen world] to carry you to the Mercy of the All-Merciful, All-Compassionate, to the Presence of our Master, the All-Affectionate, All-Munificent. Otherwise, that lion will rip us apart and eternally separate us from what we love. Decay and transience are also before us in the form of alternating day and night, and perishing and separation as seasons and years.

These things—death and separation, decay and transience—are gallows set up to hang us together with all our beloved ones. If we follow the Qur'an, all of these become a mount for a pleasant journey on the stream of time and ocean of the world to observe the operations of Divine Power through successive seasons following one another by the sun's wheel and Earth's rotation wrapping around its head the turban of days and nights and wearing the garments of summer and winter one over the other. During that journey, we can observe the continuous renewal of the Divine Names' manifestations on moving objects, in changing mirrors and on altering tablets (anything changing in parallel with the changing of days and seasons) through the alternation of days and nights.

Moreover, on our right side is the wound of infinite poverty. We are poorer than all other animate beings, while our power to satisfy all our material and spiritual needs is lesser than that of a sparrow. If we cure our wounds with the Qur'an, our painful, innate poverty changes into a pleasure-giving zeal to sit at the feast of Mercy, and into a pleasant appetite for the fruits of the Mercy of the All-Merciful, All-Compassionate. The pleasure of feeling one's poverty and impotence before the Almighty is much greater than that of being apparently rich and powerful. Otherwise, we will suffer the pain of need and the humiliation of begging from and bowing before whoever we expect to satisfy our needs.

On our left side is the deep wound of infinite impotence despite unending hostility and danger. The pain of fear destroys the worldly life's pleasure. But if we submit to the Qur'an's call, our impotence leads us to trust the Absolutely Powerful One and secures us against all hostility. Otherwise, we will continue to suffer hostility and danger in our boundless impotence.

Furthermore, our journey extends through the grave and the Resurrection to eternity. Neither the world nor human reason can illumine the veils of darkness enveloping the way, nor do they provide the necessary food. Our way is illumined only by the Qur'an's light and the food from the All-Merciful One's treasury. If you have something that will prevent our journey, provided that it is not misguidance, declare it. Otherwise, keep silent and let the Qur'an say what it says. While we are "reading" these five "verses" in the book of creation—that is, the world's decay and ephemerality, as well as each individual's death, impotence and poverty, and long journey—how can we follow you, O conceited, deceived one, especially after we hear the verse: *Let not the life of the world delude you, nor let any deluder delude in regard to God* (35:5). Only those drunk with the wine of politics or passion for fame, ambition for praise, ethnic or tribal preferences, atheism, or modern dissipation follow you.

The blows we receive must bring us to our senses. Unlike animals, who suffer only the present's pain, we suffer the present's pain, the future's anxiety and grief, and those of the past as well.

If you do not want to remain the most wretched, foolish, and misguided of all animals, keep silent and listen to the Qur'an:

> Assuredly, God's friends no fear shall come upon them, neither shall they grieve. They believe and refrain from sins in fear of God. For them is good tidings in the life of the world and in the Hereafter. No change can there be in the words of God; that is the supreme triumph. (10:62-64)

In the Name of God, the All-Merciful, the All-Compassionate.

> By the fig and the olive, and Mount Sinai, and this City secure. Surely We have created human of the best stature as the perfect pattern of creation; then We have reduced him to the lowest of the low, except those who believe and do good, righteous deeds; so there is for them a reward constant and beyond measure. What, then, (O human,) causes you, after all (these realities), to deny the Last Judgment? Is not God the Best of judges and the Most Powerful of sovereigns? (95:1-8)

KNOW, O FRIEND, that the firm and perfect artistry in everything show that the Maker of all things is present and near all things, even though He is not contained by space at the same time. As people need all things, it does not befit them to worship anything or anyone other than Him in Whose Hand is the dominion, and Who possesses the treasuries, of all things. With respect to existence, invention, and doing good, we are more impotent and powerless than an ant or a bee, and weaker than a spider or a gnat. As for destruction and evil-doing, our capacity is greater than that of the heavens, Earth, and mountains. For example, our good only extends to what our hands can reach, while our evil may have a far-reaching influence.

Denying the Almighty reduces the universe or all creatures from missives of the Lord and mirrors of Divinity to matter subject to change and decay, playthings for aimless chance. This view reduces human beings from well-composed, harmonious pieces of poetry manifesting the Divine Names; the seed of a permanent, everlasting tree; and a vicegerent of God superior to all creatures by virtue of bearing the Supreme Trust, to the lowest and most debased, powerless, and destitute mortal animate being. Our ego is given free will, but is as weak as a hair, of little capacity, faint and short-lived like a distant flash of light. However, our impotence and poverty is so great that we can be a vast mirror for the infinitely Powerful and eternally Wealthy One's manifestations.

Our worldly life, despite being like a seed endowed with innumerable parts to grow into a tree spreading throughout space, is reduced to striving, like a hen scratching the soil, to obtain some mean substances, after which we dissolve in the soil. But in our immaterial life, we are like a perpetual tree with the branches of desire extending into eternity.

Our work and effort show that we are no more than weak, impotent animals that can act only as far as our hands can reach. However, our praying and asking make us a noble guest of the All-Merciful One, Who has opened for us His Mercy's treasuries, subjugated to us all of His art's marvels, and allows us to act within a sphere that is much vaster than what we can see or imagine.

With respect to our life's pleasure and perfectibility, and its tranquility and stability, we are lower than a sparrow, for our pleasure is clouded by grief for the past and anxiety for the future. Our parts, senses, and feelings, as well as our potential's development, guide us to one task in this life: to observe, compare, and reflect upon all creatures and to witness their glorification of God. We must pray to God for our needs, and worship Him in due perception and acknowledgment of our impotence, poverty, and defectiveness.

We have such a comprehensive nature that we may worship the Creator in many ways. This makes us superior to all other creatures. A person with even a little intellect must conclude that all of our parts have been given to us for eternal life. If a master gives a servant some money to buy a garment made from a particular cloth and another servant a great deal of money to buy a garment, we would conclude that the master expected them to buy garments made from cloths of different qualities. The cloth chosen by the second servant must be far more valuable than that chosen by the first. If both servants bought the same quality of cloth, the second one certainly would be punished.

Despite (or rather because of) our lack of power and strength, we are far stronger and more powerful than other animate beings. Through our prayers and asking for help, what we cannot obtain is subjected to us through His Power. Like an infant, our tears bring to us that which we cannot reach even with a power thousands of times greater than our own. As we are superior to all other animate beings because they are subjected to us (by Him), not through our own unassisted power of grasping, overcoming, and attraction, we should admit our impotence and weakness, poverty and destitution, and implore God for help through supplication and worship.

By observing Divine Lordship's beautiful and perfect splendor, heralding His sacred Names' marvelous manifestations, perceiving the contents of His Mercy's treasuries, knowing the gems stored in the manifested Names' treasuries, studying and reflecting on the Pen of the Power's missives, and looking forward to seeing His creatures' subtleties, humanity is the noblest creation and ruler of Earth.

In the Name of God, the All-Merciful, the All-Compassionate.

O humanity! You are poor before God and in absolute need of Him. (35:15)

Flee unto God. (51:50)

O FAILING, HELPLESS, POOR SAID! With respect to your selfhood, you are constantly imperfect and have infinite helplessness and poverty, need and desire. As you are given hunger and thirst in order to know and experience the pleasure of the Almighty's bounties, you are loaded with failure and poverty, impotence and neediness so that you should view the lofty works of the All-Glorified's Perfection through your failure. Use your poverty to measure His Wealth and Mercy; your impotence, His Power and Grandeur; your need, the variety of His bounties and favors.

You were created to serve (Him), which means declaring your failure before the door of His Mercy with: "I ask God for forgiveness" and "All glory be to God"; your poverty with: "God is sufficient for us" and "All praise be to God," and begging from Him; and your impotence with: "There is no power and strength save with Him" and "God is the All-Great," and by asking Him for help. Thus the beauty and grace of His Lordship are seen in the mirror of your servanthood.

* * *

In the Name of God, the All-Merciful, the All-Compassionate.

Surely the virtuous and godly ones will be in perpetual bliss, while the wicked, dissolute ones will be in the Blazing Blame. (82:13-14)

KNOW, O HEEDLESS SAID! There are only two ways in our journey through life to the grave. They are of equal length. One is harmless, and all those with insight and discernment say that it contains great benefit. Ninety percent of those who follow it will obtain that benefit. The other way contains no benefit. In fact, those with discernment and religious scholarship say that it contains great harm. It is 99 percent harmful, but those following it do not have to carry any weapon and food (those following the first way do). They seem to bear no burden, but you do not see their hearts, which bear a burden a hundred times heavier, or their spirits carrying a burden of fright and terror. The following parable clarifies this:

You decide to go to Istanbul. There are two roads of equal length: one on the right and one on the left. Those with discernment, observation, and sufficient experience say that the right road contains many benefits and no harm. Its travelers carry weapons and food, but do not have to worry or fear about being obliged to others [for satisfying their need], which is a tremendous burden. As for the other road, millions of people of experience and religious scholarship say that it contains no benefit, although those who follow it seem to bear no burden and carry no weapons or food. But their spirits are burdened with fear, and their hearts are burdened because they must rely on others to satisfy their need. Such burdens are a thousand times heavier than carrying a weapon and food.

Those who have almost completed their journey or have seen what the travelers face both during and after their journey tell us that those following the right way travel in security and, on reaching their destination, nine out of ten of them are welcomed with great reward. Those following the left (dangerous) way suffer fear and hunger and, because of their fear and need, must humble themselves before everything or everyone. When they reach their destination, they either are called to account for their journey or killed, and only one, or at the most two, out of ten are saved. One with even a little intelligence does not choose that which is harmful for the sake of not having to carry a burden. How can something 99 percent harmful be preferred to what is 99 percent beneficial?

You are the traveler, and Istanbul is the intermediate world of the grave and the Hereafter. The right way is that of the Qur'an, which requires belief and performing the five daily Prayers. The left way is that of sin and rebellion. People of discernment and experience are saints who experience the pleasure in Islamic truths. A saint experiences what an ordinary person believes. The weapon and food are the religious obligations. These include the five daily Prayers, confirming Divine Unity, relying on God and asking Him for help, and trusting in the All-Powerful, All-Preserving, and All-Knowing One as well as on the All-Wealthy, All-Munificent, and All-Compassionate. Those following the right way are saved from humbling themselves before whatever or whoever they expect may benefit or harm them, for believing there is no deity but God means that only He can dispense harm or benefit.

* * *

In the Name of God, the All-Merciful, the All-Compassionate.

> This life of the world is but a diversion and a sport; while the home of the Hereafter, that is life if they but knew. (29:64)

KNOW, O SAID! You are journeying toward old age and the grave and eternity. Your Owner gave you this life to obtain the necessities for your life here and in the Hereafter. But you have spent everything in this transient life, which is only like an imaginary drop compared to an ocean. You should spend at least one-half or one-third of it preparing for the everlasting life. How strange that people like you are called intelligent and learned. Consider a person who is given 24 gold coins to buy provisions for a trip from Burdur to Antalya (provinces in southern Turkey), and then to Damascus, Madina, and Yemen. This traveler is told to arrange transport to Antalya, but after that to buy a vehicle. He or she then can travel in ease by ship or train or plane, and arrive in each city within a day. If this is not done, the traveler will experience great difficulty. So, this person sets out and spends 23 coins in 2 days. When told to use the rest to buy provisions, which will please the giver of the money, the traveler replies: "I will not spend it on something that probably will give no benefit." Can there be anyone more foolish?

The traveler is told: "How foolish you are! You set aside half of your money for a lottery in which 1,000 people participate, and thus take a great risk for a 1:1,000 chance. Yet you refuse to set aside one of the 24 parts of your wealth for a 999:1,000 chance, attested to by millions of people of certified knowledge. If someone tells you about a potential material benefit, you accept it. Why do you reject the tidings given to you by the suns and stars of humanity? Furthermore, the testimony of two people who confirm a thing is preferred to that of thousands who negate or deny it. For example, the testimony of two people who claim to have seen the crescent moon that marks the beginning of Ramadan is preferred to that of thousands who deny its appearance."

You are the traveler. Burdur is your world. Antalya is the grave. Damascus is the intermediate world between this world and the next. Yemen is the realms after the Resurrection. The 24 coins represent the 24 hours of a day. You spend 23 of them on this transient life, and are lazy when it comes to spending one hour for the five daily Prayers, your most essential food during the long journey.

This parable explains one of the profound meanings of: *Paradise shall be brought forward for the God-fearing pious, and the Blazing Flame will be laid open before those who rebelled and went astray* (26:90-91).

O HEEDLESS ONE who has renounced the religious life for the sake of worldly benefits. I will speak to you in a parable containing truths pertaining to both the world and the religious life.

Two brothers, one well-disciplined and well-mannered and the other badly behaved, set out on a trip. Coming to a fork in road, they saw that the right fork required obligatory observance of the law governing that road, while the left fork promised a certain kind of freedom without obligation. The first brother took the right fork, accepting dependence on law and order.

The second one took the left fork and, without undertaking any obligation, headed north. Upon reaching a desert, he heard a terrible sound and saw a lion ready to attack him. He ran away and, coming across a 60-meter-deep dry well, jumped into it. Half-way down, he grabbed onto a tree growing out of the wall. The tree had two roots at which two rats, one black and the other white, were gnawing. He saw the lion waiting for him at the top and, looking down, saw a horrible dragon almost at his feet, its mouth open to receive him. When he looked around, he saw harmful vermin everywhere. Looking again at the tree, he saw that it was actually a fig tree with a great variety of fruit.

He was very afraid. Although inwardly distressed and full of complaints, for he was under the influence of his evil-commanding soul, he pretended that he was in a garden and began to eat the fruit. As stated in a *hadith qudsi*: "I treat My servant in the way he thinks of Me,"[91] this wretched man remained in the well. He neither died nor lived well. His lack of understanding blinded him to the fact that his situation was not the result of coincidence.

The first brother, being a well-mannered man always thinking of the good, entered a garden and came across lovely flowers and attractive fruits along with some ruined or ugly things. He concerned himself with what was good and beautiful, and so found ease and was generally happy with everything.

---

[91] Muslim, hadith no. 2675; Tirmidhi, hadith no. 3538. Also recorded in Bukhari. A *hadith qudsi* is a saying from the Prophet, the wording of which belongs to the Prophet but the meaning to God. (Tr.)

Continuing on his way, all that had befallen his brother soon befell him. But there were differences. He was not so afraid when the lion roared, because he thought it might be serving the desert's ruler. Jumping into a well, he ended up just as his brother had. These strange happenings did not cause him great fear, for he thought that these were arranged by someone and were signs that he was being tested. So his fear turned into curiosity about the one who made himself known by such things. Then his curiosity aroused in him a love for the signs' owner.

His fear disappeared when he saw the fig tree bearing a variety of fruits, for he understood that there was a purpose behind everything. If not, how could the fig tree have borne the fruits of other trees? They must represent the various foods prepared by the ruler for his guests. His love for the ruler made him want to discover what the signs meant. The key to this understanding was inspired in him, and he said: "I abandon all things for your sake and rely on you." At this, the wall parted and a door opened onto a wonderful, pleasant garden. He saw the dragon and the lion change into two servants asking him to enter.

Compare the positions of these two brothers. One is about to fall into the dragon's mouth; the other is invited to enter a brilliant garden full of flowers and fruits. The former is terribly anxious and afraid; the latter studies what he witnesses and feels his fear give rise to love, respect, and knowledge. The former is lonely, full of despair and gloom; the latter sees himself in a friendly situation and is full of hope and expectation. The former is targeted for attack by terrifying enemies; the latter is welcomed and served as a guest. The former adds to his distress by eating apparently delicious (but actually poisonous) fruits that are presented only as samples, not intended to be consumed for their own sake but to persuade consumers to seek out the originals and become customers of them; the latter postpones eating and enjoys the anticipation.

Now we can interpret the parable: The first brother is the spirit and heart of a righteous believer; the second brother is the spirit and heart of a rebellious, sinful unbeliever. The right way is that of the Qur'an and belief; the left way is that of unbelief and rebellion. The desert is the world, the lion is death, the well is a person's life, and the well's depth (60 meters) is our average life span (60 years). The tree is life, the two rats are day and night, and the dragon is the grave opening on the Hereafter. The vermin are the troubles we face during life, and the fruits are this world's bounties presented as samples from the Hereafter's blessings, inviting us toward Paradise's fruits. The poisonous fruits are those that are forbidden. The sign is the wisdom in creation, and the key is God: *There is no deity but He, the All-Living, the Self-Subsistent.* That is: "O God. You are my worship's Object and (obtaining) Your pleasure is my life's aim."

The changing of the dragon's mouth into a door to the garden denotes that the grave is the door through which believers pass to reach the All-Merciful One's mercy. For the people of misguidance and rebellion, the grave is the door to dark pits of loneliness and terror in the intermediate world, which is like a dungeon, the belly of the dragon.

The ravenous lion changes into a disciplined and trained horse. For the misguided, death is an eternal separation from loved ones and a removal from their false, worldly paradise to the dungeon of the grave. For the rightly guided, by contrast, death is a means of reunion with friends and companions, of returning home, a departure from the world's dungeon for eternal gardens, and a reward for what was done in this world. This will be bestowed out of the grace of the All-Affectionate, Bounteous, the All-Requiter of good and evil, and the All-Merciful One. There is no deity but He.

KNOW, O CONCEITED SAID! You desire to be praised for even what you have not done. You have no right to be conceited and proud, for you are the origin of evil and imperfection. If there is good in your selfhood, it is only in proportion to your partial free will, while your free will causes great evil. Since your imperfection causes the fruits destined for you to fall and decay, you deserve great loss and shame.

You are like a foolish, conceited person who enters into a business deal with people on a vessel. While everybody does their job, he ignores his, which is to steer the vessel. And so the vessel sinks and they lose a great deal of money. They tell him to compensate them, but he responds: "No! Rather, we should share it among us." Later, they set out on another voyage and make a good profit. They tell him that they should share the profit according to each one's capital. But the foolish man answers: "No! I should get it all, for did you not attribute all the loss to me? Now, all the profit belongs to me." They ask: "Are you so ignorant that you do not realize that something's existence depends on the existence of all its parts and the presence of all conditions necessary for its existence?"

This is why the fruits of existence are shared among its constituents. Profit has a positive, sensed existence; loss means "non-existence." That which exists can cease to exist if even one part is destroyed or one condition necessary for its maintenance disappears.

O one whose name means prosperous (Said) but who, in truth, is wretched. One who causes something to go into non-existence is responsible for its consequences. Therefore, you have no right to be conceited and proud:

First: Evil is from you while good is from your Lord.

Second: Your evil is great and pervasive, while your good is little and restricted.

Third: You already have been rewarded for your good deeds before you do them. As your good deeds cannot pay for even one-billionth of your blessed status as a Muslim person, understand that Paradise is purely out of His Grace and that Hell is purely justice, for even the least evil act can cause global destruction.

Fourth: Something becomes good if it is done for God's sake, for only He causes something done for His sake to be realized. Therefore, as everyone is indebted to Him for his or her good deeds, thanks Him without pride or show, which change good into evil. Unaware of this, you are full of conceit. You attribute the good people do to themselves, thereby making each one a Pharaoh. You share what belongs to God among those rebelling against Him.

You seek to avoid responsibility by attributing your evil to Destiny, although it originates in you. You ascribe to yourself the good that your Creator causes to issue from you out of His Grace, and seek to be praised for what you did not do. Discipline yourself according to the Qur'an's instruction: *Whatever good visits you is from God, and whatever evil befalls you is from your self* (4:79). Take what belongs to you and do not usurp what does not. Remember that the Qur'an says that evil is returned to the same degree, while good is returned at least tenfold. Therefore, do not be excessive in your hostility to those who wrong you by extending that feeling to their relatives and ignoring their good qualities. By the same token, if you love good, righteous people, love their relatives and overlook their defects.

O HEEDLESS SAID! You abandon your duty and occupy yourself with your Lord's work, for you are unfair and ignorant. You abandon your duty of worship although it is easy for you to perform, and try to shoulder the work of Lordship that only can be done by *Him Who created and fashioned, proportioned and composed you as He willed* (82:7-8). Mind your own business, and commit His business to Him so that you may be at rest and ease. Otherwise, you will become wretched, rebellious, and treacherous.

Your situation is like that of a private whose essential duty is to train and fight when necessary. The ruler helps him to fulfill that duty by recognizing his duty to provide the necessary equipment, food and clothes, weaponry and medicine. People see the private cooking and ask him what he is doing. He answers: "Working for the state"; he does not say: "Preparing my food," for he knows that cooking is not his duty but that of the state, which must prepare his food and feed him if necessary. Thus a private seeking to earn his living through trade is ignorant, rebellious, and treacherous, and so deserves chastisement. If he neglects his training and runs away during a battle, he is a traitor and deserves severe punishment.

O wretched Said! You are that private, and the five daily Prayers are your training. Your piety, avoiding major sins, and struggling with the carnal soul and Satan is your fighting. This is why you were created, and God is the Helper Who will make you succeed. Your Creator provides your food and all that is needed for your life and maintenance, as well as for that of your family. But you must knock on the door of His Mercy's treasuries to ask Him by speech and deeds. You must follow the ways to the kitchens where His bounties are cooked to ask Him in the tongue of potential or need, or work or speech, for what He has assigned to you.

How can you accuse Him concerning your livelihood, seeing that He provided you with the best food while you were a baby with no power and will? Only He, the All-Hearing, All-Knowing, All-Powerful, All-Wealthy, Who makes Earth in summer a kitchen for His guests to pour His blessings in floods out of the envelopes of gardens and fill the pans of trees with the most delicious food, meets all creatures' needs. Besides performing your essential task, work for His sake and in His Name, and perform the task He has assigned to you. Trust Him and say: "God is sufficient for me. How good a Guardian, and how good a Helper He is."

* * *

In the Name of God, the All-Merciful, the All-Compassionate.

> When My servants question you about Me, (tell them) I am surely near. I answer the call of the caller when he calls upon Me. (2:186)
>
> Call upon Me and I will answer you. (40:60)
>
> My Lord would not care for you, were it not for your prayer. (25:77)

KNOW, O ONE WHO CLAIMS that his or her prayers are not answered. Prayer (calling to God, supplication) is a type of worship, and the fruit of worship is given in the Hereafter. The worldly results expected from worship are the occasions for it. Sunset is the occasion for the evening Prayer, and a solar eclipse (not its ending) is the reason for the eclipse Prayer. Drought is the occasion for the prayer of asking God for rain, which was not ordered so that rain would come. It is another kind of worship done purely to obtain His good pleasure, although it is necessary to continue it until rain comes. When rain comes, its appointed time ends.

When wrongdoers and misfortune assault Muslims, another kind of prayer should be offered until these conditions cease. If this is possible, it is light upon light. If not, do not say that the prayer remains unanswered; rather, say that its time has not ended yet. God promises to answer prayer in: *Call upon Me and I will answer you* (40:60), but answering does not mean accepting it and giving what is asked. Every prayer is answered, but giving what is prayed for depends on Divine Wisdom.

For example, you ask your doctor for some medicine. He or she gives you what you want, something better, or nothing at all, for it might harm you. Since we suppose that prayer is said to achieve a worldly aim, we think it has not been accepted when what we prayed for does not happen. For instance, we think that praying for rain is done so that rain may come. But if we do it for that purpose (instead of for God's sake), it is not accepted.

KNOW, O FRIEND, that revolutions open a deep rift between two sides (in conflict). A bridge is required to pass from one side to the other. However, bridges are of different kinds and shapes according to the nature of revolutions and the rifts. Sleep is a kind of bridge between this world and the World of Representations or Immaterial Forms. The Intermediate World is a bridge between the world and the Hereafter. Spring is a bridge between winter and summer. After the Resurrection, since there will be many mighty revolutions, the bridges will be extremely strange, curved, and amazing.

KNOW, O FRIEND, that in such frequently mentioned verses as: *Unto Him is your return* (6:60); *Unto Him you are returning* (2:28); *to Him is the homecoming* (5:18), and *unto Him is the return* (13:36), in addition to a threat for the rebellious, there is good news and consolation. They tell humanity that death and decay, as well as transience and separation from the world, are doors opening onto the King of Eternity's Presence. This good news saves the heart from the terrible pain of thinking of eternal separation from what is loved. Consider the hellish state that unbelief causes: According to what the Almighty decrees: "I treat My servant in the way he thinks of Me," since unbelievers suppose death to be an eternal extinction and separation, their supposition becomes a painful torment for them.

Pleasure arising from the conviction of meeting with God is superior to that of Paradise. But above that is the even greater pleasure attained by God's eternal approval and seeing Him in Paradise free of any quantitative and qualitative dimension. The physically hellish state of a sinful believer in the world is like a pleasure of Paradise compared to the spiritually hellish state of an unbeliever who does not recognize the Creator.

Even if there were no proofs for or means to obtain eternal life, the supplications of the Eternal, Beloved One's beloved, behind whom all Prophets, saints, and believers stand in lines in that supreme prayer, would suffice as a proof and means. Could the greatest, most extraordinary, and perfect beauty be marred by the greatest ugliness and most bizarre defect—that the One Who hears and meets His most secret creatures' most secret entreaty does not hear and accept the loudest voice rising from Earth to God's Supreme Throne, the most pleasant supplication, the most comprehensive prayer for meeting the greatest and most urgent needs? No, for He is the All-Hearing, All-Knowing. The Almighty's acceptance of His Messenger's entreaty is the widest, most inclusive dimension of the Messenger's intercession, and his being a mercy for creation.

KNOW, O FRIEND, that heedless people discuss Destiny and are occupied with human free will and the creation of human deeds. But they deny Destiny and attribute things and events to chance, supposing themselves independent agents and sharing what belongs to God and His works among other people and material causes. An unbelieving or heedless soul denies that God creates and administers things and events, even if they evidently confirm Him. A believing soul that knows God attributes all things and events to Him.

According to those with sufficient knowledge of God and conscious of His constant supervision, these two theological issues—Destiny and human free will—mark the final point of belief in and reliance on God, the highest degree of belief in God's Unity and of being a good Muslim. They serve as a veil between those who are aware and those who, due to their heedlessness, are far from the truth. If the believers who advance in humility and servanthood and are lost in or intoxicated with Divine love and Unity, deny free will and attribute everything to God, this is harmless. In this case, issues of denial (of human free will) or its negation and confirmation no longer concern theology; rather, they become issues pertaining to a believer's state arising from one's love and belief.

KNOW, O FRIEND, that humility sometimes contradicts one's proclaiming God's blessings upon oneself, for doing so sometimes gives rise to pride and arrogance. Thus, avoid exaggeration and excessive description. The middle way in one's proclaiming God's blessings on him or her is as follows: Every blessing has two aspects. The first pertains to the one on whom God has bestowed it. This blessing distinguishes one in a community and leads to pride and forgetting the One Who gave it. Such people arrogate it to themselves, attributing it to their abilities or merits, and become haughty.

The second pertains to the Bestower of blessings. The blessing displays His Munificence and Mercy, and testifies to His Names. By bestowing blessings, He pronounces "verses" of His manifestations. Humility should be shown in the first case, while it becomes ingratitude if shown in the second one. If one attributes all the blessings that have been bestowed to God and His Munificence, and feels no self-pride, one's proclaiming God's blessings on himself or herself becomes a praiseworthy gratitude.

O Yusuf Kishri.[92] When you wear splendid clothes, Said says to you: "How beautiful you are." You say: "Beauty belongs to the clothes, not to me." This is both humility and a proclamation of blessing.

KNOW, O FRIEND, that when people are paid and share a reward, feelings of rivalry and jealousy that are quiet while working begin to stir. Since sharing the work and responsibility lightens the burden they bring and lessens the difficulty, the weak appreciate the strong and the lazy love the hardworking. This world is the place of working for the Hereafter, of fulfilling reli-

92 Yusuf Kishri was a pupil of Said Nursi. (Tr.)

gious responsibilities to get the reward in the Hereafter. There must be no rivalry and jealousy, for such things point to insincerity and an impure intention. Such people, by looking for such worldly rewards as appreciation and praise, invalidate their good deeds, make others partners with God in giving reward, and are condemned by others.

KNOW, O FRIEND, that God's use of His servant to perform a wonder (*karama*) differs from His gradually leading another servant to perdition by enabling him or her to do extraordinary things (*istidraj*). *Karama* is an act of God. Those through whom it is done know that it originates from the All-Glorified One, that the Almighty oversees and protects them, and wills them good. This strengthens their certainty about and reliance on Him. Although they are sometimes conscious of the *karama* and how it takes place, it is safer for them and their belief that they remain unaware that God does this through them. For example, God may cause them to say unconsciously what occurs to another person's heart or mind, or reveal scenes from the Unseen so that others may be guided to the Straight Path. These beloved servants are unaware of what God does for His servants through them.

As for *istidraj*, for example, some things from the Unseen may appear to heedless or misguided people. They even may perform wonders. Attributing these to their own power or ability, they grow in conceit, vanity, and distance from God. They say: "*I have been given it only on account of knowledge I possess* (28:78), and it happened because of my purity and my heart's enlightenment."

Those who are half-way in their spiritual journey confuse *karama* and *istidraj*. Those who have attained the highest ranks and realized self-annihilation are aware of the things belonging to the Unseen with their external senses, which function as if means for God to execute His decrees.[93] Since their inner world is perfectly illumined and illuminates their outer world, they distinguish clearly between *karama* and *istidraj*.

* * *

93 As is declared in a *hadith qudsi* recorded in *Sahih al-Bukhari*: "When I love a servant of Mine, I become his (her) ears with which he (she) hears, his (her) eyes with which he (she) sees, his (her) hands with which he (she) holds, and his (her) legs on which he (she) walks.

There is nothing that does not glorify Him with His praise. (17:44)

KNOW, O FRIEND, that every creature's glorification and worship have innumerable aspects. The creature is not required to be conscious of all of them. For example, people working on a ship have to touch some of its pegs and nails. They do not know why the owner wants them to do this, only that if they do so they will be paid and feel the pleasure of earning. They even think that the work was decreed only for their pleasure. An animal is unconscious of why it mates, and does so only to satisfy its sexual desire. But this ignorance does not prevent reproduction and maintenance of its progeny and species.

For instance, while satisfying their greed, ants unconsciously clean the ground of the corpses of micro-organisms. A clock tells you how much more of your lifetime has passed, but "knows" only the pain of its own wear. A honeybee does what it does by the sweetness of Divine inspiration included in the particular pleasure it takes. Plant, animal, and even human mothers work due to the pleasure of affection, unconscious of the lofty purposes realized through them that embellish the home of the universe. It is as if their affection serves as a seed or measure for those purposes.

It is enough for those who glorify and worship God to know how to do their work. The Almighty declares: *Do you not see that all that is in the heavens and Earth glorifies God, and the birds spreading their wings. Each knows (how to do) its prayer and glorification; and God knows what they do* (24:41). They do not have to know that their actions glorify Him, or be conscious of the nature of their own specific prayer. It is enough that we, conscious beings, know that all creatures worship and glorify God. Indeed, it is enough that the Absolutely Worshipped One knows that. As non-human creatures do not have to worship God consciously, they do not have to have the intention to pray or glorify, or even be conscious of what they do. Actually, they are embodied words of glorification and, by their lives, perform another kind of glorification. They glorify (their Creator and Sustainer) in as many ways as willed by the All-Glorified, All-Pure One. There is no deity but He.

KNOW, O FRIEND, that the great variety of bounties and blessings sent to you reach you after passing through different veils and being filtered through diverse "nets" in a specific order.

KNOW, O FRIEND, that there is a very subtle point in selfhood. I think it serves as a window through which to look into eternity, for it tends to eternalize whatever it encounters. If worldly desire uses it, it attracts the building blocks of the Hereafter to the world, attempts to build a worldly palace with them, and eats up the Hereafter's fruits in this transient world before they ripen.

KNOW, O FRIEND, that selfhood is a very strange thing. If it is purified and developed, it becomes a treasury of innumerable instruments and meters to perceive the manifestations of the Divine All-Beautiful Names' treasuries. If it is seduced and stunted, it becomes a cave of snakes, scorpions, and vermin. It is preferable to maintain, rather than to annihilate, selfhood. Maintaining it in a purified form, as was done by the Prophet's Companions, is more in keeping with wisdom than is its death or annihilation, the way followed by great saints.

Selfhood has a great hunger, immense need, and strange tastes. When it is trained and purified, its blameworthy greed changes into a zeal difficult to satisfy, its vicious conceit saves one from associating any partners with God, and its intense self love changes into love of its Lord, and so on. Its evil turns into virtue.

KNOW, O FRIEND, that believers derive their value from the artistry, distinguished coloring, and embroideries of the Divine Names manifested in them. Unbelievers and the heedless only have a physical value. The world, when considered on behalf of the All-Glorified One and as the place where Divine Names are manifested, becomes infinitely valuable. If considered on behalf of itself and from the viewpoint of natural causes, as taught by philosophy, its value is reduced to its changing and lifeless material substance.

The knowledge of the universe derived from the Qur'an is infinitely superior to that taught by modern science and philosophy. For example, the Qur'an says: *He has made the sun as a lamp* (71:16). What a broad, profound view the Qur'an gives you to look at the series of the Divine Names' manifestations. Despite its huge size, the sun serves as a light to illuminate your home, a fire to ripen or cook your food, by the command of Him Who nurtures you. You have such a powerful and compassionate Owner that the sun and innumerable others like it are lamps in His guest-house.

Science or philosophy tell you that the sun is a huge mass of fire moving by itself. Our Earth and other planets were detached from it and move in their orbits determined by their attraction to the sun and gravity. This information gives you either a sense of fright or wonder.

KNOW, O FRIEND, that You cannot demand a right from God, the Ultimate Truth. Rather, you must thank Him continually, for His is the kingdom and the creation, and all praise is for Him.

> O God, All-Merciful, All-Compassionate, All-Munificent. Make this book a substitute for me to bear witness to You after my death as follows:
>
> O God, Lord of the chosen Muhammad. O Lord of Paradise and Hell, of the Prophets and the good. O Lord of the truthful and pious, of the young and old. O Lord of seeds and fruits, of lights and flowers. O Lord of rivers and trees, of what is manifest and what is secret. O Lord of day and night. We have You as a Witness. Our witnesses also include those bearing Your Supreme Throne, all Your angels and creatures, all your Prophets and saints, all Your signs of creation and verses of Your Speech, and all the universe's particles and compounds.
>
> As is also attested by Your beloved, upon him the best of blessings, the testimony containing all other witnesses, and Your Qur'an, that we all bear witness that You are God, Necessarily Existent, One and Single, Besought-of-All and Manifest Truth, All-Living and Self-Subsisting, All-Knowing and All-Wise, All-Powerful and All-Willing, All-Hearing, All-Seeing and All-Speaking. Yours are the All-Beautiful Names. We bear witness that there is no deity but You, the One, without partner. Yours is the dominion and ownership of everything, and all praise is Yours.
>
> We ask You for forgiveness and turn in repentance to You. Again, we bear witness that Muhammad is Your servant and Prophet, Your Beloved and Messenger, whom You sent as a mercy for all worlds. Bestow peace and blessings on him, his Family, and His Companions until eternity. Amen. Amen. Amen.

This explains one jewel in the treasure of: *I have not created jinn and humanity except to worship* Me (51:56).

O SAID! You have forgotten yourself and your vital duty, and are unaware of the wisdom in creating humanity, ignorant of what the All-Wise Maker has placed in those adorned creatures. The building of this universe and including the human world within it can be explained through the following parable: A king has treasuries of different jewels and buried treasures. He skillfully makes novel and magnificent things, and specializes in almost all sciences and crafts. He also wants to display his kingdom's magnificence, his wealth's splendor, his artistry's wonders, and his skills' marvels. In short, he wills that both he and everybody else see his magnificence, perfection, and graciousness.

So he builds a huge, multifloored palace, and divides each floor into different display rooms. He decorates the palace with his jewels and subtle artistry, and puts a mark or seal on each thing to display his miraculous skill, knowledge, and power. On the tables, he places innumerable kinds of delicious foods and beverages to exhibit his munificence. However, a few of the foods and beverages are forbidden for some of his subjects for certain purposes. He does many other things to show his hidden perfection.

Then he invites his subjects to have a good time. At the incomparable feast he has prepared, each morsel seems to be a product of hundreds of delicate skills and arts. Afterwards, he appoints a teacher to explain the displays and the palace's embellishments and decorations. The teacher also describes how the furniture, jewels, and embellishments point to the owner's perfection, and teaches the people how to enter the palace and how to behave toward its builder.

He says: "My master wills to make himself known to you through whatever is in this palace, so know him. He wills to make himself loved by you through these embellishments and bounties, so love him and display your love by appreciating them. He exhibits his mercy on you, so thank him. He manifests himself to you, so show zeal to enter into his presence."

The teacher says many similar things. The people enter the palace and divide into two groups. One group looks at every thing and event. Thinking that it all must signify something very important, they say to the teacher: "Peace be upon you. Everything must be as you tell us, so teach us what your master taught you." He does so, and they act in a way to please the king. The king, in return, calls them to his private, indescribably beautiful palace and, in a way befitting him, bestows all kinds of food and drink that resemble those in the other palace but which are infinitely more delicious.

The other group has eyes only for the food, and is blind and deaf to all other beauties and distinctions. They eat as if they were animals and then sleep. They drink the forbidden beverages and, getting drunk, swear and cause much harm. As a result, the king's soldiers put them in a dungeon.

You know that the king built the palace for the purposes mentioned and made their realization dependent on the teachers' existence and the people's obedience to him. Thus one can say that if there were no teacher, the king would not build the palace, and if the people ignored the teacher's words, the palace would be destroyed and a new one built for other purposes.

If you understand this parable, you can see into the truth. The palace is the world, the ceiling of which is adorned with glittering lamps and the floor with smiling flowers. The king is the Monarch of Eternity. *The seven heavens and Earth, and all that is in them, praise Him* (17:44). *God created the heavens and Earth in 6 days, then seated Himself on the Supreme Throne, covering the day with the night, each pursuing the other urgently, and the sun, the moon, and the stars subservient by His command* (7:54).

The floors are the worlds within the world, and the jewels and embellishments are His Power's miracles. The kinds of food are His Mercy's wonderful fruits. The treasuries of jewels and hidden treasuries are the Sacred Divine Names and their manifestations. All the beauties, designs, and decorations point to those Names. The teacher is our master Muhammad, upon him be peace and blessings. Other Prophets are his friends, and all saints are his students. There are many obedient servants in the palace, who are the angels. The people invited to the palace are human and other animate beings. The two groups are the people of belief and the Qur'an, which explains all "verses" of the Book of Creation, and the people of unbelief and rebellion following their carnal souls and Satan. Those in the second group are deaf, blind, and mute, *more strayed than animals which have lost their way* (25:44). They are aware only of the worldly life.

The prosperous, pious ones listened to the teacher who made his Lord known with his supplication, such as *al-Jawshan al-Kabir*, and communicated the Qur'an. They listened to the Qur'an and saw the beauty of the Divine Lordship's sovereignty. They exalted and glorified God, and proclaimed the marvels of the Sacred Names' manifestations. They glorified and praised God, recognizing the contents of His Mercy's treasuries with their senses and thanking Him. They knew the jewels in the treasuries of the Names manifested in certain measures according to their capacity to receive them, and declared God All-Holy and extolled Him. They studied, appreciated, and reflected on the Pen of Power's missives. They took great spiritual pleasure in observing creation's beauties and, filled with love for the Creator, looked forward to entering into His Presence.

They responded to the Maker's will to make Himself known through His Art's miracles, by trying to obtain knowledge of Him, and said in amazement: "Glory be to You. We cannot know You as knowing You requires, O Known One, through all Your miraculous creatures." They responded to His will to be loved by loving Him through the adornments of Mercy's fruits. They responded to His turning to them with the pleasure of His bounties, by praising and thanking Him, and said: "Glory be to You. We cannot thank You as thanking You requires, O Thanked One, through the praises of Your favors on creation, the exhibitions of Your bounties and their tastes in the market of the universe, and the testimonies of the melodies of the fruits of Your Mercy and Favoring."

They responded by prostrating in love, amazement, and humility to His display of His Grandeur and Perfection, Beauty and Grace, and Majesty throughout the universe, in the mirrors of creatures coming to and departing from the world. His display of His all-inclusive Mercy and infinite Wealth caused them to acknowledge their destitution and beseech Him. They responded to His exhibiting His Arts' subtleties with appreciation and observation, and by bearing witness to them. To His proclamation of His Lordship's sovereignty throughout the universe, they responded with belief in His Unity, obedience, and worship in acknowledgment of their helplessness, weakness, and poverty.

In short, they fulfilled their vital duties here and were perfected, more sublime than all other creatures, observing the Supreme Trust they had borne as trustworthy vicegerents. Then their Lord invited them to the Abode of Peace for eternal happiness and bestowed on them bounties and blessings beyond description.

The second group, which did not believe in the Maker, reduced creatures' value to their material substance through their unbelief, denied all of the Names' manifestations, and committed an infinitely great crime. Thus, its members deserve infinite punishment.

O WRETCHED SAID, do you think that your duty here is to maintain your life by satisfying your carnal soul, your stomach and desires? Do you suppose that all of your senses and feelings, systems and faculties, organs and limbs are to be used by your carnal soul in this fleeting life? They are not, for they were given to you so that you could perceive all the Almighty's bounties and His Names' manifestations. Use your senses and faculties as measures to appreciate the contents of His Mercy's treasuries, to discover and open the hidden treasuries of His Names' manifestations.

Your vital duty is to display His Names' marvelous manifestations, proclaim your servanthood (verbally and actively) at His Lordship's door, and then adorn yourself with the jewels of His Names' manifestations and show yourself to the Eternal Witness. You must understand the reverent glorification of living beings for the Bestower of life, testify to them, and call others to do the same. Use your attributes, qualities, and acts to compare and perceive your Creator's Attributes and sacred Essential Qualities. Considering your poverty and impotence, you must understand the extent of His Power and Wealth's manifestations.

Life serves as a treasury of senses and faculties, a map and a sample, an index and a measure to know the marvelous manifestations of the Names of the Creator of death and life. Your life is an inscribed, audible, and perceived word composed by the Divine Beautiful Names. It is a mirror for reflecting Divine Unity. Its perfection and happiness lie in its being conscious of what it embodies, and feeling love and yearning for the One Whom it serves. Other living beings have a share in some of these purposes, but not as much as you do, for you are a comprehensive mirror. The Creator Himself is said to have declared: "Neither the heavens nor Earth can contain Me, but the heart of My believing servant can."[94]

* * *

In the Name of God, the All-Merciful, the All-Compassionate.

O God, All-Merciful and All-Compassionate, Unique, All-Living and Self-Subsistent, All-Judging and All-Just, and All-Pure. For the sake of Your Greatest Name and Your wisest Criterion (the Qur'an), bestow uncountable blessings on our master Muhammad, your noblest Messenger. Send down on us, the translator and publishers of this

---

94 In *Al-Fatawa al-Hadithiya*, Ibn Hajar Haythami comments: "It is narrated by the Sufis. However, it must not be taken literally in a way to associate union (with God) and incarnation" (as asserted in Christianity and other religions). This narration means that a believer's heart is of such quality that it can know God with all His Attributes, Names, and acts and feel an overflowing love for Him. (Tr.)

book, and all other true believers the peace of reassurance, tranquility, and conviction, as You did for the Companions and Family of Your chosen Prophet, upon him be peace and blessings. Send down on us and on other believing servants of Your Religion the peace of reassurance and sincere belief, perfect certainty and pure intention, and perfect firmness in the service of the Qur'an and belief.

Secure us against our fears by removing all anti-religious elements found in the principles and public marks of Islam, and give us relief by declaring the essentials of Islam throughout the world as soon as possible. Employ us in this sacred service. Secure us, our Religion and its sincere servants, and all true believers against the attacks of heretics. Provide us and all sincere servants of Your Religion with security and safety in Religion and in both this and the other world. Cure our diseases, and make the Qur'an a cure for all our diseases and theirs as well. Include us and them among those who always praise and thank You.

Amen. All praise be to God. May God bestow blessings on our master Muhammad and on his Family and Companions. Amen.

To conclude:

- No one has the right to complain about and object to the Maker of the universe.
- The One operating in a body's cell operates in the whole body.
- He records and preserves your deeds. These are the seeds of the trees that will yield their fruit in the Hereafter, as you were a bearer of His trust and His vicegerent on Earth.
- A thing's material composition may change and be effaced, but the meaning remains. Thus your spirit will not die and, freed from its hooks and stripped of its body, will continue its journey to eternity. The strong tendency of material things (subject to decay) to remain and survive shows that such simple things as meaning, light, and spirit (inclined to permanence) will remain eternally.
- The grandeur of God's Divinity requires that everything be under His control.
- As material, solid things get larger, they lose their sensitivity to delicate, subtle things. However, when light expands and spreads, it becomes more pervasive and penetrates deeper into hidden and subtle things.
- The Qur'an, addressing itself to common people, was revealed in the language most appropriate for their level of understanding.

- A major cause of misguidance is that we think we "know" familiar and common things, and so forget that they are really miracles of Divine Power.
- The One Who prepares food for you to eat is more aware of your need to eat and of what pleases your conscience than you are.
- The human ego is the key of creation. When you fully understand its nature, creation is opened to you.
- Good deeds acquire vitality through sincere intention, and are corrupted through show, ostentation, and hypocrisy. However, sincerity or purity of intention, which is a tendency of a purified heart, is corrupted through purposefully intending to be sincere.
- The universe is a tree: The basic elements like earth and water, air and fire are its branches; plants its leaves; animals its flowers; and humanity its fruits.
- The meaning of: *We have made them (shooting stars) missiles for devils*.
- Things are recorded before and during their physical existence.
- God destines and decrees, executes His decrees, and forgives and withdraws the execution of His decrees.
- Why many Qur'anic verses end with Divine Names.
- One's acknowledgement of his or her innate helplessness and poverty before God, a path of four steps, leads to God more directly and safely than love.
- Worship is the result and price of what humanity has been given already, not a cause for future, expected reward.
- The infinite number of perfectly made and ordered creatures, especially small ones, shows that there are no limits to the Maker's manifestations, that He is absolutely different or beyond all human conceptions, and that all things are the same in relation to His Power and Necessary Existence.
- The One with the All-Beautiful Names manifests Himself in the departments of His Sovereignty with His Names. Only One Name or a few Names are dominant in a department, while the others are subordinate.
- The All-Wise Creator has included in our primordial nature innumerable meters to measure what is stored in His Mercy, and countless faculties to understand what is contained in the treasuries of His All-Beautiful Names.
- Differences among creatures show purpose and reject chance.
- God gives respite to unbelievers so that they unconsciously may manifest some of His blessings and unknowingly display the Divine Art's beauty and excellence to humanity.
- The Qur'an and the Prophet do not view the universe as do modern science and philosophy.

- Those suffering misfortune should not weaken their patience by confronting past and present misfortunes and those that might come in the future.
- Traditions some criticize as containing exaggeration contain valuable truths.
- Those enamored of themselves and relying on their physical existence are content with feeble shadows of reality.
- Every conscious being must pay attention to certain awesome issues.
- The meaning of a "letter" and a "name," and the difference between a universal having particulars or individuals and a whole formed of parts.
- When you restrict your fear or love to the created, fear becomes a pain and love an affliction.
- Although humanity, the fruit or seed of the Tree of Creation, is physically weak, impotent, and small, the All-Wise Maker has favored it with a universal disposition.
- Love of God and love of all else save Him.
- Human beings, who would give almost anything to learn about the moon and other planets, must pay attention to what God Almighty says of their future.
- The All-Wise Maker's acts contain no waste or futility. Everything that exists has a function and a purpose.
- Why the All-Wise Maker makes members of the same animal species vary greatly in size.
- Most plant and animal species try to cover as much land as possible so they can use it as a place of worship by manifesting the their Creator's Names.
- The Qur'an sometimes mentions why a certain thing exists in relation to humanity. However, it was created for many more purposes than just those mentioned.
- Glory be to Him Who has absolute power to make all things from one thing and one thing from all things.
- A brief explanation of: *Or are We the sowers?* (56:64).
- One of our tasks is to use our attributes and essential qualities to perceive the Creator's Attributes and Essential Qualities.
- An address to those who invite Muslims to the worldly life and to abandon their public marks of Islam and their own traditions.
- As human beings need all things, they should worship only God, for only He possesses and controls everything.
- Life's two roads.
- A parable on how people spend their lives.

- A parable on truths pertaining to the world and the religious life.
- The results of conceit and pride.
- That which exists only does so because all its parts and necessary conditions also exist. It ceases to exist if one part or condition no longer exists.
- Paradise is purely out of His Grace, and Hell is purely out of His justice.
- An answer to those who claim their prayers are not answered, and the meaning of answering.
- Such verses as: *To Him is the homecoming* (5:18) and *unto Him is return* (13:36) threaten the rebellious and provide glad tidings and great consolation for the believers.
- Divine Destiny and human free will.
- Humility sometimes contradicts people proclaiming God's blessings upon themselves. What is the proper way to do this?
- Rivalry and jealousy in religious service indicate insincerity, impure intention, and a desire for worldly rewards.
- The difference between saints' wonders (*karama*) and extraordinary things (*istidraj*).
- Every creature's glorification and worship, conscious or otherwise, have innumerable aspects.

The Tenth Treatise

The Tenth Treatise

A radiance from the sun of the Qur'an

Know that the All-Wise Creator gave you those senses, feelings, and systems to perceive His bounties and experience His Names' manifestations. You were created to display His Names' manifestations and exhibit their marvels. Your humanity lies in your consciousness of this duty, and your being a Muslim depends on your conviction of this honor conferred on you.

In the Name of God, the All-Merciful, the All-Compassionate.

Praise is from God and for God, as it is deserved by God. Praise be to God for "praise is for God."

O God. In the presence of all bounties and works of mercy, all favoring and wisdom, life and death; all animals and plants, flowers and fruits and works of (Your) art and fashioning; universal order and harmony; and all movement and stop in all particles and compounds, we testify that there is no deity but God. He is One with no partner. His is the kingdom of all existence and His is all praise. He gives life and death. All good is in His Hand, and He is powerful over all things. We testify that Muhammad is His servant and Prophet, beloved and Messenger, whom He sent as a mercy for all worlds.

O God. Bestow blessings on Muhammad, the ocean of Your lights, the mine of Your mysteries, the sun of Your guidance, the spring of Your Favoring, the tongue of Your proof. He represents the work of Your Power and love, is the embodiment of Your Mercy, and Your most beloved creation. Bestow blessings on all other Messengers and

Prophets, their families and Companions, and on the angels made near to You. Bless Your righteous servants in the heavens and on Earth, for the sake of Your Mercy, O Most Merciful of the Merciful.

Glory be to You, O One Whom the universe both glorifies and praises with the tongue of Muhammad, upon him be Your best blessings and peace. Glory be to You, O One Whom the world glorifies with the works of Muhammad, upon him be the most abundant of Your blessings. Glory be to You, O One before Whom Earth prostrates under the Throne of Your Grandeur and glorifies with Your praise with the tongue of its Muhammad, upon him be the purest of Your benedictions. Glory be to You, O One Whom all the believers glorify with the tongue of their Muhammad, upon him be Your blessings forever. Glory be to You. I glorify You with the tongue of Muhammad, Your beloved, upon him be Your perfect blessings and radiant peace. Accept this from me for (the sake of) Your Mercy, as You accepted it from him.

KNOW, O FRIEND, THAT THE EXTREMELY COMPREHENSIVE MEANING of: *The seven heavens and Earth and whoever is in them glorify Him. There is n othing that does not glorify Him with His praise* (17:44), requires explanation. I tried to look into it and some words of explanation dropped into my heart. If you would like to absorb those words dripping from this verse's ocean or descending from its very high heavens, listen to what follows:

Glory be to You. We, the communities of humanity, cannot know You as knowing You requires, O One known through Your works' miracles, Your creatures' descriptions, and the definitions of all existence. How immense is Your authority. How clear is Your proof.

Glory be to You. We cannot mention You as mentioning You requires, O One mentioned with all Your creatures' and works' tongues, and with the breaths of all the words of the book of Your creation. How majestic is Your mentioning.

Glory be to You. We cannot praise You as Your praise requires. You are praised through all the instances of Your Generosity displayed before the eyes of all who can see, and through exhibiting Your bounties in the market of the universe before all who witness them. You are praised through the joyful testimonies of all the fruits of Your Mercy, Which shapes them in the molds of the universal order and balance. Glory be to You. How vast is Your Mercy.

Glory be to You. We cannot worship You as Your worship requires, O One worshipped by all angels and other creatures of Yours in infinitely various ways of worshipping and praising.

Glory be to You. We cannot glorify You as Your glorification requires, O One Whom *the seven heavens and Earth and whoever is in them glorify. There is nothing that does not glorify Him with His praise.* Glory be to You, O One Whom all kinds of angels glorify in different tongues in various ways.

Glory be to You, O One Whom the universe glorifies with the mouths of its worlds, the limbs of its main parts, the cells of its limbs, and the particles of its cells, through the tongues of its purposeful order, magnificent balance, well-ordered working, and well-proportioned construction. Glory be to You, O One Whom Paradise glorifies with the mouths of its gardens through the songs of its houris, the praises of its palaces, the odes of its trees, and the hymns of its fruits resembling one another, as their resemblances in this world glorify Him.

Glory be to You, O One Who alternates day and night and subjugates the sun and the moon. You are the One Whom the heavens glorify with their systems, and the mouths of their suns or stars through the tongue of their order and harmony, well-designed adornment and majestic radiance, their absolute obedience and tranquility, and their purposeful movements.

Glory be to You, O One Whom the atmosphere glorifies with the mouths of its thunderbolts and lightning, winds and clouds, shooting stars and rain, through the words of its well-balanced order with many lofty purposes. Glory be to You, O One Whom Earth glorifies, prostrated before the immensity of His Power with its Muhammad and Qur'an, with the mouths of its seas and mountains, rivers and trees, and sounds and vibrations (the sounds of its plants and the movements of its animals). It glorifies You with its light-diffusing words and luminous letters (Prophets and saints) and through the tongue of its order and balance, life and death, poverty and dryness, rich adornment and wise art.

Glory be to You, O One Whom the seas glorify with their words of strange animals, and through their songs and the tongue of their order, balance, and the many purposes they serve. Glory be to You, O One Who has made Earth as a cradle and mountains as pegs. The mountains glorify You with their mouths of springs, rivers, and trees, and through the tongue of their balance, order, the purposes they serve, and their treasuries.

Glory be to You, O One Who has made every living thing from "water," and Whom animate beings glorify with their mouths of senses and feelings, systems and organs, artistic structures and intellects, and hearts. They glorify through the tongue of their well-proportioned designs, and they ask through their potential and the tongue of their need, prayers, their being provided, the changes they undergo, and their lives and deaths.

Glory be to You, O One Whom flying insects glorify with Your praise with their chants of thanksgiving. Birds and their chicks glorify in their nests with their songs of gratitude, through the tongue of the order and balance in their creation and movements, and of their designs and adornment. They proclaim Your favors on them and thereby manifest their gratitude when tasting the fruits of Your Generosity and being fed with the works of Your Mercy. Vermin and wild animals also glorify You through the tongue of the excellent proportion and balance in their structures and forms, and being munificently fed. Glory be to You. How fine and subtle is Your Art. How penetrating is Your Rule and Authority.

Glory be to You, O One Whom trees manifestly glorify when they blossom and give forth leaves and fruits. They glorify You through the tongue of their well-proportioned forms and designs, their taste and beautiful blossoms, fine smells, and rich adornment. They magnify You and proclaim Your Caring's perfection, describe Your Attributes' and Names' manifestations, and interpret Your making Yourself loved by Your creatures. They do so with what comes out of their fruits' limbs pertaining to the radiance of Your making Yourself loved by Your creatures and undertaking their provision. Glory be to You. How subtle is the proof of You Originating in Your Generosity. How rich is Your Graciousness in making Yourself loved.

Glory be to You, O One Whom plants glorify with perfect clarity when they blossom and produce spikes and grain, with the mouths of their flowers and spikes and with the words of their seeds and grain, through the tongue of their subtly proportioned forms and structures. They magnify and make You known, show Your "Face" which makes Yourself loved, describe Your Attributes and mention Your Names, and interpret Your making Yourself loved and making Yourself known to Your servants. Glory be to You. How subtle and varied is the evidence of You. How radiant and enriched it is.

Glory be to You, O One Who sent down iron wherein is mighty power and uses for humanity; Whom minerals glorify with all their varieties and shapes, properties and uses, and embellishments through the tongue of their well-established order and special balance. Glory be to You, O One Whom elements glorify through their coming together to make compounds by Your Command and Power.

Glory be to You, O One Whom particles glorify through their duties and the tongue of the order and balance they display. They glorify You in that, despite their absolute impotence, they perform mighty duties by Your Power. Each of them testifies to the necessity of Your Existence

> through the tongue of their essential impotence to carry out the lofty duties in creation's subtle order. For example, a tiny seed bears a huge tree in itself. Every particle indicates Your Oneness with respect to its duties, and its movements contribute to the universal order. In short, a particle testifies to both Your necessary Existence and Oneness, and every incident indicates that You are One and the Eternally-Besought-of-All. Rather, each thing indicates and bears witness that You are necessarily existent, One and Single, and Eternally Besought-of-All. There is no deity but You, One, with no partners at all.

KNOW, O FRIEND, that your body's limbs, organs, and senses belong to its Maker, Who rears and governs it. Your share in it is only your duty [to maintain and use it according to His commands]. If you use it properly, you can obtain a ray of awareness of how your body really is, for it shows that its Originator has absolute knowledge of it and that His Names and Attributes are manifested on it.

If your body serves you in some way only at this moment, it does so because it serves its Maker at all times. It displays many of its All-Wise Creator's marvelous works and, by fulfilling its "natural" tasks with perfect order and a wonderful mutual assistance, it exhibits the subtleties of the Almighty's Mercy and the "fibers" of His Wisdom.

Your share in your body and the right to control it is proportional to your knowledge of it and your share in maintaining it. All its particles, compounds, life and properties show that it belongs to its Maker and is under His absolute control. So do not overstep your limits.

Your existence has a relation to the Almighty Truth and creation. With respect to the Truth, you are a subtle work of art, a pure, clean work of the Creator of the heavens and Earth. Based on your share in your existence and its worth and perfection, it is enough for you to know that you are a work of art of the Maker Who has adorned the heavens with stars, and that you have become a beloved, honorable brother (or sister) of the universe that serves you. As for your relation to the creation, you are composed of elements that have come together and soon will part company.

Do not wrong your body by using it unjustly and breaking its relation with the Truth, for this will make it worthless. Even if it were to last millions of years, a fruitless existence cannot equal one moment of a fruitful one [that receives the manifestations of an absolute, eternal Existence]. Your Originator took material elements and kneaded them with a perfect, most valuable part of creation, to give you a particular, definite existence out of the ocean of existence. How did they come together to form you? In the market of becoming and dissolving, is there a shop selling eyes, a store selling brains and tongues, or a machine making hearts and weaving skins? No. Rather, your Originator created you in an exquisite, comprehensive form from a thing resembling nothing—or from everything—so that not even the greatest thing can create the smallest thing. That which cannot create the heavens cannot claim to create a gnat.

KNOW, O FRIEND, that the All-Skillful Maker controls matter and creates from it wonderful works of art. The value of matter cannot equal even a hundredth part of the art. An antique work of art may fetch a million dollars; its material is not even worth a few cents. If it is taken to the antiques market, it may be sold for its true value because of its art and the name of the artist who made it; in the blacksmiths' market, it may be sold only for the price of its material (iron).[95]

All creatures are embodiments of art. Living creatures, particularly small ones, display perfect art despite the density of matter. So, everything has two aspects. With respect to its material aspect and worldly life, its provision keeps it alive and gives a particular, fleeting pleasure; with respect to its aspect of displaying the Maker's manifestations, it is a wonderful treasure, a pure and marvelous treasury. It allows all the Maker's bounties to be tasted and known, manifests the Names of the All-Munificent Provider to be experienced, and causes conscious beings to be enlightened by recognizing those Names.

Consider your tongue, only one of thousands of devices receiving and recognizing provision. Despite its small size, it contains as many instruments as the different types of food and drink. If its owner becomes conscious of its significance, he or she will give thanks with each of it subtle instruments for all the bounties that the All-Providing offers him or her to taste out of His Mercy. Being thankful for the bounties, which is more pleasant than the actual bounties themselves, shows that you are conscious of being provided with them and perceive the favor or kindness of the Bestower of bounties.

---

95 In the antiques market where its art is recognized, it is sold for the price of its art and its artist's name or reputation. In the blacksmith's market, however, the value of its art cannot be recognized and so they give it the price of its material.

KNOW, O FRIEND, that everything created by Almighty God is orderly and balanced. The Originator has made it sound and well-ordered. All that is seen in this transient world is ordered according to accurate calculation, delicate balance, and careful equilibrium. This balance and order indicate the Resurrection and the awesomeness of the reckoning and Supreme Balance [by which our deeds will be weighed] in the Hereafter. Whatever we witness here as seeds or foundations serves as indications, testimonies, and signs of what will flourish in the Hereafter.

All that we see in this world is made or created. Everything contingent is too weak and impotent to be the real Maker of anything, even of itself, for making, for example, a plant or an animal requires instruments, tools, and balances like those used to prepare medicine. No contingent thing has any of these, nor does it not know how to use them, and so it cannot create anything. Whatever nearby thing that is necessary for a thing's existence and maintenance is but a radiance or manifestation of the Power of Him Whose treasures are between *Kaf* and *Nun*.[96]

Some Divine Names, such as the All-Speaking, All-Providing, All-Granting, allow apparent means to manifest themselves through veils and from behind walls. Others, such as Creator, Inventor, Bestower of life, do not. Those that admit means do so because their dignity and grandeur require them to be manifested behind veils and means, not because they need means due to incompetence.

KNOW, O FRIEND, that I saw in the desert a tree with two kinds of fruits. One resembled green grains, the other a sort of finger-sized pea or bean. They were curved and hollow, as if waiting to receive "guests." I opened one, and numerous insects flew out in lines. It was nearly sunset, and they began to dance in ecstatic movements of mentioning God Almighty—they were not playing; rather, they were rapturously mentioning the All-Merciful One Who keeps them in the air. These pods served as their nests, like a mother's warm and fortified womb in which they found delicious food.

Neither those unconscious pods nor the insects had made such a nest for forming and growing these insects, as that was obviously beyond their ability. So someone else must have done it, someone with absolute knowl-

96 *Kaf* and *Nun* are the letters forming *kun* (be), and imply God's command to anything He wills to do or create: *His command, when He wills a thing, is but to say to it "Be," and it is"* (36:82).

edge of all beans and insects, who knows all their needs and relations. Such a one only can be the One Who has absolute knowledge of and power over all things.

I ask those of you who attribute control to others apart from God in His kingdom, who accept the role of chance in the existence of His subtle works: How can that tree hear, understand, or know the tongue of those insects that lay their eggs on its branches, entrusting them to their preservation? Yet that tree provides a warm home for them, just like a mother's womb and a swinging cradle. The tree receives delicious, sufficient food from Divine Mercy's treasury, stores it in the nests on its branches, and freely gives it to another species—the guests God entrusts to its safekeeping. Such mutual assistance is a clear sign that everything serves and is directed and instructed by a single Lord, a single Instructor, Who is the Besought-of-All.

LOOK, O FRIEND, at those insects carefully, and you will see them mentioning their Creator through their manners and dispositions, well-arranged decorations and well-proportioned structures—even if you cannot understand these particular languages. It is as if each insect were an articulate word. Like those insects, all vermin in the soil glorify their Creator through their designs and decorations made by the Pen of Power, as they glorify Him in their particular languages. This reality will provide you with four benefits:

First: Confidence that you see yourself in a stronghold formed by new births and infants brought up and adorned by the All-Knowing's Caring, the All-Wise's Instruction, the All-Munificent's Favoring, and the All-Compassionate One's Compassion. You are always under the protection and consideration of that All-Knowing and All-Wise, All-Munificent and All-Compassionate One.

Second: Conviction that you are not left to do whatever you wish or left to your selfhood's compassion, unable to meet even your least need, so that you sit rebuked and denuded, frightened of your absolute impotence and unlimited need. The perfect order and delicate balance you see in the life of small creatures prevail in the whole system. Do those delicate "inscriptions," fine "books" inserted in big "letters" not tell you that you are dependent on the same order? Wake up and carefully observe the order or balance. Why do you play and amuse yourself as if trying to destroy the balance?

Third: Conviction that the One Whom you ask to meet your needs and of Whom you stand in awe is infinitely near to you although you are infinitely far from Him. He controls [all that is] in you and your environment through His Power, in relation to which everything, without exception, is the same. Nothing is difficult for Him, and His acts do not require that He be in direct contact with what He has created.

Does this mean that you should not feel awe? Wherever you are, His rules prevail; wherever you turn, there is His "Face." You are at home, even if inside the soil. He sees you even in the belly of "non-existence." The hands of compassion, munificence, and wisdom take you, by His command, from one state and stage to another. Before a hand leaves you, another is stretched to receive you in an orderly sequence. Chance cannot intervene during your journey. You are not wronged by non-existence, and mortality does not wrong you by eternal extinction. Wherever you are during your life, there is an instance of non-existence. But, also behind or beneath or within it is a treasury of Mercy full of the permanent original of that temporary and weak shadow of the thing that has perished.

Fourth: Proof, provided by those small creatures, that One Maker creates or makes everything. This evidence is strengthened in proportion to their smallness, and becomes clearer in proportion to their invisibility, for what is encompassed cannot be excluded from the Creator's control of what is encompassing. The sign of being created is clearer in small beings than in large ones.

KNOW, O FRIEND, that your heedlessness of the Creator comes from four things:

First: You are so oblivious of your own self that your hair-like ego grows into a "thick rope." When your fancies and desires cause you to forget God, He causes you to forget your own self, and so your ego grows thicker and thicker and gradually swallows you.

Second: You compare all living creatures to yourself. When you see an animal, even one innocent, secured, and happy in its life, you see it as a sorrowful person lost in thought and confused memories. You suppose its joyful dances to be no more than groaning with distress.

Third: You restrict yourself to the manifestations of the Divine Name "the Outward," and think that whatever is "excluded" from this Name's sphere of [authority and control] does not belong to the One called by It.

This is false, for the One called by this Name has many other beautiful Names. As He is above all that is above, He is also the Most Inward of the inward. He is the First and the Last, the Outward and the Inward.

Fourth: The Divine Manifestation of Oneness [the concentration of almost all or many Names on a single thing] is the highest manifestation, and also the most distant and most hidden. However, you want to see it clearly on all things. When you compare an animal to yourself, you think it suffers because it is separated from its loved ones or home, and is anxious about its future and provision. You are affected by it. However, if you consider it realistically, you see that your perception is mistaken.

Then you make a bigger mistake. When you see a honeybee, you unconsciously compare its Maker, the One, the All-Wise and Necessarily Existent Who needs no direct contact with His creatures and creates and governs with ease, to material and restricted contingent beings. Since they have to be near to and in touch with their works, and work with difficulty, this false comparison causes you to see this honeybee, on which the Maker's Pen is working as It always does, as near the All-Holy, All-Transcendent Maker.

He, exalted are His Essential Qualities, is near. He is nearer to you and every other thing than the nearest to you, nearer than your jugular vein, whereas you and that creature are infinitely distant from Him. Glass shines with the sunlight's reflection, and becomes beautiful and adorned with the sunlight's seven refracting colors. Due to its transparency, the "purity of its heart," a window or way is opened from that glass to the sun, and the sun is seen in it. However, if you stretch out your hand (to touch the sun), you cannot touch it. Only one who cherishes love for the sun in one's heart and lacks good sense wishes to reach the sun through its rays. Such people also want to see all of the original sun's properties and functions in its reflection. If this is impossible, they deny the sun's existence in its reflection or even the sun's existence.

The human heart is the mirror of the One, Eternally-Besought-of-All. However, as Imam Rabbani explains, unlike other mirrors it is conscious of and has deeply felt relations with what is manifested in it. Thus the heart can feel countless instances of happiness.

QUESTION: How can the wonderful activity in a living creature be reconciled with the silence around it, as if nothing happens or shows the activity?

ANSWER: If the activity belonged to material or natural causes or the living creature itself, every animal would have to be an independent agent with all-encompassing knowledge, and every fruit a powerful maker who could create Earth and its contents with ease. Then one could hear and observe the activity from outside. Nevertheless, consider the security and safety observed in space; the silence and tranquility observed everywhere except in the human realm; and the obedience, peace, and restfulness that pervade the universe. All of this is the work and law of the One Who *when He wills a thing, His command is but to say to it "Be!" and it is* (36:21). He says: *There is not a thing but its treasures are with Us, and We send it not down but in a known measure* (15:21). The relation between actions done by your hand and actions done with the speed of your imagination may be likened to the relation between your imagined actions and the actions of the Originator's Power.

O WRETCHED, ARROGANT SAID! You can meet only a few of your needs. The rest are committed to the care of your Creator, Who created you first like a lump of dough and then shaped you in a fluid, by His miraculous art, so that you might be a mirror reflecting His Names. He opened your ears and eyes through His Mercy so that you might hear the truth and, by seeing the created, know the Creator. He placed in your mouth, through His Favoring, a tongue so that you might mention Him. He placed your intellect in your head so that you could know Him, and entrusted your chest with a heart to love Him. He treated you kindly in the darkness of desolation (the womb) and controlled you, through His Lordship, however He willed. He formed in your body, through His Wisdom, all senses and organs so that you might perceive His bounties and recognize His Names' manifestations.

Why, after He has favored you with such blessings, do you continue to blame Him and rely on your own extremely insignificant, partial power? How much longer will you commit your affairs to your own selfhood and wrong yourself with a burden you cannot carry? Why do you refuse to rely on Him Who holds you by the forelock and meets your needs? Rely on Him. Embark on His ship floating in the flood of events and say: *In the Name of God is its course and its mooring* (11:41) so that you can rest upon the Judi of Islam and on the shore of salvation.[97] The sun of your life is about to set, the moon of

97 Referring to Prophet Noah's Ark, which after the Flood settled on al-Judi, probably a hill of Mount Ararat. (Tr.)

your body is eclipsed by old age, and your head is full of gray hair. Only the Almighty can benefit you, for whatever is outside His permission harms you. Without Him, everything is harmful and hostile, while with Him you need nobody else. So, renounce whatever or whoever is other than Him.

Without Him, the pain lying in every pleasure is more acute than the pleasure; nay, pleasure is pure pain without Him. Therefore, *flee to God* (51:50), for with Him is everything permanent; whatever perishes is with you. It perishes here, whereas it lasts with Him there. Besides, time is very limited. You will suffer the intoxication of death,[98] for your life passes in intoxication. Raise your head to free yourself from the world so that you may see Your Originator's perpetual bounties, everlasting mercy, and eternal love.

O BEWILDERED THINKER SEARCHING FOR TRUTH! When your knowledge ends in something or when you see a sign of eternality in something, glorify the Almighty with His praise, for you have approached the Truth. Being unknowable and eternality are titles or signs of His absolute Lordship's control.

O ONE IN DOUBT! When doubt attacks you, look to the right and see the spheres of His Creativity's control, from the sphere of the solar system and planets to that of atoms and particles, from the creation of the heavens to that of fruits, from the building of Earth to the invention of worms eating trees. All of this points to the fact that the Pen "drawing" them is one, and that the stamp on them is also one. You are in the middle of the conical universe, bearing the Supreme Trust and having undertaken vicegerency—[the responsibility to rule and improve Earth according to God's laws]. Then look to the left and see the universal order judging and ruling with justice, as well as the perfect balance preventing deviation. The reality of creation will blow away your doubt, and the universal order and balance will remove your confusion and bewilderment.

Afterwards look at yourself. See your self and body made or created from head to foot, from the smallest of cells to the whole body, which is like a huge cell. Look at your heart and then upwards. You will see the lights of the Light of Lights, Who has created, illuminated, and formed the light. The lights of His manifestation penetrate everything.

98 The state one feels during death is, probably because one is losing consciousness, likened to intoxication and called "the intoxication of death." (Tr.)

KNOW, O FRIEND, that using the comparative or superlative form in some Divine Names (e.g., The Most Merciful of the merciful, The Best of the creators, The Best of the judges, etc.) does not contradict Divine Unity. Rather, this expresses the Almighty's absolute, incomparable superiority over any other thing or person claimed to have Divine Attributes. Nor does this contradict the dignity of the One, the All-Overwhelming, for it does not compare the Almighty's Attributes or acts with those of the created, for in relation to the Glorified One's Perfection, all else is only a reflected shadow.

All perfection shared by the created has no right to be compared with that of the Almighty. This usage compares the particular effect of the Divine Names' manifestations on things and the extent of the things being affected by the Divine Names, and the effect of apparent means on the same things and the degree of the things being affected. For example: A private sees his corporal as the greatest person, and is both respectful and thankful to him. He is told that the king is greater and more merciful than the corporal. This does not mean comparing the king with the corporal. Rather, it informs the private that the king is more worthy of respect and thanks, and that it is only by the king's permission and to the extent of the corporal's loyalty to him that the corporal deserves respect and thanks.

We say of the Almighty, for example, The Most Affectionate of the affectionate, The Most Munificent of the munificent, or The Most Dignified of the dignified. This expresses the fact that the affection received by you from anybody cannot equal the care you receive from the infinite ocean of God's Mercy.

The One declared superior is Real, One, absolutely and incomparably superior. He has the Name or Attribute in question as essential to Him. Inferior ones are nominal or imagined, and represent what has been created. They have the attribute or name in question by accident, and appear as dim shadows or manifestations of the original possessed by the Almighty. Combined together, whatever the created has is not a real radiance of its original by itself, as God declares: *Those whom they invoke, apart from God, will never create a fly even if they combine together for the purpose* (22:73).

KNOW, O FRIEND, that the Name "God" contains the meaning of all Divine Beautiful Names and all Attributes of perfection, whereas the proper names of all other beings point only to the persons of the beings called by them. This does not include their attributes, for these are not indispensable to them, and thus their proper names do not point to their attributes or qualities. However, the All-Holy One's Names and Attributes are indispensable when describing Him, and Divinity particularly requires them. So the Name (the One) "God," the "Proper" Name of the Divine Being, necessarily contains the meaning of all other Divine Names and Attributes, points to them, and rejects all others to which divinity is attributed, as in: *There is no deity but God.*

If you understand this, you can understand that *there is no deity but God* declares absolute Divine Unity and contains all requirements or conclusions of Unity to the number of the Divine Beautiful Names. This phrase contains thousands of phrases, for such a phrase signifies confirmation and negation or rejection. Since *God* necessarily contains all other Divine Names, *there is no deity but God* also means that there is no creator, provider, self-subsistent, owner, originator, overwhelming ... but God. Therefore, one who has progressed spiritually means all of this while saying: *there is no deity but God.* This phrase implies such a person's spiritual ranks and states, and its repetition increases and improves conviction.

KNOW, O FRIEND, that if you are convinced that all things and acts are from God, you should consent to whatever happens to you, whether pleasing or harmful. If you do not, you will experience difficulties, for God Almighty decreed apparent causes that blind eyes to the truth. Displeasing things and events outnumber those that are pleasing, for the universe was not built according to the plans and desires of the wishful. If people are heedless of the role of apparent causes that belongs to the Creator of causes, they would direct improper and unjust objections and opposition, hatred and wrath, and grudges to the All-Wise Creator, the All-Munificent Master. Such people aim for either Destiny or Satan, but usually hit their own heads or souls.

KNOW, O FRIEND, that when you give due, careful consideration (to existence), you will understand that any contingent thing or being is as far from creating as the infinitude of the Power necessary for creating anything.

KNOW, O FRIEND, that there are three kinds of prayer:

First: That which people do verbally. This also includes the cries of animals, uttered in their own tongues for the needs of which they are aware.

Second: That done in the tongue of need. This includes the prayers of all plants and trees, especially those in spring, and the prayers of animals for their needs of which they are not conscious.

Third: That done in the tongue of potential. This includes the prayers of those who have the potential to grow, change, and be perfected. As everything glorifies Him with His praise, everything prays and thanks Him verbally, in person, or in the tongue of disposition or state.[99]

KNOW, O FRIEND, that a seed grows into a tree, a sperm (and egg) into a person, an egg into a bird, and a seed into a plant only by the direction, command, and control of a perfect, penetrating knowledge. This knowledge belongs only to the Knower of the Unseen, Who fashions in the wombs as He wills and knows the past, present, and future. A seed, sperm, or egg is like a prototype or an outline copied from the Manifest Book, which is one of the books of Destiny; a table of contents extracted from the Manifest Record, one of the records of the Eternal Knowledge; a set or embodiment of principles deduced from the Mother Book, a book of eternal Destiny, particularly from that Book's "chapters" of balance and order; a summary or synopsis formed by the All-Powerful, All-Knowing Lord of all things.

KNOW, O FRIEND, that a believer sees a creature as a letter meaning almost nothing by itself but serving as a complementary part of the word to which it belongs. An unbeliever considers it on behalf of itself by restricting his or her view of it to the creature itself.

Every creature has two aspects: one concerning itself and its attributes, and the other pointing to its Creator and His Names manifested on it. The second aspect is more comprehensive. Every letter in a book points to itself only as a letter, while in the book it points to and describes its author in many ways. In the same way, every creature, which is a letter from the book of Divine Power, points to itself and its apparent existence to the extent of

99 Said Nursi divides the first kind of prayer into two categories: The first category consists of supplications made in desperation or connection with natural needs. Most such supplications are accepted. The second category consists of prayers that we say every day. These are also of two types: one is active and by disposition; the other verbal and from the heart. For example, plowing the ground is an active prayer and means to knock at the door of the treasury of God's Mercy and Munificence, not to beg provision from Earth. What reaches the court of God from the whole universe is a kind of prayer. Causes are petitions to God to create the desired result. See Said Nursi, *The Letters*, The Light Inc., 2007. (Tr.)

its size, while pointing to its Eternal Designer in many respects, and sings the praises of His Names manifested on it.

A judgment cannot be given on the basis of a letter, and a letter cannot affirm or deny a conclusion. For this reason, the mind does not think about it. If the mind were to concern itself with a letter, that letter would "become" a word. This is why apparently sound and meaningful scientific or philosophical books written about the universe are of little significance concerning the Creator. By contrast, theologians use philosophical and scientific matters as arguments for the Creator's Existence and Unity. It is enough for them that, for example, the sun is a lamp, Earth a cradle, night a covering, day a time to work, and the moon a luminous, light-giving thing. It is enough for them that the mountains are as pegs for Earth's stability and freshen air, store up water and minerals, protect the soil, and calm the quaking Earth's wrath by enabling it to breathe.

However, science deals with the sun as the center of its system, a huge fire so intense that all its planets fly around it like scattered moths. The theologians' view of the universe may sometimes be contrary to reality; however, since they usually conform to what is apparent and the general viewpoint, they should not be contradicted. For this reason, even if their philosophical or scientific views may be considered weak and insignificant, their views of theology's essentials are stronger than iron.

As a result, at first the heedless and misguided may seem to have the upper hand in this world, for they incline to it with all their faculties and abilities, declaring: *(The life) is only our life of the world* (6:29). However, the end is for the righteous and God-conscious, for whom and for whose leader the Qur'an proclaims: *What is to succeed will be better for you than what is foregoing, as will the Hereafter than the world* (93:4); *The life of the world is nothing but pastime and play. But best is the home of the Hereafter for those who keep their duty in reverence for God. Still, will you not understand?* (6:32); and *The home of the Hereafter, that is life if they but knew* (29:64). God is sufficient for us. What a good Trustee, Protecting Friend, and Helper He is.

KNOW, O FRIEND, that God's forgiving is an act of extra grace, while His punishment is pure justice. If people swallow poison, they deserve to be ill according to God's established law. If they do not become ill, it is because of God's extra grace and extraordinary favoring.

The relation between sin and torment is so strong that it led the Mu'tazilites to attribute, mistakenly, evil to something other than the Almighty, and to conclude that every evil deed will be punished. But [even if it cannot be said that the Almighty must punish every evil or sin], its deserving punishment does not contradict Divine Mercy's perfection. The harm of evil, even though partial and small, affects all threads forming the universal order, which is of the absolute, great good to all. Forsaking such a good to shun a little evil or harm causes great evil or harm. This is contrary to the wisdom in the Justice of the All-Just, All-Wise, All-Munificent.

O WRONG-DOER AND IGNORANT ONE! Avoid evil as much as possible, or else you will be punished for abandoning good and not fulfilling the necessary conditions to obtain a result. Evil results in non-existence. The non-existence of a necessary part of something causes its complete non-existence, which means nullifying all other parts, for the existence of something depends on all conditions. So, God's forgiving an evil is purely an act of grace and points to His perfect graciousness. Moreover, He punishes evil with its like but rewards good tenfold at least, while their true deserts are otherwise. This shows the extent of our injustice, for we judge the other way.

KNOW, O FRIEND, that we forget, and the worst kind of forgetting is forgetting one's self. In all cases, such forgetfulness is misguidance. But doing so when being paid and rewarded is a sign of perfection. The misguided and the rightly-guided differ in forgetting and remembering.

The misguided forget themselves while working and performing their duty, and recognize no limits to their unyielding self-conceit and arrogance. Yet they remember themselves when it is time to get the fruits. The rightly-guided purify their souls and remember themselves while doing their duty, as if they know that they must set a good example for others and are responsible for fulfilling a task. Yet they forget themselves when it is time to collect the rewards and the fruits, so much so that it seems as if they are slaves sincerely and happily working for their lord (not themselves), with the results of their work mostly belonging to their lord.

KNOW, O FRIEND, that the believers' solidarity and togetherness in their congregational worship and supplications has a deep meaning. Each believer resembles a brick in a firm building benefiting from the multiplied strength of innumerable fellow believers in their worship and supplication. When belief brings them together, each works for the whole, becomes an intercessor and supplicant for them, and asks mercy for them while declaring their innocence. Together, they extol the Prophet, their leader. Every believer takes pleasure in others' happiness, just as a mother, although hungry, takes pleasure in satisfying her children, or like a compassionate brother who takes pleasure in his brother's happiness. As a result, people can worship the Creator of the universe in a comprehensive way and earn eternal happiness.

Look at the Prophet. When he calls: "O Most Merciful of the merciful," his entire community responds: "O God, bestow blessings and peace upon Your servant and beloved, Muhammad, the ocean of Your lights, the mine of Your mysteries, one diffusing remembrance of and gratitude to You, and openly proclaiming the beauty of Your Lordship's sovereignty." They declare his innocence before their Lord, make him loved by Him Who sent him as a mercy for them, and confirm his right and authority to intercede [for them with the Almighty].

They proclaim, in the tongue of their impotence and poverty, the Glorified One's Wealth in His absolute, perfect independence. They proclaim His Liberality in His majestic Dignity and His Lordship in the tongue of their servanthood. Through such exalted solidarity and mutual helping, a believer rises from complete insignificance and helplessness to being a vicegerent of God on Earth, bearing the Supreme Trust, and being an honored, respected part of creation to whom the heavens and Earth were subjugated.

KNOW, O FRIEND, that those who are far from something cannot understand it as well as those who are close to it, even if they are more intelligent. When they disagree, the closer one is preferred. European philosophers and scientists, engrossed in materialistic subjects, are extremely far from Islam, belief, and the Qur'an. Even the greatest of them cannot be on the same level as an ordinary Muslim who understands the Qur'an superficially.

This observation agrees with reality. Do not ask: "How could those who discovered such scientific realities as lightning's and steam's properties not understand the Qur'an's mysteries of truth and lights?" They cannot understand them because their minds are restricted to their eyes, and eyes cannot see what the heart and spirit see, especially when the heart has died due to heedless absorption in naturalism. *God has sealed their hearts, ears, and eyes* (16:108).

KNOW, O FRIEND, that the greatest ingratitude for bounties is not thanking the Almighty for bounties that are common to all (like hearing and sight), constant (like light and fire), and abundant and encompassing (like air and water). One can thank God Almighty for his or her own bounties, for those that are renewed or given at the time of particular need, whereas bounties given uninterruptedly and abundantly are much more important and greater. Their abundance and encompassing nature, their utmost importance, and their constancy indicate their greater value.

KNOW, O FRIEND, that: *He keeps count of all things* (72:28) implies order and harmony, equality and proportion among nearby similar things, such as human fingers, the grains in spikes or ears, fruit seeds, and flower petals. Glory be to Him Who keeps count of all things and Whose Knowledge encompasses all things.

KNOW, O FRIEND, that fertilization and birth, together with compassionate rearing, are two tasks common to everything. An immediate reward or wage is given in return for them: the pleasure they provide. The comprehensive liberality of the All-Beneficent, All-Munificent, and the intense zeal of all reproducing things to carry out these two tasks show that fulfilling each task is rewarded with a particular pleasure.

The degree of rewarding, mercy, and justice, together with the Divine declaration: *My Mercy encompasses all things* (7:156) and many Prophetic Traditions, confirm that animals will be rewarded and punished on Judgment Day, and that their souls are preserved to receive their last reward for their perfect obedience to Divine rules of life.[100] After settling mutual rights, their bodies will become dust. However, a whole species can be embodied in and represented by a blessed member, such as the camel and ram, dog and hoopoe, and ant mentioned in the Qur'an.

O WRETCHED SAID! You seek to maintain your material existence in this fleeting, decaying world that only the All-Permanent or Everlasting One can maintain. You can gain permanence only by turning toward the All-Glorified One and spending your life on His way. So why do you insist on seeking permanence here? Rather, say:

---

100 Abu Hurayra relates that God's Messenger declared: "Mutual rights will be settled on Judgment Day, to such an extent that a hornless sheep will restore (get) its right from another with horns." *Muslim*, hadith no. 2585.

As regards permanence, it is enough for me that God, the Master, is the All-Permanent. As for the pleasure of permanence, it is enough that I know Him as the All-Permanent, Worshipped One. As for the aim in seeking permanence, it is enough that I know Him as my All-Permanent Lord. As for the perfection expected from permanence, my belief in His being the All-Permanent Inventor is enough. As for existence, it is enough that I am a work of the Necessarily Existent Being. As for the worth of existence, it is enough that I am a work of the Art of the Creator of the heavens and Earth. As for the aim of existence, it is enough that I know that I am the painting of He Who adorned the heavens with stars and Earth with flowers.

With respect to the pleasure of existence, it is enough to know that I am His creature and He is my Lord and Inventor. In respect to life, it is enough that I am an object that manifests the Names of the Creator of death and life. As for life and its rights and aims, it is enough that, by virtue of my comprehensive existence, I exhibit among the perceptive people in the universe and announce in the market of the world the marvels of the works of the Names of the Creator of the heavens and Earth.

It is enough for the aim of life that I am a sample and embodiment of the works of the His Beautiful Names' manifestations. It suffices for life and its perfection that, in the tongue of my disposition and manners, I reflect the manifestations of the Names of Him by Whose command the heavens rose high and by Whose permission Earth has gained stability. It suffices for the pleasure of life that I know that I am His slave, creature, and needy servant, and that He is my Creator and God, Lord and Originator, Owner and Merciful, and the One Who sustains me. With respect to perfection, belief in God is enough, and God is sufficient for me against everything.

KNOW, O FRIEND, that belief in Divine Unity and attributing things to the One God results in such ease that existence would almost become necessary. Associating partners with God and attributing creatures to multiple creators would result in so much difficulty that existence would become impossible. While existence gains infinite worth by being attributed to the One God, it loses all value by being ascribed to multiple pseudo-creators—to themselves or nature, matter or chance, and the like. What the soldier carries is regarded as great and valuable by being attributed to the king, the soldier's speech about the king attracts attention and is given much importance, and it is easy to procure all necessities of life from the king's treasuries. However, whatever the soldier has or speaks will lose all value and importance if he rebels against the king.

KNOW, O FRIEND, that whatever comes from the Almighty is the same, whether it brings harm or benefit, good or evil, or life or death by His Power and Destiny, for death is the beginning of another life, and evil and harm end, respectively, in good and benefit.

KNOW, O FRIEND, that the human spirit, due to its comprehensive nature and numerous faculties, can experience limitless pleasure and pain. People take pleasure in the pleasures of their children, siblings, and other creatures, and suffer on account of their distress.

KNOW, O FRIEND, that if you look at things in oblivion of your self, realities change, like things beside a pool or lake seen in it as upside down. Your ignorance leads you to regard yourself as knowledgeable.

KNOW, O FRIEND, that what requires repeating parts of the Qur'an also requires repeating (religious) recitations and prayers. The Qur'an, besides being a book of truth and law, as well as of Divine knowledge and wisdom, is also a book of recitation, prayer, and call. Recitation requires reiteration, prayer requires repetition, and call requires reaffirmation.

KNOW, O FRIEND, that one virtue of the Qur'an is that it arrives at Divine Unity after mentioning the realm of multiplicity, thus summarizing after explaining. After mentioning particular things, it concludes with the principles of absolute Lordship and the rules of the encompassing Divine Attributes of perfection. Such conclusions are the results of the main parts of verses or the effects of the causes discussed in them. Thus the listener's or reciter's mind is not lost in the particulars of existence and forgetful of the Divinity's grandeur. It also shows the manner of "intellectual" servanthood to the One of Grandeur, Awe, and Greatness. It broadens your mind from those particulars to their resemblances, and teaches you that even the smallest thing contains a clear, straight way to knowing the Eternal Sovereign and observing the manifestations of the Names of the One, the Eternally-Besought-of-All.

Through this style, the Qur'an shows the "sun" in a "drop of water" or the "colors manifested in sunlight" on a "flower." It shows the sun shining with all its splendor at midday, and thereby lifts your head to the sun so that you are not bewildered amidst the multiplicity of things and do not despise the sun.

For example, after mentioning a specific minor event—Prophet Joseph's plan to retain his brother—the Qur'an concludes: *Over every man of knowledge there is one who knows (better)* (12:76). Other examples of this style are: *They do not esteem God His rightful measure* (22:74); *When the children among you come of age*... to *God is All-Knowing, All-Wise* (24:59); and *Surely the frailest of houses*... to *if they but knew* (29:41).

KNOW, O FRIEND, that the blessing and help of saints and the enlightenment they diffuse are a sort of prayer done either through disposition or actively, for the One Who actually guides and helps is God. Each person has an innermost sense or faculty that, if he or she prays through it, the prayer will be answered regardless of spiritual condition. If they swear by God through it that [something will happen], God does not disprove them.

O ONE CONVINCED of (the occurrence of) past events but doubtful about the future! In your mind, go back in time and pretend you are one of your ancestors. Look at them and then look at your descendants. Is there any difference between these two wings? You cannot see the hand of chance or something else in them, for past and future generations are creatures of God and included in the Maker's Knowledge and Sight. Resurrecting your ancestors is not stranger than creating your descendants; rather, it will be easier, as the All-Glorified One declares: *It is easier for Him* (30:27). If you compare all creation and events with this particular, minor incident, you will see that all past events are miracles testifying that their Creator brings about all events and creatures, that He has absolute knowledge of them, and encompasses them with His Sight.

All creatures and heavenly objects in the garden of the universe are miracles witnessing and clarifying that their Creator is powerful over and knows all things. Similarly, all flowering plants and adorned animals in the garden of Earth are marvels of His Art, and testify that their Maker is powerful over and knows all things. In relation with His Power, creating particles and stars, causing trees to yield fruit, and resurrecting the dead are the same. Rebuilding human beings from their rotted bones is as easy for Him as causing tree blossoms to reopen on their thin branches every year.

KNOW, O FRIEND, that like the fruits of trees, drops of water, whose forms show perfect, delicate order and balance, are among God's countless bounties. The One Who attaches infinite aims to a drop of water is He Who holds creation in His Grasp and Whose treasuries are between *Kaf* and *Nun*. A drop of water is the bounty of He Who made the order *kun* (be!) the infinitive (origin) of *kawn* (the creation). All thanks and gratitude are to Him, the All-Glorified.

KNOW, O FRIEND, that the Qur'an's frequent mentioning of Earth's revival and drawing of our attention to soil inspired in me the ideas that Earth is the universe's heart and that soil is Earth's heart. The quickest way to the target is through "soil," by way of the gate of humility and self-annihilation. Soil is nearer to the Creator of the heavens than even the highest heaven, for nothing else equals soil in receiving manifestations of Divine Lordship and the Names the All-Living and Self-Subsistent, displaying Divine Creativity, and being the object of Divine Power's activities.

As the Throne of Mercy is on water, the Throne of Life and Reviving is on soil, which is the most comprehensive mirror (reflecting the manifestations of life). However transparent the mirror of a dense thing is, it shows that thing more clearly. However dense the mirror of a luminous thing is, the Names' reflection in it is more complete. Air receives only a dim light from the sun's radiance, and water cannot reflect the sun's colors, although it shows the sun to you with its light. Through its flowers, soil shows whatever is in the sunlight. Compared with the Eternal Sun's Light, the sun is only a dense, shining drop. Soil's adornment and display of its spring finery—its flowers of various forms and colors, and its beautiful animals testifying to the Divine Lordship's perfection—are witnesses to the Creator. Look at a violet, and see how the Hand of the All-Wise Maker disposes, colors, and adorns it.

Glory be to Him Who makes Himself known to us via His subtle Art, and makes His Power known to His creatures via the marvels of His control over soil. This explains the meaning of the Tradition: "A servant is nearest to his (her) Lord while prostrate before Him."[101] Such being the truth, do not be frightened of soil and entering into it, nor fear the grave and lying in it.

KNOW, O FRIEND, that my intellect accompanies my heart in its journey, and that the heart provides its findings to the intellect, which displays them in the form of parables. For example, the All-Wise Creator is infinitely near yet infinitely far [from His creatures], the most Inward of the inward [there is none that is more subtle and penetrating than Him], the most

---

[101] Muslim, *hadith* no. 482; Abu Dawud, *hadith* no. 875.

Outward of the outward [there is none that encompasses Him], and is neither within nor outside anything.

Look at His Mercy's works on Earth's face and His Power's imprints or activities in the spheres of existence on Earth, so that you can see that manifest reality. Consider the two particles, flowers, fruits, or bees of exactly the same sort or identity but separated by great distance. With respect to apparent physical conditions, the Maker Who creates these two things at the same moment must be distant from them. From the viewpoint of creation's ease and speed and the infinite abundance of creatures, together with their absolute firmness, the Maker is infinitely near to each. This is not like the nearness seen between a concentric center's center and points, all of which have different degrees of nearness to the center; rather, all things are equally distant from the Maker Who makes everything infinitely firm and beautiful.

This arises from the Sphere of Necessity's (Divinity) qualities, the inner dimension of existence's abstraction and immateriality, and the Divine Attributes' and acts' unconditioned character. This is also due to the character of the Divine Names' simultaneous manifestations on each creature and all existence, and the complete difference between the Original Agent and the object. For example, through its images in the mirrors of transparent objects and reflections on flowers, the sun is nearer to them than even themselves, while they are extremely distant from the sun. It is almost impossible to traverse the distance between the image (of the sun) in your mirror and its original.

Glory be to Him Whose Essence and Attributes are absolutely exempt from having likes. He is the First and the Last, the Outward and the Inward, and has absolute, perfect knowledge of all things.

> O God, O All-Just, All-Wise, All-Knowing. Everything that exists testifies that You are Necessarily Existent, One and Single, Besought-of-All, and that You are (the One) God, Knower of the Unseen, the One Who brings forth grains and subjugates hearts. Everything is under Your Power. Their hearts are in Your Grasp, their forelocks in Your Hand, and their keys with You. Nothing moves without your permission.
>
> O God of those who have gone and those to come. O Lord of Muhammad, upon him be peace and blessings, and Abraham, Gabriel and Michael, upon them be peace. I ask You, for the sake of Your

Greatest Name, the Light of Your Noble "Face," Your right Religion, Your Straight Path, the Seven Doubly-Repeated Verses (*Surat al-Fatiha*), and the grand Qur'an; for the sake of uncountable "Say: 'He is God, the One'," infinite (recitations) of the Opening Chapter of the Book (*Surat al-Fatiha*); for the sake of Your All-Beautiful Names, Your Greatest Name, the Sacred Black Stone, and Your Honored House (the Ka'ba); for the sake of the Night of Power and Destiny and esteemed Ramadan; and for the sake of Your honored Prophets and Your noblest, beloved one, upon him be peace and blessings, I ask You to have mercy on Muhammad's community. Open our hearts for belief and Islam, keep us safe against heretics, protect our Religion, brighten the evidence of the Qur'an, and exalt the Shari'a of Islam. Amen, O Most Merciful of the merciful.

Addendum

In the Name of God, the All-Merciful, the All-Compassionate.

Praise be to God, and blessings be upon His Prophet.

KNOW, O FRIEND, that nothing can be veiled from the pure, all-encompassing Light, or outside the sphere of Limitless Power, for what is limitless cannot be limited.

The eternal, Divine Wisdom bestows blessing on everything according to their capacity. Small entities cannot prevent the All-Wise, All-Powerful One, Who creates everything with a certain measure, from being concerned with large entities, just as large entities cannot hinder the All-Encompassing and Immaterial, Outward, and Inward One from being interested in small entities. Something small contains great art, and there are more small creatures than large ones. Absolute Grandeur never admits partners. An infinitely abundant creation, created with absolute ease, speed, and firmness, shows that an All-Beautiful One wants to be known and have His absolute Beauty and Perfection observed. Together with this creation, the absolute Mercy and Wealth testified to by whatever exists and occurs in the universe, and the existence of an almost infinite number of reflective observers—all require the existence of micro-organisms and small, flying creatures in infinite abundance.

KNOW, O FRIEND, that if you love your self more than anything else because it is the nearest thing to you, you must love your Lord even more, for He is nearer to you than your selfhood. Do you not see that your senses and faculties, which are beyond your power and imagination, work under your Lord's guidance?

KNOW, O FRIEND, that chance has no place in the universe. Look at a garden to see its infinite orderliness in infinite mixture and perfect distinguishing amidst perfect intermixture. This points to the Wisdom of the Maker with all-encompassing Knowledge.

KNOW, O FRIEND, that if you do not attribute all things to the One Being, you must accept the existence of as many divinities as required by the number of God's manifestations throughout the universe. This would be like closing your eyes and ignoring the sun, but still seeing its image reflected in drops of water. If you think that they exist independently, you must accept the existence of as many suns as those drops. But a drop cannot contain the smallest star, let alone the lamp of the world.

KNOW, O FRIEND, that all creatures compete enthusiastically to present their adornments and subtleties of beauty to the Majestic Observer Who constantly watches them, for they all bear subtleties of the firm, amazing art attracting all beholders. They compete to present their beauty and adornments to the Eternal Witness, because He created every creature to see in their mirrors the manifestations of the lights of His Beauty and Grace, Majesty and Perfection. Then He calls all other conscious witnesses to see them so that they will know Him and discern that Secret Treasure.

A thing's highest purpose, its loftiest right of life, is to present itself to its Creator's view and to be watched by Him, for it is a work of His Names. The greatest pleasure for a living being is its being conscious of being watched by Him. Another purpose for its existence is to be seen by its fellow creatures. However, the first purpose is infinitely greater.

Life has the right to be preserved and maintained in people's eyes. However, among life's innumerable rights, this is the smallest and least significant, for life is among the highest and most elevated, amazing and noblest miracles of the Power of the All-Living and Self-Subsistent, the One and Eternally Besought-of-All. Maintaining life only allows this miracle to be recognized and fulfill its functions. Therefore, as it is valuable only as a means, it cannot be elevated to an end or an aim. Do you think that a pomegranate, an amazing work of Divine Art, is only for eating quickly? It is a word displaying the All-Glorified One Who forms it, [and so requires reflection on it to know and love its Creator.]

The One Who has the most superior Beauty takes true, sacred pleasure in observing His Beauty and showing It to His creatures.[102] The pleasure of relative superiority cannot be felt with the same strength. The One with essential Perfection and eternal, true, pure Beauty is loved because of Himself, Who has the absolutely sublime Attributes, and Who informed us through His Messenger that He created creation to be known. That is, He fashioned mirrors so that manifestations of His Beauty, Who is loved because of Himself, may be observed.

O MORTAL ONE! After your death you will continue to exist in His Knowledge and before His eyes. Give all things to their true Owner, and attribute them to Him to acquire satisfaction. Otherwise, you will have to accept as many deities as God's manifestations or particles in the universe or soil, for many living things come into existence by means of soil.

Glory be to Him Who has no like in His Essence and Attributes, to Whose Oneness His creatures bear witness, to Whose Lordship His signs testify, and Whose Knowledge and Power encompass all things. Exalted is His Majesty. There is no deity but He.

To conclude:

- An explanation of: *The seven heavens and Earth and whoever is in them glorify Him. There is nothing that does not glorify Him with His praise* (17:44).
- Your body, with respect to it and to its Creator.
- What we see here as seeds or foundations indicates what will flourish in the Hereafter.
- Four things that cause one to be heedless of the Creator.
- Without Him, the pain in each pleasure is more acute than the pleasure itself, and pleasure becomes pure pain. So flee to God, where everything is permanent.

---

102 The Almighty is free of all needs. Just as parents take pleasure in seeing their children happy and prosperous, the Almighty takes infinitely more sacred pleasure, unique to His Holiness, in seeing His creatures perfect, beautiful, and adorned. This is why the beauty, perfection, and adornment reflected by creatures are the results of the manifestations of His perfect, All-Beautiful Names and Attributes. The imperfection seen in all creatures is due to themselves and because they should serve as a unit of comparison so that the Creator's absolute Perfection can be perceived. This is also for the good of creatures, for their denial of the Creator results in their infinite perishing. The more creatures display the Divine manifestations on them, the greater perfection they acquire. However, their "perfection" is always relative compared to the absolute Perfection of God, the Creator. (Tr.)

- The use of the comparative or superlative form in some of the Divine Names.
- The Name "God" contains the meaning of all Divine Beautiful Names and all Attributes of perfection.
- If you are convinced that all things and events come from God, you should accept everything, whether pleasing or otherwise.
- Three kinds of prayer.
- Believers see a creature as a letter, which means almost nothing by itself but complements the word to which it belongs. Unbelievers see a creature on behalf of itself, and so restrict their view of it to the creature itself.
- God's forgiving is an act of extra grace, while His punishment is pure justice.
- The misguided and the rightly-guided differ in forgetting and remembering (themselves) at the time of work, duty, and reward.
- The virtue of praying in congregation.
- European philosophers and scientists engrossed in materialistic subjects cannot equal ordinary Muslims' understanding (even if superficial) of the truths of Islam and the Qur'an.
- Why insist on seeking permanence in this (impermanent) world?
- Elevated virtues in the ways the Qur'an concludes its verses.
- All creatures and heavenly objects in the garden of the universe are miracles bearing witness and clarifying that their Creator is powerful over and knows all things.
- Earth is the universe's heart, and soil is Earth's heart. The quickest way to the target goes through "soil" via the gate of humility and self-annihilation, for soil is nearer to the Creator of the heavens than even the highest heaven. The Throne of Mercy is on water, while the Throne of Life and Reviving is on soil.
- The All-Wise Creator is infinitely near and infinitely far (from His creatures). He is the most Inward of the inward, the most Outward of the outward, and is neither within nor outside anything.
- Small entities cannot prevent the All-Wise, All-Powerful One from being concerned with large entities; large entities cannot hinder the All-Encompassing and Immaterial, Outward and Inward One from being interested in small entities.
- If you do not attribute all things to the One Being, you must accept the existence of divinities equal to the number of God's manifestations on all individual existents in the universe.
- A thing's highest purpose in life is to present itself to its Creator's view and be watched by Him. The greatest pleasure of life is that a living being is conscious of being watched by Him.

The
Eleventh Treatise

The Eleventh Treatise

A point from the light of knowledge of God, exalted is His Majesty

When I enter a garden, I choose its most beautiful flower or fruit. If it is difficult for me to pick it, I take pleasure in looking at it. If I come across a rotten one, I pretend not to notice it, according to the rule: Take what pleases and leave what does not. This is my style, and I request my readers to behave in the same way.

People say that what I write cannot be understood clearly. I agree. I write whatever occurs to my heart in the way it occurs. I feel as if I sometimes speak from the top of a minaret and sometimes from the bottom of a well.

As you read this treatise, consider the following:

The one that speaks is my wretched heart.
The one I address is my rebellious selfhood.
The one who truly listens is one in search of the truth.

I believe in God, His angels, Books, Messengers, and the Last Day; and in Destiny, good and evil, being created by Almighty God. Revival after death is true. I bear witness that there is no deity but God, and that Muhammad is His Messenger, upon him be peace and blessings.

In the Name of God, the All-Merciful, the All-Compassionate.

Praise be to God, the Lord of the worlds, and peace and blessings be upon Muhammad, the Seal of the Prophets, and on all his Family and Companions.

Our aim and goal is God. *There is no deity but He, the All-Living, Self-Subsistent* (2:255). Among countless proofs of Him, we give only four here.

- The first proof is Prophet Muhammad, upon him be peace and blessings. We explained this proof in the treatise *Gleams from Knowledge of the Prophet* [and also in the second treatise of this book: *Droplets from the Ocean of Knowledge of the Prophet*].
- The second proof is the universe, the macro-cosmos or macro-human, the observed, great Book of Creation.
- The third proof is the Qur'an, the book in which there is no doubt and which is the Sacred Word.
- The fourth proof is the human conscience or consciousness, the juncture of the Unseen and the material, visible worlds. A human being's consciousness or conscience influences the intellect from which the ray of belief in Divine Unity issues.

First proof: The Muhammadan Truth [103]

This proof is furnished with Messengership and Islam. Messengership contains the testimony of the greatest consensus and most comprehensive agreement of all Prophets, and Islam bears the spirit of the Divinely revealed religions and their confirmation based on the Revelation.

The noble Messenger explains the existence of God and His Unity to humanity. His truthful words are affirmed by his manifest miracles, the Prophets' testimony, and the confirmation of all Divinely revealed religions. The Prophet manifests that light (of Divine Unity) in the name of those purified, excellent men and women who agree on this call. Falsehood cannot have a hand in this pure, clear, evident truth, which enjoys such strong confirmation and is discerned by eyes penetrating all truths.

Second proof: The Book of Creation

All letters and points of this book, individually and collectively and in its particular tongue, say: *There is nothing that does not glorify Him with His praise* (17:44), and proclaim the All-Great Creator's Existence and Unity. Every

---

[103] The Muhammadan Truth is the truth represented by Prophet Muhammad, upon him be peace and blessings, as a servant and Messenger of God Almighty, as well as the truth of which he is the unique embodiment. (Tr.)

particle testifies truthfully to the All-Wise Creator's necessary Existence. While hesitating among endless possible destinations, if they will constitute building blocks of a being and in what kind of being they will be put, each particle takes a particular route and assumes particular attributes. It is directed to a specific goal in accordance with certain established laws and ends in many amazing, purposeful consequences. It strengthens belief in God, which God implanted in our inner faculty so that we may find Him, and which is a sample in us of the unseen worlds.

Does a particle proclaim the purpose of its All-Majestic Maker and His manifest Wisdom in its particular tongue? Through its individual existence, particular attributes, and definite nature, every particle points and testifies to the All-Wise Creator. It acts as a building block in forming compounds; taking a route among countless possibilities, it assumes its proper position in a compound. This position has relations with all other positions, and the particle fulfills many tasks issuing from those relations. As there is a strict balance and perfect harmony among positions, each task the particle fulfills yields numerous, wise fruits.

As all of this corroborates the particle's testimony of the Creator, the particle proclaims the proofs of its All-Majestic Maker's necessary Existence and displays its All-Wise Creator's purpose in the tongue of its acts and the task it fulfills. It is as if it recites the verses declaring Divine Unity, just as a soldier is charged with particular duties and has relations with all army divisions in respect of those duties.

Then, are the proofs of Almighty God's (Existence and Unity) not more than all of creation's particles? The Tradition "The roads leading to God are as many as His creatures breaths" expresses a pure truth.

QUESTION: Why are we unable to find the All-Great Creator with our intellects?

ANSWER: Because of His manifestation's perfection and His having no opposite.[104]

Reflect upon the lines of the [Book of the] Universe,
for they are letters to you from the Highest Realm.

The Book of Creation displays orderliness as clearly as the midday sun and exhibits the Power's miracle in every word or letter. Its composition is so

104 Everything is known through its opposite. Only the Almighty has no equal or opposite. (Tr.)

miraculous that, even supposing that each natural cause were a free agent, each cause would prostrate humbly before this miraculousness, acknowledging: "Glory be to You. We have no power. Surely, You are All-Mighty, All-Wise."

This Book's order is so subtle and delicate that inserting a new point in its exact place requires an absolute power that can create everything, for each letter—especially living ones—has inner relations with sentences and a strong connection with all other words. Thus, whoever created a gnat's eyes created the sun, and whoever ordered a flea's stomach ordered the solar system. Refer to: *Your creation and resurrection are but like (those of) a single soul* (31:28), and see how truthful a witness comes from a bee's tongue, which is only one of the Power's miracles or represents a small word in this Book.

Ponder over a micro-organism that, although invisible to the naked eye, is a sample of creation. The One Who "wrote" it in that miraculous fashion also "wrote" the universe. If you study it and discern its subtle mechanisms and wonderful systems, you will be convinced that its existence and life cannot be attributed to lifeless, simple, natural causes that cannot distinguish between possibilities. Otherwise you must admit that each particle contains the consciousness of sages, the knowledge of scientists, and the genius of statesmen or administrators, and that they communicate with each other directly. Even the superstitious are ashamed of such a claim.

There is no explanation other than to regard it as a miracle of Divine Power, the invention of the One Who invented and arranged the universe. If this were not so, it would be impossible for the two most important natural causes or laws, gravity and repulsion, to come together in an atom. Gravity and repulsion, motion and similar phenomena, are names of Divine principles or ways of operating represented as laws. They may be accepted as laws, provided they are not promoted to being the foundation of an agent nature. Being only names or titles or having nominal existence, they should not be accorded real, external existence.

QUESTION: Why do people believe in matter's eternity and attribute all species' formation to random motions of particles or similar things?

ANSWER: Reasoning or rational judgment does not always lead to belief, as being rationally convinced does not mean believing in God. They cannot perceive their mistake, as their reasoning is based on a superficial view and imitation. If they inquire into the matter closely in pursuit of the truth, they will see how illogical and irrational such a belief is. If, despite this, they still hold such a belief, they are heedless of the Creator. Such a strange deviation! How can those who find it hard to accept the eternity of God, the Glorified, and attribute creation to Him—although eternity and creativity are among the Divine Essence's indispensable Attributes—attribute eternity and creativity to countless particles and helpless things?

Recall this well-known incident: Once, people were scanning the sky for the new crescent moon to mark Ramadan's beginning. An old man claimed he had seen it, when what he had really seen was a downward-curving white hair from his eyebrow. It is that hair-like thing that blinds people to the truth. Humanity is of noble character by creation. While pursuing truth, people sometimes encounter falsehood and keep it in their hearts; or while digging out the truth they come across misguidance and, supposing it to be the truth, accept it.

QUESTION: What are those things called "nature," "laws," and "forces," and how are people deceived by them?

ANSWER: Nature is the comprehensive Divine Shari'a (assembly of laws) established for the order and harmony among everything contained in the visible, material world. This law of creation also is called the "way of God." Nature is the result of all nominal laws in creation. Forces are the principles of this Shari'a, and laws are elements of the same Shari'a. The regularity of its principles and elements leads people to see it as "nature" with a real, external existence, and, after that, as an agent. Although the human heart or mind cannot be convinced that nature is a true agent, those who deny the All-Majestic Creator and refuse to understand the Divine Power's miraculous works may see this blind, ignorant nature as the origin of things.

Nature is something printed, not a printer; a design, not a designer; an object acted on, not an agent; a rule or measure, not an origin; an order, not an orderer. It is a principle without power, a set of laws without real or external existence that issues from the Divine Attributes of Will and Power.

Suppose a young person comes to this exquisite world from another one and enters a beautiful, richly adorned palace. No one to whom this building and decoration can be attributed is seen. So this person, after seeing a comprehensive book containing the blueprint and information on how the palace was built and furnished, and due to his or her ignorance and obsession with the builder, thinks that the book built the palace. In the same way, the heedlessness of some people concerning the All-Majestic Creator allows them to deceive themselves into accepting the natural world as its own originator.

God has two kinds of Shari'a. One issues from the Divine Attribute of Speech and regulates or orders the acts of servants issuing from their free will. The other issues from the Divine Attribute of Will and Power, comprises the Divine commands of creation, and is the result of the Divine Way of acting. The first one comprises comprehensible laws, while the second one consists of nominal laws, wrongly called "laws of nature." They have no creative or inventive part in existence, for that is unique to the Divine Power.

Everything that exists is connected to all other things; nothing can exist or survive by itself. The one who created a single thing created all things, and can only be the One, Eternally-Besought-of-All. By contrast, natural causes, to which the misguided ascribe creativity, are numerous, do not know one another, and are blind. Attributing creativity to them means accepting that innumerable blind, lifeless things have come together by chance and formed that vast, orderly universe, [the existence, order, and harmony of which manifestly require absolute knowledge and will, power and wisdom]. *Then leave them to plunge and play* (6:91).

To sum up: The Book of the Universe's observed order and regularity, and the manifest miraculousness in its composition, are two proofs of Divine Unity showing that the universe and its contents are works of the absolute Power, infinite Knowledge, and eternal Will of God.

QUESTION: How can the order, harmony, and regularity be established?

ANSWER: Sciences, which function as if humanity's senses, have discovered this order by deduction and induction. Each branch of science is based upon or studies one aspect of existence. Science's universal principles originate in this order, harmony, and regularity. Each branch comprises the universal principles and rules prevalent in the species it studies. Those principles' universality and uniformity point to the order's magnificence, for without it universal rules or what they call laws could not be inferred. Scientists discover that order through science, and by it see that the macro-human being (the universe) is as orderly as themselves. There is wisdom in everything, for nothing is purposeless or left to its own devices.

The Book of Creation, with all its systems, worlds of living creatures and particles, proclaims Divine Unity. Altogether they declare: *there is no deity but God*.

Third proof: The Qur'an

When you listen to this articulate proof, you will hear it repeat: *there is no deity but God*. This proof is like an enormous tree whose branches hang down with innumerable, splendid fruits of truth. Since such a tree cannot grow from a rotten seed, all can see that its seed (Divine Unity) is sound and lively.

The branch of this tree stretching into the visible, material world bears fruits of the most sound and realistic commands and rules, while its other great branch, extending into the Unseen, is laden with ripe fruits yielded by Divine Unity and belief in the Unseen.

If this comprehensive proof is studied closely, one will have to admit that the one who communicated it was absolutely certain of its result (Divine Unity), and felt no hesitation about its truth. He based his other claims on this firm result, and made it a criterion to judge whatever exists. Such a basis, established so firmly and bearing a manifest seal of miraculousness, has no need for show and pretension, and is independent of being pronounced true by others. All that it says and declares, and all its tidings, are true.

All six sides of this luminous proof are transparent and clear. On it is the seal of manifest miraculousness, beneath it are logic and evidence, to its right is the assent of intellect, to its left is the testimony of conscience, in front of it is good and happiness in both worlds, and it is founded on pure Revelation. How can doubt enter such a formidable citadel?

There are four paths leading to the throne of perfection, which is knowledge of God:

First: The path of Sufis, which is based on purifying the carnal soul and spiritual illumination.

Second: The path of theologians who, to prove the Necessarily Existent-Being's Existence, depend on the argument that everything comes into existence contingently, in time and space. Thus its existence or non-existence is equally possible, which means that there must be an Eternal One Who prefers their existence and brings them into existence by His Will.

Although both paths are deduced from the Qur'an, their followers have complicated them a bit and thus caused some doubt to enter.

Third: The path of philosophers contaminated with doubt, hesitation, and fancies to some extent.

Fourth (and best): The path of the Qur'an, which clearly shows the throne of perfection with its miraculous eloquence, beautiful style, directness, and incomparable comprehensiveness. It is the most direct and inclusive, as well as the shortest, path to God.

There are four means to reach that throne: inspiration, learning or study, purification, and reflection.

The Qur'an follows two ways to knowledge of God, glory be to Him, and to prove God's Unity.

The first is the argument of favoring and purposiveness

All Qur'anic verses that mention the benefits or uses of things, and the wisdom in or purposes for their existence, "weave" this argument and serve as mirrors in which it is reflected. This argument can be summarized as follows: Everything is made firmly and artistically. The perfect orderliness in creation, which is for certain purposes and uses and is evident in everything's existence, indicates that the All-Wise Creator created them for a basic purpose. Such clear will leaves no room for chance and coincidence. Any science dealing with creation testifies to this orderliness, points to the uses and fruits hanging from the branches of existence like clusters, and reveals the wisdom and beneficial results behind daily, monthly, and seasonal changes.

Take zoology and botany. The world contains hundreds of thousands (even millions) of plant and animal species, each of which had a first, original ancestor. For humanity, this was Adam. Each member of these species is like an exquisite, amazing mechanism. How can one claim that the so-called laws of nominal existence and ignorant, blind natural causes could create these innumerable chains of beings? Each species and each member proclaim that they issued from the Hand of the wise, Divine Power.

The Qur'an teaches us this argument: *Then, look again! Can you see any rifts?* (67:3). By commanding us to reflect on creatures and mentioning their uses or benefits as Divine bounties, the Qur'an seeks to establish this argument in the human mind, and then calls upon reason to ponder over them in the conclusions and divisions of verses. It illuminates the role of reason and stirs up conscience in such conclusions as: *Do they not know? Will they not reflect and learn the lesson?*

The second is the argument of invention

God Almighty has given each species and each member an existence particular to the tasks it will fulfill and the perfections it will achieve. No species comes from eternity, because every species has a beginning and its existence is not absolutely necessary. Everything exists by the Necessarily Existent One's will and preference, while it was equally possible for it to exist or not. This truth cannot be changed.

Evolution is also impossible, for mutations occur only within a species, and there are no intermediary species. If God changed one species into another to punish it, that species did not survive. As matter is changeable and not independent of time and space, it has a beginning. Forces and forms are accidental and cannot be the origin of a species' diverse essences or substances, for something accidental cannot be a thing's essence or substance. Thus the substances of all species, with their diverse and distinguishing attributes, were created while they did not exist. Generation or reproduction is only a later condition for their continuance.

How strange it is that those who deny the All-Majestic Creator's Eternity—although eternity is one of His indispensable Attributes—attribute it to matter, which is contained in time and space. Where can the tiniest blind, ignorant, and helpless particle find the power, stability, and firmness before which the universe bows in submission and veneration? How can creating and originating, attributes of Divine Power, be attributed to natural causes, the most impotent and weakest of things?

The Qur'an establishes this argument when mentioning creation and invention, and confirms that only God, the One, has creative power. Causes are only veils before the Divine Power and Its Grandeur to prevent the mind from drawing wrong conclusions about the All-Holy Divine Being by seeing with a superficial view the Hand of His Power involved in mundane affairs.

Every thing has two aspects. One is its apparent aspect, which is like a mirror's dense, black face in which opposites—small and great, good and evil, beautiful and ugly—exist side by side. Here, causes display the Almighty's Grandeur and Dignity. The other is the inner, immaterial aspect, which is like a mirror's polished or transparent face. This aspect is pure and absolutely beautiful and, as required by Divine Unity, has no room for causes. Since things like life and spirit, as well as light and existence, were created by the Hand of Power without the "help" of causes, both their outer and inner aspects are beautiful.

Fourth proof: The human conscience (conscious nature)

FIRST: The natural or inborn qualities of things do not lie. A seed has an inclination to grow as if to say: "If I am planted, I will grow and yield fruit." It says the truth. An egg has an inclination toward life as if to say: "I will become a chick," and becomes so. When a handful of water has an inclination to freeze and then expand, it says: "I will cover a broader space" and cracks even iron, despite the latter's hardness and firmness. Such inclinations manifest the commands of creation issuing from Divine Will.

SECOND: Human senses are not restricted to the five known ones. Each person has many "windows" opening on the Unseen, and many other senses of whose nature he or she knows or does not know. For example, *drive* and *energy* are two other senses that do not lie.

THIRD: Something imagined and only of nominal existence cannot be the origin of external, visible existence. *The point of reliance* (or support) and *the point of seeking help*, both of which people necessarily feel within themselves, are two essential aspects of their conscience or conscious nature. The absence of these two points, which is irreconcilable with the wisdom, order, and perfection in creation, would mean that human beings, noble creations with an essentially pure spirit, would be reduced to the lowest of the low.

FOURTH: Even if reason does not work properly and cannot see the truth, the human conscience does not forget the Creator. Even if one's selfhood denies Him, the conscience sees Him, reflects on Him, and turns toward Him. Intuitive perception stirs it up, and inspiration illuminates it. Love of God urges the conscience to obtain knowledge of the Almighty. This love, one's strong yearning for Him that issues from a strong desire based on a strong inclination, is innate in the human conscience. The attraction (toward Him) ingrained in this conscience is due to the existence of One Who really attracts.

After these preliminary notes, look into the conscience and see how it is a proof, entrusted to the soul of every person, proclaiming Divine Unity. Just as the heart pumps life throughout the body, knowledge of God, the source of its (spiritual) life, energizes and vitalizes all human ambition and inclinations. It also pours pleasure and joy into them, increases their value, expands or develops, and sharpens them. This is the point of seeking help.

Knowledge of God is a point of support and reliance upon which people base their lives. If people do not believe in the All-Wise Creator, Whose every act contains order and wisdom, but attribute things and events to blind coincidence (which cannot resist misfortune), they will live in a hellish state. This cannot be allowed, for humanity is a noble creation and has the potential to achieve perfection. This also goes against the universe's prevailing, firm order. These two points are necessary for one's spirit, because the All-Munificent Creator uses them to diffuse the light of His knowledge into the conscience of every person. Even if the eyes of reason are blind, the eyes of conscience are always open.

The testimony of these four comprehensive arguments show that as the All-Majestic Creator is the Necessarily Existent Being and Eternal, One and Single, Unique and Eternally-Besought-of-All, All-Knowing and All-Powerful, All-Willing and All-Hearing, All-Seeing and All-Speaking, All-Living and Self-Subsistent, He is also qualified with all Attributes of Majesty and Grace. Whatever creatures have in the name of perfection comes from the shadowy manifestation of the Majestic Creator's Perfection. Beauty, Grace, and Perfection are infinitely greater than the sum of the beauty, grace, and perfection shared by creation. Also, the All-Glorified Creator has no defect, for defect originates from the imperfect inborn capacities of material beings. The All-Glorified One is free from materiality, and exempt from the qualities essential to the nature of the created.

> There is nothing like Him; He is the All-Hearing, the All-Seeing. (42:11)
>
> Glory be to Him Who keeps concealed because of the intensity of His manifestation, Who is hidden because of the lack of His opposite, and Who is veiled by natural causes because of His Dignity.

QUESTION: What about the doctrine of the Unity of Being (*Wahdat al-Wujud*)?

ANSWER: The doctrine of the Unity of Being comes from absorption in Divine Unity. This is experienced inwardly and deeply and cannot be a matter of theory and thought. Profound absorption in Divine Unity (following belief in God's Unity as Lord and Deity) engenders belief in the Power's unity (only God creates). Belief in the Power's unity engenders belief in the unity of dominion and ruling, which, in turn, ends in seeing what is witnessed as united (Unity of the Witnessed) and finally in the Unity of Being. This leads to seeing existence as one or united, and then seeing what exists as united.

The ecstatic sayings of some Sufis that go beyond what is really intended must not be taken as proofs for this way's truth. If people who have not saved themselves from the sphere of cause and effect, who organize their lives considering the law of causality, speak about the Unity of Being (inclusive of created entities), they exceed their limits. Those who really sense and speak about this unity restrict themselves to the Necessarily Existent Being in isolation from the created, and see God as the only truly existent being.

Seeing the result together with or contained in the evidence leading to it, that is, seeing the All-Majestic Maker as the only truly existent being, comes from absorbing the view and experience of the Divine Being's existence. It is the result of seeing or perceiving Divine manifestations in the channels of existence and the flux of Divine effulgences in the inner dimension of things, and the manifestation of Divine Names and Attributes in the mirrors of creatures.

My personal view is as follows: This perception pertains to inner experience and sensing. However, as such belief or inner experience cannot be expressed exactly, those who follow the Unity of Being interpret it as pervading Divinity and permeating Life in creatures. Philosophers or those who try to find the truth with their intellects or sense impressions have made this way a philosophical or intellectual topic, and thus a source of false ideas and concepts.

Some materialist, pantheistic philosophers also believe in the Unity of Being. However, both groups understand this phrase in mutually exclusive terms. There are five significant differences between them:

First: Sufi scholars restrict their view to the Necessarily Existent Being and reflect on Him so strongly that they do not accept the universe's existence, for, in their words, only the Necessarily Existent Being truly exists; everything else is illusory. Materialist philosophers and those with weak belief concentrate on matter and are far from perceiving Divinity. They give priority to matter and say that only matter or material things exist. Due to their unbelief, they see Divinity as contained in or embodied by matter, or prefer to remain indifferent to Divinity by restricting their view to the universe.

Second: Sufis who believe in the Unity of Being see the universe as something witnessed or only sensed. However, the others regard the universe as really existent and believe in the unity of what exists materially.

Third: The way of Sufi saints pertains to inner experience, while the others follow a purely rationalistic way.

Fourth: Sufi saints are lost in the Truth, the Almighty, and consider the universe from the viewpoint of Divinity. The others are absorbed in creatures and reflect on them for their sake and from within that absorption.

Fifth: Sufi saints worship God and love Him deeply, while the others adore their selves and follow their fancies.

These two ways are as different as the highest heaven and Earth, bright light and thick darkness.

A note for further enlightenment

If Earth were made up of pieces of different-colored glass, each piece would receive sunlight and reflect it accordingly. Although what each piece would receive and reflect is neither the sun nor its light itself, if each piece could speak, it would say: "I am a sun." Similarly, if the colors of those smiling, brilliant flowers were to speak, although they are manifestations of sunlight's seven colors, each would say: "The sun resembles me" or "The sun belongs to me exclusively."

> Those illusions are traps for saints,
> Whereas in reality they are reflections of the
> radiant-faced in the garden of God.[105]

Those who believe in the Unity of the Witnessed (or sensed) in the name of existence follow sobriety, wakefulness, and discernment. As the Unity of Being is a way of spiritual intoxication, the Unity of the Witnessed is a safer way.

> Think about the bounties and blessings of God. Do not think about
> His Essence, because you are unable do that.[106]

---

[105] Mawlana Jalal al-Din al-Rumi, *Al-Mathnawi al-Kabir*, 1:3.

[106] A Prophetic Tradition. Tabarani, *Al-Mu'jam al-Awsat*, 6456.

The reality of humanity: While humanity cannot perceive it,
how can humanity perceive how the Eternal All-Compelling is?
He is the One Who originated things and built them.
How can one who is a breath created perceive Him?

To conclude:

- Four proofs of God Almighty are Prophet Muhammad, upon him be peace and blessings, the observed Book (of the Universe), the Qur'an, and the human conscience or consciousness, which is the juncture of the Unseen and the material, visible world.
- Can people find the All-Great Creator with their intellects?
- The Book of Creation's order is so subtle and delicate that placing a point in its exact place requires an absolute knowledge and power that can create everything.
- Gravity and repulsion, as well as motion and similar phenomena, are names of Divine principles or ways of operating represented as laws.
- Why do some believe in matter's eternity and attribute the formation of all species to the random motions of particles or similar things?
- Humanity is a noble creation. While pursuing truth, people sometimes find falsehood and keep it in their hearts.
- God has two kinds of Shari'a: one regulates or orders the acts done through one's free will, and the other comprises the Divine commands of creation and operation of the universe and life.
- How can the order, harmony, and regularity observed in creation be established?
- The Qur'an is like an enormous fruit-laden tree with two great branches: one in this world and the other in the Unseen.
- Four ways lead to the throne of perfection (knowledge of God): that of the Sufis, theologians, philosophers, and the Qur'an.
- The Qur'anic arguments of favoring and purpose and invention.
- Everything has an apparent and an inner spiritual aspect.
- The natural or inborn qualities of things do not lie.
- The point of reliance (or support) and the point of seeking help are two essential aspects of the human conscience or conscious nature.
- People have many other senses, the nature of which they are aware or unaware.
- Knowledge of God is a point of support and reliance for people.
- The truth of the Unity of Being (*Wahdat al-Wujud*), and its difference from pantheism and similar doctrines.

The Twelfth Treatise

The Twelfth Treatise

A light from the lights of the verses of the Qur'an

In the Name of God, the All-Merciful, the All-Compassionate.

. . . and from Him we seek help.

Praise be to God Who has guided us to this. We could not have found guidance if God had not guided us. Assuredly, the Messengers of our Lord brought the truth. (7:43)

Peace and blessings be upon the Argument of the Truth to the creation, the greatest of the Prophets, proof of the purified scholars, and the beloved of the Lord of the worlds, and on his Family and all His Companions.

KNOW, O FRIEND, THAT ALL OF EARTH'S FEATURES BEAR VARIOUS stamps of the One, Eternally-Besought-of-All. A mountain shows that it is the All-Glorified One's property by the many animals and trees that live on it, which are the All-Glorified's property. It is a creature of the Almighty, as testified to by the brilliant stamps of plants and birds on it. It is also one of His missives, as testified to by the seals the All-Glorified placed on its corners, such as adorned flowers and beautiful fruits. When you know that a palm-tree and bee are the All-Glorified's property and creatures, you will understand that all palm-trees and bees are also His property.

All such stamps and seals belong to the One Sovereign and the Owner, Eternally-Besought-of-All, for all things are found almost world-wide at the same moment. The identity in existence and invention, form and making, as well as time, show that their Maker is the One and Single, Who can do or say many things at once and can hear and meet many needs without becoming confused.

KNOW, O FRIEND, that if you would like to hear about the Qur'an's miraculousness as it flows into me from the ocean of the Qur'an, listen to the following, which I address to myself:

O Said! Heedless of your self and your heedlessness! Heedlessness, ingratitude, and unbelief arise from groundless conceptions or notions. If you do not attribute something—especially something that is alive—to the Almighty, you must attribute divinity to all particles and compounds of soil, air, and water, and admit as many deities as God's manifestations. Each soil particle serves for the growth of plants and trees, flowers and fruits. Put some soil in a pot. If you then put in fig, pomegranate, or apple seeds, you will get, respectively, a fig, pomegranate, or apple tree. These trees are very different from each other. If the mechanism of Destiny operating in a fig seed is like, say, a sugar factory, the machine of Power working in a pomegranate seed may be like a textile factory. If you put flower seeds in the same pot, you will have flowers.

Know, O owner of the pot, that if your heedlessness leads you to follow materialists, you will have to admit that your pot contains as many factories as there are fruit-bearing trees in order to make all the parts of infinitely various trees, and as many mechanisms as there are flowers. Soil particles also must have as much knowledge and power needed to grow each tree and flower, and the necessary capacity to distinguish them.

If you attribute the existence of trees and flowers to nature, you have to admit that nature has numberless printing machines in each soil particle. Seeds are material things of almost the same structure and contents, and resemble one another in formation and shape. So, their growing into different trees or flowers is like a few grams of cotton being woven into rolls of silk or satin, broadcloth or wool. Such verses as: *He created you from a single soul* (4:1) and *God has created every moving creature of water* (24:45) point to the fact that the simple substance from which you were created, not compound or composite like you, cannot be your origin. Seeds, which include all the details of the tree or flower that will grow from it, are simple and small. However, each one is like a plan made by Destiny, an origin or nucleus containing all principles of its tree's or flower's existence. As a result, they are a most evident testimony that their Creator can only be the One Who has created the heavens and Earth, and in relation to Whose Power everything, without exception, is the same.

If your heedlessness arises from materialism, you must admit that your pot contains a wonderful, intelligent power that can make and form all fruit-bearing trees and flowers; knowledge that encompasses all of their features and properties; a will with the knowledge of all principles and necessities of their existence; and the capacity to perform the functions of other Names of the One *Who will roll up the heavens as written scrolls are rolled up* (21:104), Who holds Earth in His Hand and controls it as He wills, Who holds the human heart between His two fingers and turns it however He wills, and Who is not hindered by something big or significant when it comes to being concerned with what is small or insignificant.

He manifests His Power's light on the Supreme Throne, the sun, and particles with the same facility, as the sun is reflected simultaneously in an ocean's surface, a mirror, and in drops or bubbles of water with the same ease and the same extent of radiance. The only exception is that things vary in receiving its manifestations because of the differences of their capacities of receiving. This is observed especially in spring, when innumerable kinds of flowers and plants, trees and animals burst forth almost at the same time in great abundance and with absolute ease and firmness.

Each flower and fruit, animal and micro-organism is like a drop formed of constituents taken from all parts of existence with exact and subtle measures and according to precise calculations. Only He Who holds existence in His Grasp, controlling it as He wills and extracting this drop from existence with such measures and according to such calculations, can make each flower, fruit, or animal a miniature of existence when He wills to create that drop from non-existence.

Just as it is necessary to admit the existence of as many suns as there are transparent objects, when images of the sun are not attributed to the sun in the sky, so too do unbelievers have to accept as many deities as there are particles of existence, or as there are manifestations of God. If you have understood this, you will have perceived only one of the innumerable rays of the lights of the Qur'an's miraculous explanations from the viewpoint of its meaning.

KNOW, O FRIEND, that some human artifacts may be worth thousands of dollars because of their art, while their material costs are next to nothing. Similarly, belief is an elixir changing humanity's decaying, coal-like substance into an enduring, bejeweled diamond by connecting its members to the All-Permanent or Everlasting Maker. By contrast, unbelief reduces humanity to a lump of coal that decomposes in the ground.

Humanity is the most amazing artifact of the Eternal Maker *Who created the heavens and Earth in 6 days* (7:54), and adorned the sky with stars and Earth with flowers. Created of clay and subject to rapid disintegration, human beings' material constituents are worth very little. But when the art they contain is considered, their worth increases infinitely, for human beings are pieces of poetry composed with the subtleties of the Divine Beautiful Names' manifestations, polished mirrors reflecting the Eternal Sun's rays.

Belief connects human beings to their Owner and reveals the Divine art in humanity. It shows that humanity is an artifact of God, which causes a human being's value to increase to the extent that Paradise will become its price. Through belief, humanity assumes the role of God's vicegerent on Earth and bears the Supreme Trust. Unbelief cuts this connection, causes this Divine art to be concealed, and reduces humanity to its material substance. In other words, unbelief renders humanity so valueless that unbelievers would wish not to exist or to become dust.

In short: Human beings are like machines furnished with millions of measuring tools to weigh and experience the contents of Divine Mercy's treasury and the Hidden Treasure's jewels.[107] So that they might taste all varieties of the Truth's bounties, as many devices of tasting as there are edibles were set in their tongues. When this machine is used according to and guided by the requirements of belief, it yields fruits preserved by the One Who never errs or forgets. If this machine falls into the hand of unbelievers, it is like an invaluable, matchless machine in the hands of those who do not recognize it and so use it to light a fire or make it burn more brightly.

> O One in Whose Hand is the dominion and keys of all things, Who grasps all things by the forelock and with Whom are the treasuries of all things. Do not leave us to ourselves. Have mercy on us and illuminate our hearts with the light of belief and the Qur'an.

---

[107] Alluding to the *hadith qudsi*: "I was a hidden treasure. I willed to be known and [so] created the universe." (Tr.)

> God's promise is true, so let not the life of the world delude you, nor let any deluder delude you in regard to God. (31:33)

O YOU WHO ARE MISGUIDED! You have drowned in the marsh of the world and desire to lead people astray by presenting that marsh as the source of happiness to console yourself. If you can change the nature of the following four realities, do whatever you wish:

First: Death, which you cannot change or remove from life. Believers see it as a changing of residences. But you see it as eternal extinction.

Second: Your innate helplessness, limitless need, and hostilities towards you invite you to rely on the absolutely Powerful One. But you make your innate helplessness absolute [through unbelief], for you deprive it of reliance and support.

Third: Your innate poverty, which is a means of appealing and an invitation to the absolutely Wealthy One's treasure. But you make it a painful destitution increasing with the mistaken habits of modern civilization.

Fourth: Decay or disappearance, which in the case of pleasure brings permanent pain. Disappearance or decay actually is a means of reaching everlasting pleasure, but you make it a painful decay leaving behind only sin and remorse.

You can die at any time, are enveloped by helplessness, and surrounded by poverty. You are on a continuous journey, and can be deceived in your sophistries only while drunk (with this temporary life). But this drunkenness only lasts for a while. The happiness of this life is wretchedness and may be possible only by killing or totally ignoring death, removing helplessness, pursuing extreme vanity, eliminating poverty, complete madness, acquiring eternal life, or stopping the wheel of existence.

May God awaken us from the sleep of heedlessness, which you accept as wakefulness (although it is the deepest sleep), and bring us to our senses by curing us of our so-called intellectual enlightenment.

SEE, O FRIEND, how the All-Powerful Maker has spread millions of worlds of plants and animals on Earth's face. Every world is like a sea whose drops are charged with cleaning. For example, ants are charged with cleaning Earth's face of various corpses.

Similarly, water and air, light and earth, especially snow, are like oceans whose drops have specific duties. The All-Wise Maker, Who has placed these worlds one within the other, distinguishes each one with particular properties and duties. He displays infinite distinguishing amidst infinite mixture.

For example, He places the world of ants or flies in worlds of other living creatures by creating and causing them to die in a specific way. It is as if Earth's face is only their home. No confusion is observed in their coming into existence and death. As each world subsists amongst other worlds, each individual member of each species is brought up among other individuals. Maintaining one world does not prevent the Maker from maintaining others, nor does bringing up one individual hinder Him from rearing others.

O, ONE WHOSE EYES ARE BLIND because of naturalism and whose heart has been sealed. If you think of nature as a printer and a maker, even though it is something printed and made, you must admit that each piece of soil contains perfect printing machines that are more in number than all printing machines in the world.

O ANIMALS! Do not be proud that you are greater than plants, for the art in plants is not inferior to yours. Do you not see that while the fleshy parts of all animal species are almost of the same constitution and quality, the pulpy parts of fruits are different from one another? This shows that the Pen of Divine Power works more deeply and delicately in them. Also, animals and human beings have, on the average, seven offspring during their lives. Fish, due to their weak animal senses, are an exception, for they reproduce abundantly. Plants, however, usually reproduce by 70, 700, or 7,000. Such abundant reproduction signifies the degree of importance attached to plants.

O ANIMAL PROUD OF ITSELF! Plants and trees rely only on God, and so their food comes to them and their offspring. It is as if the roots of every plant and tree were connected directly to the Mercy's treasury. Mercy shares each tree's food among its parts according to each part's need. While giving the "parents" pure "milk," it gives the daughters (fruits) pure sherbet, and the sons (olives) blessed oil.

* * *

Human has been created weak. (4:28)

O HUMANITY! Do not be proud that you are superior to animals, for our superiority is based on our weakness and impotence, just as an infant commands its elders by its impotence and weakness. What animal is more unable than you to satisfy its needs? An animal can acquire what it needs to maintain its life in 20 days, 20 hours, or 20 minutes after its birth, while it takes you 20 years of study and experience. If you form a community and help each other, you can acquire only what it takes one animal to acquire for itself. But by virtue of the perfection you can attain by servanthood to God, you, an individual being, can equal a species of animals.

We have two alternatives: We will be either the lowest or the highest species. Choose whichever you wish. Be aware of your impotence and weakness, and know that your power and strength lie in prayer and weeping before your Owner. Whatever you take pride in is the work of His inspiration and favoring. He has made you a specimen of all species so that He may show His marvelous Beauty and Creativity through you and cause you to taste His bounties.

KNOW, O ONE WHO DOUBTS the authenticity of the Prophetic Traditions about the Mahdi,[108] the approaching of the Last Hour, and the great tumults predicted to occur after the Prophet. Do you seek conviction in all issues, even secondary ones unconcerned with the fundamentals of belief? Some issues do not require conviction so that you need evident proof, as they are not concerned directly with belief. Simple acceptance or non-rejection is enough.

Just as the Qur'an's profound, allegorical statements require interpretation, seemingly ambiguous, parable-style Traditions also require interpretation and commentary. When you find an apparently illogical narration attributed to the Prophet, consider the following: It may have been borrowed from commentaries on the Torah or related by Jewish converts whose narrations were mistakenly thought to belong to the Prophet, upon him be peace and blessings. Or a narrator's explanatory addition could, later on, have been taken as belonging to the Tradition itself. Or it may have been deduced from the Tradition by the narrators, a saying of an inspired Traditionist mistakenly attributed to the Prophet. Or a proverb in circulation among the people which the Prophet mentioned on an occasion for a certain purpose might have been taken to be a Prophetic Tradition.

So, such narrations should not be restricted to their apparent meaning. Rather, people should ponder over them and either accept them as sayings uttered to guide to a truth, or think that they may have subtle meanings requiring interpretation. Your heedless interpretation will be like a sleeping person's interpreting what is seen by a person who is not asleep. O awake

---

108 The Mahdi, literally meaning "one who guides," is the Muslim Messiah who is expected to come toward the end of time to deliver the oppressed. (Tr.)

one, you can interpret what a sleeping person sees [while asleep]. So too, asleep in the heedlessness of this life, you cannot interpret what was seen by one who was always awake, whose heart never slept, and about whom God says: *The eye did not swerve nor waver* (51:17).

Each person's appointed hour is hidden so that he or she always will watch out for it and strive for the afterlife. The Last Hour, this world's appointed hour, is kept hidden for the same reason. This is why the people in every century from the Age of Happiness to the present have watched for it. Thus we wait for it with alertness, a condition that removes our heedlessness.

Narrations concerning the Mahdi are ambiguous so that people in every age will expect him. This strengthens the believers' resistance and morale, and removes their despair when misguidance spreads and gains strength. It also encourages Muslim scholars who strive to revive Islamic principles and guide people to truth in a way expected from the Mahdi, their illustrious leader.

KNOW, O MUSLIMS who are Muslim in name and appearance only. Your imitation of unbelievers and opposition to Islamic injunctions makes you resemble clan members who blame their clan, despise their chief, and scorn their customs because they see someone from a different and hostile clan who is proud of its virtues. Such people think that such misguided actions will make them like members of the other clan. They do not realize that such rejection and apostasy disgraces them and causes them to lose all support.

Westerners who reject Prophet Muhammad, upon him be peace and blessings, console themselves with Christianity and Western civilization, which contain elements of their nation's customs. They can preserve in their spirits some laudable virtues and make praiseworthy efforts to improve their worldly life. This consolation keeps them from seeing the veils of darkness in their spirits and the loneliness they must otherwise feel.

Know, O apostates, that those who deny Prophet Muhammad and his accomplishments cannot accept another Prophet, their Lord, or any real perfection. Look at the terrible ruin in their spirits. See the intense darkness in their conscience, and the gloom and despair in their heart. The ugliness of their inner world soon will become manifest, and it will become clear that the superficial attractiveness of apostasy is uglier than an unbeliever's ugliness. They will be like carriers of poison, harmful to themselves and to the community.

KNOW, O YOU WHO FIND it hard to understand some of the Qur'an's awesome truths, such as: *He created the heavens and Earth in 6 days* (10:3); *The Hour's affair is but like the eye's twinkling* (16:77); *Your creation and resurrection are but like (those of) a single soul* (31:28); *Then it will be breathed into it a second time and lo! they have all stood up, staring* (39:68); and *On that day We will roll up the heavens as written scrolls are rolled up* (21:104).

The Book of Creation interprets these Qur'anic verses clearly and offers them to your understanding by showing you many comparable physical realities that you observe regularly [as, for example,] in the alternation of day and night and the changes of seasons and centuries. If you seek conviction, open the treasure of: *Look at the imprints of God's Mercy, how He revives Earth after its death. Surely He is the Reviver of the dead (in the same way)* (30:50), so that you can see innumerable examples of the awesome realities that you deem unlikely.

For example, each spring you witness the resurrection of thousands of plant and animal worlds that died during the winter. All are brought back to life within a few days, in a definite order, and in appointed particular measures. Most of them are found in and adorn almost all regions of Earth. There are innumerable other examples.

Consider the world of trees, which contain many kinds of apple trees, and each individual member of each kind. You will see three incidents of resurrection: The tree bursts into beautiful blossoms, produces well-proportioned leaves, and yields beautiful, delicious fruits. The One Creator does all these things on Earth's face and, turning over winter's sheet, fills thousands of sheets (each the size of Earth's sheet) with marvelous "words." He introduces Himself as the One *Who created the heavens and Earth in 6 days*, Who does all things mentioned in the verses above.

KNOW, O FRIEND, that everyone feels love and affection for their relatives; clan members; members of their nation, race, and species (humanity); and for all parts and particles of existence. Even if unconsciously, they are sad when others are sad and happy when others are happy. They feel that they are with the community of Prophets, saints, and pious people because of their perfection. A mother, for example, disturbs her rest and peace for a relative or a loved one.

However, due to what the surrounding world presents to them, the heedless cannot rid themselves of distress. They are crushed by spiritual pain and inner unrest. Even if placed in a paradise, they would be like a firefly that gives out a brief, dim flash of light and then is enveloped by darkness. Even this fleeting light harms them by illuminating the distressing scenes around them.

But if they get rid of this heedlessness and consider all things and events in the light of belief in the Owner of existence, Whose every act is good by itself or by its consequences, a window will open from their hearts to the lights of the Everlasting Sun that illuminates the past and the future. They will discern that their love for other things is really love for the One Who suffices and substitutes for all things, and causes them to forget all others. Nothing can substitute for Him or for one manifestation of His love. Even if believers convinced of this were placed in Hell, they would enjoy some feeling of Paradise knowing that all their loved ones were saved from eternal extinction and separation and blessed with perpetual happiness.

O HEEDLESS SAID! Give up the idea that you own yourself. Give your loved ones to their All-Munificent and All-Compassionate Owner, and secure their salvation and happiness.

KNOW, O FRIEND, that God creates everything. However, evil and defect, as well as fault and vice, are the result of the created thing's nature and imperfect capacities. The All-Generous Creator creates whatever the created things ask of Him in the tongue of their potential and disposition. Good and beauty are from Him, for He creates and requires them. He also creates ugliness and defect, but does not require them. All praise is due to Him, for asking Him for beauty and good is like an answer from Him and His Names. All glorification is due to Him, and He has no defect and ugliness. Creatures seek out and engage in vice and ugliness, and the Almighty creates them. However, He attaches many beautiful consequences to what seems ugly. *Whatever good visits you is from God, and whatever evil befalls you is from yourself* (4:79).

KNOW, O FRIEND, that all species, especially plants and animals, are like threads of an embroidery spread like garments on Earth's face. Some are thinner, shorter, or more loosely knitted, while others are torn in winter and renewed in spring. However, all are woven with perfect order and perfect proportions. All species embrace one another and help one another. Their members come together and separate on good terms.

Whatever exists is the textile of a Single Weaver and the servant of a Single Master. Everything is woven specifically for itself and with fibers fitted for itself, and without any confusion or flaw. This testifies, with a certainty based on observation, that it is a work of the art of the One Whose Power and Wisdom have no limit.

The purposeful, specific adornment and furnishing of all creatures shows that the One Who adorned and furnished the palace of the world with such different species is He Who created whatever is necessary to maintain the palace. One of the most important purposes for its rich adornment is making its Maker known, and that adornment is one of the most polished mirrors reflecting the truth that the Maker wills to make Himself known and loved.

Look at a yellow sunflower that closes at night and opens in daytime. Its Maker makes it a pleasant home for tiny organisms or animals glorifying their Creator. A group of them inhabit it, and it becomes like a garden, a palace, or a village for them.

Glory be to Him Who manifests His Grace in all things, makes His Power known by His creatures, and makes Himself loved by His servants through the rich adornment of His works of art. There is no deity but He. *His word is true, and for Him is the whole creation and His is the dominion over them* (6:73). *He is not questioned concerning what He does* (21:23).

KNOW, O FRIEND, that no one has the right or a pretext to question Him. In His kingdom, He controls as He wills. He is All-Knowing, All-Wise, and knows what we do not. Our ignorance of an event's or a creature's wisdom does not mean that there is no wisdom in it, for the wisdom observed in the absolute majority of things testifies to its existence in all things and events.

For example, we grieve when living things die. We may not discern any beauty or good in the short lives of some fine beings, or perceive any mercy in the decay of living creatures in autumn or winter. However, such objections or grief arise from our ignorance of the reality that a living being is like a soldier or servant charged with many tasks that glorify and praise the Creator of life and death. The purposes for their lives pertain to Him. So, their short existence or their innate intention to fulfill their functions—like the intentions of seeds to grow into plants or trees—may be sufficient to perform what is expected of them.

Death is only a changing of abodes, a discharge from duties, and a call to the presence of the Creator, as the Creator Himself decrees: *Then, they are resurrected and gathered in the Presence of their Lord* (6:38). It is a sign of His Mercy's perfection that He usually does not allow His creatures to live to the unbearable period of old age and to remain in the most severe, troublesome hardships of life. He discharges lovers of flowers and those taking pleasure in vegetation from their duties. The Maker of those creatures, their Master, employs them during their lives according to the ease with which they fulfill their tasks. When the frown of life's unbearable conditions, because of old age or winter, consume them and they no longer have any enthusiasm, the Mercy of the All-Merciful One discharges them. In their place, He dispatches their likes, woven after their example, so that they glorify their Master. These newcomers start their tasks where their predecessors completed theirs.

O heedless, conceited ones who think that you own your selves and your lives, and assume that happiness lies in a continuous, easy life—you are wrong. You compare your self-forgetting selfhood to an animal contented with its life. However, it fulfills its tasks. The shouts of joy caused by universal Mercy's manifestations sound like lamentations to you. Do not grieve for them, because grief arises from compassion and pity. Rather, pity and grieve for your self. Some animals are allowed to attack others so that the latter can develop their agility and potential or capacity to defend themselves, and learn to know their faculties. You see this clear wisdom when you compare domesticated and wild members of the same species.

WHY, O FRIEND, do saints differ in the conclusions they draw through inspiration and spiritual unveiling, while agreeing on the fundamentals of the Religion? Why did saints and Prophets preceding the Last One [Prophet Muhammad], only elaborate on Divine Unity, while the Qur'an and Prophet Muhammad explained all pillars of the religion so clearly that they need no further clarification? The reason is the intervention of certain veils between those pillars, saints, and previous Prophets. Another reason is each one's capacity to receive the Divine Names' varied manifestations.

For example, the sun has a universal manifestation on all flowers, as well as a particular manifestation upon each species and individual flower. According to a well-known theory, every flower receives its color from sunlight's refraction. The sun has a universal manifestation of light on planets and the moon, which reflects the sun's light on the sea and its bubbles and drops, on land and the transparent things on it, and on air and its particles. The sun also has a pure, universal reflection in the atmosphere's "mirrors" and the sea's surface, and particular reflections or images in the bubbles on the sea's surface, drops of water, air molecules, and snowflakes.

The sun's manifestation on all of these things takes two forms: direct (Prophethood) and indirect (sainthood), with the intervention of veils and media. In this way, its manifestations are received according to the capacity and nature of the "mirrors."

With respect to the first way, each thing can say: "I am a mirror of the sun of the world," while, with respect to the second, they can only say: "I am a mirror of my particular sun or the sun of my species." In the second way, the "sun" manifests itself behind or is obstructed by veils. Thus this manifestation cannot possess the properties of the sun of the world, which causes the planets to revolve around itself, heats and illuminates Earth, and moves the wheels of the lives of plants and other things.

O friend, let's imagine ourselves in their places. This dense carnal self will become the flower that assumes a color as an effect produced by a ray of sunlight. This philosopher drowned in natural causes will be the drop that receives from the moon a shadow of the sun's light. The dewdrop, without color, will hold the sun's image in the "pupil of its eyes."

The love of Him Who, out of His Grace, illuminates and adorns us, has moved us to approach Him and see Him. You, the flower, represent all flowers. But as a flower is a dense mirror that refracts light and dissolves its seven colors, it veils the sun's reflection. And so you cannot be saved from separation, are confused between the colors' qualities, and suffer from the separation caused by interposing barriers. You can be freed if you give up your love of selfhood, stop looking at the merit and beauty you ascribe to your selfhood, and look at the sun. Also turn your face, which is fixed on soil to attract your sustenance although in reality it is hastened to you, up to the sun. You are a mirror of it, as it is a drop-like mirror shining in the heavens to a gleam from the lights of the Light, the Truth.[109] You cannot

---

109 As the flower receives its sustenance from the soil, it turns its face to it. But its sustenance is sent to it through the soil. Therefore, since the real origin of its sustenance is not the soil, it should turn its face to the sun. The flower is a mirror of the sun, as the sun itself is a tiny mirror (tiny compared to the vastness of the heaven, to a gleam of the lights of the Light—God.)

see it in its real identity, but only painted with your own attributes' colors and restricted by your limited capacity.

O drop, you have advanced as far as the moon by science and philosophy, and found it dense and dark, without light or life. Your endeavor has been in vain, and your knowledge has proven fruitless. You can be saved from the darkness of hopelessness, the desolation of loneliness, and the terror of that frightening solitude only if you abandon the night of naturalism and turn toward the sun of truth. Believe with certainty that the lights of that night are only shadowy reflections of the lights of the sun of daytime. However, you cannot see the sun clearly, but only from beyond the veils woven by your knowledge and philosophy, and in a color produced by your capacity.

As for you, O weak and poor dewdrop, you advance by evaporating and rising into the air. The dense matter in your structure burns and changes into light, after which you hold on to a ray of the light's manifestations. In whatever station you reach during your journeying upward, a window is opened to you from the sun. You see with certainty that it deserves the attributes it has, and no veil or barrier, limited capacity or smallness of mirrors can restrain you from attributing to it all the works of its essential sovereignty. You have understood that what appears in the objects and is observed in the mirrors is not the sun itself, but rather manifestations or colored reflections of it.

The three groups represented by the flower, drop of water, and dewdrop differ in the merits of the perfection they have obtained and in the rank of certainty they have reached. But they all agree on affirming the truth.

KNOW, O HUMANITY, that you serve as a unit of comparison in five ways:

First: You are a comprehensive index of the marvelous works of the Divine Beautiful Names' manifestations. With your attributes and supposed lordship in your own sphere, you are a measuring instrument to know God's all-comprehensive Attributes.

Second: You are a measure to reject any association of partners with Him. When you are convinced that you belong only to Him and are His property, you believe that He has no partners. If you give a third of your existence to Him, a second third to natural causes, and the last third to your own selfhood, this sharing occurs throughout the universe. When you attribute even the smallest part of His property to your ego, you have to admit that every being and natural cause has a thing of the same size. Thus you share God's property among others.

Third: When your ego is unveiled to you, the true map of the "natural" sciences and the knowledge of the outer world are opened to you. When you forget your self, this knowledge becomes closed or changes into ignorance and sophistry.

Fourth: You hold the keys of the Divine Names' hidden treasuries. If you perceive your limitless impotence, you will discover that your Creator has limitless power; if you discover your infinite poverty, you will see that your Provider has infinite wealth. In such ways, His Names' manifestations become luminous letters inscribed in the darkness of your existence. The more intense that darkness is, the more luminous they are.

With respect to these four ways, you can only receive—you have nothing (good) by yourself. You are a eulogy written in the language of *"Be!" and it is*.

Fifth: You are an agent, an effective cause, asking in the tongue of potential and need, action and word. Concerning this aspect, you are the origin of all vice, defect, and sin; your Creator is the source of all good and beauty, perfection and light.

The first four ways manifest the essence of everything with respect to your Creator and your relation with Him, while the fifth one shows the degrees of His Names' manifestations.

* * *

> Surely God has bought from the believers their selves in return for Paradise. (9:111)

KNOW, O FRIEND, that: *What deceives you with respect to your All-Munificent Lord* (82:6) means that He buys the property He entrusted to you for your benefit and for a high price.[110] He buys it, while you hold it in your hand and benefit from it, to preserve it from being lost and so that it may grow in value. Profit upon profit!

But you reject this transaction and break His trust in you. You decrease its value from the highest height to the lowest depth, and then it goes in vain. You are deprived of the great price He offers, and endure suffering and

110 Your selfhood, body, and life, which are in fact His property. (Tr.)

difficulty, pain and hardship to maintain it for a very short time. You also endure the sins you commit thereby. Loss upon loss!

You resemble a person standing on a mountain top. An earthquake occurs, causing you to fall into crevice and lose whatever is in your hand. You are like one "just about to fall into a pit of fire or an abode of ruin from the brink of a crumbling precipice." Yet you still hold the marvelous device entrusted to you that can produce limitless fruit and benefit. At this time, the device's true owner, purely out of compassion, offers to buy it from you:

> To preserve it and return it after you are saved, I will buy this piece of my property as if it belonged to you. Use it in my infinitely spacious gardens to recognize and measure the contents of my overflowing treasures so that its value may increase. In return, you will receive very high wages. Otherwise, it will become a lowly, ordinary device of the kind used in your abdomen's narrow cavities that, compared with my gardens and treasures, are worthless. How can those cavities contain the device entrusted to you, which not even the world can contain? I will give you a very high price for it.
>
> As long as you are on this mountain, I will not take possession of it, but only preserve and manage it so that you can maintain it easily. If you accept, use it in my name and on my behalf, as a soldier controlling what he holds in his hand in the king's name or on his behalf, without fear of what will occur or grief for what has taken place. If you do not agree, you will suffer great loss and be treated as a breacher of trust responsible for its perishing.[111]

The Qur'an describes this transaction and warns: Buy it and gain an extremely high profit: *The home of the Hereafter, that is life if they but knew* (29:64). Modern civilization and materialistic philosophy say: *Appropriate it. It*

---

111 Some may see a threat here. However, human existence here is a reality out of human will. Therefore it is much more than a bargain, for God's creation of us is a pure blessing. How many people complain of being in the world? Is there anybody who does not love life? Only those misusing their willpower and engulfed in dissipation complain about life. No true believer complains. Whatever we do not like in life and in the world is due to the fact that we neglect our responsibilities as the most honored of beings. God's informing us of how to act in life and then rewarding us with eternal happiness is as great and infinite a blessing as eternity. If some still see a threat, that threat is also pure blessing, as it compels us to find the straight way and attain happiness in both worlds, where a promise is not enough for weak-willed, spiritually corrupt, obstinate persons to change their ways. (Tr.)

is but our life of the world (6:29). Consider the difference between the illuminating Divine guidance and misleading human genius.

KNOW, O FRIEND, that the All-Glorified One is near but you are distant from Him. He is as near to you as He is to all people, and is as near to all people as He is to all living beings and all creatures, from the tiniest particles to ether and spirit beings and to those you cannot imagine.

If you want to be near to Him, develop and expand so that you can represent humanity, and then acquire a universal existence to represent creation. Go beyond 70,000 veils. As He is near to you and near to everything else at the same time, you will have to be near to everything. Thereafter, you encounter an infinite space between contingency (the sphere of creation) and Necessity (the sphere of Divinity). How can you reach the One infinitely distant in His nearness? If you desire to be near to Him, renounce and annihilate your selfhood to remove the intervening distance, gain permanence with Him, and acquire nearness to Him.

Know, O friend, that God is nearer to us than ourselves, while we are infinitely distant from Him. Among the evidence of His nearness is His control of us. If we look for Him near what He controls, we will find Him near all things. If we could reach Him by representing creation, we would find Him beyond veils of light in the sphere of Necessity formed of the "worlds" of the Names, Attributes, and Essential Qualities in His Dignity, Grandeur, and Magnificence. But if we look for Him through His nearness by renouncing and annihilating our selfhood, it is easy to find Him, if He wills. There is no strength and power save with Him.

KNOW, O YOU WHO DESIRE to know the difference between the Qur'an's wisdom and philosophy's viewpoint. Imagine that there is a copy of the Qur'an written in letters of different precious jewels—gold and silver, diamond and emerald, agate and others. Two people, after seeing and admiring it, decide to write a book on its merits. One is a foreigner who does not understand the text's meaning. The foreigner is an expert jeweler and a specialist in engineering, geometry, and painting, and so his book discusses the visible beauties of the Qur'an's jeweled letters. The other one realizes what the Qur'an is, and so ignores its physical jewels and concentrates on the jewels of its meaning, the lights of its mysteries, and the truths of its verses, which are infinitely loftier.

O you with little sense and intellect! Which book deserves to be recognized as containing some of the Qur'an's wisdom? If you understood this analogy, you will realize that copy of the Qur'an is the universe, the first person represents philosophers and scientists, and the second person represents students of the Qur'an.

* * *

> Whoever puts his (or her) trust in God, He is sufficient for him (or her). (65:3)

O SAID! Happiness lies in trusting in God, so trust in Him so that you may find peace and rest in this world and a great reward in the next.

Those who trust in God and those who do not are like two people carrying heavy loads who board a ship. One puts his load down and sits on it, his mind at peace. The other one does not, and when told to put it down, responds: "I am strong enough to carry it." They explain to him:

> This ship is stronger and better able to carry it. As the journey proceeds, your load will grow heavier, so put it down and be relieved of your burden. If the ship's owner sees you, he will either think that you are mad and order your off, or that you are mocking his ship and ridiculing him. With that, he will put you in the brig. You will be a laughing stock to everyone. And when you can no longer carry your load, you will have to pretend to be strong (ostentation or false show) or display arrogance or conceit (weakness and impotence).

Finally, the man agrees with them, places his load on the deck, and sits on it. Relieved, he says: "May God reward you, for you have guided me to that upon which my ease, salvation, and honor rest."

KNOW, O FRIEND, that Qur'anic verses often end by mentioning the Divine Beautiful Names or with phrases implying them, ordering reflection and contemplation or calling to one's reason. Sometimes they conclude with a general expression containing a purpose of the Qur'an—as if rays from the light of elevated wisdom or sprinkles from the pure water of Divine guidance. That is, with its miraculous expressions, the Qur'an expounds the Maker's works and acts and then concludes with the relevant Divine Names, affirmation of the Resurrection or Divine Unity, or another pillar of belief.

For example:

> He created for you all that there is on Earth; then He turned to the sky, fashioning it into seven heavens. He is the Knower of all things. (2:29)

> Have We not made Earth a cradle, and the mountains as pegs? And We have created you in pairs. We have made your sleep for repose. We have made night a cloak, and We have made the day (a means or time of earning) livelihood. We have made above you seven strong (firmaments), and We have made a lamp therein blazing with splendor. We have sent down from the condensed clouds pouring water, so that We may bring forth grain and plants, and gardens thick with foliage. Surely the Day of Judgment is a fixed time. (78:6-17)

The Qur'an spreads before our eyes His art's textiles and then concludes with the Divine Names or with a reference to reasoning:

> Say: "Who is it that provides for you from the sky and Earth, possesses hearing and sight, brings forth the living from the dead and the dead from the living, and directs all affairs?" They will surely say: "God." Then say: "Will you not then improve your ways in reverence for Him? Such then is God, your True Lord." (10:31-32)

> In the creation of the heavens and Earth, and in the alternation of night and day, and in the ships sailing through the ocean for the benefit of humanity, and in the water which God sends down from the sky and with which He revives Earth after its death, and dispersing over it all kinds of beasts, and in the ordinance of the winds and clouds subjugated between Earth and sky are signs for people who reason. (2:164)

It explains God's acts and then concludes with His Names or Attributes:

> Thus Your Lord will choose you and teach you the interpretation of things and events, including dreams. And He will perfect His grace upon you and upon the family of Jacob as He perfected it to your forefathers Abraham and Isaac before you. Assuredly, your Lord is All-Knowing, All-Wise. (12:6)

> Say: "O God, absolute Master of dominion! You bestow dominion on whom You will, and take it from whom You will; You exalt whom You will and abase whom You will. In Your hand lies all good. Surely You are Powerful over all things." (3:26)

The Qur'an mentions creatures and then employs the order and harmony, proportions and fruits of their existence as mirrors to reflect the Names manifested on them as if they were words, and as if the Names were their meanings or water of life, seeds or essences:

> Surely We created people from an extract of wet earth; then We placed him (or her) as a drop (of seed) in a safe lodging. Then We have created the drop into a suspended clot, and We have created the clot into a shapeless lump, and We have created the lump into bones. Then We clothed the bones with flesh, and then built it as another creation. So Supreme and Blessed is God, the Best of creators! (23:12-14)

> Assuredly Your Lord is God, Who has created the heavens and Earth in 6 days, then established Himself on the Supreme Throne, covering the night with the day, each pursuing the other urgently, and has made the sun and the moon and the stars subservient by His command. Beware, His is creation and commandment. Supreme and Blessed is God, the Lord of the worlds. (7:54)

The Qur'an mentions particular, changeable events and things and then concludes with universal, luminous, established Names or phrases urging reflection or learning:

> He taught Adam the names, all of them, and then presented them to the angels: "Tell Me the names of these, if you are truthful." "Glory be to You" they replied; "We have no knowledge save what You have taught us. Surely You are the All-Knowing, the All-Wise." (2:31-32)

> And for you there is a lesson in the cattle (too). We give you to drink of that which is in their bellies, between bowels and blood, pure milk, palatable for those who drink. And of the fruits of the date-palm and grapes from which you derive strong drink and (also) good nourishment. Surely in this is a sign for a people who reason and understand. And Your Lord inspired the bee: "Build your homes in the mountains and in the trees, and in what they build. Then eat of all the fruits, and returning with your load follow the ways your Lord has made easy for you." There comes forth out of their bellies a fluid of many hues, wherein is healing for humanity. Indeed in this is a sign for a people who reflect. (16:66-69)

The Qur'an mentions vast things or things found in multiplicity, places on them the signs of Divine Unity, and concludes them with a general rule:

> His Supreme Seat embraces the heavens and Earth, and it tires Him not to uphold them both. He is the All-Exalted, the Supreme. (2:255)

> God has created the heavens and Earth, and sends down from the sky rain, with which He brings forth fruits to be your sustenance. He makes the ships be of service to you, that they may run upon the sea at His command, and has made the rivers be of service to you. He makes the sun and the moon, both constant in their courses, to be of service to you; and has made of service to you the night and the day. And He gives you of all that you ask Him; and if you were to reckon the favors of God, you would never be able to count them. Surely humanity is a wrongdoer, ungrateful. (14:32-34)

It mentions apparent causes for creating things and then draws attention to the real Agent Who creates them and their fruits, thus pointing out that lifeless causes cannot know those fruits and purposeful results. Even if the causes seem to be near to the effects, there is a very great distance between them. That is where the Divine Names show forth in their splendor. Even the largest cause cannot create the smallest effect, just as the horizon, which seems to touch the mountains, in reality is separated from them by a vast distance—the distance in which the stars reside:

> Let humanity reflect on the food it eats: How We pour water in showers, then split the ground in clefts, and cause the grain to grow on it, and grapes and fresh herbage, and olive trees and palm trees, and enclosed gardens dense with lofty trees, and fruits and pasture, as provision (from God) for you and your cattle. (80:24-32)

The phrase *provision (from God)* and mentioning plants and trees, each an exquisite work of art with many uses, show that apparent causes cannot create anything.

> Do you not see that God gently drives the clouds, then joins them together, (completing the formation of a circuit between them,) and then turns them into a thick mass, and consequently you see rain-drops issue out of their midst? He sends down hail out of snow-laden mountains (of clouds) from the sky, and smites with it whom He wills and averts it from whom He wills. The flash of its lightning almost takes away the sight. God alternates night and day, and in

> this is a teaching for people of insight. He has created every creature of water; some go upon their bellies, others on two feet, and still others on four feet. God creates what He wills. Surely God is Powerful over all things. (24:43-45)

The Qur'an mentions God's extraordinary feats to prepare our minds to accept His wonderful acts in the Hereafter, or mentions His future acts in the Hereafter to point to their likes in this world:

> Has human not considered that We have created him from a drop of (seminal) fluid? Yet, he turns into an open, fierce adversary. And he coins a comparison for Us, having forgotten his own origin and creation, saying, "Who will give life to these bones when they have rotten away?" Say: "He Who produced them in the first instance will give them life. He has full knowledge of every creation." He Who has made for you fire from the green tree, and see, you kindle fire with it. Is not He Who has created the heavens and the earth able to create (from rotten bones) the like of them (whose bones have rotted under the ground)? Surely He is; He is the Supreme Creator, the All-Knowing. (36:77-81)

> When the sun is folded up ... (81:1)

> When the heaven is cleft open ... (82:1)

> When the heaven is split asunder ... (84:1)

The resurrection [of countless animal and plant species] during spring displays numerous analogies for the Resurrection. For example, you see the likes of: *When the pages (records of our deeds) are laid open* (81:10) in the germination and growth of seeds the records of the deeds of their "mothers" and their life-histories.

The Qur'an mentions particular purposes or events, and then confirms and corroborates them with the Names as if they were universal rules:

> God has heard the words of her who disputed with you concerning her husband and made her complaint to God. God has heard the arguments of both of you. Surely God is All-Hearing, All-Seeing. (58:1)

> Glory be to Him Who carried His servant by night from the Sacred Mosque (Masjid al-Haram) to the Farthest Mosque (Masjid al-Aqsa') whose surroundings We have blessed, that We might show him some of Our signs. Surely He is All-Hearing, All-Seeing. (17:1)

> Praise be to God, the Creator of the heavens and Earth, Who appoints the angels (as) messengers having wings two, three, or four. He multiplies in creation however He pleases. Surely God is Powerful over all things. (35:1)

The Qur'an mentions the acts of ungrateful people with the doom threatened for those acts. Afterwards, it consoles them with the Names pointing to mercy:

> Say: "If there were other gods besides Him, as they say, they would certainly have sought out a way to the Owner of the Supreme Throne." Glorified is He, and High Exalted above all that they say. The seven heavens and Earth, and all that is in them glorify Him. There is nothing that does not glorify Him with His praise, yet you cannot understand their glorification. Surely He is All-Clement, All-Forgiving. (17:42-44)

An important topic

The Qur'an says:

> Say: "If the ocean were ink for the words of my Lord, assuredly the ocean would be used up before the words of my Lord were finished, even if We brought another (ocean) like it, for its aid." (18:109)

If you ask how the Qur'an is superior to all speech, whether spoken or written, the answer will be: It is God's Word on account of His being the Lord of the worlds having the title "Deity of the worlds," and the Name "Lord of the heavens and Earth," and in respect of His absolute Lordship and universal Sovereignty. It is God's Word by reason of the all-embracing Mercy, because of Divinity's magnificence and grandeur, and because it issues from the all-encompassing field of the Greatest Name and addresses the circle encompassed by the Supreme Throne.

Other words of God are words of God because of the particular manifestations of His Lordship and Divinity with particular Names and titles, and as part of particular Sovereignty and Mercy. They are like most Divine inspirations. For this reason, a saint can say: "My heart informs me from my Lord," but not: "My heart informs me from the Lord of the worlds."

A Prophet receives radiance and enlightenment from the Lord of the worlds' manifestation with His Greatest Name in the mirror of the Supreme

Throne, the "mother" of thrones. Compared to this, a saint's particular enlightenment and radiance, received from the Lord's manifestation in the mirror of his or her heart, is limited to the heart's capacity. Consider the difference between the sunlight reflected in your little, dim mirror, and the light the sun provides to the solar system. Another example is the difference between a king's address to a subject on a particular matter specifically for that subject, and a royal decree issued to all subjects by his envoys, due to his supreme authority and its full majesty.

This also explains why most Divine Revelations come through the greatest angels, while inspirations come without mediation, and why even the greatest saint cannot reach the rank of a Prophet. It also explains the Qur'an's supremacy and incomparable dignity and sacredness, as well as the sublimity and beauty of its miraculous conciseness. In addition to many other mysteries, it explains why the Seal of the Prophets had to ascend to the heavens as far as the Farthest Lote Tree, why he ascended to the nearness of "two bows' length" to supplicate Him Who is nearer to him than his jugular vein, and then returned to the world in the twinkling of an eye.

Like Knowledge and Will, God's Speaking to Himself is one of His eternal Attributes. Its existence is known and its nature is unknown. His words are without end.

> Glory be to You. We have no knowledge save what You have taught us. Surely You are the All-Knowing, the All-Wise.

* * *

In the Name of God, the All-Merciful, the All-Compassionate.

From Him we seek help.
In the Name of God.

KNOW, O FRIEND, that everything says, either verbally or via the tongue of disposition or potential: *In and with the Name of God.* It does so because, despite its essential impotence, every thing that exists, without exception, performs astonishing tasks of which, on its own, it could not perform even the smallest part. This shows that it does them by the Strength of an All-Strong, All-Mighty One, and that it undertakes those tasks in and with the Name of the All-Powerful, the All-Wise One.

Despite its complete ignorance, it does those tasks so wisely and orderly and in such a beneficial and fruitful way. However, on its own it cannot do even the smallest part of any action. This shows that it assumes those purposeful tasks in and with the Name of an All-Tremendous, All-Wise One. Every object works for the use of living creatures in and with the Name of an All-Merciful, All-Compassionate One, and on behalf of an All-Knowing, All-Munificent One.

See how each seed results in a tree or a plant. Look at trees and their fruits, at micro-organisms and other animals, and the tasks they do. When you see a private gathering people in a certain place and dispatching them to different places to do certain tasks, you conclude that he is working on behalf of the king or government and enjoys its authority.

In the same way, one with knowledge understands that those impotent, ignorant creatures can perform their tasks so wisely, orderly, and fruitfully only in the Name of an All-Powerful, All-Knowing One. They act on behalf of an All-Mighty, All-Wise One, offering the fruits of their tasks in the Name of an All-Merciful, All-Compassionate One. Whatever task a creature does and produces fruits thereby is such that the universal Divine Mercy gives a particular pleasure in return for it. It is like the pleasure a mother takes in her compassion for her children, the delight a bee has in obeying the Divine inspiration to do what it does, or the pleasure in sexual intercourse. It is like the pleasure every living organism takes in eating, drinking, and resting, or the pleasure a creature takes in putting its potential into effect, as in the germination and growth of plants. The All-Wise Creator, All-Munificent Owner, assigns such pleasures as wages for the services rendered and as appetites urging their actions.

Now, O bearer of the Supreme Trust! Why do you not obey a law encompassing all things from the Supreme Throne to the tiniest creature? Why do you rebel against a principle of the One Who subjugated the sun and moon and employs stars and particles in His service?

KNOW, O FRIEND, that the difference between belief in Divine Unity and atheism and heresy is like that between Paradise and Hell, between what is absolutely necessary and what is [or should be] inconceivable. Consider the following: Belief in Divine Unity attributes all things to One Being, thereby decreasing the difficulty and expenditure of everything's creation, for, in relation to that Being's Power, there is no difference between one thing and another.

Also, belief in Divine Unity unveils the many purposes of their Maker in creating them. One purpose is that a thing manifests the Creator's Names as if it were a comprehensive word bearing the meanings and pointing to the Names. But heedless and misguided people attribute a thing's existence to other things, to impotent and lifeless elements, and to deaf and blind forces and laws. They make the existence of things so difficult that it is equally difficult for one or all things to be created. They consider things only with respect to their benefits for people, which is only one of their purposes.

An atheist and a believer are like two people who see a date-palm seed. The believer says: "It is an index of innumerable other indexes called seeds. It reveals the meaning and essence of the tree destined to grow from it, and describes the life-history of the tree that produced it. It is a map showing the nature of the tree's potentials and functions as a sort of machine weaving a date-palm." The atheist says: "All of the date-palm's parts and leaves have gathered together to make and equip this seed with what it needs. But it is of no use, for the tree's only purpose is to produce this seed, which will finally be eaten by an animal or rot in the soil."

All things occur with great ease despite their abundance. Despite their intermingling, each thing can be distinguished easily, and an all-embracing order prevails in the universe. This being so, how can you attribute even one thing to lifeless causes? Most things that exist cooperate for that single thing, which is a sample of all things, to exist. Was a pomegranate created only for eating?

Universal wisdom has assigned many tasks to a person's head and the senses it contains. If each assigned task required a different mustard seed-sized instrument, your head would be as big as Mount Sinai. Consider your tongue and its tasks. Tasting and measuring the contents of all treasures of Divine Mercy is only one of its tasks. Has this universal wisdom (which charges a thing, however small, with numerous duties) assigned only one purpose to that pomegranate, a miraculous work of art—your eating it in a moment of heedlessness? Can something the size of your head yield a fruit as large as a mountain, or something as large as a mountain yield a fruit like your head? If you answer "yes," it means that you see no difference between wisdom and futility and absurdity, that you see infinite wisdom as identical with infinite futility and absurdity. In reality, like all fruits, that pomegranate contains a long poem on the Divine Beautiful Names, explaining their meanings. Glorified be Him in Whose work minds are amazed.

The following is a blossom of the tree of: *The seven heavens and Earth and all that is in them glorify Him. There is nothing that does not glorify Him with His praise* (17:44). The meaning of this verse was unveiled to me when trees blossomed in the spring. I went into ecstasies and reflected on their glorification. The following lines occurred to me:

* * *

In the Name of God, the All-Merciful, the All-Compassionate.

Praise be to God, Whom all things glorify with their own visible and perceptible words. For example, lights, rivers, and rain clouds are the words of the source of light, water, and air, respectively.

Glory be to Him Whom praise:
the source of light with lights;
water and air with rivers and clouds...
earth and plants with rocks and flowers...
the atmosphere and trees with birds and fruits...
clouds and sky with rain and moons...
Light shines by His illuminating and displaying it.
Air produces waves by His controlling
and charging it (with tasks).
Water bursts forth and flows by His subjugating and depositing it,
which is praise for the One Who determines all things and appoints
for each thing a particular nature.
Stones are adorned by His shaping and arranging them.
Flowers smile by His making them adorned and beautiful.
Fruits appear richly adorned by His favoring and graciousness, which
is a manifest, comely praise for the One Who creates every thing
with a particular nature.
Birds sing by His enabling them to speak
and making them lovely.
Rain trills by His sending it down and making it vital for beings.
Moons move by His determining and directing,
which is an eloquent glorification for the All-Determining,
a luminous sign for the All-Overwhelming.
Glory be to Him Whom praise:
the heavens with constellations and light-giving objects...
the planetary systems with suns, stars, and moons...

the atmosphere with thunderbolts, lightning, and rain...
Earth with animals, plants, and trees...
Trees praise Him with leaves and flowers,
then with well-proportioned fruits.
When flowers stop praising, fruits begin to speak
with an eloquent, light-diffusing praise.
A seed hymns silently by heart, full of mysteries;
a book is inscribed in it—the record of its tree's life-history.
It voices the praise of the Splitter of grains, the Originator.
All plants praise and worship, glorify and
prostrate before the All-Determining.
The smiles of plants through their flowers are
praise manifest for one able to discern.
Their sprouts and spikes are their mouths, seeds and
grains the words of the poetry they recite...
Their proportions and orderliness are another tongue, and their
design is by the designing of the All-Illuminating.
Each is a work of art adorned by the All-Radiating.
With their being sustenance, their colors and smells, they describe
and praise the Originator.
They describe His Attributes, make His Names known, and
interpret His will to make Himself known and loved.
The grains in the ears and flowers like eyes are "drops" of
the manifestations of the Originator...
So His servants may love Him and His creatures may know him.
A tree in blossom is an expression of praise in verse,
with many "eyes" that have opened.
It has adorned its green parts for its festive day,
in order that its Lord may watch His illustrious works.
It exhibits the gems attached to it to those with eyes to see;
and proclaims to humanity the wisdom in its creation,
with the treasury deposited in it by
the Munificence of the Lord of fruits.
Glory be to Him Who does good whatever He does:
how illustrious His proof, how clear His explanations!
Who is the All-Shaping Originator, All-Able Creator,
All-Illuminating Fashioner, Who creates each thing
with a nature particular to it.
Look at His Mercy in the season of spring to see His art:
the season of spring is a festive day for His servants...
the day when His creation—trees and plants—adorn themselves...
Each plant manifests to the degree of its rank

the sovereignty of its King and the gifts of its Owner...
It is ready to receive and fulfill His orders;
renders much service in His Name...
It blossoms and yields fruits by His leave,
resembling a clean table for His guests...
Light and air, soil, and water are conveyors of His
commands and bearers of His Throne,
publicizing His Art, illustrating His Wisdom.
Knowledge and Wisdom: light is their throne.[112]
Grace and Mercy: water is their throne.
Preserving and reviving: soil is their throne.
Command and Will: air is their throne.

KNOW, O FRIEND, that all those elements are objects on which His Names are manifested; they are media, not sources or origins; they are acted on, not agents. They are conveyors by His Strength and carry what they carry by His leave, by His Names... they do what they do by His Power.

If what falls to the part of things did not consist of being objects where His Names are manifested, being passive media, it would have been necessary for soil and air, light and water to have in each of their particles or atoms or molecules an infinite knowledge, power, and creative ability. For example, air passes through the atmosphere and visits the particles of all plants destined to grow. Its passing causes countless marvels—miracles of the art of Him Who has created the heavens—to appear.

If it were possible for a simple, lifeless, ignorant particle to build those trees, attach those fruits to them, and to shape those flowers—in short, to invent all those things—and if it were able to bear this Earth, you would have the right to doubt the Oneness of Him Who has no partners. Otherwise, it is beyond doubt that only He Who holds all creation in His Power's grasp, in His Wisdom's grasp, can claim any ownership and dominion of things.

Every grain, drop, or particle works in the service of plants, fruits, or flowers. If they were not employed by the Lord of the heavens, each grain, drop, or particle would have enough art, power, and wisdom to invent and direct all of those creatures.

Glory be to Him Whom trees praise with their leaves,
blossoms, and fruits...

112 They pervade existence or manifest themselves through light (light conveys them). The thrones to follow should be taken in the light of this explanation. (Tr.)

Bursting of blossoms amidst multiplicity of leaves
to lead the way to the growth of fruits,
and the growth of fruits in the lap of the flowers—
which are daughters of trees—
dancing in the hands of green branches,
moved by enlivening breezes—
all is an eloquent speech extolling Him Who has built them,
Who is One, Overwhelming.
Their mouths, letters, and words...
are leaves, flowers, and fruits.
Leaves dance in delight at mentioning the Creator...
Flowers smile in gratitude to the All-Able One
for their adornment...
Fruits joy in what Mercy provides for them,
singing sweet melodies,
well-ordered, well-proportioned, in shining colors...
artistically designed and embroidered,
with wonderful shape;
richly adorned and marvelously painted,
delicious in the eating.
The marvelous art they display, their being in great variety
and with diverse skins—all this is in praise of the Originator
and describes the All-Able.
They describe His Attributes and make His Names known,
interpreting that He wills to be loved
and manifests His Affection.
The drops of the Creator's manifestations come out
of the mouths of fruits that He wills to be known
and loved by His servants, and manifest
His Compassion for His creatures in poverty.
Glory be to Him. How clear His proof, how vast His Power,
how manifest His Mercy.
He is All-Building and All-Shaping, All-Composing and
All-Arranging, All-Spreading and All-Promising.
Glory be to Him: How gracious His Majesty,
how majestic His Grace, how great His Sovereignty.

LOOK AT EARTH AND SAY: *God is the All-Great.* Look at the universe and say: *God is the All-Great*, He is the Creator and All-Acting, All-Opening and All-Knowing, All-Giving and All-Diffusing, All-Mighty and All-Wise, All-Munificent and All-Compassionate.

To know the meaning of *God is the All-Great*, look at the universe. It consists in shadows of His Lights, results of His acts, lines of the Pen of His Decree and Destiny, embroideries of His Names, and mirrors of His Attributes.

KNOW AND SAY: *God is the All-Great*. Look at the worlds. They are held in the grasp of His Knowledge and Power, Justice and Wisdom, and are well-ordered, measured, harmonious.

He orders the universe and determines the measure, for order and measure are two handfuls of the All-Merciful, and the titles of two chapters from the Manifest Record and the Manifest Book. That Record and this Book are titles of the Knowledge and Power of the All-Knowing and All-Able, All-Just and All-Wise. Nothing is outside this order and measure. This shows that nothing in space and time is excluded from the All-Merciful's disposal.

LOOK AND SAY: *God is the All-Great*. He is All-Just and All-Ruling, All-Wise and All-Independent, Single and One. He dispenses justice and acts wisely, for He created the universe by measuring with the rule of Will and the ordering Wisdom. The principles of His Wisdom link everything that exists.

He distinguished all things and beings as individuals by the principle of His Decree and the law of Destiny (His Determining), which appoint all distinguishing lines. He ordered the universe and its creatures by the principle of His way of acting and the law of His practicing. He does what He wills, and decrees what He wills in the heavens and Earth with Mercy's grace and Favoring's kindness. He adorned the universe by Mercy's laws and Favoring's principles, in which all beauty seen in creatures has its source. He illuminated the universe by manifesting His Names and Attributes, which form the lamps of creatures in the heavens and Earth.

UNDERSTAND THIS AND SAY: *God is the All-Great*. He is the All-Knowing Creator, All-Wise Maker. The world and this normo-world (humanity) are works of His Power, inscriptions of His Determining. He created the world and made it a place of worship; He created men and women and made them worshippers. He constructed the former (His property) and built the latter (His servants). His art in the former was manifested as a book, and His painting in the latter appeared as speech. His Power manifested on the former displays His Might and Honor, and His Mercy in the latter arranges His bounties. His stamp in the former is visible on wholes and parts, and His seal on the latter on the body as a whole and on its parts.

LOOK AND SAY: *God is the All-Great*. He is All-Able and Enduring, Originator and All-Knowing, All-Subtle and All-Munificent, All-Loving and All-Compassionate, All-Beautiful and Tremendous, and Designer of the universe. The universe consists of parts, each of which is a sample of the whole. It also consists of worlds that, both as wholes and parts representing wholes, are lines and inscriptions of His Decree, pictures of His Determining.

Then limits are appointed according to dimensions, and with the ruler and compasses of Destiny, the Power individualizes forms according to each thing's purposes. Considering benefits with respect to each testifies that each thing's particular, distinguishing lines are drawn by the Pen of an All-Knowing, All-Wise One. After individualization, Favoring adorns the forms with Its shining hand and in the best way conceivable. This shows that adornment and beauty are works of His Grace, signs of His Munificence.

After adornment, His Munificence embellishes and makes beautiful to show that the All-Munificent wills to be loved by His creatures. He displays His desire to be known by humanity and jinn. All beauty and kindness originate from His will to be loved and known, which is why He made all of His works beautiful. The All-Able shows His desire to be known by embellishing His works. After the will to be loved comes His Mercy, which sends bounties and maintains His creation. He spreads His tables for the pleasure of living beings. The Creator's Mercy is apparent in His works, and the All-Providing shows His Pitying in His fruits.

To sum up: This world consists of the lines and inscriptions of His Determining (Destiny) and embroideries of His Pen, embellishments of His Munificence, and flowers of His Generosity. For believers, it consists of the fruits of His Mercy and gleams of His Beauty, manifestations of His Majesty and mirrors of His Perfection. All that is seen in the name of beauty and displayed in the name of perfection are moving and changeable mirrors, shadows of His Light, signs of His Perfection, and point to His works' perfection.

A perfect work testifies to a perfect act, which points to a perfect title, which indicates a perfect attribute, which shows a perfect essential quality or potential, which points to the Being Who is the Manifest Truth and then establishes the degrees and raising by them—the Creator of the universe. This shows that the beauty apparent on things does not belong to them.

Mirrors disappear and creatures decay, but Divine Names and Attributes continue to manifest themselves and create new creatures. This is one of the clearest, most articulate proofs of the absolute Beauty and ever-renewed gifts of the Necessarily Existent, All-Permanent, All-Loved One.

KNOW AND SAY: *God is the All-Great.* He is Creator and All-Great, All-Acting and All-Powerful. Worldly objects and earthly adornments, heavenly bodies and pearl-like stars in the garden of the universe are miracles of His Power, witnesses of His Wisdom, and proofs of the One and Unique, All-Able and Eternally-Besought-of-All.

Glory be to Him Who has made the garden of Earth display His art. Blooming plants and fruit-bearing trees, adorned animals and beautiful birds are marvels of His art, witnesses of His Knowledge, evidence of His Generosity. The smiles of flowers, ornaments of fruits in these orchards, display the will of the All-Merciful to be loved, the desire of the All-Benevolent to be known by jinn and humanity, spirits and animals, and the compassion of the All-Pitying toward them.

Flowers and fruits, grains and seeds are miracles of Wisdom, gifts of Mercy, evidence of Unity. They are presents offered in this world to give the good tidings that their likes will be given in the next. They are truthful witnesses that their Maker has full knowledge of all things, is powerful over all things, and that He embraces all things with mercy and knowledge, kindness and prearrangement (of all necessities for their lives). The sun or a tiny particle, a star or a flower, Earth or an egg—nothing is difficult for Him to create and maintain, to preserve and shape, to make and equip.

UNDERSTAND THIS AND SAY: *God is the All-Great.* He is the eternal Sovereign, Ruler of eternity, everlasting Lord. Look at the sky's face. You will see silent peace and purposeful movement, splendid radiation and smiling ornaments, and a perfect, inviolable order. The glittering of its stars proclaims the eternal Sovereignty. These luminous objects and revolving planets are radiant evidence and light-diffusing witnesses proclaiming the Divine Grandeur's might and dignity, displaying the majesty of the Lord's Sovereignty, revealing His Power's magnificence and vastness, and pointing to His all-comprehensive Wisdom.

BELIEVE AND SAY: *God is the All-Great.* His is the grandeur in the heavens and Earth, and He is All-Mighty, All-Wise. Glory be to You, O One for Whose Necessary Existence and Unity there are two witnesses in everything, for Whose Oneness and being the Eternally-Besought-of-All there are two signs in everything, and Whose stamp is placed on the forehead of creatures as a truthful witness and an articulate evidence.

Look at His works. You will see as bright as morning an absolute abundance in absolute order. In the creation and administration of all things, you will see absolute order and balance despite absolute ease; absolutely beautiful art despite absolute speed; absolute firmness despite absolute abundance; absolute ease despite absolute value; absolute mingledness despite absolute distinguishment; absolute agreement despite absolute distance; and absolute perfection despite absolute multiplicity. This shows you that the Truth is One, having absolute Power, absolute Knowing.

THINK ABOUT THIS AND SAY: There is no creator but He... There is none other than He, Who originates each thing with its own specific nature.

* * *

In the Name of God, the All-Merciful, the All-Compassionate.

> Do you not see that all who are in the heavens and on Earth, the sun and the moon, the stars and the mountains, the trees and the beasts, and many human beings prostrate before God? And many have been destined to punishment. Whoever God makes lowly, there is none to give him honor. Surely God does what He wills. (22:18)

KNOW, O FRIEND, that the Qur'an declares that everything worships God and prostrates before Him, and praises and glorifies Him in its own specific way. We will point to only a few. For example, when a great king wants to have a vast city and a magnificent palace built, he employs four kinds of workers:

First: Slaves who are not paid. They take pleasure in whatever they do by his command, always praise him, and are content with the honor of being attached to him and working on his behalf.[113]

Second: Ordinary people who are paid according to their task. They do not know what great purposes are intended. Some even think that there is no purpose other than their being paid.

---

[113] This is only a comparison. However, for example, the sincere followers of a Prophet or a saint take great pleasure in serving them, for the Prophet's or saint's being pleased with them is enough reward for them.

Third: Animals belonging to the king. They are paid in terms of fodder and the pleasure they take in performing suitable tasks and thereby putting their potential into effect, which also gives them pleasure.

Fourth: Workers who understand what they and others are doing, why it is being done, and why the king is doing it. They supervise the others and are paid according to their rank.

In the same way, the Owner and Builder of the heavens and Earth employs and causes angels and animals, inanimate objects, and plants and human beings to worship Him. He does not do this out of need, for He is the Creator of them and their acts, but because it is required by His Dignity, Grandeur, and His Lordship's essential qualities.

Angels are not promoted because of their endeavors. Each one has a fixed, determined rank, and receives a specific pleasure from its task and a radiance suited for the act of worship it does. Their reward is in the service itself. Just as people are nourished with and derive pleasure from air and water, light and food, angels are nourished with and receive pleasure from the lights of remembrance and glorification, praise and worship, knowledge and love of God. Since they are created of light, light and things close to it (e.g., fragrant scents) sustain them. They feel great happiness in performing the tasks commanded by the One Whom they worship, in their actions for His sake, in the service they render in His Name, and in the supervision they exercise through His view. They find great bliss in the honor they gain through their connection with Him, in the "refreshment" they find in studying His Kingdom's material and immaterial dimensions, and in the satisfaction they have in observing the manifestations of His Grace and Majesty.

Animals, which have an appetitive soul and partial will, do not work purely for the sake of God. Therefore, their Munificent Owner pays them for their work. For example, the All-Wise Creator employs the nightingale, renowned for its love of roses,[114] to proclaim the intense relationship between

---

114 In Eastern literature, a rose symbolizes a beloved woman and a nightingale is a young man who loves her. Its singing symbolizes the heart-rending songs sung for the beloved, especially laments of separation. In the Twenty-fourth Word, Said Nursi treats the nightingale as the representative of animals that offer God, on their behalf, their thanks for the flowers and other plants they consume. Every species has a "nightingale" doing the same task on behalf of its species. According to him, Prophet Muhammad is the nightingale of humanity who sings the praises of God on our behalf and conveys our worship and thanks to God. (Tr.)

plants and animals. The nightingale is an orator of the Lord among animals, which are guests of the All-Merciful One, and is charged with acclaiming their Provider's gifts and announcing their joy therein. It announces the welcome offered to plants in return for the help they offer animals, and declares on beautiful plants the animals' intense need of plants—a need in the degree of love and passion. It offers a most beautiful gratitude to the All-Majestic, Gracious, and Munificent Lord of all kingdoms, with a most pleasing yearning and in a most delicate form.

A nightingale performs this task for the sake of the All-Glorified One. It speaks in its own tongue; we understand these meanings from it, even if it does not know the meaning of its melodies. The nightingale's ignorance of those aims does not mean that it is not employed for them. It is like a clock that tells you the time, even though it is unaware of what it does. The nightingale's wage is the delight it derives from looking on smiling flowers, the pleasure it receives from conversing with them. Its touching songs are not complaints arising from animal grief, but rather are thanks for the All-Merciful One's gifts.

Compare a nightingale with a bee or a spider, an ant or the "nightingales" among insects. Each receives a particular pleasure, included in their duties, as its payment. Like a private employed on an imperial vessel, they serve certain important aims and the Lord's art. They observe God's commands of creation and operation of the universe in perfect obedience, thereby displaying in the best way the purposes for their creation in His Name. They spend their lives fulfilling their tasks by His Power in the most wonderful fashion. In this manner, they present the gifts of their worship and virtues of their submission to their Creator, which are the true reasons why the Bestower of life created them.

As plants and inanimate objects have no free will, they are not paid. Whatever they do, they do by God's Power and in His Name, purely for God's sake, and to fulfill what Divine Will requires of them. We can see that plants derive some sort of pleasure from fulfilling their tasks but, unlike animate beings with free will, they do not suffer pain. The results of the works of plants and inanimate objects are more perfect than those of animals, because they are in complete submission to the Creator, with free choice having no part in them. Among animals having some sort of choice, the work of those like bees and others similar to them, which are equipped with a kind of inspiration, is more perfect than the work of those that rely on their partial will and power.

Human beings resemble angels in the universality of their worship, extent of their supervision, comprehensiveness of their knowledge, and their role as heralds of Divine Lordship. Indeed, they are more comprehensive in nature than angels. Since their drives are not restricted and their appetitive souls are disposed toward evil, they have a capacity for almost both boundless advance and decline. In their quest for self-pleasure in their work and a share for themselves, they resemble animals. So, they receive two kinds of wages: one animal (insignificant and immediate) and the other angelic (universal and postponed).

A complementary note for the discussion on the nightingale

The nightingale is not the only creature that sings and announces the praise and glorification of God Almighty. Rather, every species has its own "nightingale" to represent its finest feelings with the finest glorification in the finest verse. The "nightingales" of vermin and insects, who sing their glorification in fine poetry and give pleasure to those who hear them, are particularly numerous and various.

Some of these nightingales are nocturnal. As if each were the leader of a circle reciting God's Names by heart, the poetry-reciting friends of all small animals glorify God and sing His praises in the night's peaceful silence. Their song is like a common language understood by all who can hear and feel. Another group is diurnal. During daytime in spring and summer, as if each were the leader of a circle reciting God's Names aloud, they proclaim the glorification in fine verse to all living beings from the "pulpits" of trees, and arouse those hearing them to ecstasy.

Prophet Muhammad, upon him be peace and blessings, is the most virtuous being and the most excellent and noble, illustrious and profound, the greatest and the most honorable nightingale. His voice is the loudest and most lyrical, his attributes the most brilliant, his recitation of God's Names the most perfect and comprehensive, and his thanks the most universal. Prophet Muhammad is the nightingale of humanity—singing in the garden of the universe, who, through his most-pleasant tunes, has become the nightingale of all creatures in the heavens and Earth. Upon him, his Family, and his peers—the other Prophets—be the best of blessings and peace.

KNOW, O FRIEND, that the fact that animals are born with the skills and practical knowledge they need to survive shows that they are sent here only to work (or to serve the purposes of their lives), not to be perfected through learning. Human beings, however, are born ignorant and impotent, and need to learn throughout life how to survive. This shows that we are sent here to be perfected through learning and worship, not to work only for this life. We are to arrange the "actions" of plants and animals, which God has subjugated to us, and benefit from the laws of Mercy. Our real duty is to worship, pray, and supplicate to the One Who has put creation in our service because of our infinite weakness and impotence, poverty and need. We must acquire knowledge of Him Who made us the most honored member of creation and equipped us with what we need to worship. We must find happiness by studying creation and the wisdom in it to learn about the Creator with His Names and Attributes, Majesty and Grace, and Perfection. Any study that does not produce this knowledge is useless and causes deviation.

> O God, make us Your servants who sincerely worship You wherever and in whichever rank we are. Make us supplicate to You as our God and be occupied with acquiring knowledge of You.

KNOW, O FRIEND, that since the All-Munificent Creator is free from any impotence and is perfectly munificent, He creates a particle as He creates the sun; He gives a particle the same sort of existence as He gives the sun. He creates the smallest plant as He creates the largest tree. He creates the angel who supervises and manages the sun's movement as He creates the angel who supervises and manages a single raindrop. He creates the largest animal as He creates the smallest animal. All creatures, regardless of size and number, worship and obey Him, and have specific tasks to perform. They are appointed by the One: *When He wills a thing, His command is but to say to it "Be!" and it is. Glory be to Him in Whose Hand is the dominion of everything, and unto Him you are returning* (36:82-83).

KNOW, O MUSLIMS, that the Islamic Shari'a enables you to turn all of your daily acts and deeds into a treasury for your afterlife. Your most ordinary actions can become acts of worship. For example, if you say the words decreed by the relevant Shari'a ordinance while shopping or doing some business, you will feel a sort of exhilaration because it becomes an act of worship for which you will receive a (spiritual) reward. Prosperous are those who do so, for they become more enlightened by observing even the secondary ordinances of that Shari'a.

Happy are those whom God enables to follow the Prophet in all their acts and deeds, and thereby make their transient life yield innumerable eternal fruits. How unfortunate are those whom God debases because they follow their animal desires and fancies, and take their carnal desires and whims for their god. Their lives pass in vain.

Know, O friend, that among people are shepherds who supervise animals' lives and functions, and farmers who grow plants. Similarly, some angels supervise animals scattered over Earth's face and so can be called "shepherds." But their supervision differs from that of human shepherds, for they do it purely in God's Name, for His sake, and by His command and Power. They observe the Divine Lordship's manifestations on the animals, and study the acts of the Power and Mercy on them. They inspire the Divine commands into them so that they can conduct their lives.

Some angels supervise the spreading of plants by God's permission, power and command, and in His Name. They represent and proclaim all plants' glorification of their All-Mighty Creator and their obedience to Him, in addition to arranging and protecting their use of the systems granted to them.

Angels have no true control over animals and plants with a creative effect, for everything has a special stamp showing that it is the Creator of all things Who has created and controls it; the angels' supervision is their worship of God. Archangel Michael, who is among those carrying the Throne of Divine Providence and conveying Divine bounties to creatures by His Will, Power, and permission and in His Name, does his duty of worship by supervising plants. Many other angels supervise a particular species under his command. There are other angels who supervise animals.

Look at Earth, how the All-Wise Creator made it a vast field and a wide pasture for plants and animals. Then look at the species of plants astonishingly distributed over Earth in an amazing order by scattering around their seeds according to the All-Wise, All-Knowing Creator's Wisdom. Look at the animals distributed in a wonderful, astonishing way. They live on land or in water in an orderly fashion by their All-Wise, All-Munificent Creator's Favoring. Exalted is His Majesty. There is no deity but He.

In the Name of God, the All-Merciful, the All-Compassionate.

O God. O All-Merciful and All-Compassionate, All-Independent and All-Living, Self-Subsistent and All-Wise, All-Just and All-Pure, and All-Holy. For the sake of Your Greatest Name, place the students of the *Risale-i Nur* who publish and translate this *al-Mathnawi al-Nuri* in *Jannat al-Firdaws*—the Highest Floor of Paradise—and grant them eternal happiness there. Make them always successful in the service of belief and the Qur'an. Record in their registers of deeds many (spiritual) rewards for each letter of this book. Amen. Amen. Amen, for the sake of Your Mercy, O Most Merciful of the Merciful.

— Said Nursi

To conclude:

- All of Earth's features bear various stamps of the One, Eternally-Besought-of-All.
- Heedlessness, ingratitude, and unbelief arise from groundless conceptions or notions.
- Some of humanity's artifacts may be worth thousands of dollars because of their art, while their material costs are negligible. Humanity's real worth lies in belief, which connects it to the All-Permanent Maker, while unbelief reduces humanity to the level of coal, which decays in the ground.
- There are four realities that humanity cannot change.
- What is referred to as "happiness" in this world is deceiving, temporary, and short-lived.
- The All-Powerful Maker has spread millions of plant and animal worlds on Earth's face. Every world is like a sea whose drops are charged with cleaning.
- What about the Prophetic Traditions concerning the Mahdi, the approaching of the Last Hour, and the great tumults predicted to occur?
- God created everything. Evil and defect, fault and vice are the results of the created thing's nature and imperfect capacities, and their misuse of their willpower.
- All species embrace and help each other. Their members come together and separate on good terms.
- God's acts are not open to question.
- Saints differ in the conclusions they draw through inspiration and spiritual unveiling, but agree on the fundamentals of the Religion. Why saints and Prophets preceding Prophet Muhammad only elaborated upon Divine

Unity, while the Qur'an and Prophet Muhammad explained all pillars of belief so clearly that they do not require further clarification.

- Humanity serves as a unit of comparison in five ways.
- Why are you reluctant to sell to your All-Munificent Lord that which is already His property—your selfhood and life?
- A person who refuses this bargain.
- If you want to be near to Him, you must develop and expand so that you can represent humanity, and acquire an absolutely universal existence, which is almost impossible, or renounce and annihilate your selfhood so that He may be "seen" in it.
- An analogy to understand the difference between the Qur'an's wisdom and philosophy's viewpoint.
- Those who trust in God, and those who do not.
- Qur'anic verses end in specific ways. What do these endings signify?
- Everything says *In and with the Name of God* either verbally or through the tongue of disposition or potential.
- The difference between belief in Divine Unity, atheism, and heresy.
- A blossom of the tree of the verse: *The seven heavens and Earth and all that is in them glorify Him.*
- Meaning of *Glory be to Him* and *God is the All-Great.*
- All things worship God, prostrate to Him, and praise and glorify Him in their own specific ways.
- Every species has a "nightingale" that represents it. Prophet Muhammad is the most honorable nightingale.
- An animal is born with the skills and practical knowledge needed for its survival. This shows that it is sent here only to work. Human beings need to acquire such knowledge and petition God to meet their needs. This shows that we are sent here to be perfected through learning and worship.
- Since the All-Munificent Creator is free of any impotence and is perfectly munificent, He creates a particle as He creates the sun and gives both the same sort of existence.
- The Islamic Shari'a enables people to change their daily acts and deeds into a treasury for their afterlife. Our most ordinary actions can become acts of worship.
- Among angels are those resembling human shepherds and farmers. They superintend animals and the spreading and growth of plants. However, they differ from their human counterparts in one important aspect: They do it purely in the Name of God, for His sake, and by His command and Power.

Index

A

B

C

D

E

F

G

H

I

J

L

M

N

O

P

R